LEADERSHIP EDUCATION AND TRAINING (LET 2)

With material selected from:

Health: Skills for Wellness, Third Edition
by B.E. Pruitt, Ed.D., Kathy Teer Crumpler, M.P.H.,
and Deborah Prothrow-Stith, M.D.

World Geography: Building a Global Perspective, Second Edition
by Thomas J. Baerwald and Celeste Fraser

CUSTOM EDITION FOR ARMY JROTC
A Character and Leadership Development Program

PEARSON
Custom
Publishing

Cover images courtesy of Army JROTC.
Content created by JROTC unless otherwise credited.

Text excerpts taken from:

Health: Skills for Wellness, Third Edition
by B.E. (Buzz) Pruitt, Ed.D., Kathy Teer Crumpler, M.P.H., and Deborah Prothrow-Stith, M.D.
Copyright © 2001 by Prentice-Hall, Inc.
A Pearson Education Company
Upper Saddle River, New Jersey 07458

World Geography: Building a Global Perspective, Second Edition
by Thomas J. Baerwald and Celeste Fraser
Copyright © 2002 by Prentice-Hall, Inc.

Copyright © 2008, 2006, 2005, 2002 by Pearson Custom Publishing
All rights reserved.

This copyright covers material written expressly for this volume by the editor/s as well as the compilation itself. It does not cover the individual selections herein that first appeared elsewhere. Permission to reprint these has been obtained by Pearson Custom Publishing for this edition only. Further reproduction by any means, electronic or mechanical, including photocopying and recording, or by any information storage or retrieval system, must be arranged with the individual copyright holders noted.

All trademarks, service marks, registered trademarks, and registered service marks are the property of their respective owners and are used herein for identification purposes only.

Printed in the United States of America

10 9 8 7 6 5

ISBN 0-536-85201-4

2007420578

SB/MJ

Please visit our web site at *www.pearsoncustom.com*

PEARSON CUSTOM PUBLISHING
501 Boylston Street, Suite 900, Boston, MA 02116
A Pearson Education Company

Brief Contents

Table of Contents

Wellness, Fitness, and First Aid

Unit 4

Chapter 1

Achieving a Healthy Lifestyle

Lesson 3

You Are What You Eat

Key Terms

calories
carbohydrates
deficient
diabetes
fats
fiber
metabolism
minerals
nutrients
osteoporosis
protein
stimulant
vitamins

What You Will Learn to Do

- Evaluate how diet impacts life

Linked Core Abilities

- Take responsibility for your actions and choices

Skills and Knowledge You Will Gain along the Way

- Explain how calories consumed verses calories used affects body weight
- Identify the daily-required food and portions
- Identify sources and benefits of fiber in diet
- Describe the importance of water

- Describe the possible effects of a diet high in fat and cholesterol
- Explain why salt, sugar, and caffeine should be used in moderation
- Define key words contained in this lesson

Introduction

A healthy lifestyle includes good nutrition as well as exercise. You need to eat well to maintain an exercise program. After all, just as a car will not run without fuel, your body will not work properly without the right **nutrients**. Eating a balanced diet also helps you maintain proper weight and lowers your risk of disease. This lesson explains the importance of a proper diet to your health.

Americans live in a fast-paced environment and frequently eat on the run. Eating on the run too often, however, may affect your nutrition and weight. You can end up consuming too many **fats** and too few vegetables and fruit, leaving you overweight and/or **deficient** in certain nutrients. Learning to eat balanced meals, even on the run, contributes to your overall well-being by:

- **helping to maintain proper weight**
- **providing energy for physical activity**
- **supplying nutrients for good health**

> ### Note
> Although too many fats can be bad for you, your body needs a certain amount of fat from the foods you eat. Many necessary vitamins are fat-soluable only, and without fat, these vitamins cannot be absorbed.

Balancing Calories

You must eat to fuel your body. The more active you are, the more fuel your body requires. Even if you remain very still, your body uses a certain amount of energy, or **calories**, on basic functions that work automatically all the time to keep you alive—such as your heart beating, your lungs inhaling, and your nerves delivering information. You do not have much control over the amount of calories used for these basic functions. Some people's bodies naturally use more calories to sustain their basic functions some people use less. It's often said that those who use more have a high **metabolism**, meaning they can eat more and not gain weight.

Key Note Term

nutrients – substances found in food that allow the body to function properly.

deficient – having too little of something, such as a nutrient in the body.

fats – nutrients made up of fatty acids that are insoluble in water and provide energy to the body.

Key Note Term

calories – the amount of energy it takes to raise the temperature of one kilogram of water one degree Celsius; a measurement of energy.

metabolism – the chemical process by which the body produces energy and maintains vital functions.

Your body also uses calories to do everything else throughout the day, from brushing your teeth, to studying, to stretching. Unlike your basic functions; however, you can control how many calories you voluntarily use throughout the day by how active you are. For example, you will use more calories if you choose to walk for an hour instead of watching television for an hour. Also, the more effort you put into an activity, the more calories you burn. For example, walking at a brisk pace uses more calories than walking at a leisurely pace.

When your body uses the same amount of calories daily than you eat daily, your weight stays the same. If you eat more calories than your body uses, your body stores the unused calories as fat and you gain weight. If you eat fewer calories than your body needs, your body uses the stored fat for energy and you lose weight. It's a balancing act between numbers of calories eaten and calories used.

Karen wonders why she keeps gaining weight—10 pounds over the last year. One Saturday, she and her friend, Andrea, meet at the local fast food restaurant for lunch. While they wait in line, Andrea says she played tennis that morning. Karen admits she slept late and watched television. Andrea orders a small soda and a salad with grilled chicken and light Italian dressing; then Karen orders a double hamburger with mayonnaise only, large French fries, and a large chocolate milkshake.

Andrea shakes her head and asks Karen if she ever eats fruit or vegetables. Karen shrugs and says "sometimes." Andrea explains that she eats hamburgers and French fries every once in a while—in fact, she had that for lunch a few days ago, which is why she ordered a salad today. Andrea tells Karen that eating fruit and vegetables more often than fried foods and sweets helps her maintain her desired weight, and she feels better, too. Karen thinks about this for a moment as they sit down to eat.

Perhaps if Karen had access to the following calorie counts, she would reconsider what she ordered. Keep in mind that most people need only between 2,000 and 3,000 total calories a day. Table 1.2.1 shows the difference between the two food orders.

> **Note**
>
> The calories listed here are approximate; actual calories of these food items at different restaurants may vary.

Table 1.2.1: Karen and Andrea's lunch orders

Karen's Order	Calories	Andrea's Order	Calories
Plain double hamburger with bun (¼ pound of beef)	540	Salad with grilled chicken	200
Mayonnaise (1 tablespoon)	100	Light Italian salad dressing (2 tablespoons)	50
French fries (large order)	360		
Chocolate milkshake (large)	540	Soda (small)	150
TOTAL	1540	TOTAL	400

Even if Karen did not want a salad, she could cut her calories considerably by ordering a single hamburger with mustard and ketchup, a small milkshake, and a regular order of fries. She could also have lettuce and tomato on the burger to eat some vegetables. Her new calorie intake would look simliar to Table 1.2.2.

If Karen really wants to lose those extra 10 pounds, however, she should skip the milkshake and replace the fries with a small salad and light dressing. This would reduce her calorie intake to about 400 for lunch. She should then get some exercise like her friend Andrea. Playing tennis for an hour uses three

Table 1.2.2: An alternative to Andrea's lunch order

Andrea's order	Calories
Plain single hamburger with bun (2 ounce patty)	275
Lettuce (½ cup)	5
Tomato (1 slice)	5
Mustard (1 tablespoon)	8
Ketchup (1 tablespoon)	15
French fries (regular order)	220
Chocolate milkshake (small)	330
TOTAL	**858**

times as many calories as watching television for an hour. If Karen sticks to eating sensibly and exercises daily, she will start using more calories than she eats, losing those extra pounds.

The Importance of a Proper Diet to Your Health

Just as important as eating the correct amount of calories to supply your body with energy and maintain proper weight is what you eat to get those calories. If you eat like Karen every day, you are giving your body too much fat, cholesterol, salt, and sugar, and denying your body many necessary nutrients. Many health problems are related to poor diets, and these problems can start when you are young. At your next physical examination, ask your doctor about your cholesterol, blood pressure, and blood sugar levels. You may be surprised to find you need to change your diet to improve your health.

What Should You Eat?

The United States Department of Agriculture (USDA) developed the Food Guide Pyramid to indicate how many servings of six different food groups you should eat daily to get the nutrients your body needs. If you follow these guidelines, you will get enough **vitamins** and **minerals** to keep your body's processes functioning properly, and you will have enough **carbohydrates**, **protein**, and fat to supply your body with energy. When you do not get enough of certain nutrients, you increase your risk of disease. For example, if you do not get enough calcium, a mineral found in milk products, almonds, sardines, leafy vegetables, and beans, you can develop **osteoporosis.**

> ### Note
> To see the current Food Guide Pyramid as offered by the USDA, check out http://www.nal.usda.gov/fnic/Fpyr/pyramid.html.

Your body also needs fiber, the only form of carbohydrate that is not an energy source. Fiber aids in digestion. It prevents cholesterol, fats, and other toxic materials from entering the bloodstream, and for this reason may lessen your chances of cancer and heart disease. It also helps balance your blood sugar levels, so it helps control **diabetes**. To obtain fiber, eat raw or lightly cooked vegetables, fresh fruit, beans, nuts, and whole wheat or bran breads, cereals, and crackers.

One final nutrient that you do not get from food that is vital to keeping you alive is water. More than 65 percent of the body is water, and, as the body loses water through normal activity and exercise, it must be replaced. Water aids in digestion, regulates temperature, carries vitamins and minerals to all parts of the body, and is important for the removal of waste products from the kidneys. Drink a minimum of five to six glasses of water a day. On the days you exercise, you may need to drink more.

Key Note Term

carbohydrates – one of the various neutral organic compounds composed of carbon, hydrogen, and oxygen (including starches and sugars) produced by plants and used to provide energy necessary for growth and other functions.

minerals – natural chemical elements of the earth used by the body to supply necessary nutrition.

osteoporosis – a condition characterized by a calcium deficiency in the bone mass. The body pulls calcium from the bones, causing them to lose their density and possibly leading to fractures.

protein – nutrients that are made of amino acids and that maintain body tissues and supply energy to the body.

vitamins – nutrients that occur naturally in plant and animal tissue and are required for proper function of the body.

diabetes – a disease in which the body is unable to use sugars properly.

Eating in Moderation

Key Note Term

fiber – coarse food made mostly of carbohydrates, such as bran or broccoli, that serves to stimulate and aid the movement of food through the digestive tract.

stimulant – an ingredient found in beverages, food or drugs that speeds up the activity of the mind or body; a drug that speeds up the activities of the central nervous system, the heart, and other organs; for example, caffeine in tea or chocolate.

Your body needs fat for energy, but too much fat in your diet can make you gain weight and can lead to high cholesterol. Cholesterol, a type of fat, is a natural, waxy substance produced by your body and found in animal products. Your body needs some cholesterol to remain healthy, but too much is harmful. As shown in Figure 1.2.1, cholesterol forms plaque on artery walls, restricting the flow of blood within blood vessels. This leads to high blood pressure and an increased risk of heart disease. To lower cholesterol levels, lower your intake of fat by eating less meat, using oil-free dressings, avoiding fried foods, eating low-fat dairy products, and consuming lots of **fiber**.

Many foods, especially prepackaged foods and restaurant foods, already have added salt, so do not shake on more. Too much salt in your diet forces your body to retain unnecessary water and may contribute to high blood pressure.

Sugary foods like candy, soda, syrup, and table sugar supply you with calories and few (if any) nutrients. These foods contain "empty calories"—they give your body calories and nothing else. Avoid them while dieting, and do not eat them as a replacement for other foods that provide nutrition. Many fruits and vegetables naturally contain sugar, but they also provide many other important nutrients.

Limit your intake of coffee, tea, and sodas that contain caffeine, a **stimulant**. Although caffeine temporarily reduces drowsiness and makes you more alert, in large quantities it can upset your stomach, make you nervous and irritable, keep you awake when you want to sleep, and give you diarrhea.

Figure 1.2.1: Cholesterol shown in artery walls.

Clot

Conclusion

Your body needs food for energy, just like a car needs fuel to run. How much food your body needs depends on how active you are and how many calories your body uses to keep its basic functions operating. You know you are getting the right amount of calories from food when you maintain your ideal weight. Not only does food supply you with energy, but the right foods also provide the nutrients your body needs to operate properly and lower your risk of disease. Eating a healthy, balanced diet and exercising regularly increase your chances of a long, strong, and disease-free life.

Chapter 1

Lesson Review

1. **Think about what you had for breakfast. How could you have balanced your calories better?**

2. **Do you feel you have a slow or fast metabolism? How can you plan your meals with this in mind?**

3. **Looking at the food pyramid, what food group do you need to eat more or less of?**

4. **Define the term "metabolism."**

Lesson Review

Lesson 4

Nutrition– Nourishing Your Body

Key Terms

amino acids
complex carbohydrates
fat soluble vitamins
mono-unsaturated fats
poly-unsaturated fats
Referenced Daily Intake (RDI)
saturated fats
simple carbohydrates
water soluble vitamins

What You Will Learn to Do

- Analyze how well you meet nutrient guidelines

Linked Core Abilities

- Take responsibility for your actions and choices

Skills and Knowledge You Will Gain along the Way

- Explain the six nutrients your body requires
- Explain the difference between simple and complex carbohydrates
- Describe the role fat and cholesterol play in body functioning
- Compare saturated and unsaturated fats
- Describe ways to reduce cholesterol levels

- Compare the functions of vitamins, carbohydrates, fats and proteins
- Identify food sources of vitamins and minerals
- Define key words contained in this lesson

Introduction

Nutrition is the science of nourishing the body properly to reach the higher levels of dynamic living. This lesson will introduce you to the six nutrients, and show you how to best provide them in a diet that is well rounded yet diversified. You will learn the newest methods available in how to choose your foods and how to read labels. Finally, you will better understand how to maintain a lean body, free from the damaging effects of carrying too much personal fat.

Our diets have radically changed during the past 35 years. With the advent of fast-food outlets, an increase in dual-career parents, and sky-rocketing numbers of single-parent households, most Americans now have a hurry-up lifestyle where proper eating habits take a back seat to convenience and lack of time.

Knowing that our lifestyles are busy and sometimes hurried, it is very important that young adults have at least a basic understanding of nutrients, how to obtain them, and how to control fat. This knowledge will lead to a more dynamic life and a higher quality lifestyle. The six types of nutrients are carbohydrates, fats, proteins, vitamins, minerals, and water.

We also refer to the first three nutrients, carbohydrates, fats, and proteins, as foodstuffs. They give us the energy for all of the bodily processes. When our body uses the foodstuffs, it releases energy. We measure this energy in calories.

> **Note**
>
> To learn more about calories, see Unit 4, Chapter 1, Lesson 2, "You Are What You Eat."

Carbohydrates

Carbohydrates are the starches and sugars found in fruits, grains, and vegetables. They have a caloric value of four calories per gram and supply us with short- and long-term energy to accomplish everything from thinking and breathing to running a race.

Key Note Term

simple carbohydrate – a sugar that is found in food and the body in its simple state which supplies the body with short-term energy .

complex carbohydrates – a carbohydrate that is formed by the body or by plants after the conversion of simple carbohydrates, which supplies the body with long-term energy.

Key Note Term

fat soluble vitamin – a vitamin that is absorbed through the intestinal tract with the help of fats and is stored in the body.

mono-unsaturated fats – oil or fat that is liquid at room temperature, is low in hydrogen, and can lower the level of blood cholesterol.

poly-unsaturated fats – an oil of fatty acid containing more than one double or triple bond and is therefore cholesterol defensive.

saturated fats – a fat that does not melt at room temperature and can raise the blood cholesterol level.

The short-term carbohydrates are the sugars, or **simple carbohydrates**, which are quickly digested and absorbed into the blood. The most important simple sugar is glucose, or blood sugar. Before the body's cells can use other simple sugars (such as fructose, sucrose, and lactose) for energy, a change must occur converting them into glucose. Many sugary foods are sources of simple carbohydrates; however, those such as soda and candy have few other nutrients while fruit is an excellent source of simple carbohydrates and contains many other vitamins and minerals as well.

The long-term carbohydrates are starches, or **complex carbohydrates**, which are made up of combinations of simple sugars. They take longer to digest because the body must break them into simple sugars (glucose) before they can enter the bloodstream. When your body has extra glucose that it does not need immediately for energy, it converts it into the complex carbohydrate glycogen and stores it in the muscles and liver to be released later when energy is needed, usually for short periods of strenuous activity. After your muscles and liver store as much glycogen as they can hold, your body changes the rest to body fat for long-term energy. Long distance runners use carbohydrate loading (eating large quantities of carbohydrates) to have the long-term energy they need to complete the race.

Good sources of complex carbohydrates are grains (such as bread, cereal, pasta, and rice) and starchy vegetables (such as peas, corn, beans, and potatoes). These starchy foods are also important sources of vitamins, minerals, and fiber. Fiber provides no calories, but is roughage that aids in the movement of food through the digestive system.

Nourishing Your Body's Fuel with Fats

Fats, or lipids, perform the vital roles of maintaining body temperature, insulating body organs, providing the body with stored energy, and carrying the **fat soluble vitamins** A, D, E, and K to the cells. One gram of fat is the equivalent of nine calories of energy, more than twice the amount of carbohydrates; therefore, minimum consumption of fats is the most sensible approach to maintaining a lean body fat content.

Triglycerides are the primary fats in the foods we eat, as well as the fats stored in body tissue. They include saturated fat, which mainly comes from animal sources and does not melt at room temperature, and **mono-unsaturated** and **poly-unsaturated fats**, which are usually liquid oils of vegetable origin. When you eat too many calories, your liver changes them into triglycerides and stores them as fat. When you eat too many saturated fats, your liver makes more cholesterol than your body needs, which is unhealthy.

Cardiovascular disease is the main killer of Americans

Your liver already produces about 1,000 milligrams (mg) of cholesterol daily and diet adds another 400 to 500 mg. Cholesterol, a waxy, sticky substance found in animal and human tissue, insulates nerves and forms hormones, cell membranes, vitamin D, and bile to aid in food digestion.

Your blood carries cholesterol by way of lipoproteins, with low density lipoproteins (LDL) carrying cholesterol from the liver to the cells to accomplish the functions mentioned. Unfortunately, the LDLs deposit any cholesterol that is not needed by the cells in the arteries, giving them the nickname of the "bad guys." Cholesterol accumulated on the inside walls of the arteries is a factor in the development of atherosclerosis. Eventually, cardiovascular disease, in the form of a heart attack or stroke, may result.

The high density lipoproteins (HDL) carry the extra cholesterol in your blood to the liver to dispose of it, thus preventing cholesterol from building up in the arteries. For this reason, HDLs are known as the "good guys." To keep cholesterol at a normal level in the body, you must lower LDL levels and raise HDL levels. Steps you can take to accomplish this are to eat less fat, especially saturated fat, maintain appropriate body weight, and participate in a regular exercise program. Eating more fiber will also help because it binds with cholesterol and carries it out of the body; and consuming mono-unsaturated fats, such as olive, canola, and peanut oils, raises HDLs.

Nourishing Your Body with Proteins

The body contains substances called proteins in every cell. They aid in the development and maintenance of muscle, bone, skin, and blood. Proteins are also the key behind keeping the immune system strong. They control the chemical activities in the body that transport oxygen, iron, and nutrients to the body cells. The body can also use protein for energy if it is low on carbohydrates and fats; but in most cases, its role as an energy source is minor. Proteins, like carbohydrates, contain four calories per gram.

The building blocks of protein are the **amino acids**. These chains of carbon, hydrogen, oxygen, and nitrogen linked together in different ways control all of the activities mentioned above. There are 22 amino acids found in the human tissue, but the body cannot manufacture all of them. Eight (nine for children) amino acids, known as the essential amino acids, must come from the food we eat since the body cannot produce them. We refer to the food products that contain all eight essential amino acids as having complete proteins. The best sources of complete proteins are meat, fish, poultry, and dairy products. Plant foods generally contain incomplete proteins since they are either low on or lack an essential amino acid. However, plant foods can be combined easily, such as rice and beans or peanut butter and bread, to include all essential amino acids in high enough amounts to form a complete protein.

The remaining 14 amino acids are known as the nonessential amino acids. They are still necessary for bodily functioning, but are called "nonessential" because they do not have to be supplied in the diet. Instead, the body manufactures nonessential amino acids itself.

Key Note Term

amino acids – the basic units of proteins, produced by living cells or obtained as an essential component of a diet.

Keep in mind that although animal and dairy products are sources of complete proteins, many are often high in fat as well. As you will read later in this text, Americans get most of their protein from animal sources instead of from combinations of complex carbohydrates. You will have a healthier diet and still meet your protein needs if you consume less fatty foods and more carbohydrates in the forms of grains and vegetables.

Regulating Your Body with Vitamins, Minerals, and Water

Key Note Term

water soluble vitamin – a vitamin that is dissolved in the water of tissues.

Referenced Daily Intake (RDI) – standards developed by the United States government for the regulation of vitamin and mineral requirements.

Vitamins are promoters of health and wellness. Unlike the carbohydrates, fats, and proteins, the body does not digest vitamins; instead, food products release them and your body tissues absorb them. Vitamins are classified as either fat soluble or water soluble. With the help of fats, the intestinal tract absorbs fat soluble vitamins (A, D, E, and K) and stores them in the body. The water in the tissues dissolves the **water soluble vitamins** (B complex and C).

Many countries have standards for vitamin and mineral requirements to recommend daily amounts needed for good health. For example, the standards for the United States are the **Referenced Daily Intakes (RDI)**. From time to time, the federal government reviews these standards and proposes new ones as research continues and more complete information about vitamins and minerals is discovered. Table 1.3.1 shows the current U.S. RDI for vitamins and minerals.

Minerals

Minerals are elements found in the environment that help regulate the bodily processes. Without minerals, the body cannot absorb vitamins. Macrominerals, shown in Table 1.3.2, are minerals that the body needs in large amounts. These are calcium, phosphorus, magnesium, potassium, sulfur, sodium, and chloride.

Although sodium is a macromineral, many Americans consume too much of it, which can contribute to high blood pressure. High blood pressure, in turn, can contribute to cardiovascular disease. On the other hand, many Americans do not consume enough calcium, and a calcium deficiency can lead to osteoporosis later in life.

Although the body only needs trace minerals (such as selenium, manganese, molybdenum, iron, copper, zinc, iodine, and chromium, shown in Table 1.3.3) in very small amounts, they are also essential for proper functioning of the body. For example, an iron deficiency can reduce the number and size of red blood cells, causing weakness, sleepiness, and headaches.

Table 1.3.1: Vitamins

Vitamin	U.S. RDI	Functions	Sources
A	5000 International Units (IU)	Helps maintain eyes, skin, and linings of the nose, mouth, digestive, and urinary tracts	Liver, dairy products, fortified margarine, orange fruits and vegetables, dark-green vegetables
B-1 (Thiamin)	1.5 mg	Helps convert carbohydrates into energy	Yeast, rice, whole-grain and enriched breads/cereals, liver, pork, meat, poultry, eggs, fish, fruits, vegetables
B-2 (Riboflavin)	1.7 mg	Helps convert nutrients into energy; helps maintain skin, mucous membranes, and nervous structures	Dairy products, liver, yeast, fruits, whole-grain and enriched breads/cereals, vegetables, meat, poultry
B-3 (Niacin)	20 mg	Helps convert nutrients into energy; essential for growth; aids in synthesis of hormones	Liver, poultry, fish, milk, eggs, whole-grain and enriched breads/cereals, fruit, vegetables
B-5 (Pantothenic Acid)	10 mg	Helps convert nutrients into energy	Liver, yeast, whole grains, eggs, beans, milk
B-6 (Pyridoxine)	2.0 mg	Aids in more than 60 enzyme reactions	Milk, liver, meat, green, leafy vegetables, whole-grain and enriched breads/cereals
B-7 (Biotin)	0.3 mg	Helps convert nutrients to energy	Liver, yeast, milk, oatmeal, beans, nuts, egg yolk
B-9 (Folic Acid)	0.4 mg	Aids in blood cell production; helps maintain nervous system	Liver, green, leafy vegetables, beans
B-12 (Cobalmin)	6 micrograms (mcg)	Helps form new cells	Meat, seafood, poultry, dairy products, eggs
C	60 mg	Helps maintain and repair connective tissue, bones, teeth, cartilage; promotes wound-healing	Broccoli, brussels sprouts, citrus fruit, tomatoes, potatoes, peppers, cabbage, other fruits and vegetables

continued on next page

Table 1.3.1: Vitamins (continued)

Vitamin	U.S. RDI	Functions	Sources
D	400 IU	Helps regulate calcium and phosphorus metabolism; promotes calcium absorption; essential for development/maintenance of bones and teeth	Fortified milk, eggs, fish-liver oils, sunlight on skin
E	30 IU	An antioxidant (prevents oxygen from interacting destructively with other substances) that helps protect cell membranes, maintain fats and vitamin A, and increase blood flow	Green, leafy vegetables, whole grains, seeds, nuts, vegetable oil/shortening, liver, egg yolks
K	60 – 80 mcg*	Helps in blood clotting	Green, leafy vegetables, liver, tomatoes, egg yolks, milk

* No U.S. RDI established. Amount is an estimated recommendation for dietary intake.

Points of Interest: Vitamins

According to a 10-year study of 11,348 U.S. adults, vitamin C was effective at cutting death rates from heart disease and stroke. The study tested three groups getting:

- 50 mg or more a day in food, plus an average supplement of 500 mg
- 50 or more mg and no supplement
- less than 50 mg with no supplement.

Men in Group 1 had a 35 percent lower mortality rate and 42 percent lower death rate from heart disease and stroke. Women in Group 1 were 25 percent less likely to die of heart disease or stroke and had a 10 percent lower mortality rate.

Taking supplements of 2,000 mg of vitamin C daily might be helpful to allergy sufferers.

A new study also found vitamin E cuts the risk of certain cancers. Plus, two other studies with 130,000+ people reported vitamin E helps prevent coronary heart diseases.

Table 1.3.2: Macrominerals

Mineral	U.S. RDI	Functions	Sources
Calcium	1000 mg	Structure of bones and teeth; muscle contraction; maintenance of cell membranes; blood clotting; nerve impulse transmission; heart activity Helps convert carbohydrates into energy	Dairy products, small fish (such as sardines) with bones, dark-green vegetables, dried beans and peas
Phosphorus	1000 mg	Structure of bones and teeth; muscle contraction; maintenance of cell membranes; blood clotting; nerve impulse transmission; heart activity Helps convert carbohydrates into energy	Dairy products, small fish (such as sardines) with bones, dark-green vegetables, dried beans and peas
Magnesium	400 mg	Structure of bones and teeth; release of energy from nutrients; formation of enzymes	Meat, poultry, fish, eggs, dried beans and peas, dairy products
Potassium	3500 mg*	Building bones; release of energy from muscle glycogen; conduction of nerve impulse to muscle	Green, leafy vegetables, nuts, soybeans, seeds, whole grains
Sulfur	140 mg*	Muscle contraction; maintenance of fluid and electrolyte balance; transmission of nerve impulse; release of energy from nutrients	Orange juice, bananas, dried fruit, meat, bran, peanut butter, potatoes, coffee, tea, cocoa
Chloride and Sodium	No more than 2400 mg*	Part of sulfur-containing amino acids; firm proteins of hair, nails, and skin	Meat, wheat germ, dried beans and peas, peanuts
		Regulate blood and fluids; nerve impulse transmission; heart activity; metabolic controls	Table salt (sodium chloride), many canned soups and processed foods, pickles, soy sauce, sauerkraut, celery

* No U.S. RDI established. Amount is an estimated recommendation for dietary intake.

Table 1.3.3: Trace Minerals

Mineral	U.S. RDI	Functions	Sources
Selenium	50–75 mcg*	Prevents breakdown of fats	Seafood, whole-grain cereals, meat, egg yolk, milk, garlic
Manganese	5 mg*	Central nervous system; normal bone structure; reproduction	Nuts, whole grains, vegetables, fruits, tea, cocoa powder
Fluoride	1.5 to 4 mg*	Tooth and bone formation	Drinking water in some places, seafood, tea
Molybdenum	75–250 mcg*	Part of enzymes	Legumes, cereals, liver, kidneys, dark-green vegetables
Iron	18 mg	Formation of hemoglobin; part of enzymes and proteins	Liver, kidneys, meat, egg yolk, green, leafy vegetables, dried fruit, dried beans and peas, whole-grain and enriched cereals
Copper	2 mg	Formation of red blood cells; part of respiratory enzymes	Oysters, nuts, cocoa powder, liver, kidneys, beans, corn oil, margarine
Iodine	150 mcg	Functioning of the thyroid gland and production of thyroid hormones	Iodized salt, seafood
Chromium	50–200 mcg*	Helps the body use carbohydrates and fats; aids in digestion of protein	Liver, nuts, whole grains, Brewer's yeast, meat, mushrooms, potatoes, apples with skin, oysters
Zinc	15 mg	Part of many enzymes; essential to synthesis of DNA and RNA; metabolizes carbohydrates, fats, and proteins; dispose of carbon dioxide; strengthen immune system; helps wounds heal; helps body use vitamin A	Meat, liver, eggs, poultry, seafood

* No U.S. RDI established. Amount is an estimated recommendation for dietary intake.

> ***Point of Interest: Minerals***
>
> A study has found that heart-disease patients who received 150 mcg of chromium per day had a dramatic jump in the HDL cholesterol, the good stuff that helps keep arteries clear.

Water

About 60 to 70 percent of your body is water, with most of your blood, brain, and muscles being water and even 20 percent of your bones. Water carries the other nutrients, when dissolved, to all parts of the body where and when needed. It also aids in digestion, regulation of temperature, removal of wastes, joint lubrication, and biochemical processes taking place in the body all the time. Without water you would die in a few days. To maintain all the bodily functions water helps carry out, you need to consume the equivalent of six to eight glasses of water a day. If you exercise regularly, you may need as many as ten glasses, especially on the days you exercise.

Hunger and Malnutrition

As long as people can easily obtain an abundant and varied diet, it is not difficult for them to meet their nutritional needs. When such fortunate people become hungry, they can usually satisfy their need for food. However, many people in the world cannot obtain enough of the right foods—and in some cases cannot get much food at all. For them, hunger is a way of life—an ongoing, painful condition over which they have little control. Poor nutrition is a serious, worldwide problem.

Malnutrition

Technically, malnutrition is any condition in which a person's nutrient consumption is inadequate or unbalanced. Most cases, however, are the result of consuming too little of one or more nutrients. Malnutrition harms every system of the body and also damages emotional well-being.

When people are malnourished, they do not have the energy to perform well in school or at work. Malnourished people are also more susceptible to disease than those who eat a healthy diet. Malnourished children usually grow much more slowly than children whose diet is adequate. If malnutrition occurs during pregnancy, the baby may weigh less than normal and have serious health problems.

Figure 1.3.1: Famine victims, such as this Somalian woman, search in vain to try to find food. Source: Jean-Claude Coutausse/ Contact Press Images

There are various types of malnutrition, including the vitamin and mineral deficiencies discussed earlier in this lesson. In one especially serious condition known as protein-energy malnutrition, the diet does not contain adequate protein, nor does it supply enough calories to meet the body's energy needs. The effects of this condition are especially severe on children because their bodies need protein and calories for growth. Severe cases can cause death, either directly through starvation or indirectly through the diseases to which its victims become susceptible. Protein-energy malnutrition is the most serious nutrition problem affecting people in developing countries today.

Malnutrition has various causes. In some cases, people may be undernourished because they are unaware of the foods that they need for good health. Also, diseases and other conditions may prevent the digestive system from absorbing nutrients. But indirectly, poverty is by far the most common cause of malnutrition. Victims of severe poverty cannot afford to buy or grow the food they need.

A World Problem

Hunger and malnutrition are an especially severe problem in many of the world's poorer nations. Severe famines, for example, have devastated countries such as Somalia and Bangladesh. However, hunger is also a problem in more prosperous countries, including the United States. Although few people starve in the United States, many are not receiving adequate nutrition. Hungry people in the United States are those who have little or no income, such as homeless people, teenage runaways, families dealing with unemployment, and some elderly people.

Various programs and organizations are trying to solve the problem of malnutrition and provide food for those who need it. For example, the Food and Agriculture Organization of the United Nations combats hunger by helping people improve methods of agriculture and food distribution. The United States government sponsors the Food Stamp Program that enables low-income people to purchase the food that they need. Volunteers also work hard to help those who are hungry. For example, soup kitchens, which are often staffed by volunteers, provide meals for those in need.

Conclusion

Understanding what nutrition your body needs is essential to maintaining both physical and emotional health. Without the proper balance of carbohydrates, fats, proteins, vitamins, and minerals, you open the door to all kinds of health problems—some possibly fatal. Even with a fast-paced lifestyle, it's still possible to eat correctly and give your body the fuel it needs.

Lesson Review

1. **How do carbohydrates help the body?**

2. **Compare and contrast mono-unsaturated fats and poly-unsaturated fats.**

3. **What roles do proteins play in nutrition?**

4. **What are the effects of malnutrition?**

Chapter 2

First Aid for Emergency and Non-Emergency Situations

Lesson 1

The Need for First Aid/Your Response

Key Terms

cardiopulmonary resuscitation (CPR)
catastrophe
consent
emergency medical service
evaluate
first aid
Good Samaritan Law

What You Will Learn to Do

- Assess first aid situations

Linked Core Abilities

- Do your share as a good citizen in your school, community, country, and the world

Skills and Knowledge You Will Gain along the Way

- Assess the need for knowing how to perform first aid
- Explain the significance of the Good Samaritan Law
- Identify the steps of first aid intervention
- Identify the information needed when calling an emergency number such as 911
- Identify the steps for checking the ABCDs
- Define key words contained in this lesson

Chapter 2

Introduction

Most people encounter at least one situation requiring the use of first aid at some time in their lives. Whether a friend falls when rollerblading and breaks an arm, or your younger brother cuts himself on broken glass and requires stitches, someone should administer first aid until the injured person receives proper medical attention. That someone can be you if you acquire basic first aid knowledge of what to do and not to do in different accident situations. Remember that first aid may mean the difference between life and death, permanent and temporary disability, or long- and short-term recovery for an accident victim.

In addition to the first aid taught in this text, consider taking a first aid class from a qualified instructor. Many schools, hospitals, and fire departments offer first aid classes that provide demonstrations and hands-on experience with medical models of victims. Hands-on training is especially important before actually performing mouth-to-mouth resuscitation and **cardiopulmonary resuscitation (CPR)**, both of which can be hazardous to a victim if performed improperly.

Definition of First Aid

First aid is the immediate care given to an injured or ill individual to keep him or her alive or stop further damage until qualified medical treatment can be administered. It is caring for people involved in accidents, **catastrophes**, and natural disasters such as hurricanes, tornadoes, and earthquakes. First aid includes dealing with the situation, the person, and the injury, as well as encouraging the victim and showing a willingness to help.

Good Samaritan Law

The **Good Samaritan Law** is designed to protect the rescuer and encourage people to assist others in distress by granting them immunity against lawsuits. This law protects people from lawsuits as long as the rescuer is acting in good faith, without compensation and administers first aid correctly and without malicious misconduct or gross negligence.

First Aid Kit

Administering first aid is easier with a first aid kit. It is a good idea to keep one in your house and car and take one along on camping trips and hikes. A well-stocked first aid kit contains an assortment of bandages, Band-Aids, tape,

Key Note Term

cardiopulmonary resuscitation (CPR) – an emergency method to keep blood and oxygen flowing through a person whose heart and breathing have stopped.

first aid – the immediate care given to a victim of injury or sudden illness before professional medical help arrives.

catastrophe - a great and sudden misfortune.

Good Samaritan Law – a law enacted in most states that protects people from lawsuits if medical complications arise after they have administered first aid correctly.

aspirin or aspirin substitutes, antiseptic cream and cleanser, safety pins, scissors, tweezers, cotton, and tissues. To protect against infectious diseases, include rubber gloves and face shields in the kit. Rubber gloves will keep you from contact with blood and body fluids, and face shields will allow you to give mouth-to-mouth resuscitation and CPR without direct contact.

Evaluating the Victim

When you encounter an injured person, you must **evaluate** that person to determine what kind of first aid, if any, is needed. This preliminary check of the person follows a series of steps designed to pinpoint and correct the most serious health risks first and then continue with less life-threatening problems. These steps are explained in more detail later in this lesson. Basically, check for breathing and heartbeat first, for severe bleeding second, then for signs of shock, and finally for broken bones, burns, and head injuries. Depending on what problems your evaluation of an accident victim reveals, perform the life-saving steps in a sequence that parallels this evaluation sequence:

1. **Open the airway**
2. **Assess breathing**
3. **Assess circulation**
4. **Assess disability**

When evaluating a conscious victim, ask the victim if you can help and get **consent** to provide first aid; then get as much information as possible about the situation and how the victim feels. If the victim is unconscious and others witnessed the accident, get as much information from the witnesses as possible. Check the victim for medical alert identification. Many people with heart disease, epilepsy, diabetes, and allergies to medications wear medical alert identification bracelets or necklaces that can give you a clue as to their medical condition.

Have someone at the scene dial 911 for **emergency medical services** (**EMS**). If you are alone and the victim's condition is life-threatening, give first aid first, and then call 911. When calling 911, calmly state your name and exact location, the telephone number from which you are calling, details of what has happened, and the condition of the victim or victims.

Other important rules to follow at the scene of an accident include:

- **Remain calm, but act quickly. This will reassure the victim and help him or her to remain calm as well.**

- **Do not move an injured person. If the person has a neck or spine injury or broken bones, moving him or her could worsen the condition. Only move a victim if there is potential danger in remaining at the accident location. If you must move the victim for this reason, pull him or her in a straight line from the shoulders keeping the head and body in line. Support the head and pull the victim as short a distance as possible.**

Key Note Term

evaluate – to determine if an act, process, or method has been attained; to assess; to determine he significance of by careful appraisal and study.

Key Note Term

consent – to get approval for what is to be done or proposed by another.

emergency medical service (EMS) – medical professional dedicated to the reduction of morbidity and mortality of residents through the provision of Advanced and Basic Life Support care, medically directed rescue, and transportation of the ill and injured.

- If there is more than one injured person at an accident scene, evaluate them quickly; then help the most seriously injured first. For example, help the person with severe bleeding before you help the person with a broken arm.

The Life-Saving Steps

The following steps list evaluation procedures and specify treatment if necessary.

1. Check to see if the victim is conscious. To do so:

   a. Ask in a loud but calm voice, "Are you okay?"

   b. Gently shake or tap the victim on the shoulder.

   c. Watch for response. If the victim does not respond, go to Step 2.

   d. If the victim is conscious, ask where he or she feels different than usual or where it hurts. Go to Step 3.

   e. If the victim is conscious but is choking and cannot talk, stop the evaluation and begin treatment for clearing the airway of a conscious victim.

2. Check for breathing and heartbeat.

   a. Look for rise and fall of the victim's chest.

   b. Listen for breathing by placing your ear about one inch from the victim's mouth and nose.

   c. Feel for breathing by placing your hand or cheek about one inch from the victim's mouth and nose.

   d. At the same time, check for a pulse in the victim's neck.

   e. If there is a pulse but no breathing, stop the evaluation and begin treatment to restore the breathing.

   f. If there is no pulse, stop the evaluation and begin CPR.

3. Check for bleeding.

   a. Look for spurts of blood and blood-soaked clothing.

   b. Look for entry and exit wounds.

   c. If bleeding is present, stop the evaluation and begin treatment for stopping the bleeding.

4. Check for the following signs of shock:

   a. Sweaty, but cool skin

   b. Paleness

   c. Restlessness or nervousness

   d. Thirst

   e. Loss of blood

   f. Confusion

   g. Faster than normal breathing rate

   h. Blotchy or bluish skin

   i. Vomiting or nausea

If any of these signs are present, discontinue the evaluation and treat for shock.

5. **Check for fractures (broken bones).**

   a. **Check for the following signs of neck or back injury:**

      • **Pain or tenderness of neck or back area**

      • **Wounds of neck or back area**

      • **Paralysis**

   b. **Ask the victim if he or she can move.**

   c. **Touch the victim's arms and legs and ask whether he or she can feel it.**

   d. **If you suspect a neck or back injury, immobilize the victim by doing the following:**

      • **Tell the victim not to move.**

      • **If you suspect a back injury, place padding under the natural arch of the lower back.**

      • **If you suspect a neck injury, place padding under the victim's neck and place objects such as rocks or shoes on both sides of the head.**

   e. **Check the victim's arms or legs for fractures or broken bones. Signs are:**

      • **Swelling**

      • **Discoloration**

      • **Unusual angle or position of arm or leg**

      • **Bones sticking through the skin**

If you suspect a fracture, stop the evaluation and begin treatment for fractures.

6. **Check for burns. If you find burns, cover them with a clean dry cloth.**

7. **Check for head injury. Some possible signs of head injury are:**

   a. **Pupils of eyes unequal size**

   b. **Fluid from ear(s), nose, mouth or wounds to the head or face**

   c. **Slurred speech**

   d. **Confusion**

   e. **Sleepiness**

   f. **Loss of memory or consciousness**

   g. **Staggering when walking**

   h. **Headache**

   i. **Dizziness**

   j. **Vomiting**

   k. **Paralysis**

   l. **Convulsion or twitching**

When first aid is administered correctly and in a timely manner, it could mean the difference between life and death for the victim. Figure 2.1.1 shows emergency medical personnel assisting with an injured person.

Figure 2.1.1: Emergency personnel are trained to help victims of all types of injuries.

If a head injury is suspected, keep the person awake. Watch the victim for signs that would require restoring breathing or treating for shock.

When to Call 911 or Your Local Emergency Number

Call for an ambulance if the victim:

- Is or becomes unconscious
- Has trouble breathing
- Has persistent chest pain or pressure
- Is bleeding severely
- Has persistent pain or pressure in the abdomen
- Is vomiting
- Has seizures, slurred speech, or persistent severe headache
- Appears to have been poisoned
- Has injuries to the head, neck, or back
- Has possible broken bones

Also call if there is:

- A fire or explosion
- A downed electrical wire
- Swiftly moving or rapidly rising water
- Poisonous gas present
- A vehicle collision

Call the Emergency Number

Call or send someone to call for an ambulance. Calling your emergency number is often the most important thing you can do in an emergency. It is often critical to get professional medical help on the scene as soon as possible. In many communities, you can dial 911 for help in any type of emergency; otherwise, dial your local police or sheriff for medical emergencies, or dial 0, the operator, for assistance. Be prepared to follow the steps given below.

1. **Speak slowly and clearly.**
2. **Identify yourself and the phone number from which you are calling.**
3. **Give the exact location of the accident. Give the town, street name, and number. If you are calling at night, describe the building.**
4. **Describe what has happened. Give essential details about the victim(s), the situation, and any treatments you have given.**
5. **Ask for advice. Let the person on the other end ask you questions and tell you what to do until help arrives. Take notes, if necessary.**
6. **Hang up last. The person on the other end may have more questions or advice for you. And they might want you to stay on the phone with them until help arrives. Whatever the case, let the other person hang up first.**

Conclusion

First aid is the help that you give an injured person until qualified medical personnel can administer treatment. In other words, think of first aid as aid given first before actual medical treatment. The type of first aid required by an individual depends on his or her injuries, and you determine what those injuries are by carefully and quickly evaluating the person. This evaluation and the administration of first aid follow a sequence that deals with the most life-threatening problems first—breathing and heartbeat, followed by bleeding; then other health problems—shock, broken bones, burns, and head injuries.

Lesson Review

1. **Do you know how to perform CPR? If so, where did you learn this skill? If not, where can you learn it?**
2. **What is the meaning of the Good Samaritan Law?**
3. **Why is it important to have rubber gloves and a face shield in your first aid kit?**
4. **What skill can you use to remain calm and aware in a medical emergency?**

Chapter 2   Lesson Review

Lesson 2

The First Life-Saving Steps

Key Terms

automated external defibrillators
cardiac arrest
cardiopulmonary resuscitation (CPR)
Heimlich maneuver
rescue breathing
stroke

What You Will Learn to Do

- Demonstrate life-saving skills in an emergency situation

Linked Core Abilities

- Do your share as a good citizen in your school, community, country, and the world

Skills and Knowledge You Will Gain along the Way

- Describe how to perform rescue breathing
- Identify the steps for performing CPR
- Explain how CPR can keep a victim's heart and brain alive
- Identify the steps for performing the Heimlich maneuver
- Define key words contained in this lesson

Introduction

In emergency situations, the people involved may find it difficult to remain calm and think clearly. In the midst of this confusion, one simple trick you can use to remind yourself of the first and most important problems to check for and steps to take are the letters A-B-C.

- **A** stands for airway. Is the victim's airway blocked? If so, clear the airway.
- **B** stands for breathing. Is the victim breathing? If not, restore breathing.
- **C** stands for circulation. Is the victim's heart beating? If not, restore the heartbeat.

Clearing the Airway of a Conscious Victim

Choking occurs when a person inhales something into the airway leading to the lungs, blocking the airway off and preventing breathing. In many choking cases, people inhale particles of food while eating. In an accident, injured people may choke on dirt, broken teeth, or dentures.

A person whose airway is completely blocked off cannot make any sound because no air is getting to the vocal cords. If a person can speak or cough, some air is getting through to the vocal cords and lungs, and you should let the person try to clear the airway on his or her own. If the person can make no sound and indicates choking by grabbing the throat, the best method to clear the person's airway is the **Heimlich maneuver**, shown in Figure 2.2.1. After performing the Heimlich maneuver, be sure the victim seeks professional medical help.

> ### Key Note Term
>
> **Heimlich maneuver** – an upward push to the abdomen given to clear the airway of a person with a complete airway obstruction; procedure used to expel an object lodged in the airway of a choking victim.

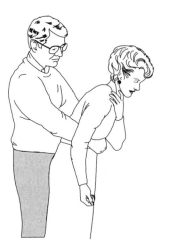

Figure 2.2.1: The Heimlich maneuver can save the life of a choking victim.

To perform the Heimlich maneuver on a choking victim, follow these steps:

1. **Stand behind the victim and wrap your arms around the victim's waist.**

2. **Make a fist with one hand and place the thumb side of the fist against the victim's abdomen slightly above the navel and well below the breastbone. Grasp the fist with the other hand.**

3. **Give six to ten quick backward and upward thrusts; repeat this until the airway is clear.**

For an exceptionally overweight person or pregnant woman, use the same procedure, except place the fist in the middle of the breastbone.

If you are the victim of an airway obstruction and no one is around to help, lean forward over a railing, sink, or the back of a chair as shown in Figure 2.2.2, and thrust yourself down until you dislodge the obstruction.

> **Note**
>
> Don't slap the victim's back. This could make matters worse. For more information about the Heimlich maneuver, check out
> http://www.heimlichinstitute.org/howtodo.html.

Clearing the Airway of an Unconscious Victim

If a person is unconscious and you know that individual has an obstructed airway, perform the following maneuver with the victim lying on his or her back. Figure 2.2.3 shows the position for this action.

1. **Kneel astride the victim's thighs. Place the heel of one hand against the victim's abdomen, slightly above the navel, but well below the victim's breastbone, with your fingers pointing towards the victim's head.**

2. **Place your other hand on top of your first hand and press into the abdomen with a quick forward and upward thrust. Repeat this six to ten times.**

Figure 2.2.2: You can save your life when choking if you know how to dislodge the obstruction.

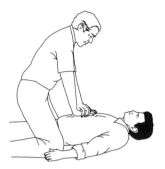

Figure 2.2.3: Kneel over an unconscious victim to clear the airway.

3. **Open the victim's mouth and sweep out any foreign matter using a hooked finger. Be careful not to push anything down the throat.**

For an obese individual or a woman in the advanced stages of pregnancy, use the following procedure:

1. **Kneel to the side of the victim's body. Locate the lower edge of the victim's ribs, and run the fingers up along the rib cage to the notch where the ribs meet the breastbone.**

2. **Place the heel of the hand two finger widths above the notch, and place the other hand over the first, interlocking the fingers.**

3. **Position your shoulders over your hands, and with the elbows locked, press down 1½ to 2 inches, six to ten times.**

4. **Open the victim's mouth and sweep out any foreign matter using a hooked finger. Be careful not to push anything down the throat.**

Restoring the Breathing

If you discover a victim who is not breathing, it is necessary to start breathing for the victim by forcing oxygen into his or her lungs as soon as possible. This process, called **rescue breathing** or mouth-to-mouth resuscitation, can prevent brain damage and death. By applying this first aid step it will most likely start the victim breathing independently; if not, continue it until you are replaced by a qualified person or medical help arrives. When you are giving mouth-to-mouth resuscitation to a victim, you are a life-support system! Figure 2.2.4 shows the basic position for applying mouth-to-mouth resuscitation.

The following steps describe how to give mouth-to-mouth resuscitation to adults. Procedures that are different for infants and small children are italicized.

1. **Roll the victim gently over if he or she is not already facing up. Open the mouth and check to see if it is clear. Using a hooked finger, sweep out anything you find in the mouth, being careful not to push anything down the throat.**

Key Note Term

rescue breathing – the act of forcing air into and out of the lungs of a person by another person.

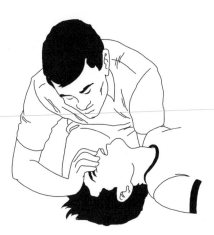

Figure 2.2.4: Tilt the victim's head and pinch the nose to perform rescue breathing.

2. Tilt the victim's head back sharply by pressing down on the forehead and lifting on the jaw. This straightens out the passageway to the victim's lungs. *For infants and small children, do not tilt the head back. Instead, place a finger under the chin and lift it slightly.*

3. Keeping the victim's head tilted sharply back, pinch the nose closed, cover the victim's mouth completely with your mouth, and give the victim two full breaths. *For infants and small children, do not pinch the nose closed. Instead, cover both the mouth and nose with your mouth and give small, slow, gentle breaths.* Each breath should last 1 to 1½ seconds. Pause between breaths to let the air come out of the victim and to breathe in yourself. If the victim's chest does not rise when you breathe into his or her lungs, reposition the head slightly farther back and repeat the breaths. If the victim's chest still does not rise, perform abdominal thrusts to clear the airway as described in the previous section, "Clearing the Airway of an Unconscious Victim;" then repeat the breaths.

4. After the two breaths, listen and feel for breathing by placing your cheek close to the victim's mouth. At the same time, check the victim's pulse by placing two fingers in the groove of the neck next to the Adam's apple, as shown in Figure 2.2.5. This is the location of the carotid artery, which normally produces a strong pulse.

5. If there is no pulse, start CPR immediately as described in the next section.

6. If there is a pulse but no breathing, continue mouth-to-mouth resuscitation at the rate of one breath every five seconds or 12 times a minute. *For infants and small children, give one slow breath every three seconds.*

7. If the victim starts to breathe, stop mouth-to-mouth resuscitation and let the victim breathe on his or her own. Check for other injuries, treat as required, and observe the victim closely until medical help arrives.

Cardiopulmonary Resuscitation (CPR)

As in mouth-to-mouth resuscitation, when you perform **cardiopulmonary resuscitation** (CPR), you are a life-support system for the victim. CPR is a first aid procedure performed to restore breathing and heartbeat. It is a combination

Key Note Term

cardiopulmonary resuscitation (CPR) – an emergency method to keep blood and oxygen flowing through a person whose heart and breathing have stopped.

Figure 2.2.5: After two breaths, check for a pulse as you check for breath sounds.

of mouth-to-mouth resuscitation and a procedure known as closed chest heart massage. Mouth-to-mouth resuscitation supplies oxygen to the lungs, while the closed chest heart massage manually pumps blood through the victim's body, circulating it to the heart and brain. These actions help keep the heart and brain alive until the heartbeat is restored or medical help arrives.

CPR can be performed by a single rescuer or by more than one rescuer because CPR can be tiring and is easier if two rescuers are available. The CPR procedures discussed in this lesson are for a single rescuer. Before beginning CPR, you should turn the victim face up, clear the airway, give two full breaths as described in mouth-to-mouth resuscitation, and check for a pulse. Only proceed if there is no pulse, and therefore, no heartbeat present.

Performing CPR on an Adult

To perform CPR on an adult, follow these steps:

1. **With the middle and index fingers of the hand nearest the victim's legs, locate the lower edge of the rib cage on the side of the victim's chest closest to you.**

2. **Slide your fingers up the edge of the rib cage to the notch at the lower end of the breastbone. Place your middle finger in the notch and the index finger next to it on the lower end of the breastbone.**

3. **Place the heel of the hand nearest the victim's head on the breastbone next to the index finger of the hand used to find the notch.**

4. **Place the heel of the hand used to find the notch directly on top of the heel of the other hand. Only let the heel of your hand touch the victim's chest; keep your fingers lifted off of the victim's chest. If you place your hands correctly, they will be positioned slightly above the lowest part of the breastbone, known as the xiphoid process. Avoid pressing on the xiphoid process because it breaks easily.**

5. **Position your shoulders over your hands, with elbows locked and arms straight.**

6. **Press down on the breastbone 1½ to 2 inches at a very quick, continuous rate. This squeezes the victim's heart against the spine and forces blood through the body.**

7. **While compressing, count aloud "one and two and three and four . . ." until you get to 15. It should take you about ten seconds to do 15 compressions. Push down as you say the number and release the pressure as you say "and." Compress up and down smoothly without removing your hands from the chest.**

8. After the fifteenth compression, give the victim two full breaths. Be sure to pinch the nose closed and tilt the victim's head back to straighten the airway. Then return to the chest compressions.

9. When you complete four cycles of 15 chest compressions and two breaths, check for a pulse again. If there is no pulse, continue CPR.

Performing CPR on an Infant

Performing CPR on an infant is slightly different than performing it on an adult. To do so, follow these steps:

1. Place your hand closest to the infant's head gently on the infant's forehead and leave it there throughout the procedure.

2. Place the middle and ring fingers of the hand nearest the infant's legs on the infant's breastbone about one finger width below the infant's nipples.

3. Give five compressions with those two fingers at a rapid pace, pushing the chest down about ½ to 1 inch.

4. Follow the five compressions with one breath as described in the italicized text in Step 3 of mouth-to-mouth resuscitation. Rapidly repeat the five compressions and one breath 20 times a minute until breathing and heartbeat resume.

Performing CPR on a Child

To perform CPR on a child, follow these steps:

1. As with an adult, find the notched center of the child's ribcage with the hand closest to the child's legs. Measure two finger widths above the notch using the other hand, and then place the heel of the hand used to find the notch on the child's breastbone above the two fingers.

2. Place the hand that you used to measure two finger widths gently on the child's forehead and leave it there throughout the rest of the procedure.

3. Using the heel of your hand and keeping your fingers off of the child's chest, give five compressions 1 to 1 ½ inches deep, followed by one breath as described in the italicized text in Step 3 of mouth-to-mouth resuscitation. Repeat this sequence 12 times a minute until breathing and heartbeat resume.

Heart Attacks

A heart attack occurs when the blood supply to part of the heart muscle is severely reduced or stopped. That happens when one of the coronary arteries (the arteries that supply blood to the heart muscle) is blocked by an obstruction or a spasm. Common signs and symptoms so of a heart attack include:

- Uncomfortable pressure, fullness, squeezing, or pain in the center of the chest that lasts more than a few minutes or that goes away and comes back.
- Pain spreading to the shoulders, neck, or arms.
- Chest discomfort with lightheadedness, fainting, sweating, nausea, or shortness of breath.

When a person's heart stops beating, the victims is said to be in **cardiac arrest**. Cardiopulmonary resuscitations (CPR) can keep the individual alive. If a person has a heart attack, call Emergency Medical Services (EMS). Monitor the ABC's and give CPR as necessary.

Stroke

A **stroke** occurs when blood vessels that deliver oxygen-rich blood to the brain rupture or when a blood clot forms and blocks the flow of blood to the brain. Common signs and symptoms of a stroke include:

* **Paralysis on one side of the body**

* **Blurred or decreased vision, pupils of unequal size**

* **Problems speaking, slurred speech**

* **Difficulty breathing**

* **Mental confusion**

* **Dizziness or loss of balance**

* **Sudden, severe, or unexplained headache**

* **Loss of consciousness**

If a person has a stroke, call Emergency Medical Service (EMS). Lay the victim down on one side and cover with blanket. Monitor the ABC's and give CPR as necessary.

> **Note**
>
> To learn more about strokes, check out www.strokeassociation.org to see the American Stroke Association website.

Automated External Defibrillators (AED)

Recently there has been a breakthrough in how Emergency Medical Technicians (EMTs) treat victims of sudden cardiac arrest. The **Automated External Defibrillator (AED)** is a device that uses a computer chip to analyze the heart rhythm and determines whether a shock is needed. This device allows victims suffering a sudden cardiac arrest a greatly improved chance of survival. Because of the ease of operation, people can be trained in AED use in a few hours, and some say the techniques are easier to learn than CPR. Many AEDs offer voice prompts, which provide operators with clear and concise instructions. Most AEDs have only three buttons: On/Off, Analyze, and Shock. Many airlines have installed AEDs on all their planes, and several cities are locating them in areas where there are large concentrations of people, such as malls, arenas, and stadiums.

Key Note Term

cardiac arrest – the sudden stoppage of the heart.

Key Note Term

stroke – a reduction of blood flow to a part of the brain.

Key Note Term

automated external defibrillator – a device used to treat a patient with cardiac arrest whose heart is beating irregularly.

Conclusion

This lesson presents the correct techniques for dealing with the most life-threatening conditions of an accident victim—loss of breathing and heartbeat. Use the letters **A-B-C** to remind yourself of the first problems to check for on an injured person: Airway blocked, loss of Breathing, and lack of Circulation. Perform the Heimlich maneuver to clear a victim's airway, mouth-to-mouth resuscitation to restore breathing, and CPR to restore circulation (heartbeat). For the best and safest results, take a class from a qualified instructor before performing mouth-to-mouth resuscitation or CPR on an injured person.

Lesson Review

1. What are the A-B-Cs of life-saving steps?

2. Discuss the Heimlich maneuver, both performing it on another and performing it on yourself.

3. When performing CPR, what are the differences between performing this on an adult, an infant, and a child?

4. What are the common signs of a stroke?

Lesson 3

Controlling Bleeding

Key Terms

arteries
dressing
elevated
hemorrhage
pressure bandage
pressure point
veins

What You Will Learn to Do

- Determine first aid procedures for bleeding victim

Linked Core Abilities

- Do your share as a good citizen in your school, community, country, and the world

Skills and Knowledge You Will Gain along the Way

- Identify the three types of bleeding
- Identify the best way to control most cases of bleeding
- Distinguish among direct pressure, pressure points and a tourniquet to control bleeding
- Describe how to clean wounds
- Define key words

Chapter 2

Introduction

In an accident situation, you may encounter injured persons bleeding from wounds such as scrapes, cuts, or punctures as well as tears or gashes in the skin. The deeper a wound goes, the more serious it is. Mild wounds to the outer layer of skin do not bleed heavily but still require cleaning to avoid infection. Deeper wounds in which **arteries** and **veins** are cut can be life-threatening. These kinds of wounds may involve great amounts of blood, and blood may often pulse or spurt out of the wound. Severe bleeding, or **hemorrhage**, can result in shock or death if not treated promptly. It is essential to stop the loss of blood in these cases. If a victim loses too much blood, even CPR will not keep the person alive because there will not be enough blood to deliver oxygen from the lungs to the body.

Types of Bleeding

There are three types of bleeding you may encounter in an emergency situation. These are:

- **Arterial bleeding is the loss of blood from an artery. Characterized by bright red blood that spurts with each heartbeat, arterial blood loss is severe and hard to control. Give it first priority for treatment.**
- **Venous bleeding is blood loss from a vein. Venous bleeding is characterized by a steady flow of dark blood.**
- **Capillary bleeding is the loss of blood from the capillaries (the smallest blood vessels), and is usually characterized by a slow flow of blood.**

First aid treatment in all of these cases includes stopping the flow of blood and preventing infection.

Direct Pressure

In most cases, applying continuous, direct pressure to a wound is the best way to control bleeding. To apply direct pressure, place a **dressing** over the wound and apply pressure to the dressing, as shown in Figure 2.3.1. A dressing should be:

- **As sterile as possible. If a sterile dressing is not available, use a clean cloth (a washcloth, towel, or handkerchief).**
- **Larger than the wound.**
- **Thick, soft, and compressible so pressure is evenly distributed over the wound.**
- **Lint free.**

Key Note Term

arteries – blood vessels that carry blood away from the heart to all parts of the body.

veins – blood vessels that carry blood from all parts of the body to the heart.

hemorrhage – heavy or uncontrollable bleeding

Key Note Term

dressing – ointment and bandages applied to a wound.

Figure 2.3.1: Apply direct pressure to the bandage to stop bleeding.

If a clean cloth or gauze is not available, use clothing or your bare hands or fingers—whatever is the cleanest. Continue applying pressure and the bleeding should begin to slow or stop within 30 minutes.

Stopping Infection

Even the slightest wound requires immediate cleansing. The best way to clean wounds is to wash them with soap and water. At home, use water from the faucet. On a hike, use water from a canteen or the clear running water of a stream. If available, use an antiseptic cleanser instead of soap. Wait until the skin around the wound dries and then put on a bandage. If available, apply an antiseptic cream to the wound before bandaging it.

For a minor wound, cleaning and bandaging it is probably all that is required. Deep wounds, wounds made by animal or human bites, and wounds contaminated by dirt, rust, or other items require medical treatment. Clean and bandage these wounds, and get medical assistance as soon as possible. If a wound contains glass or other objects stuck into the flesh, do not remove them unless they wash out of the wound easily.

Controlling Bleeding to Extremities

In most cases, direct pressure is the best way to stop bleeding of wounds to the extremities (arms and legs). As you apply direct pressure, keep the injured limb **elevated** above the heart to slow the flow of blood out of the body.

After initially applying direct pressure, you may want to apply a **pressure bandage** by wrapping a bandage snugly around the limb, using overlapping turns with a roll of gauze. Do not tie the pressure bandage so tightly that it restricts blood flow to the lower part of the limb. If fingertips or toes appear bluish or if

Key Note Term

elevated – raised up.

pressure bandage – a snug bandage used to control bleeding.

Key Note Term

pressure point – a point on the body where a major artery lies near the skin surface and passes over a bone.

there is no pulse below the dressing, loosen the material used to secure the dressing immediately. After you apply a pressure bandage, only qualified medical personnel should remove it.

Pressure Points

In the case of severe bleeding that does not slow or stop using direct pressure, finger pressure may be applied to the **pressure point** on the injured limb between the wound and the heart. Pressure points, shown in Figure 2.3.2, are locations on the body where arteries are close to the surface. By applying pressure at these points, you slow or stop the flow of blood through the artery.

Figure 2.3.2: Use pressure points on the body to help slow or stop bleeding.

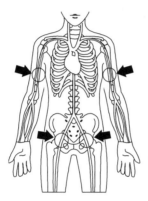

As with mouth-to-mouth resuscitation and CPR, it is better to have first aid training on pressure points before actually using this technique to stop bleeding. If done incorrectly, you may damage healthy tissue fed by the artery you are constricting.

Tourniquet

If heavy blood loss continues, as from amputation, it may be necessary to use a tourniquet.

> **Caution:** Because a tourniquet is a constricting band that stops the flow of blood below it, it can kill the limb to which it is applied; therefore, only use a tourniquet if no other method works to stop the bleeding and you believe the injured person's life is in danger.

To apply a tourniquet, follow these steps:

1. **Fold a cloth until it is approximately two inches wide and long enough to go around the injured limb (see Figure 2.3.3).**

2. **Tie the material in a loop and position it two to four inches above the wound, but not over a joint.**

3. **Pass a rigid object, such as a stick, under the tourniquet loop and twist it until the bleeding stops (see Figure 2.3.4).**

Figure 2.3.3: Fold a cloth so it is long enough to go around the injured limb.

Figure 2.3.4: Use a stick or other rigid object to tie off the tourniquet.

Figure 2.3.5: Secure the end of the stick to keep the tourniquet from unwinding.

4. **Tie off the end of the stick with another piece of cloth or string to prevent it from unwinding (see Figure 2.3.5).**

5. **Mark the victim's forehead with a "T" to alert medical personnel that you have applied a tourniquet.**

If it is necessary to cover the victim with a blanket, do not cover the tourniquet to make it easier for medical personnel to spot. After you apply a tourniquet, do not loosen or remove it. As with a pressure dressing, only qualified medical personnel should remove a tourniquet.

Note

Remember—use a tourniquet only as a last resort when all other attempts to stop the bleeding fail.

Controlling Bleeding to the Head and Torso

There are different ways to control head and torso bleeding. This section details how to use the methods.

Scalp Injuries

For wounds to the scalp, use a pressure dressing. If brain tissue is exposed, tie the dressing loosely over the wound. Do not press the brain tissue back into the open wound.

Facial Injuries

Control bleeding from facial wounds by using a pressure bandage. Position the victim to prevent him or her from breathing blood. Victims who have sustained a severe blow to the head should be kept under close observation as they may have brain damage and could require rescue breathing.

Chest Injuries

A chest injury may result in an open chest wound, which could lead to air leaking from a lung and the collapse of a lung. If conscious, have the victim breathe out and apply some material such as plastic wrap or foil to the wound. Bind a pressure bandage tightly to the wound to prevent leakage of air and slow down blood loss. Have the victim sit up, if possible, or lay that person on the injured side.

Abdominal Injuries

When an open abdominal wound has exposed visceral (internal) organs, cover the abdomen loosely with dressings. Do not force the organs back into the body cavity and do not give victims with abdominal wounds any food or water.

Conclusion

Severe bleeding from wounds in which arteries or veins are cut can be life-threatening to an injured person; therefore, controlling the loss of blood is second in importance only to restoring breathing and circulation. In most cases, applying direct pressure to a wound is the best way to control bleeding. Cleansing a wound to stop infection is also extremely important. If you know these two facts, and the other details on controlling bleeding to the extremities, head, and torso, you can successfully accomplish the second life-saving step in an emergency situation.

Lesson Review

1. List and explain the three types of bleeding.
2. How does direct pressure help stop bleeding?
3. Why is it important to use bandages that are as clean as possible?
4. Define the term "hemorrhage."

Lesson 4

Treating for Shock and Immobilizing Fractures

Key Terms

clammy
closed fracture
dislocation
fainting
ligament
open fracture
splint
sprain
strain
trauma

What You Will Learn to Do

- Determine first aid treatment for shock, fractures, strains and sprains

Linked Core Abilities

- Do your share as a good citizen in your school, community, country, and the world

Skills and Knowledge You Will Gain along the Way

- Explain causes and effects of shock
- Identify the signs of shock
- Demonstrate how to treat for shock

- Distinguish between closed and open fractures
- Identify procedures for immobilizing fractures using splints and slings
- Distinguish between strains and sprains
- Define key words contained in this lesson

Introduction

Whenever you treat someone for a severe injury, you must also treat them for shock. Even if an injured person shows no signs of shock, treat them anyway; shock can follow all major injuries. By treating for shock, you lessen its severity. If left untreated, shock can become life-threatening. There have been cases where people died from shock even though their injuries would not have killed them. Knowing how to deal with shock is a very important part of first aid.

After treating for shock, take care of broken bones or suspected broken bones. If there is a question of whether a bone is broken, treat it as if it were broken. Follow the first aid procedures for splinting a fracture carefully because more damage can occur if a fracture is handled improperly.

Shock

Shock from an injury is different from electric shock, although it can be brought on by electric shock, as well as blood loss, burns, psychological **trauma**, heart attack, and other injuries involving pain. Shock disrupts circulation. In an attempt to correct damage from an injury and to protect its blood supply, the body routes blood away from outer tissues to organs inside the body. This may keep adequate blood, and therefore oxygen, from reaching the brain. In severe cases, the injured person can lose consciousness and blood supply to vital organs like the heart, causing death.

Shock usually occurs within the first hour after a severe injury. How severe shock becomes depends on several factors including the type of injury, how much blood is lost, and characteristics of the injured person's nervous system. Increased pain, rough handling, delayed treatment, and emotional reactions such as fear and panic can worsen shock.

Signs of Shock

When a victim is in shock, the skin is pale or bluish and cold to the touch. For a victim with dark skin, check the color of the mucous membranes on the inside of the mouth or under the eyelids, or check under the nail beds. The skin may be **clammy** from perspiration. Other signs that may develop in the early stages of shock include:

Key Note Term

trauma – a behavioral state resulting from mention or emotional stress or physical injury that has a lasting effect on the mind; a physical wound or injury.

Key Note Term

clammy – damp, soft, sticky, and unusually cool.

- **Restlessness or nervousness**
- **Thirst**
- **Bleeding**
- **Confusion or loss of awareness**
- **Breathing rapidly**
- **Nausea and/or vomiting**
- **Blotchy or bluish skin around the mouth and lips**
- **Fainting**

Key Note Term

fainting – to lose consciousness briefly because of temporary decrease in the amount of blood that flows to the brain.

Fainting, or "blacking out," is a mild form of shock caused by a lack of blood to the brain. Fright, bad news, breathing polluted air, or standing too long can result in fainting. Before fainting occurs, a shock victim may turn pale, shake, or suddenly fall to the ground.

Treating Shock

Procedures for treating shock include improving circulation of the blood, ensuring an adequate supply of oxygen, and maintaining normal body temperature. To treat a victim for shock, follow these steps:

1. **Position the victim on his or her back, unless a sitting position allows easier breathing. If the victim is vomiting, position that person on the side to let fluid drain from the mouth.**

2. **Elevate the victim's feet higher than the heart, unless the victim has an abdominal or chest wound or an unsplinted leg fracture.**

3. **Loosen clothing that may bind around the neck and waist.**

4. **Keep the victim from becoming cold or overheating.**

5. **Reassure the victim, and do not give him or her any food or drink; however, if you know that help is not going to arrive for over an hour, give the victim small amounts of fluids, at room temperature, every 15 minutes. Add an eighth of a teaspoon of salt, if available, to each half glass of fluid. This will help the victim retain more fluids in his or her system.**

Fractures

Key Note Term

closed fracture – a fracture in which the broken bone does not push through the skin's surface.

open fracture – a fracture in which the broken end of a bone pierces the skin.

Bone fractures resulting from falls are common injuries. A **closed** or simple **fracture** is a break in the bone that does not penetrate the skin. An **open** or compound **fracture** occurs if the sharp edges of a splintered bone have cut through the skin. Both types of fractures are shown in Figure 2.4.1.

In the case of an open fracture, it is obvious that a bone is broken. In the case of a closed fracture, indications of a broken bone include swelling, discoloration, and unusual positioning of the limb in question.

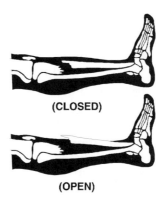

Figure 2.4.1: Closed (simple) and open (compound) fractures.

Do's and Don'ts

When treating fractures, what you do is important, and what you don't do is equally as important.

- **Do call for medical assistance immediately.**
- **Do keep the victim from moving.**
- **Do treat for shock while waiting for medical assistance.**
- **Don't try to set the bone.**
- **Don't put the victim in a car to rush him or her to a hospital. That is the easiest way of turning a closed fracture into an open one.**
- **Don't give stimulants if there is severe bleeding.**

Splints

The most important action to take when dealing with a fracture is to immobilize the injured bone to prevent further damage. The best way to immobilize bones is with a **splint**, shown in Figure 2.4.2.

Key Note Term

splint – to support and immobilize a body part with a stiff material.

Figure 2.4.2: Splints help immobilize bones to prevent further injury.

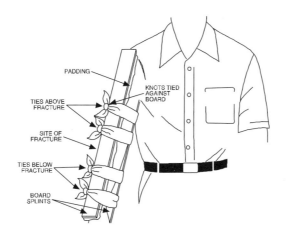

For open fractures, control the bleeding before splinting. Keep the exposed bone moist by covering it with a moist, sterile dressing. The rules of splinting are:

1. **Pad all splinting material. Make splints from sticks, boards, cardboard, rolled newspaper, or any other unbendable material.**

2. **Splint the broken leg or arm in the position in which you found it. Do not try to straighten or reposition the fracture. In most cases, support an arm from above and below and a leg from the sides.**

3. **Use splinting material that is long enough to immobilize the joint above and below the break. For example, immobilize the ankle and the knee for a fracture in the vicinity of the calf.**

4. **Tie the splints above and below the suspected fracture. Make two ties above and two below the break. Never make a tie directly over the break.**

5. **Tie all knots on the outside of the splints.**

6. **Check that circulation is not restricted by splints tied too tightly.**

If no splinting material is available, immobilize a leg fracture by placing padding between the injured leg and the uninjured leg and tying them together. Using the uninjured leg as the splint, draw two ties above and two below the suspected break.

Slings

For arm fractures in which the entire arm is not splinted, use a sling (see Figure 2.4.3) to support the weight of the arm. If necessary, pin the victim's shirttail up to serve as a field expedient sling.

Figure 2.4.3: Placing a sling on an injured arm can support the injury.

Joint Injuries

Joint injuries occur when excess stress or strain is placed on the joint. This can happen during normal activities such as walking or running, and is common in sports activities. Dislocations and sprains are the most common joint injuries.

Dislocations

A **dislocation** occurs when a joint comes apart and stays apart with the bone ends no longer in contact. The shoulders, elbows, fingers, hips, kneecaps, and ankles are the joints most frequently affected. Dislocations have signs and symptoms similar to those of a fracture: severe pain, swelling, and the inability of the victim to move the injured joint. The main sign of a dislocation is deformity; its appearance will be different from that of a comparable uninjured joint. The procedures for treating a dislocation include:

1. **Do not try to set the joint. Immobilize and support the injured joint as if treating for a fracture.**
2. **Use the RICE procedures (discussed later in this lesson).**
3. **Seek medical attention.**

Sprain

A **sprain** is an injury to a joint in which the **ligament**s and other tissues are damaged by violent stretching or twisting. Attempts to move or use the joint increase the pain. The skin about the joint may be discolored because of bleeding from torn tissues. It is often difficult to distinguish between a severe sprain and a fracture, because their signs and symptoms are similar. If you are not sure whether an injury is a sprain or a fracture, treat it like a fracture. It is better to immobilize a sprain than to take the chance of a victim sustaining further damage from an unsplinted closed fracture.

Treatment for a sprain consists of rest, ice, compression, and elevation (RICE). Seek medical attention.

Muscle Injuries

Muscle injuries are as common as joint injuries. These can be very painful and need treatment as soon as possible after the injury occurs. The most common muscle injury is a strain.

Key Note Term

dislocation – the separation of a bone from its joint.

Key Note Term

sprain – an injury caused by twisting a ligament or tendon around a joint.

ligament – a fibrous band of tissue that holds bones together at a joint.

Strain

Key Note Term

strain – an injury caused when a muscle or tendon is overstretched.

A muscle **strain**, or muscle pull, occurs when a muscle is stretched beyond its normal range of motion, resulting in the muscle tearing. Signs and symptoms include: sharp pain, extreme tenderness when the area is touched, slight swelling, and difficulty moving or using he affected part. Treatment for a strain consists of rest, ice, compression and elevation (RICE).

RICE Procedures for Bone, Joint and Muscle Injuries

RICE is the acronym for the first aid procedures—Rest, Ice, Compression, and Elevation—for bone, joint, and muscle injuries. What is done in the first 48–72 hours following such an injury can greatly affect the recovery.

1. **Rest—Injuries heal faster if rested. Rest means the victim stays off the injured part.**

2. **Ice—An ice pack should be applied to the injured area for 20–30 minutes every 2–3 hours during the first 24–48 hours. When the skin becomes numb, remove the ice pack.**

3. **Compression—Compression of the injured area may squeeze some fluid and debris out of the injury site. Compression limits the ability of the skin and of other tissues to expand. Applying compression may be the most important step in preventing swelling. The victim should wear an elastic bandage continuously for 18–24 hours.**

4. **Elevation—Gravity has an important effect on swelling. The force of gravity pulls blood and other tissue to the lower parts of the body. After fluids get to your hands or feet, they have nowhere else to go; therefore, those parts of the body tend to swell the most. Elevating the injured areas, in combination with ice and compression, limits circulation to that area, which in turn helps limit internal bleeding and minimize swelling. Whenever possible, elevate the injured part above the level of the heart for the first 24 hours after an injury.**

Conclusion

This lesson explained the first aid procedures for treating shock and fractures. Remember that shock can follow severe injuries and can be life-threatening if left untreated. Treating a victim for shock involves improving circulation, ensuring an adequate oxygen supply, and maintaining normal body temperature. For fractures, the most important action to take is immobilizing the broken bone using splints. By following these first aid procedures, you can lessen the severity of shock caused by an injury and ensure that no further damage occurs to a victim because of a broken bone, sprain, or strain.

Lesson Review

1. List one 'do' and one 'don't' when treating fractures.

2. What causes fainting?

3. What are the signs of shock?

4. Define the differences between a strain and a sprain.

Lesson 5

First Aid for Burns

Chapter 2

Key Terms

acids
alkalis
bases
caustic
compresses
flush
mottled
neutralized
scalding
smoldering
systemic

What You Will Learn to Do

- Determine first aid treatment for burns

Linked Core Abilities

- Do your share as a good citizen in your school, community, country, and the world

Skill and Knowledge You Will Gain along the Way

- Characterize degrees of burns
- Describe how to treat first, second, and third-degree heat burns

- **Describe how to treat electrical burns**
- **Describe how to treat chemical burns to the eyes and skin**
- **Define key words**

Introduction

Burns can result from sources of heat, electricity, and chemicals. In situations where people are injured by these sources, your first aid knowledge should include how to treat them. This lesson covers different types of burns, how to treat them, and ways to prevent them.

Burns

There are several types and degrees of burns that require different treatments. Heat, electricity, and chemicals can produce burn injuries; their severity depends upon the burn's depth, size, and location. Burns can be painful and may result in shock and infection. They can be very serious if they are spread over a large area of the body, there are other injuries involved, or the victim is very young or very old.

Degrees of Burns

For burns caused by heat sources, there are different degrees (first, second, or third) based on the burn's depth. The deeper the burn, the more severe and the higher the degree. All electrical burns are third degree.

Characteristics of First-Degree Burns

There are several characteristics of first-degree burns. These include:

- **Least severe**
- **Injure only the top layer of skin**
- **Redden the skin**
- **Produce mild swelling**
- **Cause pain due to irritated nerve endings**
- **Heal quickly and completely if properly treated**
- **Caused by brief contact with hot objects, brief exposure to hot water or steam, and overexposure to sun (light sunburn) or wind**

Characteristics of Second-Degree Burns

There are several characteristics of second-degree burns. These include:

- Involve deeper layers of skin
- Cause skin to turn red and/or **mottled**
- Appear moist and oozing from the loss of fluid through damaged skin layers
- Produce blisters and swelling
- Usually the most painful type of burn because nerve endings are still intact even though tissue damage is severe
- Burns covering a large area may cause shock due to extensive loss of fluid from the burned skin
- Smaller second-degree burns that are properly treated should heal within two weeks with little or no scarring
- Caused by a deep sunburn, prolonged contact with hot objects, **scalding**, and flash burns from flammable liquids suddenly bursting into flame

Characteristics of Third-Degree Burns

There are specific characteristics of third-degree burns. These include:

- Deepest and most severe type of burn
- May look white or charred (may appear to be a second-degree burn at first)
- Result in deep tissue destruction, reaching all layers of the skin and sometimes structures below the skin
- Often cause little or no pain since nerve endings are destroyed
- Often cause shock
- When healed, will be covered by scar tissue
- Caused by immersion in extremely hot water, prolonged contact with flames, and electric shock

Treatment of Heat Burns

Treat heat burns based on their degree; therefore, before treating a burn, determine its degree and treat accordingly. When deciding the degree of a burn, in addition to the previous descriptions, it may help to know the source of the burn and/or how hot the source was, as well as how long the victim was exposed to it. If a victim appears to have a combination of burns of different degrees, determine the degree of the most burned part—usually in the middle of the burned area—and treat for that degree. If you are not sure about the degree of a burn, treat it as a third-degree burn.

Keep in mind that the goal of burn treatment is to relieve the victim's pain, prevent him/her from going into shock, and prevent infection of the burned area.

Key Note Term

mottled – marked with irregular spots or splotches of different colors or shades of color.

scalding - the burning of the skin by a substance that is near boiling in temperature.

Treating First-Degree Burns

To treat first-degree burns, follow these steps:

1. **Loosen tight clothing and remove jewelry from the burned area before it swells. Have the victim put his/her jewelry in a safe place after removal.**

2. **Cool the burned part with water by either holding it under cold, running water, pouring cold water over it, immersing it in cold water, or applying cold, wet compresses to it. Cooling the burn with water helps remove heat from the skin, relieves pain and swelling, and cleans the injury. Continue this cooling treatment for between five and 15 minutes until the pain subsides.**

3. **Gently pat the burned area dry with a clean cloth.**

4. **Cover the injury with a sterile bandage or clean cloth to keep air off of it, thereby reducing pain, and providing protection against infection. Keep the bandage loose to keep pressure off of the injury.**

5. **After a first-degree burn is completely cooled, especially a sunburn, use a lotion or moisturizer to relieve pain and prevent drying of the skin.**

Key Note Term

compresses – folded clothes or pads applied so as to press upon a body part to stop bleeding or cool a burn

Treating Second-Degree Burns

To treat second-degree burns, follow these steps:

1. **For second-degree burns, follow steps one through four for treating first-degree burns. If you use running water to cool the injured part, ensure the water is not so forceful that blisters on the burned skin are broken.**

2. **Elevate the burned part.**

3. **Ensure the victim drinks plenty of liquids to avoid dehydration.**

4. **Seek medical treatment for second-degree burns to the face, hands, feet, or genitals, or that are more than two to three inches in diameter.**

Note

For extensive second-degree burns, monitor the victim for signs of shock and treat accordingly until he/she receives medical treatment. See Lesson 4 for signs and treatment of shock. For second-degree burns to the face, especially if accompanied by smoke inhalation, the victim may have respiratory burns that can lead to swelling and blockage of his/her airway. Monitor the victim's breathing and treat accordingly until he/she receives medical treatment.

Treating Third-Degree Burns

To treat third-degree burns, follow these steps:

1. **Remove the victim from the source of heat if he/she is still in contact with it. (See the following section for removing a victim from a source of electricity.)**

2. **Call for Emergency Medical Services (EMS). All third-degree burns require medical treatment regardless of their size. Until the victim receives treatment, follow steps 3 through 9.**

3. **Ensure that the victim is breathing. If not, begin mouth-to-mouth resuscitation.**

Key Note Term

smoldering – burn-
ing slowly without
flame, but often with
much smoke.

4. Remove any clothing that is still **smoldering** to stop further burning. If the victim is wearing jewelry that is near or on a burned area, remove it if it comes off easily. Place the jewelry in the victim's pocket, purse, and so on, if available. If not, reassure the victim that you will give his/ her jewelry to emergency medical personnel when they arrive.

5. If necessary, expose the burned area by cutting and gently lifting away any clothing. If any cloth sticks to the burn, leave it in place. Note: If you are in a chemically contaminated area, do not expose the burned area; simply apply a dressing over the victim's clothing.

6. Cover the burned area loosely with cool, moist compresses, sterile bandages, or clean cloth.

> ### Note
>
> Unlike treatment for first and second degree burns, do not cool a third-degree burn with water because this can increase the risk of shock.

7. Elevate the burned part.

8. Treat the victim for shock. Pay special attention to the victim's body temperature, which can change rapidly due to the skin being burned.

9. Monitor the breathing of victims with burns to the face and burns resulting from fire accompanied by smoke inhalation. Treat accordingly.

"Don'ts" When Treating Burns

It's important to know what to do when treating burns, but it's just as important to know what not to do. The following list details actions that should never be done when treating burns.

- Do not put butter, oil, or grease on a burn; they can keep heat in the burn and cause more damage, as well as increase the chance of infection.

- Do not use cotton or cottony bandages on burns as they may stick to the injury.

- Do not put ice or ice water on a burn; this can result in frostbite and cause more damage to the skin.

- Do not break any blisters that have formed; blisters help protect against infection.

- Do not put pressure on a burn.

- Do not try to remove stuck clothing, debris, or loosened skin from a burn.

- Do not try to clean a wound with soap, alcohol, or any other antiseptic product; only water should be used and only on first- and second-degree burns.

- Do not let a victim walk on burned feet even if he/she tells you it does not hurt; third-degree burns can cause little pain since nerved endings are destroyed, but damage is severe and pressure from walking will only increase it.

Prevention of Heat Burns

There are many things you can do to prevent heat burns. Some of these include:

- Use caution when handling matches and starting a fire, particularly with a flammable liquid.

- If you have young brothers and sisters, store matches out of their reach.

- Use caution around hot liquids, steam, and heating and cooking equipment.

- Ensure hot tap water is not scalding before stepping into a tub or shower or putting your hands under a running faucet.

- Ensure your home has a fire extinguisher and smoke alarms.

- Never use water on an electrical fire; use a chemical fire extinguisher.

- If anyone in your household smokes, remind them not to smoke in bed.

- Keep a box of baking soda in the kitchen to smother grease fires.

- Turn pot handles on the stove so they are not sticking out where someone may bump them in passing.

- For electric cookware, do not let cords hang off the counter where they can be caught and pull the cookware off as well.

- If a pilot light goes out on a gas appliance, make sure all burners and the stove are turned off and ventilate the area before relighting it or before using electrical switches, which make tiny sparks.

- Do not leave flammable items (such as newspapers or dishcloths) near the fireplace or on or near the stove.

- Turn off space heaters before going to sleep or leaving the house.

- Know what actions to take if a fire starts in your home and practice them with family members.

Treatment of Electrical Burns

Although an electrical shock will often produce only a minor mark on the skin, the injury can be a serious, deep-tissue burn, so treat all electrical burns as third degree. The current from an electrical shock passing through a victim's body can also result in unconsciousness and may slow or stop his or her breathing and/or heartbeat; therefore, treat electrical shock as a potentially life-threatening injury.

If you believe a person has been electrocuted, assess the situation first before touching the victim. He or she may still be in contact with the electrical current, and if you touch him or her, you could become a victim of electrical shock as well. Follow these steps to avoid a double accident and provide first aid treatment:

1. **If the victim is still in contact with the source of electricity, stop the current.**

   Shut off the electrical current by unplugging a cord, removing a fuse from the fuse box, or turning off the circuit breaker, as appropriate. Note: In many cases, just turning off a wall or appliance switch does not stop the electrical flow. Even though you have shut off the electrical current, to be completely safe, move the victim away from the electrical source before continuing. Proceed to step 3.

   If you cannot turn off the electricity or you are outside and the shock is due to a downed power line, either call the power company yourself if you have a phone near you, or if there are other people around, have someone else call the power company. Meanwhile, since it may take you less time to separate the victim from the current than to wait for the power to be cut off, proceed to step 2. Or, if

you are alone and/or there is no phone readily available in this situation, proceed to step 2.

2. **Separate the victim from the source of electrical current.**

   Push the victim off of or away from the source of electricity—or push the source of electricity off of or away from the victim—using a dry non-conducting material (wood, plastic, cardboard) like a broom, stick, or chair. If available, also stand on something dry and non-conducting, like newspaper or a rubber mat, as you disengage the victim.

   If pushing does not work, use a dry rope or dry clothing to lift or drag the victim off of or away from the source of electricity. This method works better if there are two rescuers: one to lift the victim off and the other to push the electrical source away.

Note

Special Precaution: If the ground is wet, do not attempt to move a victim in contact with an electrical current. Water conducts electricity, and you can be electrocuted as well. In this case, the current must be stopped before you can administer first aid.

---

3. **Check the victim's breathing and pulse. Be prepared to administer mouth-to-mouth resuscitation or cardiopulmonary resuscitation (CPR) if the victim's breathing is shallow or nonexistent or his/her pulse is dangerously slow or non-existent.**

4. **After you are sure the victim is breathing, take the time to call EMS if you or someone else has not already done so.**

5. **Check the victim for two burn sites—one where the electricity entered the body and one where it exited the body. Treat the burns by following steps 4 through 9 for treating third-degree burns, including treating for shock and monitoring breathing.**

Note

About 1,000 people die each year in the United States due to electrical shock.

Prevention of Electrical Burns

Electrical burns can be prevented if you know what to do. To prevent electrical burns:

- **Do not use electrical appliances in the tub, while showering, or in or near swimming pools.**
- **Do not use electrical equipment outdoors if it is raining or the ground is wet.**
- **Ensure electrical equipment you use outdoors is made for outdoor use, with three-way ground plugs and heavier wiring.**
- **Ensure outdoor electrical outlets have weatherproof covers.**
- **If you have very young brothers or sisters, ensure there are child safety plugs in all electrical outlets.**

- Do not overload an outlet by plugging in several appliances in a "piggy-back" fashion.

- Do not use electrical appliances or equipment that have exposed wiring or frayed cords, or that overheat or create sparks.

- Do not climb trees that have wires running through or near them.

- Look for overhead wires before using long tools like tree trimmers, pool skimmers, or ladders.

- Stay inside during electrical storms; keep away from windows; do not use appliances or the phone, since lightning can travel through wires; and do not take a shower or bath, since lightning can also travel through pipes.

- If you are caught outside during an electrical storm, avoid trees, poles, and metal objects; find low ground and crouch down.

Treatment of Chemical Burns

Chemical burns occur when the skin or eyes come in contact with liquid or dry chemicals that are **caustic** or irritating. You may have products around your house, such as rust and paint removers and drain and cement cleaners that contain **acids** designed to eat away certain materials and **bases** (also called **alkalis**) used to cut through grease. If used carelessly or improperly, these products may also do the same to your clothes and skin.

The seriousness of a chemical burn depends on the:

- **Length of time the chemical is in contact with the skin or eyes**

- **Concentration of the chemical—the more concentrated, the more damaging**

- **Temperature of the product containing the chemical—the higher the temperature, the quicker the damage**

Treatment of chemical burns involves stopping the chemical action immediately by removing the chemical from the skin or eyes and by removing contaminated clothing that can transmit absorbed chemicals to the skin. Treatment will vary depending on the type of chemical involved, so if there are first aid instructions on the label of the chemical product causing the burn, follow those instructions. If not, use the following basic guidelines for treatment.

Treating Chemical Burns to the Skin

To treat chemical burns to the skin, follow these steps:

1. **Depending on the extent of chemical coverage on the victim or in the area, consider wearing gloves and/or safety goggles, if available, to protect yourself from chemical injuries while assisting the victim.**

2. **Remove any contaminated jewelry or clothing from the victim, including shoes and socks where chemicals can collect.**

3. **Remove the chemical from the skin.**

   - **For liquid chemicals, flush them from the contaminated skin with large amounts of cool running water for at least 15 minutes.**

Key Note Term

caustic – capable of destroying or eating away by chemical action; corrosive.

acids – chemical compounds with a sour taste that react with bese to form salt, have a pH value of less than 7, react with metals to form hydrogen gas, and have the capability to eat away or dissolve metals and other materials.

bases – chemical compounds with a slippery or soapy feel that react with acids to form salt, have a pH value above 7, and are used as cleaning materials.

alkalis – any base, as soda, potash, and so on, that is soluble in water, combines with fats to form soap, neutralizes acids, and forms salts with them.

flush – to cleanse or wash out with running water or another liquid.

- For dry chemicals, brush them off the skin using a clean, dry cloth. Take care to keep the chemicals from blowing into your eyes or the victim's eyes, and avoid brushing the chemicals onto your own skin. Then, if large amounts of water are available, flush the contaminated area for at least 15 minutes. If large amounts of water are not available, do not apply any water to the contaminated area, since small amounts of water can react with dry chemicals causing more burning.

Note

If the victim says he/she feels the burning has intensified after you have finished flushing the contaminated area, flush for several more minutes, or longer, as necessary.

4. **Cover the burned area loosely with dry, clean bandages or cloth.**

5. **Minor chemical burns generally heal without further treatment; however, call for Emergency Medical Services for:**

   - **any chemical burn to the face, hands, feet, genitalia, or joints**

   - **second-degree chemical burns over two to three inches in diameter**

   - **all third-degree chemical burns**

   - **if there is a systemic reaction to the chemical burn and/or chemical exposure**

Key Note Term

systemic – affecting the body in general; acting throughout the body after absorption or ingestion.

Note

For extensive or severe chemical burns, monitor the victim for signs of shock and treat accordingly until he/she receives medical treatment. For a victim with chemical burns to the face or who may have inhaled chemicals, monitor his/her breathing in case of possible respiratory burns and swelling. Treat accordingly until medical help arrives.

Treating Chemical Burns to the Eyes

To treat chemical burns to the eyes, follow these steps:

1. **Position the victim's head so that the injured eye is lower than the uninjured eye. This will prevent the chemical from getting into the uninjured eye. If both eyes are injured, proceed to Step 2.**

2. **If there is only one injured eye, hold the eyelids of the injured eye open and flush with water from the inner corner of the eye (closest to the nose) to the outer corner (closest to the ear). Flush for at least 15 minutes. If both eyes are injured, flush both at the same time.**

3. **To keep the victim from moving his/her injured eye(s), have the victim close both eyes, then cover them with cloth pads or gauze taped loosely into place. Because eyes move together, both eyes must be closed and covered to keep the injured eye still.**

4. **Call for Emergency Medical Services or transport the victim to the emergency room.**

Key Note Term

neutralize – to counteract the activity or effect of; to make chemically neutral.

"Don'ts" When Treating Chemical Burns

Follow the "don'ts" listed earlier in this lesson in "Don'ts When Treating Burns." In addition, do not put any other chemicals on a chemical burn in an attempt to

neutralize the chemical causing the burn—for example, putting an acid on an alkali and vice versa.

Prevention of Chemical Burns

Chemical burns can be prevented, if you know what to do. To help prevent chemical burns:

- **Before using any chemical product, read the label—including precautions or warnings—then follow the instructions for use.**

- **If you have younger brothers or sisters, ensure chemical products are stored out of their reach.**

- **Use chemical products in a well-ventilated area.**

- **Do not mix different chemical products; they may react with each other causing hazardous conditions; for example, mixing bleach and ammonia results in dangerous fumes.**

- **To avoid confusion and accidental misuse of chemical products, leave them in their original containers with their labels intact.**

Conclusion

You have just learned important procedures for treating burns as well as when to apply basic first aid and life-saving skills in these situations. Remember, although it is important to administer first aid treatment as quickly as possible in most situations, for your safety, some rescue situations require careful assessment before adminstering first aid. Remaining calm, thinking logically and clearly, and knowing what steps to take and when to take them will help you to successfully perform first aid. In addition, this lesson provided many tips on how to prevent accidents from occurring in the first place.

Lesson Review

1. **What are some of the characteristics of first, second, and third-degree burns?**

2. **How can you prevent electrical burns?**

3. **What determines the seriousness of a chemical burn?**

4. **Define the term "systemic."**

Chapter 2

Lesson Review

Lesson 6

First Aid for Poisons, Wounds, and Bruises

Chapter 2

Key Terms

abrasions
amputation
avulsion
incisions
lacerations
solvents

What You Will Learn to Do

- Determine first aid treatment for wounds, bruises and poisoning

Linked Core Abilities

- Do your share as a good citizen in your school, community, country, and the world

Skills and Knowledge You Will Gain along the Way

- Identify the causes and symptoms of poisoning
- Describe how to treat a poison victim
- Distinguish among the four types of wounds
- Describe how to treat minor wounds and bruises
- Define key words contained in this lesson

Introduction

Whenever there are small children left alone in the kitchen, accidents can happen, especially when cleaning products are left out in the open. The first section of this lesson introduces the treatment and prevention of injury from poisons. As an addition to your first aid abilities, the lesson ends with a discussion of different types of wounds and their treatments, as well as the treatment of bruises.

Poisons

As consumers, we buy more than a quarter of a million different household products—materials used in and around the house for medication, cleaning, cosmetic purposes, exterminating insects, and killing weeds. These items are valuable in the house and for yard maintenance, but misuse, especially when products are used in inappropriate applications or quantities, can cause illness, injury, and even death.

Each year more than 6,000 people die and an estimated 300,000 suffer disabling illnesses as a result of unintentional poisoning by solid and liquid substances. Poisonings can happen to anyone, at any time, in any situation.

Poisonings at home; however, can be prevented. Although child-resistant packaging has greatly reduced the number of fatalities among children under five years of age; parents, grandparents, and other caregivers must still be cautious. Following label directions for all products, including medication dosages, and proper storage of potentially toxic products are important precautions to heed.

- **Poisonings from solids and liquids such as drugs, medicines, poisonous houseplants, and commonly recognized poisons caused 6,300 deaths in the home in 1998 alone.**

- **An additional 500 deaths in the home in 1998 were due to poisonings from gases and vapors such as carbon monoxide.**

- **These deaths are not all among children. Another age group at risk is adults age 25 through 44. Many adults are unintentionally poisoned when they do not follow label directions on medications or household chemicals.**

Poisoning is the effect of one or more harmful substances on the body. Poisons can be inhaled or ingested. Fortunately, most poisonings happen with products of low toxicity or with amounts so small, that severe poisoning rarely occurs; however, the potential for severe or fatal poisoning is always present.

Inhaled Poisons

Inhaled poisoning occurs when a person breathes a poisonous substance into his/her lungs. Inhaled poisons include:

- Smoke
- Gas used in outdoor cooking equipment and appliances in homes and recreational vehicles
- Hazardous fumes from household products such as paint and paint thinners, gasoline, **solvents**, and glues, as well as from chemicals used in industrial processes
- Carbon monoxide, which is always produced by wood, coal, and charcoal fires, and by gasoline engines, can also be produced by gas, oil, and kerosene appliances such as furnaces, space heaters, water heaters, and stoves

Key Note Term

solvents – liquid substances capable of dissolving or eliminating something unwanted.

Carbon monoxide, in particular, is a very dangerous poisonous substance, because it is odorless, colorless, and tasteless, making it difficult to detect. When a person inhales carbon monoxide, it replaces oxygen in the blood, which results in oxygen starvation throughout the body. Exposure to low amounts of carbon monoxide can cause flu-like symptoms; continued exposure can cause permanent brain, nerve, and heart damage; exposure to very high concentrations can kill a person in a few minutes.

Running a car engine in a closed garage, using a charcoal grill indoors, and burning a fire in a fireplace with a blocked chimney can all result in carbon monoxide poisoning. In addition, because carbon monoxide forms when there is a lack of oxygen resulting in incomplete fuel combustion, operating fuel-burning equipment without an adequate supply of oxygen (proper ventilation) can result in carbon monoxide poisoning. For example, hundreds of people in the United States each year suffer carbon monoxide injuries from using portable heaters, lanterns, and camping stoves inside tents, campers, and vehicles.

Symptoms of Inhaled Poisoning

Symptoms of inhaled poisoning may not show up immediately. If you suspect inhalation poisoning, keep the victim under observation. If you know the victim has inhaled a poisonous chemical, get medical help whether or not symptoms are present. Symptoms will vary depending on the type and amount of poison inhaled, but can include any of the following:

- Dizziness
- Weakness
- Drowsiness
- Headache
- Mental confusion
- Breathing difficulties
- Heartbeat irregularities
- Unusual breath odor
- Discoloration of the lips and mucous membranes
- Nausea

- **Vomiting**
- **Rashes or burns on the skin**
- **Unconsciousness**

Treatment for Inhaled Poisons

Before rushing in to rescue a victim in a smoke, gas, or fume-filled environment, quickly assess the situation so that you do not end up a victim as well. If the poisonous substance is overwhelming and the danger to you is too great, do not attempt to rescue the victim unless you have been trained for rescue in this type of situation. Immediately call EMS and stay clear of danger.

However, if after assessing the situation you believe you can safely remove the victim from the poisonous environment, do so by following these steps.

1. **If you are alone, call for help first before attempting the rescue. This will notify others of the situation—a precaution that will ensure help is on its way in case you are also overcome by the poison.**

2. **Take several deep breaths of fresh air, then take a final deep breath and hold it as you go in. If available, a damp cloth held over your nose and mouth is a good safety precaution.**

> **Note**
>
> Do not use light switches, light a match, or use any other equipment or appliance that produces flames or sparks while you are in a gas or fume-filled area.

3. **If you can see fumes or smoke, keep your head out of them. For example, fumes from car exhaust are heavy and settle near the floor, so keep your head above them; but in the case of smoke, which rises, keep your head below it.**

4. **Move the victim out into the fresh air. If for some reason this is not possible, open doors and windows to ventilate the area, returning out into the fresh air as necessary to ensure your safety. Do not administer first aid until you and the victim are out of the hazardous environment or the area is ventilated.**

Check the victim's airway, breathing, and circulation (ABCs), and perform mouth-to-mouth resuscitation and CPR as necessary. After you are sure the victim is breathing, call EMS if you or someone else has not already done so. Even if the victim seems fine after he/she is in fresh air, call for medical help as symptoms may show up later. While you are waiting for medical help, treat the victim for any burns he/she may have suffered and monitor for shock.

Oral Poisoning

Oral poisoning occurs when a harmful substance, such as a common household cleaning product, is swallowed. First aid for oral poisoning depends on the substance swallowed.

Symptoms of Oral Poisoning

Symptoms will vary depending on the type and amount of poison inhaled but can include any of the following:

- **Abdominal pain and cramping**
- **Nausea or vomiting**
- **Diarrhea**
- **Burns, odor, stains around and in mouth**
- **Drowsiness or unconsciousness**
- **Poison containers nearby**

Treatment for Oral Poisons

Procedures for treating oral poisoning:

1. **Determine critical information:**

   - **Age and size of victim**
   - **What was swallowed**
   - **How much was swallowed**
   - **When was it swallowed**

2. **If a corrosive or caustic substance was swallowed, immediately dilute it by having the victim drink at least one or two eight-ounce glasses of water or milk.**

3. **For a responsive victim, call a poison control center immediately. More than 70 percent of poisonings can be treated through instructions taken over the telephone from a poison control center.**

4. **For an unresponsive victim, or if the poison control center number is unknown, call EMS and monitor the ABCs.**

5. **Place the victim on his or her left side to position the end of the stomach where it enters the small intestine straight up. Gravity will delay advancement of the poison into the small intestine, where absorption into the victim's circulatory system is faster.**

6. **Induce vomiting only if a poison control center or physician advises it. Inducing must be done within 30 minutes of swallowing.**

7. **Save poison containers, plants, and so on to help medical personnel identify the poison.**

Wounds

Wounds are soft tissue injuries that break the skin. Generally, they can be classified as follows:

- *Scrapes* (**abrasions**) are caused by sliding contact between the skin and a rough surface. They are generally shallow injuries with little bleeding.

- *Cuts* (**incisions**) are straight, even wounds made with sharp objects like knives or razor blades.

- *Tears* (**lacerations**) are caused by objects with sharp, irregular edges or by exerted force that leaves jagged, torn tissue.

- *Punctures* are caused by pointed objects such as pins and nails that make small holes in tissue, often with little bleeding.

All wounds can be minor or serious depending on their size, depth, location, and source. Minor wounds involve only the outer skin layer. They stop bleeding in a few minutes on their own or with gentle pressure and can be treated with just first aid. Serious wounds require first aid followed by medical treatment. Consider a wound serious if:

- **The skin is cut or torn all the way through so that it gapes open.**

- **Fat, muscle, or tendons are visible.**

- **Bleeding is heavy and does not slow or stop after applying pressure for 15 to 20 minutes.**

- **Soil or other debris cannot be washed from the wound.**

- **There is loss of function such as the inability to move a cut finger.**

- **It is on the face; even a small wound may leave a scar.**

- **It is on the bottom of the foot.**

- **Its source is a rusty or dirty object, or an animal or human bite.**

Some extremely serious injuries that generally contain a combination of the four kinds of wounds and always require immediate medical attention are **amputations**, **avulsions**, and crushing injuries. They are generally the result of motor vehicle or industrial machinery accidents or explosions.

- **An amputation is the complete removal of an extremity, such as a finger or leg.**

- **An avulsion is tissue torn from or pulled away from and hanging off of the body. This type of injury may also result from an animal bite.**

- **Crushing injuries occur when parts of the body are caught between heavy objects or when the body is thrown against a heavy object or vice versa. In addition to wounds, crushing injuries include bone fractures, as well as possible injuries to internal organs and internal bleeding.**

Treatment of Wounds

For a minor wound, clean it by flushing it with cool water and washing it with mild soap. Dry it thoroughly with a clean cloth, apply a thin layer of antibiotic

---

Key Note Term

abrasion – a part of the skin that has been lightly torn or scraped.

incision – a wound that is made by cutting into the body.

laceration – a wound that is torn and ragged.

Key Note Term

amputation – the removal of an external part of the body, most often a limb or part of it, when it has been severely crushed or following the death of an extremity due to impaired blood circulation.

avulsion – the tearing away of a body part accidentally or surgically.

ointment to keep the wound moist and protect against infection, and cover it with a bandage to keep it clean. Change the bandage whenever it gets wet or dirty, and consider leaving the bandage off at night when sleeping since exposure to air also helps the healing process. Contact a doctor if the wound does not appear to be healing after several days or shows signs of infection like redness, draining, or swelling.

For any wound caused by a rusty or dirty object or an animal bite, ask if the victim has had a tetanus shot within the past 10 years. If not, suggest that he/she get one to guard against tetanus infection.

For extremely serious injuries such as amputations, avulsions, or crushing injuries, call EMS, control the bleeding, monitor breathing, treat for shock, and provide comfort to the victim until medical help arrives. Remember that tourniquets should only be used in extreme, life-threatening situations, and pressure points should only be used if you are trained to do so.

Bruises

Bruises are injuries that discolor but do not break the skin tissue. They can be caused by a fall, a blow, or bumping into something. Though sometimes very ugly and lasting for several weeks, they are usually not very serious.

Wrap ice or an ice pack in a clean towel and apply it to the bruise. To reduce swelling, elevate the bruised part for 20 to 30 minutes if the injury is mild or for a few hours if it is severe. Seek medical attention if swelling increases unusually, pain increases, the bruise site appears deformed, or there is an inability to move a body part associated with the bruise.

Conclusion

You have just learned important procedures for treating poisons, wounds, and bruises, as well as when to apply basic first aid and life-saving skills in these situations. Remember that while it is important to administer first aid treatment as quickly as possible in most situations, some rescue situations require careful assessment before you jump in to save someone, so that you do not become a victim yourself. Remaining calm, thinking logically and clearly, and knowing what steps to take and when to take them will help you to successfully perform first aid. In addition, this chapter provided many tips on how to prevent accidents from occurring in the first place.

Lesson Review

1. What are common types of inhaled poisons?

2. How can some in-home poisonings be prevented?

3. Compare and contrast scrapes, cuts, tears, and punctures.

4. How would you treat a bruise?

Chapter 2

Lesson Review

Lesson 7

Heat Injuries

Key Terms

dehydration
fatigue
heat exhaustion
heatstroke
heat cramps
perspiring
ventilation

What You Will Learn to Do

- Determine first aid treatment for heat related injuries

Linked Core Abilities

- Do your share as a good citizen in your school, community, country, and the world

Skills and Knowledge You Will Gain along the Way

- Explain the causes and effects of heat injuries

- Associate the symptoms of the three types of heat injuries

- Explain how to treat heat cramps

- Explain how to treat heat exhaustion

- Explain how to treat heatstroke

- Define key words contained in this lesson

Introduction

Participating in any vigorous outdoor exercise or activity on an extremely hot day can lead to serious injuries if you are not prepared. Knowing how to recognize the signs and symptoms of heat related injuries can help you prevent a life-threatening accident.

Causes

For your body to work properly, its temperature must be normal, which is around 98° Fahrenheit. You risk health problems, and even death, if your body gets too cold or too hot.

Heat injuries can occur when people are exposed to high temperatures and high humidity. When it is hot, your body cools itself by **perspiring**—sweat evaporates carrying heat away from your body. However, you risk heat injuries when you lose large amounts of water, salt, or both through perspiring, and do not replace the lost fluid, resulting in **dehydration**. You also risk injury in high humidity when sweat does not evaporate as rapidly as needed to keep the body cool, causing heat to build up. The body will then perspire even more in an attempt to cool itself, losing dangerous amounts of fluids in the process.

People who may be at risk of heat injuries include those who exercise or work outside in high temperatures and high humidity, or those whose bodies do not regulate heat well, such as older people, overweight people, or babies.

Factors to Consider

When perspiring, the body can lose more than a quart of water per hour. Therefore, since the body depends on water to cool itself, you should drink plenty of water when working or playing in hot weather. Salt, which helps the body to retain water, is also lost through perspiring. In most cases, however, you do not need to consume extra salt because you obtain adequate amounts through a balanced diet. In fact, consuming salt during hot weather activities may pull water away from muscles and other tissues where it is needed and into your digestive tract.

In addition to water intake and diet, consider the type of clothing you wear in hot weather. Wear clothes that fit loosely but also protect the body from sunburn. Wear natural fabrics, like cotton, through which perspiration evaporates better. Some activities require extra clothing or equipment, such as football or hiking with full camping gear. Soldiers may have problems acclimating to hot weather because of the type and amount of clothing and equipment they must wear. In all of these cases, protective gear and equipment may reduce **ventilation** needed to cool the body. So, ensure clothing or uniforms fit well but are not tight, and remove extra pieces of clothing and equipment as soon as they are no longer needed.

> **Key Note Term**
>
> **perspiring** – giving off moisture through the pores of the skin.
>
> **dehydration** – the condition that results when fluids are lost from the body and are not replaced; symptoms can include thirst, weakness, exhaustion, confusion, and may result in death.

> **Key Note Term**
>
> **ventilation** – circulation of air; a system or means of providing fresh air.

Types of Heat Injuries

Key Note Term

heat cramps – a condition that is marked by the sudden development of cramps in the skeletal muscles and that results from prolonged work in high temperatures accompanied by profuse perspiration with loss of sodium chloride from the body.

heat exhaustion – a condition that occurs when a person is exposed to excessive heat over a period of time, caused by the loss of water and salt from the body through excessive perspiration.

heatstroke – a life-threatening condition caused by prolonged exposure to high heat.

Overheating of the body progresses through stages. At first, a person may suffer **heat cramps**. If the person ignores the symptoms and continues exercising, working, or playing in the heat, he or she may experience **heat exhaustion**. If heat exhaustion is left untreated, **heatstroke** may follow and can be fatal.

Heat Cramps

Heat cramps are muscular pains and spasms caused by the loss of salt from the body through heavy perspiring. Other symptoms may include stomach cramps, wet skin, and extreme thirst. To treat heat cramps:

1. **Move the victim to a shady area, or improvise shade.**
2. **Loosen the victim's clothing.**
3. **Give the victim large amounts of cool water slowly.**
4. **Monitor the victim and give more water as needed.**
5. **Seek medical aid if cramps continue.**

Heat Exhaustion

When people work or exercise heavily in high temperatures or in a hot, humid place, the body loses fluids through heavy sweating. Heat exhaustion occurs when fluids are not adequately replaced or when sweat does not evaporate because of high humidity or too many layers of clothing, causing the body to sweat even more. When the body loses a great amount of fluid, less blood flows to vital organs, resulting in a form of shock. The symptoms of heat exhaustion are:

- **Heavy sweating**
- **Weakness or faintness**
- **Dizziness or drowsiness**
- **Cool, pale, moist skin**
- **Headaches**
- **Loss of appetite**
- **Heat cramps**
- **Nausea with or without vomiting**
- **Confusion**
- **Chills**
- **Rapid breathing and pulse**
- **Body temperature above normal but below 102°F**

Treat heat exhaustion as follows:

1. **Move the victim to a cool, shady area, or improvise shade.**

2. **Loosen the victim's clothing.**

3. **Pour water on or apply cold, wet cloth to the skin. Fan the victim if it is a hot day.**

4. **Have the victim slowly drink at least one quart of water.**

5. **Elevate the victim's legs.**

6. **Monitor the victim until symptoms are gone. If symptoms continue, seek medical aid.**

7. **If possible, keep the victim from participating in heavy activity for the rest of the day.**

Heatstroke

Heatstroke, also known as sunstroke, is a medical emergency that can be fatal if not treated as soon as possible. The victim's cooling mechanism stops working when the body perspires so much that no fluids remain to produce sweat. Because the body can no longer sweat and sweating is its defense against overheating, body temperature rises and skin becomes red and flushed. If body temperature rises high enough, brain damage and death can occur; therefore, when you encounter a heatstroke victim, you must cool the victim as fast as possible.

Symptoms of heatstroke are:

- **No sweating**
- **Hot, dry, red skin**
- **Headache, dizziness, nausea, and vomiting**
- **Fast, weak pulse and shallow respiration**
- **Seizures and mental confusion**
- **Unconsciousness or sudden collapse**
- **Very high body temperature**

Treat victims of heatstroke as follows:

1. **Move the victim to a cool, shady area, or improvise shade.**

2. **Loosen the victim's clothing. Remove any outer garments and protective clothing.**

3. **Pour water on the victim or immerse in water, and fan the victim so sweat can evaporate. If you cannot immerse the victim, massage arms and legs with cool water.**

4. **If the victim is conscious, have him or her slowly drink at least one quart of water.**

5. **Seek medical aid and transport the victim to a medical facility as soon as possible. Perform any necessary life-saving measures.**

Prevention of Heat Injuries

Key Note Term

fatigue – weakness or exhaustion due to hard work or mental effort.

You can prevent heat injuries by taking just a few simple precautions and exercising a little common sense. If possible, limit your exposure to high temperatures and avoid working or exercising outside in hot, humid weather. During work or training periods, or in extremely hot climates, drink at least one quart of water every hour. Also, remember to dress for the hot weather and the activity being performed.

In the military or in the field, prevention of heat injuries is both an individual and leadership responsibility. Leaders should identify people who have a high risk of injury—basic trainees, overweight individuals, and individuals who have symptoms of **fatigue** or a previous history of heat injury. If possible, leaders should schedule heavy or strenuous activities during cooler morning or evening hours.

Conclusion

Vigorous exercise in hot weather can lead to heat cramps, heat exhaustion, or heatstroke. Familiarize yourself with the symptoms of these injuries, which can be serious or even fatal if left untreated. By knowing the signs of heat injuries, and taking precautions, you should be able to enjoy exercising outdoors, even in hot weather.

Lesson Review

1. What are the causes of heat injuries?
2. What are the types of heat injuries?
3. How would you treat heat exhaustion?
4. What are the symptoms of heat stroke?

Chapter 2

Lesson Review

Lesson 8

Cold Weather Injuries

Key Terms

dehydration
frostbite
hypothermia
insulate
precipitation
subcutaneous
superficial

What You Will Learn to Do

- Determine first aid treatment for cold weather injuries

Linked Core Abilities

- Do your share as a good citizen in your school, community, country, and the world

Skills and Knowledge You Will Gain along the Way

- Describe factors to consider in cold weather situations
- Explain causes and effects of cold weather injuries
- Identify symptoms of cold weather injuries
- Explain how to treat frostbite, immersion foot/trench foot, hypothermia, and snow blindness
- Define key words contained in this lesson

Chapter 2

Introduction

It is common to think that only in areas where snow and frost are present, people are susceptible to cold weather injuries. Prolonged exposure to low temperatures, wind, or moisture—whether it be on a ski slope or in a stranded car—can result in cold related injuries such as **frostbite** and **hypothermia**, no matter where you live if you are not prepared.

Factors to Consider

When thinking about cold weather injuries, there are several factors you need to consider. These factors include weather, stress, clothing, physical makeup, psychological factors, and more. This section discusses these factors.

Weather

Low temperature, high humidity, **precipitation**, and high wind may affect the loss of body heat. Wind chill (the temperature of both the wind speed and air temperature combined) speeds up the loss of body heat and may aggravate cold injuries. By studying the Wind Chill Chart shown in Figure 2.8.1, you can determine the chilling effect that wind speed has on temperature.

Stress

When in a stressful situation, people are more likely to experience fear, fatigue, **dehydration**, and lack of nutrition. These factors increase the possibility of cold injury.

Clothing

When in cold weather, you should wear several layers of loose-fitting clothing and dress as lightly as the weather permits. This reduces the danger of excessive perspiration followed by chilling. It is better if the body is slightly cold and producing heat rather than overly warm and sweltering toward dehydration. Wet clothing adds to the possibility of cold injury.

Physical Makeup

Physical fatigue leads to inactivity, personal neglect, carelessness, and less heat production. These, in turn, increase the risk of cold injury. Individuals who have had a cold injury before have a higher risk of being injured again.

Psychological Factors

Mental fatigue and fear lessen the body's ability to re-warm itself and thus increase the possibility of cold injury. Depressed or unresponsive individuals

Key Note Term

frostbite – an injury caused to body tissue by frost or extreme cold.

hypothermia – too little body heat with abnormally low internal body temperature.

Key Note Term

precipitation –Any form of water, such as rain, snow, sleet, or hail, that falls to the earth's surface.

Key Note Term

dehydration – the condition that results when fluids are lost from the body and not replaced; symptoms can include thirst, weakness, exhaustion, confusion, and may result in death.

Figure 2.8.1: The Wind Chill Chart.

HOW TO USE THE WIND CHILL CHART

Find the wind speed in the left-hand column, then read across to the column under the actual temperature. This number is the equivalent temperature which would be acting on any exposed skin. For example, if the wind is blowing at 20 mph and the actual temperature is 10° F, the effect on bare skin would be the same as a temperature reading of –25° F under calm conditions. Any movement has the same cooling effect as the wind. Running, skiing, or riding in an open vehicle must be considered in using the wind chill chart.

★GPO : 1983 0 - 417-503

WIND CHILL CHART FOR FAHRENHEIT TEMPERATURES

ESTIMATED WIND SPEED IN MPH	ACTUAL THERMOMETER READING (° F)											
	50	40	30	20	10	0	-10	-20	-30	-40	-50	-60
	EQUIVALENT TEMPERATURE (° F)											
CALM	50	40	30	20	10	0	-10	-20	-30	-40	-50	-60
5	48	37	27	16	6	-5	-15	-26	-36	-47	-57	-68
10	40	28	16	4	-9	-24	-33	-46	-58	-70	-83	-95
15	36	22	9	-5	-18	-32	-45	-58	-72	-85	-99	-112
20	32	18	4	-10	-25	-39	-53	-67	-82	-96	-110	-124
25	30	16	0	-15	-29	-44	-59	-74	-88	-104	-118	-133
30	28	13	-2	-18	-33	-48	-63	-79	-94	-109	-125	-140
35	27	11	-4	-21	-35	-51	-67	-82	-96	-113	-129	-145
40	26	10	-6	-24	-37	-53	-69	-85	-100	-116	-132	-148

WIND SPEEDS ABOVE 40 MPH HAVE LITTLE ADDITIONAL EFFECT.	LITTLE DANGER FOR THE PROPERLY CLOTHED PERSON; MAXIMUM DANGER OF FALSE SENSE OF SECURITY.	INCREASING DANGER OF FREEZING EXPOSED FLESH.	GREAT DANGER

TRENCH FOOT AND IMMERSION FOOT MAY OCCUR AT ANY POINT ON THIS CHART.

are also at a higher risk of cold injury because they are less active and tend to be careless about protecting themselves.

Other Factors

Individuals are also at risk of cold injury if they are:

- **In contact with the ground for an extended period**
- **Immobile for long periods of time, such as while riding in a crowded vehicle**
- **Standing in water**
- **Out in the cold for days without being warmed**
- **Deprived of an adequate diet and rest**
- **Careless about personal hygiene**

Types of Cold Injuries

People exposed to severe cold can suffer from the following conditions: frostbite, immersion foot/trench foot, hypothermia, snow blindness, and dehydration.

Frostbite

Frostbite is the most common injury resulting from exposure to the cold. Ice crystals form in body tissues exposed to temperatures below freezing. The crystals restrict blood flow to the injured parts and are like daggers that puncture cell membranes as they grow larger. Body parts most easily frostbitten are the cheeks, nose, ears, chin, forehead, wrists, hands, and feet. People suffering from frostbite may not realize it because the injured part may be numb from the cold.

There are different degrees of frostbite depending on the extent of tissue damage. A **superficial** cold injury can usually be characterized by numbness and tingling or "pins and needles" sensations. It involves the skin and the tissue just beneath the skin. Deep frostbite, on the other hand, involves freezing of the **subcutaneous** tissue, and possibly even muscle and bone. With a deep cold injury, victims are often unaware of a problem until the affected part feels like a stump or block of wood. Severe frostbite may result in infection or gangrene and may require surgical removal of the injured part.

Signs of Frostbite

Signs of superficial frostbite include:

- **Redness of the skin on light-skinned individuals; grayish coloring of the skin on dark-skinned individuals**
- **Blisters appearing in 24 to 36 hours**
- **Sloughing of the skin**

Signs of deep frostbite include:

- **Signs of superficial frostbite**
- **Painless or numb unthawed skin that is pale-yellowish and waxy looking**
- **Frozen, swollen tissue that is similar to wood to the touch**
- **Blisters in 12 to 36 hours**

Treatment of Frostbite

Treat superficial frostbite as follows:

1. **Move the victim out of the cold and wind.**
2. **Keep the victim warm; re-warm the affected parts gently and slowly. Explain to the victim that he or she will experience pain when warmth restores feeling to the injured part.**

   - **Cover cheeks, ears, and nose with the victim's and/or your hands.**
   - **Put fingertips under the victim's armpits.**
   - **Place the victim's feet under the clothing of another person next to that person's belly.**

Key Note Term

superficial – not serious; on the surface; shallow.

subcutaneous – beneath the top layer of skin.

3. **Insulate** injured parts by covering them with a blanket or dry clothing.

4. **Loosen tight clothing and remove wet clothing.**

5. **Encourage the victim to exercise carefully, avoiding further injury.**

6. **Seek medical treatment.**

Deep frostbite is very serious and requires extra care to reduce or avoid losing all or parts of the fingers, toes, hands, or feet. If possible, transport the victim to a hospital or contact emergency medical services immediately; it is preferable that deep frostbite injuries be re-warmed under medical supervision. If this is not possible, re-warm the injured parts, protect them from re-freezing, and seek medical help as soon as possible.

The Don'ts of Treating Frostbite

Although there are many things you can do to help a frostbite victim, there are also several things you should not do.

- **Do not attempt to thaw the affected part if you believe you cannot keep it warm until the victim receives medical treatment. It is extremely dangerous for an injured part to re-freeze after warming. It is less dangerous to leave the part frozen than to warm it and have it re-freeze.**

- **Avoid having the victim walk on frostbitten feet, especially if they thaw. If the victim must walk, it is less dangerous while his or her feet are frozen.**

- **Do not rub the injured part with snow or apply cold water packs.**

- **Do not warm the injured part by massage; ice crystals in the tissues will damage more cells when rubbed.**

- **Do not expose the injured part to open fire; the frozen part may burn because of lack of feeling.**

- **Do not have the victim move the injured part to increase circulation.**

- **Do not break any blisters.**

- **Do not use ointments or other medications.**

- **Do not let the victim use alcohol or tobacco. Alcohol reduces the body's resistance to cold, and tobacco decreases blood circulation.**

Immersion Foot/Trench Foot

Immersion foot and trench foot result from long exposure of the feet to wet conditions at temperatures between approximately 32° and 50°F. Keeping your feet in damp or wet socks and shoes or tightly laced boots for long periods of time may affect circulation and contribute to injury. Inactivity also increases the risk of immersion foot/trench foot. This injury can be very serious, leading to loss of toes or parts of the feet.

Signs of Immersion Foot/Trench Foot

Symptoms of immersion foot/trench foot in the primary stage include affected parts that are cold, numb, and painless. These parts may then begin to feel hot with burning and shooting pains. In the advanced stage of immersion

Key Note Term

insulate – to use materials to protect or isolate from the elements of weather.

foot/trench foot, the pulse decreases and the skin becomes pale with a bluish cast. Redness, blistering, swelling, heat, hemorrhages, and gangrene may follow.

Treatment of Immersion Foot/Trench Foot

Treat immersion foot/trench foot as follows:

1. **Gradually re-warm the affected foot by exposure to warm air. Explain to the victim that he or she may experience pain and burning when you re-warm the foot.**

   - **Do not massage or moisten skin.**
   - **Do not apply ice.**
   - **Do not expose injured parts to open fire or other sources of heat. Warm by covering with loose, dry clothing or other coverings instead.**

2. **Protect the affected foot from trauma or infection.**

3. **Elevate the foot to relieve swelling.**

4. **Dry the foot thoroughly; avoid walking.**

5. **Seek medical treatment.**

Hypothermia

Hypothermia is a general cooling of the body to a temperature below 95°F caused by continued exposure to low or rapidly dropping temperatures, cold moisture or wind, snow, or ice. With hypothermia, the body loses heat faster than it can produce it. Inadequate insulation, fatigue, poor physical condition, dehydration, faulty blood circulation, alcohol, trauma, and immersion in cold water can bring on this condition. People at high risk of hypothermia include infants, older people, people with limited mobility due to illness or other medical conditions, very thin people, and people with heart and lung problems.

Remember, cold weather affects the body slowly and almost without notice. Even when well-protected by clothing, a person may suffer cold injuries if exposed to low temperatures for long periods of time. As the body cools, it goes through several stages of discomfort and problems.

Signs of Hypothermia

The signs of hypothermia include:

- **Shivering or trembling, which indicates mild hypothermia and will eventually stop as body temperature drops**
- **Cold skin**
- **Weakness**
- **Dizziness**
- **Drowsiness and mental slowness or confusion**
- **Uncoordinated movements and slurred speech**
- **Low body temperature; in severe hypothermia, 90°F or below**
- **Stiff or rigid muscles**

- **Decreasing pulse and breathing rate**

- **Unconsciousness**

- **Shock, coma, and death, which may result as body temperature drops and the body freezes.**

Treatment of Hypothermia

Except in the most severe cases, the treatment for hypothermia is directed toward re-warming the body evenly and without delay. Treat mild hypothermia as follows:

1. **Re-warm the victim slowly.**

   - **If possible, move the victim inside, remove any wet clothing, and cover him or her with blankets. Avoid warming the victim quickly with hot baths, electric blankets, or heat lamps.**

   - **If you cannot move the victim inside, remove any wet clothing and re-warm him or her beside a campfire or using the body heat from another person.**

2. **Keep the victim dry and protected with clothing, blankets, towels, a sleeping bag, or even newspapers.**

3. **Keep the victim awake.**

4. **Do not raise the victim's feet or legs, since blood in the extremities is colder than in the rest of the body and may further chill the body's core.**

5. **Give the victim warm liquids gradually. Do not give the victim alcohol. Do not force liquids on an unconscious victim.**

6. **Be prepared to start basic life-support measures.**

7. **Seek medical treatment immediately.**

Treating a person with severe hypothermia is extremely dangerous because of the possibility of shock and disturbances of the heartbeat while re-warming. If possible, as you begin to re-warm the victim, transport him or her to a hospital or contact Emergency Medical Services immediately. If this is not possible, treat the victim gently because the heart is weak when the body is cold. Stabilize the victim's body temperature by keeping him or her from losing more body heat, and continue to keep the victim warm until you can get him or her medical treatment.

Snow Blindness

Snow blindness is the effect that the glare from an ice field, or snowfield, has on the eyes. It is more likely to occur in hazy, cloudy weather because people tend to protect their eyes when the sun is shining and believe protection is unnecessary on cloudy days. If a person waits until he or she feels discomfort or pain to use protective eyewear, a deep burn of the eyes may have already occurred.

Signs of Snow Blindness

There are several signs of snow blindness. These include:

- **A sensation of grit in the eyes**

- **Pain in and over the eyes made worse with eye movement**

- Watery and red eyes
- Headache
- Increased pain with exposure to light

Treatment of Snow Blindness

Treat snow blindness as follows:

1. **Cover the eyes with a dark cloth to discourage painful eye movement.**

2. **Try to give the eyes complete rest without exposure to light. If this is not possible, protect the eyes with dark bandages or very dark glasses.**

3. **Seek medical treatment. In most cases, once exposure to sunlight stops, the eyes heal in a few days without permanent damage.**

Dehydration

Dehydration from cold weather occurs when the body loses too much fluid, salt, and minerals. As mentioned in the previous lesson, you can lose large amounts of fluid and salt through sweating. This loss creates an imbalance of fluids, and dehydration occurs when fluids are not replaced.

Dehydration can occur in both hot and cold climates. In cold weather, sweat evaporates quickly and heavy layers of clothing absorb it, making dehydration more difficult to detect because the signs of sweating are less noticeable; therefore, the danger of dehydration during strenuous cold weather activities can become a serious problem.

The symptoms of cold weather dehydration are similar to those of heat exhaustion. Treat dehydration as follows:

1. **Move the victim out of the wind and cold, and keep him or her warm.**

2. **Loosen the victim's clothes to promote circulation.**

3. **Ensure the victim receives proper fluid replacement, rest, and prompt medical treatment.**

Prevention of Cold Injuries

You can prevent many cold weather injuries by taking proper care and precautions when participating in cold weather activities. Be sure to receive adequate nutrition, hot meals, and warm fluids. Get enough rest. Practice good hygiene. Wear the right clothing and protective gear. Do not forget to protect your eyes, ears, and face. Wear layers of clothing so you can remove outer layers if you begin to perspire. Avoid tight clothes that interfere with circulation. Replace or remove any clothing that gets wet as soon as possible.

You may not feel cold injuries because of cold's numbing effect, so always try to go out into cold weather with a partner. You can check each other for signs of injury. Exercise and keep active to maintain steady circulation and improve resistance to the cold. Many cold weather injuries can be avoided by planning ahead, staying alert, and using common sense.

Conclusion

Whether or not snow and frost are present, cold weather injuries such as frostbite or hypothermia can be a threat to safety. Knowing the proper ways to treat these injuries is very important because although it might seem like a good idea to re-warm the victim, you may in fact be making the injury worse. Read the first aid measures outlined in this lesson, consider how to prevent these injuries in the first place, and you will not be caught off-guard when you are exposed to the cold.

Lesson Review

1. **What factors should you consider when preparing for cold weather?**
2. **What are the signs of frostbite?**
3. **How would you treat hypothermia?**
4. **List the symptoms of cold weather dehydration.**

Chapter 2

Lesson Review

Lesson 9

Bites, Stings, and Poisonous Hazards

Key Terms

allergic reaction
antivenim
calamine
discoloration
rabies
tetanus
venom

What You Will Learn to Do

- Determine first aid treatment for bites, stings, and poisonous hazards

Linked Core Abilities

- Do your share as a good citizen in your school, community, country, and the world

Skills and Knowledge You Will Gain along the Way

- Identify types of venoms
- Relate snakes to their bites
- Explain the effects of animal and human bites
- Identify the symptoms of insect bites and stings
- Associate the types of poisonous plants to the reactions they cause
- Determine how to treat for contact with poisonous plants
- Define key words contained in this lesson

Chapter 2

Introduction

With so many outdoor activities to participate in, such as hiking, camping, bicycle riding, skate boarding, and skiing, it is common to come across emergencies involving bites, stings, and poisonous hazards. It is estimated that one of every two Americans will be bitten at some time by an animal. Dogs are responsible for about 80 percent of all animal bite injuries. Too, bee, wasp, and other types of insect stings can be not only painful, but fatal if the person is allergic. Depending upon where you live, the type of first aid you need to know for snakebites and plants will vary. Knowing what to do when outdoors can mean the difference between life and death.

Snakebites

If you spend much of your time outdoors, it may be common for you to come across snakes; however, your chances of a snakebite are remote if you remain alert and careful. There are both poisonous and nonpoisonous snakes, so the severity of a snakebite depends on whether the snake is poisonous or not. Beyond that, the severity of a snakebite depends on the type of snake, location of the bite, and the amount and type of venom injected.

Types of Snakes

There are approximately 130 different varieties of nonpoisonous snakes in the United States. They have oval-shaped heads and round pupils. Unlike pit vipers, nonpoisonous snakes do not have sensory pits with which to sense the body heat of their prey.

Poisonous snakes exist throughout the world, primarily in tropical to moderate climates. In the United States, there are four kinds of native poisonous snakes. Three of these four—the rattlesnake, copperhead, and cottonmouth (water moccasin)—are pit vipers. Pit vipers in other parts of the world include the bushmaster and fer-de-lance in Central and South America, the tropical rattlesnake in Central America, and the Malayan pit viper in eastern Asia. These snakes are shown in Figure 2.9.1.

Pit vipers have slit-like pupils; flat, triangular-shaped heads; small, deep, heat-sensing pits between their nostrils and eyes; and in most cases, hemotoxic **venom**. When a pit viper bites, it injects this venom from sacs through long, hollow fangs. This produces a severe burning pain, along with **discoloration** and swelling around the fang marks. The hemotoxin destroys blood cells, which causes the discoloration of the skin. Blisters and numbness in the affected area follow this reaction. Pit viper bites attack the circulatory system, possibly causing weakness, rapid pulse, and shortness of breath; as well as nausea, vomiting, and shock.

Key Note Term

venom – a poison produced by animals such as snakes and spiders that is transmitted by a bite or sting.

discoloration – altered or changed in color.

Figure 2.9.1: Common pit vipers.

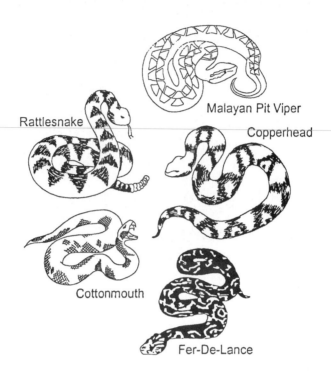

Corals, cobras, kraits, and mambas belong to the cobra family (see Figure 2.9.2). The coral snake is the only one native to the United States. Rings of red, yellow, and black color encircle its body. Although other nonpoisonous snakes have the same colors, only the coral snake has a red ring next to a yellow ring. The cobra, found in Africa and Asia, forms a hood with its neck when on the defensive. The krait, found in India and southeast Asia, is brightly banded; the mamba in Africa is either almost black or green.

Figure 2.9.2: Members of the cobra family.

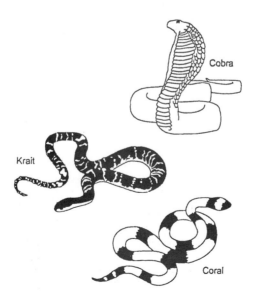

These snakes look very different, but all four inject their venom—a neurotoxin—through short, grooved fangs leaving a characteristic bite pattern, shown in Figure 2.9.3. There is minimal pain and swelling compared to a pit viper bite, but because their powerful venom affects the central nervous system, it can cause blurred vision, drooping eyelids, slurred speech, drowsiness, and increased salivation and sweating. Nausea, vomiting, shock, respiratory difficulty, paralysis, convulsions, and coma develop if the bite is not treated promptly.

Sea snakes are found in warm water areas of the Pacific and Indian Oceans. They have small heads, thick bodies, and tails flattened along the sides. Their fangs are only ¼ inch long, but their venom is very poisonous.

Types of Venoms

Basically, venoms are categorized as neurotoxins that affect the nervous system and can cause death by paralysis, hemotoxins that digest tissue including blood cells, or cardiotoxins that affect the heart directly.

Treating Snakebites

Snakebites are rarely fatal if treated within an hour or two, but they can cause pain and illness and may severely damage a bitten hand or foot. Although snakes do not always inject venom, all snakes may carry tetanus (lockjaw); therefore, anyone bitten by a snake, whether poisonous or nonpoisonous, should receive immediate medical attention.

One of the most important parts of treating a snakebite is identifying the type of snake making the bite. The type of **antivenim** used in medical treatment of snakebites varies depending on the type of venom injected. If you can identify the type of snake causing the injury, let Emergency Medical Services know when you call for help or phone the information ahead to the hospital if you plan to transport the victim yourself. If you cannot identify the snake, try to kill it without risk to yourself or delaying first aid; then show it to emergency medical personnel or take it to the hospital along with the victim for identification.

To treat snakebites, follow these steps:

1. **Get the victim away from the snake.**
2. **Reassure and keep the victim quiet and still. This will keep circulation to a minimum and keep the venom from spreading.**
3. **Immobilize the affected part in a position below the level of the heart.**

> **Key Note Term**
>
> **antivenom** – an anti-toxin used to counter-act venom.

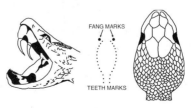

FANG MARKS

TEETH MARKS

Figure 2.9.3: Poisonous snakebites leave characteristic bite patterns.

4. Remove rings, bracelets, watches, and other jewelry from any affected limb. In case of swelling, this will make the victim more comfortable and will keep the affected limb from losing blood flow.

5. Wash the bite thoroughly with soap and water. Do not apply any ointments.

6. Place an icepack or freeze pack, if available, over the area of the bite. Do not place ice directly on the skin or wrap the limb with ice. You are only trying to cool the bite area, not freeze it.

7. For bites to the arms, legs, hands, or feet, apply constricting bands two to four inches away from the bite (see Figure 2.9.4). For an arm or leg bite, place one band above and one below the bite. For a hand or foot bite, place one band above the wrist or ankle. To ensure a band is not too tight, you should be able to insert a finger between the band and the skin.

8. If swelling from the bite reaches the band, tie another band a few inches farther away from the bite and the old band; then remove the old band.

9. Do not give the victim any food, alcohol, tobacco, medication, or drinks with caffeine.

10. Seek medical aid immediately.

Prevention of Snakebites

Most snakes are shy and passive. Unless they are injured or disturbed, they tend to avoid contact with humans. You can prevent a snakebite by using caution and common sense. If you are working outside clearing dense undergrowth, wear gloves, long sleeves, long pants, and boots for protection. When hiking in the wilderness, wear boots and long pants. Try to walk in open areas or stay on established paths. Look where you are stepping or placing a hand if climbing or pushing away tree limbs. Check before sitting on a rock or fallen tree. If possible, stay away from brush, rocks, and undergrowth. If you must handle a snake, even a freshly killed one, use a long tool or stick.

Human and Animal Bites

Mouths of people and animals are full of bacteria, so human and animal bites that break the skin spread germs and may result in serious infection and disease.

Figure 2.9.4: Place constricting bands on either side of the snakebite.

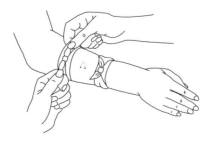

A person bitten by a diseased animal may come down with **tetanus**, **rabies**, and various types of fevers. If you think an animal is carrying a disease, notify the proper authorities to have it captured.

To treat a victim of an animal bite, follow these steps:

1. **If bleeding is severe, control it first before continuing with other first aid. Refer to the lesson on Controlling Bleeding for procedures to control bleeding.**

2. **Cleanse the wound thoroughly with soap or a detergent solution and water. Continue to cleanse and flush the wound with water for five minutes.**

3. **If there is minor bleeding, cover the wound with gauze or a clean cloth, press firmly on the wound, and if possible, raise the injury above the level of the victim's heart.**

4. **When minor bleeding stops, cover the wound with a sterile dressing and secure the dressing in place.**

5. **Immobilize an injured arm or leg.**

6. **Seek medical assistance as soon as possible.**

Insect Bites and Stings

In the outdoors, you may come in contact with various types of biting and stinging insects—bees, mosquitoes, ticks, fleas, spiders, and so on. Most of these insect bites and stings result in minor reactions, such as itching, redness, swelling, and irritation; however, scorpions and certain spiders can inject powerful poisons when they bite, and some people may have an **allergic reaction** to an insect bite or sting, particularly made by bees or wasps. In these cases, seek medical treatment immediately.

The black widow and brown recluse spiders, tarantulas, and scorpions, shown in Figure 2.9.5, are some of the more harmful insects you may encounter. Venom from the black widow is neurotoxic and may cause stomach and muscle cramps, breathing difficulties, nausea, sweating, vomiting, and convulsions. Tarantula venom is basically neurotoxic and may produce symptoms similar to that of a black widow bite, but in some cases can affect the heart and may digest tissue producing a severe local wound. The brown recluse spider can produce severe tissue damage around the bite, possibly leading to gangrene. Although stings from certain types of scorpions are painful but not dangerous, some can cause nausea, fever, stomach cramps, and possible convulsions and shock.

In most cases, bee and wasp stings produce minimal swelling, pain, redness, itching, and burning at the site of the sting. Multiple stings may cause headaches, fever, muscle cramps, and drowsiness. Symptoms from an allergic reaction may include:

- **Extreme pain at the site of the sting**
- **Itching and hives**
- **Weakness**

tetanus – (also called lockjaw) an acute infectious disease caused by the poison of a certain bacterium that enters the body through a wound, resulting in muscle contractions, rigidity, and death; it is preventable by immunization.

rabies – a viral disease affecting the central nervous system of mammals that is transmitted by a bite from an infected animal; it can result in paralysis and death if left untreated.

allergic reaction – a physical reaction, often marked by sneezing, breathing difficulties, itching, rash, or swelling, that some people have when the come in contact with certain substances.

Figure 2.9.5: Some biting and stinging insects can cause serious health problems.

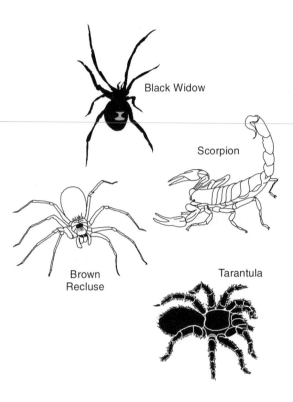

- **Anxiety**
- **Headache**
- **Breathing difficulties**
- **Nausea and vomiting**
- **Diarrhea**
- **Collapse, shock, and even death from a serious allergic reaction.**

Take the following basic first aid measures regardless of what caused the bite or sting:

1. **Remove any stinger left in the skin by scraping the skin's surface with a fingernail or knife. Do not squeeze the stinger because it may inject more venom.**

2. **For tick bites, remove the tick with your fingers if it will come off the skin easily. Do not pull the tick off if it will not come easily; this may leave the head of the tick in the skin which can cause infection. Instead, cover the tick with vaseline or thick oil to make it let go and then remove it.**

3. **Wash the area of the bite/sting with soap and water. Apply an antiseptic, if available, to minimize the chances for infection.**

4. **Use an icepack or cold compresses on the site of the bite/sting to help reduce swelling. Do not apply the ice directly to the skin.**

5. **Apply calamine lotion or a baking soda and water paste to the bite to relieve pain and itching.**

6. **Treat more serious allergic reactions as you would a snakebite.**

    - **Apply constricting bands above and below the site.**
    - **Be prepared to perform basic life-support measures.**

Key Note Term

calamine – a pink powder consisting of zinc oxide and some ferric oxide used in lotions and ointments.

- **To positively identify the insect, attempt to capture it without putting yourself at risk.**

- **Seek medical aid right away.**

7. **If signs of infection such as pus, red streaks leading away from the bite, swollen glands, or fever occur within hours or several days after an insect bite, seek medical attention.**

Prevention of Insect Bites and Stings

Wear insect repellent when outside in areas where biting insects are present. Reapply repellent every few hours when participating in activities that cause heavy perspiration. Wear appropriate protective clothing when hiking or camping in the wilderness or working in a yard, garden, or other woodsy or overgrown area.

Poisonous Plants

Most plants are harmless, but a few can cause allergic reactions upon contact (see Figure 2.9.6). For example, plants of the poison ivy group, including poison oak and poison sumac, produce an oily substance that irritates the skin of many people. Reactions to this substance include a rash characterized by redness, blisters, swelling, and intense burning and itching, as well as headaches and fever. Although the rash usually begins within a few hours after contact, it may appear 24 to 48 hours later.

In general, treat someone who has come in contact with a poisonous plant as follows:

1. **Remove contaminated clothing. Set it aside to be washed.**

2. **Wash all exposed areas of the skin thoroughly with soap and water, then apply rubbing alcohol.**

3. **Apply calamine or other soothing skin lotion to relieve itching and burning. Avoid covering the rash with a dressing.**

4. **Seek medical treatment if a severe rash occurs, if the rash is on the face or mouth which may interfere with breathing, or if there is a known history of allergic reactions.**

Prevention of Exposure to Poisonous Plants

Become familiar with what poison ivy and other poisonous plants look like so you can recognize a poisonous plant and avoid contacting it. The following are other precautions you should take to limit your exposure to poisonous plants:

- **Dress appropriately when participating in outdoor activities.**

- **Avoid areas where you aware that poisonous plants grow.**

- **Do not eat plants or parts of plants that you do not recognize.**

- **Do not put grass, twigs, stems, or leaves in your mouth.**

Figure 2.9.6: Poison ivy, oak, and sumac can cause severe allergic reactions in some people.

COMMON POISON IVY

° Grows as a small plant, a vine, and a shrub.

° Grows everywhere in the U.S. except California and parts of adjacent states.

° Leaves always consist of three glossy leaflets.

° Also known as Eastern three-leaf ivy, poison creeper, climbing sumac, poison oak, markweed, picry, and mercury.

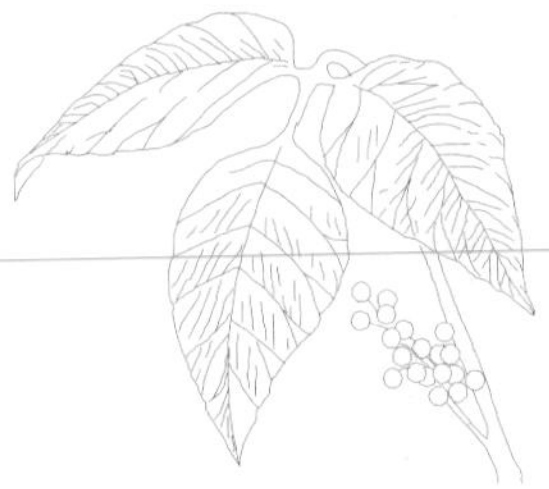

Poison Ivy

WESTERN POISON OAK

° Grows in shrub and sometimes vine form.

° Grows in California and parts of adjacent states.

° Leaves consist of three leaflets with wavy edges.

Poison Oak

POISON SUMAC

° Grows as a woody shrub or small tree from 5 to 25 feet tall.

° Grows in most of the eastern third of the U.S.

° Leaflets grow opposite each other with one leaflet at the tip.

° Also known as swamp sumac, poison ash, poison dogwood, and thunderwood.

Poison Sumac

Conclusion

Being able to adjust to new environments and protect yourself from harmful conditions is very important when participating in outdoor activities. Factors in nature such as extreme temperatures and humidity; animal, snake, and insect bites; and poisonous plants can pose a threat to you if you do not take precautions to guard against the possibility of injury. By being aware of potential hazards, knowing how to treat outdoor-related injuries, and exercising common sense, you can cope successfully with the environment and enjoy your time in the great outdoors.

Chapter 2

Lesson Review

Lesson Review

1. What are the three types of snake venom?
2. Why is it important to try and determine what type of snake caused the bite?
3. What are the symptoms of an allergic reaction to an insect bite or sting?
4. How would you treat someone who has come in contact with a poisonous plant?

Drug Awareness

Lesson 1

Use and Effects of Drugs, Alcohol, and Substances

Key Terms

abuse
addiction
alcohol
controlled substance
dependency
depressed
drugs
distilled
ethyl alcohol
ferment
gateway
hallucinogens
inhalants
intoxicated
misuse
narcotics
nicotine
stimulants
substance
tobacco

What You Will Learn to Do

• Assess the impact of drug and substance abuse on life today

Chapter 3

Linked Core Abilities

- Communicate using verbal, non-verbal, visual, and written techniques
- Do your share as a good citizen in your school, community, country, and the world

Skills and Knowledge You Will Gain along the Way

- Identify commonly abused substances
- Recognize the difference between drug use, misuse, and abuse
- Describe reasons why people might use, misuse, or abuse alcohol or drugs
- Identify the risks associated with alcohol and various drugs
- Associate the consequences of alcohol and drug use, misuse, and abuse to life
- Define key words contained in this lesson

Introduction

Data presented by the teenGetgoing website (www.teengetgoing.com) advocated by the JROTC Program notes that teen alcohol and drug trends suggest that 90 percent of teens will use alcohol and/or other **drugs** during adolescence. Fifty percent of teens will abuse alcohol and/or drugs, and 15 percent will become addicted while still in adolescence. Look around your classroom. What kind of numbers does this represent? This lesson presents the latest information about alcohol and drugs, defines drugs, and explains the differences between drug use, drug **misuse**, and drug **abuse**. You will learn several types of drugs that people abuse, their side effects, indications of overdose, and you will learn to process it in a way that is meaningful both to you and your community.

Key Note Term

drugs – chemicals that cause a change in a person's body or behavior.

misuse – the incorrect or improper use of a substance.

abuse – improper or excessive use or treatment.

substance – something, such as a drug or alcohol, deemed harmful and usually subject to legal restrictions.

controlled substance – a substance whose manufacture, possession, or sale is controlled by the law.

Drug Use, Misuse, and Abuse

Used under proper conditions, drugs can relieve pain, cure illness, and save lives. When abused; however, drugs can ruin lives and even cause death.

Think about the word "drug" for a moment. It can bring many images to mind—over-the-counter aspirin to stop a headache, a news report about someone arrested for cocaine possession, a prescription for antibiotics from your doctor, a drug-related death covered on the front page of the paper, medical research to develop drugs to cure illnesses, the war on drugs, etc. So exactly what is a drug?

Broadly defined, a drug is any **substance** taken into the body that changes how the body functions, whether mentally or physically. This includes medications used for the prevention and treatment of disease, as well as any **controlled**

substance to which a person can become addicted. Whether or not a drug is legal or illegal is no indication of whether or not it is addictive. For example, alcohol and the nicotine in tobacco products are addictive drugs. And, just because a drug has a medical purpose does not mean it is not addictive. Many medications, when misused or abused, can cause **addiction**.

Drug use is taking a legal drug as recommended or prescribed for medical reasons. Drug misuse is taking a legal drug for medical reasons but not as recommended or prescribed. For example, a person who doubles the recommended dosage of a pain reliever because they think it will make their headache go away quicker is misusing a drug. Drug abuse is taking a legal or illegal drug for a non-medical reason in a way that can injure your health or ability to function.

> ### Key Note Term
>
> **addiction** – physically or psychologically dependent on a substance, habit, or behavior that can lead to health, social, or economic problems; dependence on a drug.

Why Do People Abuse Drugs?

Some people try drugs out of curiosity or as an act of rebellion. Others cannot resist the peer pressure to try drugs. After people have tried a drug, whether or not they continue to abuse it depends on their individual personalities and situations and on the kind of drug abused.

Most drugs that people abuse produce feelings of pleasure and well-being. When people are unhappy, lonely, or stressed; or are missing something in their lives such as friends, love, or satisfying work, they may abuse drugs to avoid their problems or fill a void. But when the effects of the drug wear off, they realize the problems and the void are still there. So, they turn to the drug again.

This cycle is what leads to addiction, a trap that can ruin a person emotionally, socially, economically, legally, and physically. Some drugs are far more addictive than others. For example, a first-time user of crack cocaine has a one in three chance of becoming an addict. This is why it is important to stop before you ever start taking drugs.

> ### What Can You Do to Remain Drug-Free?
>
> - Fill your life with activities and people you enjoy.
> - Believe in yourself.
> - Practice saying no before you are actually in a situation where someone offers you drugs, so you will not hesitate to say no when the time comes.
> - Think through the consequences of abusing drugs. Where will drugs lead you in life? How long will your body remain healthy if you abuse drugs? How many of your plans can drugs ruin?
> - Remember that drugs do not solve problems; they create them.

Many people take drugs without knowing what effect they have on the mind and body. Knowing ahead of time what a drug can do is often enough to convince a person not to try it, especially if one of the potential dangers of abusing a drug is death. This lesson covers a variety of drugs, including alcohol and tobacco, and gives you an overview of what the dangers and effects are for each.

Alcohol

Alcohol, legal for those 21 years of age and older, is the most widely consumed and abused drug in the United States. It is socially acceptable in our society for adults to drink in moderation. In excess, however, alcohol is a dangerous drug.

Alcohol is a natural substance formed when sugar and yeast react and ferment. Some alcohols are **distilled**; other are simply **fermented**. Alcohol is a drug—a depressant that is absorbed into the bloodstream and transmitted to virtually all parts of the body. Many people don't realize that alcohol is a drug. Some hold the view that experimentation with or use of alcohol is considered normal or acceptable behavior. However, the use of alcohol can cause alcohol addiction, and often progresses to further drug abuse. Accordingly, some experts attach the term **gateway** to this substance. Use of drugs such as cocaine and heroin is unusual in those who have not previously used alcohol.

Alcohol abuse can cause serious chemical dependencies, harmful physical and psychological effects, and much suffering by family and friends. As awareness of these ill effects reaches new heights, more and more Americans are joining forces to fight alcohol abuse everyday.

When a person drinks alcohol, it follows the same pathway as food through the digestive system. Unlike food, however, alcohol does not have to be digested by the stomach to be absorbed into the blood. After alcohol reaches the blood, it is circulated throughout the body and affects every part, including the brain and the rest of the nervous system.

Key Note Term

alcohol – a beverage containing ethanol or ethyl alcohol which causes intoxication.

distilled – heated and condensed to purify, form a new substance, or concentrate.

ferment – to produce a chemical change in a carbohydrate material resulting in alcohol.

gateway – a term attached to alcohol and tobacco due to the fact that their use often leads to further drug abuse.

Alcohol Statistics

- Ninety percent of teenage automobile accidents involve alcohol.
- Drinking and driving accidents are the leading cause of death among 15- to 24-year-olds.
- Seventy percent of teenage suicide attempts involve alcohol.

Key Note Term

ethyl alcohol – the type of alcohol found in beer, wine, and distilled spirits.

Alcohol's Effects on the Body

The effects of **ethyl alcohol** on the human body can range greatly depending on:

- **Size of the individual**
- **How empty the stomach is at the time of alcohol consumption**

- **State of health and fatigue**
- **Mental attitude**
- **Speed and amount of consumption.**

Although alcohol may make a person feel "high," alcohol is actually considered a "downer" drug. It slows down or depresses the central nervous system causing slowed reactions, slurred speech, impaired coordination and judgment, and sometimes unconsciousness. Because alcohol affects reaction time, coordination, and judgment, people under its influence are more accident-prone and less likely to make wise decisions. For these reasons, drinking and driving are a very dangerous combination—and illegal.

Long-Term Effects

Long-term effects of alcohol abuse include alcoholism; cancers of the liver, stomach, colon, larynx, esophagus, and breast; high blood pressure; heart attacks; strokes; stomach ulcers; birth defects; premature aging; and a diminished immunity to disease due to non-function of infection-fighting cells. In men, hormone levels change causing lower sex drives and enlarged breasts; women's menstrual cycles become irregular, possibly resulting in infertility.

The list of effects goes on to include shrinking of the muscles, including the heart; kidney, bladder, and pancreas damage; brain damage affecting vision and memory; depression; and mental illness. Obviously, long-term damage from alcohol abuse can be irreversible and result in death.

TOLERANCE

When the body becomes accustomed to or builds up a resistance to a drug, the body has developed tolerance to the drug. Tolerance causes a drinker's body to need increasingly larger amounts of alcohol to achieve the effect that was originally
produced.

DEPENDENCE

When the body develops a resistance to a drug and requires the drug to function normally, dependence occurs. The drinker's body develops a chemical need for alcohol. Dependence occurs as tolerance builds. Dependence is also called addiction.

A dependent person who stops taking a drug will suffer from withdrawal. Signs of alcohol withdrawal include shakiness, sleep problems, irritability, rapid heartbeat, and sweating. The drinker also may see, smell, or feel imaginary objects.

The major psychological symptom of dependence is a strong desire or emotional need to continue using a drug. This need is often associated with specific routines and events. For example, some people drink whenever they face a difficult task or when they feel angry about something.

BRAIN DAMAGE

Long-term alcohol abuse destroys nerve cells in the brain. Destroyed nerve cells usually cannot grow again. The loss of many nerve cells causes forgetfulness, an inability to concentrate, and poor judgment. These losses interfere with normal everyday functions.

DIGESTIVE PROBLEMS

Ongoing drinking irritates the tissues lining the mouth, throat, esophagus, and stomach. The irritation can cause the tissues to swell and become inflamed. Repeated irritation increases the risk of cancers of the mouth, tongue, esophagus, and stomach. Alcohol also affects the intestines and can cause recurring diarrhea. Large amounts of alcohol cause the stomach to produce too much stomach acid. The overproduction of acid may lead to indigestion, heartburn, or ulcers.

LIVER DAMAGE

Alcohol interferes with the liver's ability to break down fats. As a result of heavy drinking, the liver begins to fill with fat. The excess fat blocks the flow of blood in the liver, and the fat-filled liver cells die. Cirrhosis of the liver is a disease in which useless scar tissue replaces normal liver tissue. Since there is no blood flow in the scarred area, the liver begins to fail. Heavy drinkers suffering from cirrhosis may have high blood pressure, get infections easily, have swelling of the abdomen, and show a yellowing of the skin and eyes. Cirrhosis is the last stage of liver disease and can result in death.

Heavy drinkers often develop alcoholic hepatitis, or inflammation of the liver, caused by the toxic effects of alcohol. Hepatitis causes weakness, fever, yellowing of the skin, and enlargement of the liver. Recovery may take weeks. Sometimes hepatitis can lead to liver failure and even death.

HEART DISEASE

Excessive drinking contributes to increased blood pressure and heart rate, and irregular heartbeat. These problems can cause disruption in blood flow and possible heart damage. Also, alcohol causes fat to be deposited in heart muscle. Fatty heart muscle, in turn, causes the heart to pump blood through the body less efficiently. Alcohol abuse leads to heart disease, the leading cause of death in the United States.

FETAL ALCOHOL SYNDROME

Pregnant women who drink put the health of their child at risk. A disorder called fetal alcohol syndrome (FAS) refers to the group of birth defects caused by the effects of alcohol on the unborn child. FAS occurs when alcohol in the mother's blood passes into the fetal, or unborn baby's, blood. Babies born with FAS often suffer from heart defects, malformed faces, delayed growth, and poor motor development. Alcohol prevents FAS babies from ever developing the reasoning abilities of healthy babies. Tragically, it is the leading preventable cause of mental retardation in America.

If a woman who is pregnant does not drink, her baby will not be born with FAS. Any woman who is pregnant or planning to become pregnant should not drink alcohol at all.

Short-Term Effects

The short-term effects of alcohol include those that happen within minutes, and sometimes within days, of drinking alcohol. Figure 3.1.1 identifies the short-term effects of alcohol on the body.

BLOODSTREAM

When alcohol enters the blood, it causes the blood vessels to widen. More blood flows to the skin's surface. The drinker feels warm for a short time as the skin flushes; however, the drinker's body temperature drops as the increased blood flow to the surface allows body heat to escape. People who drink alcohol in cold weather to get warm actually accomplish the opposite.

BRAIN

Upon reaching the brain, alcohol immediately has a depressant effect and slows the speed of some brain activities. People who drink alcohol may describe the change as relaxing. What they actually experience are physical changes such as a loss of sensation and a decrease in sharpness of vision, hearing, and other senses. Alcohol also affects the parts of the brain that control muscle coordination, which is why drinkers may lose their balance or stumble.

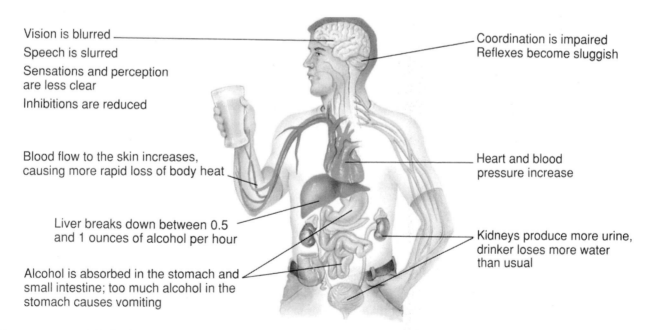

Figure 3.1.1: How the body reacts to the toxic effects of too much alcohol in the stomach.

If drinking continues, alcohol depresses the part of the brain that controls breathing and heartbeat. Breathing rates, pulse rates, and blood pressure, which initially increased, now decrease. A drinker may lose consciousness, slip into a coma, or die from alcohol poisoning.

Heavy drinkers and many first-time drinkers may suffer blackouts. Blackouts are periods of time that the drinker cannot recall. Other people recall seeing the drinker talking, walking, and in control. The following day, however, the drinker has no memory of some events from the day before.

LIVER

In the bloodstream, alcohol is carried to the liver. The liver chemically breaks down alcohol into energy and the waste produces carbon dioxide and water. The carbon dioxide is released from the body in the lungs. The water passes out of the body as breath vapor, perspiration, or urine. When people drink alcohol faster than the liver can break it down, they become **intoxicated**.

KIDNEYS

Alcohol prevents the release of body chemicals that regulate how much urine the kidneys make. The kidneys produce more urine than usual, and the drinker loses more water than usual. The drinker becomes very thirsty. In extreme cases, a drinker may lose water needed for the body to function properly.

MOTOR-VEHICLE CRASHES

Almost half of the fatal crashes and about two-thirds of all crashes involving personal injury in the United States are related to alcohol use. In addition, more than one-third of pedestrians who are struck and killed by motor vehicles are drunk.

Driving while intoxicated is illegal in all of the 50 states. Driving while intoxicated means a driver exceeds the level of blood alcohol concentration allowed by law in a state. Drivers who cause motor-vehicle crashes usually undergo blood, urine, breath, or saliva tests to determine their blood alcohol concentration (BAC, discussed later in this section). If their BAC is above the legal limit, drunk drivers can have their driver's license taken away and can be prosecuted.

SYNERGISM

Some drugs can interact to produce effects that are many times greater than either drug would produce by itself. When drugs increase each other's effects when taken together, the interaction is called synergism.

As previously stated, alcohol is generally a depressant drug. When a person drinks alcohol and takes another depressant, such as sleeping pills, the combination can cause drastic changes in the body. Together the depressants' effects are more than doubled and can cause a dangerous slowing of breathing and heart rates. In extreme cases, synergism of alcohol and other depressants can lead to coma or death.

Key Note Term

intoxicated – drunk; affected by alcohol to the point that physical and mental control are significantly impaired

OVERDOSE

Taking an excessive amount of a drug that leads to coma or death is called an overdose. Severe intoxication causes the heart and breathing to stop, resulting in death from alcohol overdose. Many drinkers assume that they will pass out before drinking a fatal amount. This is not necessarily true. Alcohol continues to be absorbed into the blood for 30 to 90 minutes after the last drink. The drinker's BAC can increase even if the drinker becomes unconscious. First-time drinkers who participate in a drinking contest may die from alcohol poisoning.

Blood Alcohol Concentration

The amount of ethanol in a person's blood is expressed by a percentage called the blood alcohol concentration (BAC). BAC measures the number of milligrams of ethanol per 100 milliliters of blood. A BAC of 0.1 percent means that 1/10 of 1 percent of the fluid in the blood is ethanol. A BAC of 0.1 percent reduces a person's muscle coordination, perception, and judgment.

A variety of factors can affect a person's BAC, including:

- **gender**
- **age, weight, and height**
- **amount of food in the stomach**
- **concentration of alcohol in beverages consumed**
- **volume of alcohol consumed**
- **rate of consumption and absorption**

The rate at which a person's liver can break down alcohol is fairly constant. In one hour, the liver can break down the amount of ethanol in a can of beer, a shot of liquor, or a glass of wine. Thus, someone who has three cans of beer in the last 45 minutes of a three-hour party will become more intoxicated than someone who drinks those three cans of beer over the three-hour period. The effects of BAC on the body are shown in Figure 3.1.2.

Provided the person does not continue to drink, the BAC decreases. The intoxicating effects of alcohol slowly diminish. As reflexes and coordination return to normal, a person gradually becomes steadier. Many people refer to this process as "becoming sober" or "sobering up."

You may have heard that cold showers, exercise, fresh air, or coffee will help a person sober up more quickly. But this is not true. Nothing can speed the liver's ability to break down alcohol. Coffee or fresh air may keep a person awake, but they do not eliminate the intoxicating effects of alcohol.

Behavioral Effects

In addition to the physical effects of alcohol, certain behavioral, or learned, effects are connected to drinking. A person's mood and reason for drinking can alter the effects of alcohol. Sometimes the person's mood and reason for drink-

Blood Alcohol Concentration: Effects on the Body

Number of Drinks	Effects	BAC Range*	Approximate Time to Eliminate Alcohol
	Inhibitions, reflexes, and alertness diminished. Judgment and reasoning affected.	.02–.03%	11/2 hours
	Drinker gets the mistaken idea that his or her skills and abilities have improved. Self-control declines.	.04–.06%	3 hours
	Unable to think clearly. Judgment, reasoning and muscular coordination is impaired.	.06–.09%	4 to 5 hours
	Most behaviors, including hearing, speech, vision, and balance, are affected.	.08–.12%	5 to 7 hours

*The BAC will vary depending on the alcohol content of the drinks and rate of consumption.

Figure 3.1.2: In some states, a person with a BAC of 0.1 percent is legally drunk. Other states have lowered the legal BAC to 0.08 percent.

ing make the effects stronger; sometimes they make the effects weaker. The environment in which alcohol is consumed may influence its effects as well.

At a quiet family dinner, family members may consume wine with no negative effects. The calm nature of the event and the fact that both parents and children expect each other to behave politely creates an environment in which people drink responsibly.

At a party in which "getting drunk" is the main theme, alcohol consumption often leads to negative behaviors. The loss of coordination may be exaggerated for comic effect. People who have been drinking may insist that they are still perfectly able to drive. They may not want to admit that they cannot drink as much as others.

As alcohol takes effect, drinkers begin to lose judgment and self-control. At the same time, alcohol decreases drinkers' natural fears. When these two effects are combined, the person's inhibitions are reduced. Inhibitions are the controls that people put on their emotions and behavior in order to behave in socially acceptable ways.

After they lose their inhibitions, drinkers may behave in ways they normally would never consider. For example, a person under the influence of alcohol may express anger in violent or destructive ways. Shy people may behave in outgoing ways, and serious people may act foolishly.

Alcoholism

Some drinkers cannot control their drinking. Their major goal in drinking is to get drunk. People who have an addiction to alcohol suffer from the disease of

D E C I D E

DEFINE the problem	
EXPLORE alternatives	
CONSIDER the consequences	
IDENTIFY values	
DECIDE and act	
EVALUATE results	

Drinking and Driving?

Janelle attended a party with some of her friends. She planned to get a ride home with Dave, but she had seen him drink four beers since he arrived. Dave was showing some signs of intoxication, and Janelle was not sure if he should drive. Unfortunately, she did not know anyone else at the party who could give her a ride, and Janelle knew that her parents had gone out with friends for the evening. Besides, three of her friends were getting a ride from Dave. "I'm probably getting worried for nothing," thought Janelle. "What could happen in the few miles to my house?"

1. Use the DECIDE process to decide what you would do if you were in Janelle's position. Explain your decision.

2. What role might peer pressure play in influencing Janelle's decision?

3. Suggest a realistic plan that you and your friends could use to avoid situations like the one described above.

Source: Ken Karp

alcoholism. Psychologically, alcoholics consider drinking a regular, essential part of coping with daily life. Physically, an alcoholic's body requires alcohol to function. An alcoholic's drinking patterns eventually control every aspect of life.

No one is sure why some drinkers become alcoholics, but anyone who drinks—even one drink—is at risk of becoming an alcoholic. Because alcoholism tends to run in families, there appears to be some genetic basis. On the other hand, the attitudes in the home in which a person grows up may play a role in whether or not a person develops a drinking problem

Drugs

A drug is any chemical substance that changes the function of the mind or the body. Aspirin is a drug; allergy medication is a drug; marijuana is a drug; beer is a drug; the nicotine in cigarettes is a drug. A drug is neither good nor bad—it is what a person does with a drug that makes the difference.

Use, misuse, and abuse are terms thrown around quite a bit when talking about drugs. Use is taking a legal drug as prescribed or recommended for medical reasons. Misuse is taking a legal drug for medical reasons but not as recommended or prescribed. Abuse is taking any drug, legal or illegal, for a nonmedical reason in a way that can injure your health or ability to function. Taking drugs is a serious matter; there is no such thing as "recreational drug use."

Abusing drugs is not a sport or a hobby and always involves an unnecessary risk to your health.

When people talk about drugs, you often hear that someone is a drug addict or that a drug can or cannot cause dependence. Addiction and drug dependence mean basically the same thing; however, the term "addict" tends to make people think of a desperate individual living in the back alleys of a big city. But anyone from any background in any place can be addicted or drug dependent. People who are dependent cannot refuse the drug they have been abusing.

A person has a physical dependence on a drug when, after being deprived of the drug for any length of time, he or she experiences symptoms like nausea, vomiting, anxiety, watery eyes and nose, and an overwhelming desire to use the drug. Such symptoms are typical of withdrawal sickness. Withdrawal happens because the body's chemistry has been changed, causing the user to be unable to function comfortably without the drug.

Most people who are physically dependent are also psychologically dependent. Some have psychological dependence without the physical dependence, which can be an equally strong dependence. With this type of dependence, the user feels a powerful motivation to continue abusing a drug for the temporary pleasure or relief of discomfort the drug gives. Because the mind and the body work together very closely, it is often difficult to tell the difference between physical and psychological dependence. The mental craving for a drug may be so powerful that it seems to be a physical need.

Marijuana (Pot, Grass, Weed, Dope, Reefer)

Marijuana (Acapulco Gold, Ganga, Grass, Mary Jane, Pot, Weed, Reefer, Stick, Smoke) comes from the dried flowers, leaves, and small stems of the cannabis plant. It is smoked in cigarettes, known as joints, and also in pipes. Marijuana use is illegal in the United States, but in the past was used medically to reduce swelling of the eyes caused by glaucoma and to counteract the intense nausea brought on by certain cancer treatments. Its legalization, especially for these medical purposes, has been a controversial subject in this country for years.

The chemical tetrahydrocannabinol (THC) produced by cannabis is the main psychoactive substance that produces marijuana's mind-altering effects. THC is quickly absorbed into the lungs and then travels through the blood to affect the brain. It distorts the senses, including hearing, taste, touch, and smell, and alters sense of time and place, as well as feelings. THC affects sleep patterns and remains in body fat for at least a month after only one joint has been smoked. It causes users to crave food (getting the munchies) and to enjoy eating, which is unusual for a drug. It also tends to dull sexual urges and pleasure.

There are several hundred other chemicals in marijuana that vary between different types of cannabis plants and between plants grown during different seasons. The active chemicals in marijuana affect the brain, altering hearing, taste, touch, smell, and sense of time and space. The effects of marijuana vary from person to person depending on each person's expectations and how much they smoke, and because the chemicals in different marijuana plants vary. People may experience anything from a mild euphoria to uncontrollable laughter to hallucinations. Marijuana can also contain dangerous substances such as pesticides and molds, and is sometimes mixed with PCP to make the user believe it is more potent.

Because marijuana is widely abused today and has been around for thousands of years, many people believe that its use poses no harm. However, research studies prove this notion wrong. Effects include:

- **Short-term memory loss and shortened attention span, both of which interfere with the ability to learn. Heavy, long-term use is often called "burn out" because the user's thinking is slow and confused.**

- **Increased heart rate and irregular heartbeat.**

- **Weakening of the immune system.**

- **Reduced hormone levels resulting in lower sperm counts in males and irregular menstrual cycles in females.**

- **Development of "amotivational syndrome," which results in apathy and loss of ambition and drive.**

- **Impaired judgment, unsteadiness, lack of coordination, and slowed responses, which make driving a dangerous activity.**

- **Lung damage and increased risk of lung cancer. This risk is higher than that of smoking tobacco cigarettes, since marijuana is inhaled more deeply and then held in the lungs for a longer period of time. Joints also lack filters to cut down on harmful chemical effects.**

- **Possible depression and moodiness. Some users feel tired and unhappy the morning after smoking marijuana and may respond by smoking a joint to feel better. This cycle may lead to psychological dependency.**

- **Possible intense fear and anxiety, called a "pot panic" and even paranoia and psychosis. This may occur if the marijuana contains higher levels of THC.**

- **Development of a tolerance to marijuana resulting in the need for greater amounts in order to feel any effects. This may also contribute to psychological dependence.**

> ### Key Note Term
>
> **dependency** – addiction to a substance.

Harmful health effects of marijuana use may include rapid and irregular heartbeat, short-term memory loss, shortened attention span, a weakened immune system, fatigue, and a higher risk of lung cancer. In extreme cases, marijuana abuse can result in paranoia and psychosis. Similar to alcohol, marijuana abuse can affect driving ability. As with any illegal drug, marijuana is not tested for safety and purity. It may contain pesticides and molds and may be mixed with other dangerous drugs.

Because of all the effects marijuana has on the mind, body, and the ability to learn, its use may be particularly harmful to young people since they are still maturing physically, sexually, and mentally. Marijuana's effects may prevent you from becoming a healthy, normal adult.

Cocaine, Crack, and Bazuco

Cocaine hydrochloride (Cocaine, Coke, Snow, Flake, Rock, White, Blow, Nose Candy) comes from the leaves of the coca bush and is an illegal drug that looks like white crystalline powder. It is often diluted with other ingredients and then inhaled through the nose, injected, or smoked.

It is a stimulant that affects the nervous system providing short bursts of euphoria, a feeling of excitement, increased blood pressure and pulse rate, and alertness. People often use it to increase mental activity and to offset drowsiness, fatigue, or as an appetite suppressant; however, the intense high of cocaine is followed by an intense low. Repeated abuse of cocaine can result in a strong physical and psychological dependency. The body will ignore all other drives, including hunger, in its drive for cocaine.

Regular use can lead to hallucinations of touch, taste, sound, or smell. Tolerance develops rapidly with repeated use. As cocaine's effects wear off, the user feels exhausted, **depressed**, and sometimes paranoid, similar to the crashing of amphetamines. Cocaine is considered to be one of the most potentially addictive drugs.

Cocaine stimulates the central nervous system. Immediate effects include dilated pupils and elevated blood pressure, heart rate, respiratory rate, and body temperature. Occasional use results in a stuffy nose, while chronic use decays the mucous membranes of the nose. Injecting cocaine, or any drug, with a shared needle may spread AIDS, hepatitis, and other diseases. Cocaine produces both psychological and physical dependency.

Dealers cut cocaine with other substances, usually table sugar, mannitol, lactose, dextrose, and other drugs (PCP, lidocaine, amphetamines). Strychnine, a poison, has been found in cocaine; talc, which damages the lungs, is also often used.

Occasional use of cocaine can lead to heavy, uncontrollable use, with the dependence becoming so strong that users will not quit even when cocaine severely damages their lives. When users do quit, they may not experience strong physical withdrawal symptoms, but they do become depressed, irritable, tired but unable to sleep, and constantly crave the drug.

Crack (Crack, Freebase Rocks, Rock) looks like brown pellets or crystalline rocks that resemble lumpy soap and is often packaged in small vials. It is smoked. Bazuco is a drug similar to crack. Both of these drugs are illegal.

Crack is street cocaine commonly processed with boiling water and baking soda, which produces a very pure form of cocaine. The effects and the risk of addiction to crack are so great, however, that it is like a completely different drug. It is many, many times more dangerous than cocaine hydrochloride. Its effects are felt within 10 seconds. Cocaine in this form creates a very intense high and a fast, strong addiction. The user also experiences an incredible low after the high has worn off, often throwing him or her into a deep depression. To offset this depression, the user then smokes more crack, starting the compulsive cycle that leads to a severe dependency. The only person who benefits from this vicious cycle is the drug dealer who now has a desperate customer in constant need of his or her product.

Physical side effects of crack include dilated pupils, increased pulse rate, elevated blood pressure, insomnia, loss of appetite, hallucinations of touch, paranoia, and seizures. A major concern with crack is that dependency is almost immediate. The first experience is often very pleasurable. Then, the extreme low

Key Note Term

depressed – low spirits; sadness; dejection.

afterwards is a strong motivator to use the drug again right away, this time to relieve bad feelings. Users of crack are addicted before they know it, turning their lives upside down.

Bazuco, another form of cocaine, is equally if not more dangerous and addictive than crack. Its use originated in Colombia and other South American countries and has now made its way to the United States. It is made from the intermediate step between the coca leaf and the cocaine hydrochloride, called cocaine sulfate. It is mixed with a number of other substances, among them marijuana, methaqualone, and acetone. Its effects are similar to those of crack, as are its dangers and its quick addiction.

The use of any type of cocaine can cause death by disrupting the brain's control of the heart and respiration.

Amphetamines and Methamphetamines (Speed)

Amphetamines (Speed, Uppers, Ups, Black Beauties, Pep Pills, Copilots, Bumblebees, White Crosses, Benzedrine, Dexedrine, Footballs, Biphetamine) look like capsules, pills, or tablets. Methamphetamines (Crank, Crystal, Meth, Crystal Meth, Methedrine, Ice) can be in the form of a white powder, pills, or a rock which resembles blue paraffin. Forms of both drugs are used medically to treat obesity, narcolepsy, and hyperactivity in children.

Amphetamines

Similar to cocaine, amphetamines are **stimulants**. They stimulate the nervous system, increasing physical activity, energy, mental alertness, and self-confidence, and producing euphoria. Medically, amphetamines are used to treat obesity, narcolepsy, and hyperactivity in children. For example, the amphetamine Ritalin is used to stimulate the brain center that helps hyperactive children sit still and pay attention.

As a drug of abuse, amphetamines are often referred to as "speed." Many people abuse amphetamines to increase energy and alertness, and in some cases to combat fatigue brought on by use of alcohol, marijuana, or depressants. The body builds up tolerance to amphetamines, however, and greater and greater doses are required to achieve the same effects. Addiction may become severe.

Medically, amphetamines are taken orally, but many abusers inject the drug directly into a vein increasing the risk of overdose and infection. Needles shared to inject the drug can spread hepatitis and HIV. After an injection of amphetamines, the user experiences intense, short-lived euphoria. An addict may inject the drug several times a day for several days feeling little need for food or sleep. Mental depression and overwhelming fatigue follow abuse, which may cause the abuser to turn to amphetamines again for relief.

In addition to fatigue and depression, other side effects of amphetamine abuse include extreme anxiety, temporary mental illness, and malnutrition. High doses can cause hallucinations, increased body temperature, high blood pressure, convulsions, kidney failure, lack of oxygen, bleeding of the brain, and death. Withdrawal symptoms include irritability, depression, disorientation, long periods of sleep, and not caring about anything.

Key Note Term

stimulants – drugs, drinks, or other substances that speed up the activity of the mind or body; a drug that speeds up the activities of the central nervous system, the heart, and other organs.

Methamphetamines

Methamphetamine is a nervous system stimulant similar to amphetamines that is used medically in much the same way as amphetamines. This drug is abused to produce heightened awareness, alertness, and self-confidence. A smokable form of methamphetamine is "ice." Like crack, it produces an intense high without the use of needles and is extremely addictive. Abuse of methamphetamine may result in bizarre behavior, sleeplessness, depression, high blood pressure, increased body temperature, convulsions, heart problems, seizures, and strokes.

Methcathinone, also called "cat" and "star," is a designer drug similar to methamphetamine that can cause paranoia, slurred speech, tremors, extreme weight loss, and sleeplessness

Barbiturates, Methaqualones, and Tranquilizers

Barbiturates (Downers, Barbs, Blue Devils, Red Devils, Yellow Jacket, Yellows, Nembutal, Seconal, Amytal, Tuinals, Luminal, Amytal, Pentothal, Phenobarbital) look like red, yellow, blue, or red and blue capsules. Methaqualones (Ludes, Quaaludes, Quads, Sopors, Sopes, 714s) look like tablets. Tranquilizers (Valium, Librium, Equanil, Miltown, Serax, Tranxene, Thorazine) look like tablets or capsules.

Barbiturates

Barbiturates are a group of depressant drugs that include phenobarbital (goofballs), pentobarbital (yellow jackets), amobarbital (blue devils), and secobarbital (red devils). They lower body temperature and blood pressure, slow breathing and heart rate, and as such, have many medical uses. For example, doctors prescribe phenobarbital to reduce the frequency of convulsions in epileptics. Barbiturates are also used medically as an anesthetic and to treat insomnia. Barbiturates' effects vary from person to person and even change within one person from one time to the next.

When abused, the symptoms they produce are similar to those of alcohol. Small amounts can produce calmness and relaxed muscles, but larger doses cause slurred speech and staggering walk. Like alcohol, they distort perception and slow reaction time, which can cause serious accidents like car crashes. Very large doses can cause respiratory depression, coma, and death.

Signs of barbiturate abuse include fatigue, blurred vision, confused or slurred speech, lack of coordination and balance, a reduction of mental and physical activity, and decreased breathing. Abusers will often act like they are drunk, but there will be no smell of alcohol. Long-term abuse may result in double vision, depression, and forgetfulness.

Signs of an overdose of barbiturates include dilated pupils, a rapid pulse, shallow breathing, and clammy skin. An overdose can cause coma and death. Because barbiturates cause confusion and forgetfulness, accidental death occurs when a person has taken barbiturates, becomes confused, forgets, and takes more barbiturates. Accidental poisoning occurs when barbiturates are combined with alcohol. Withdrawal symptoms include anxiety, insomnia, tremors, delirium, and convulsions.

Barbiturate abusers often become extremely depressed, tired, and hopeless. They may reach for the rest of the bottle to "end it all" when in this mental state, or they may become confused, forget how many pills they have taken, and accidentally overdose. For this reason, barbiturates are one of the leading causes of drug-related deaths. The combination of barbiturates and alcohol can multiply the effects of both drugs, thereby multiplying the risks. This multiplication of the effects of two separate drugs when taken together is called the synergistic effect. It can be fatal.

Methaqualone

Methaqualone production has been banned in the United States since 1984 due to its widespread misuse and minimal medical value. Abusers take it to produce a feeling of elation; however, its side effects are headaches, nosebleeds, dizziness, loss of coordination, and leg and arm pain. Tolerance and psychological dependence can develop when used regularly. Using methaqualone with alcohol is known as "luding out" and can cause death.

Tranquilizers

Tranquilizers are used medically to treat anxiety, insomnia, and convulsions. It is very easy to become both physically and psychologically dependent on them. When mixed with alcohol, they can cause death.

Narcotics

Most **narcotics** are opiates, which come from the seed pods of opium poppies. Many are used medically to relieve pain and treat insomnia. Narcotics abuse initially produces a feeling of euphoria that is often followed by drowsiness, nausea, and vomiting. Users also may experience constricted pupils, watery eyes, and itching. An overdose may produce slow and shallow breathing, clammy skin, convulsions, coma, and death. Tolerance develops rapidly and dependence is likely. The use of contaminated syringes to inject certain kinds of narcotics may result in diseases such as AIDS and hepatitis. Narcotics include opium, codeine, morphine, and heroin. Other types of opiates include Percocet, Percodan, Tussionex, Fentanyl, Darvon, Talwin, and Lomotil and come as tablets, capsules, or liquids.

Opium

Opium (Paregoric, Dover's Powder, Parepectolin) can look like dark brown chunks or a powder. It comes from a specific type of poppy, generally grown in the Middle East. Opium is one of the weaker narcotics, but it has side effects that make it undesirable as a medication, including slowed heart rate, breathing, and mental abilities, and loss of appetite.

Codeine

Codeine comes in different drugs such as Empirin, Tylenol, and certain cough medicines. It is either a dark liquid varying in thickness or comes in capsules or tablets. Similar to opium, codeine is one of the weakest narcotics. Doctors prescribe it for coughs and pain relief.

> ## Key Note Term
>
> **narcotics** – a drug medically used to relieve pain, produce sleep, and dull the senses.

Morphine

Morphine (Pectoral Syrup) is an opium derivative, and comes in the form of white crystals, hypodermic tablets, and injectable solutions. Morphine is a very strong painkiller, but because it is also very addictive, it is used in medicine only for severe cases, such as in the later stages of terminal cancer when patients are in extreme pain. Unfortunately, as a drug of abuse, morphine usually results in addiction. Withdrawal from it has painful and severe effects and generally requires the help of a professional to get an addict off the drug.

Heroin and Methadone

Heroin (Smack, Horse, Junk, Harry, H, Brown, Black Tar, Antifreeze) looks like a white to dark brown powder or a tar-like substance. Methadone Hydrochloride (Dolophine, Methadose, Methadone) comes in the form of a solution.

Heroin is a concentrated form of morphine and is so addictive that it is illegal in the United States even for medical use. Unfortunately, it is the most abused narcotic in this country, and its use is on the rise as of the late 1990s. Users of heroin often start by sniffing or smoking the drug in powdered form. Because tolerance develops quickly, they often turn to "mainlining," the practice of injecting a heroin solution into their veins to intensify the drug's effects.

Heroin dulls the senses, easing tensions, fears, and worries. A stupor follows that lasts for several hours in which hunger and thirst are reduced. After 12 to 16 hours without heroin, the user will experience severe withdrawal symptoms, including sweating, shaking, chills, nausea, diarrhea, abdominal pain, leg cramps, and severe mental and emotional pain. To relieve these symptoms, the user must take another dose of the drug. People addicted to heroin often die young, some from overdoses caused by unreliable drugs, others because they cannot distinguish between safe and dangerous doses.

Signs of an overdose include shallow and slow breathing, clammy skin, and convulsions. An overdose can result in a coma and death. When addicted, a person must have more of the drug to keep from experiencing withdrawal symptoms, which are severe and can include panic, shaking, chills, sweating, cramps, and nausea.

Hallucinogens

Key Note Term

hallucinogens – drugs that cause hallucinations.

Hallucinogens alter the physical senses, producing visions, sounds, and smells that are not real, and distorting the concepts of time and space in the user's mind. Because these drugs confuse fact and fantasy, a user may become irrational and resort to violence or suicide to avoid an imagined situation or attacker. Hallucinogens are not physically addictive, but users often become psychologically dependent on these drugs.

Lysergic Acid Diethylamide (Acid)

Lysergic acid diethylamide (LSD, Acid, White Lightning, Blue Heaven, Sugar Cubes, Microdot) can come as brightly colored tablets, imprinted blotter paper, thin squares of gelatin, or as a clear liquid.

A "trip" from an average dose of LSD can last as long as 8 to 10 hours. LSD's effects are unpredictable, tolerance to it develops quickly, and its use frequently results in psychological dependence.

LSD is a powerful hallucinogen that scrambles and confuses the senses. A tiny drop taken with sugar or food can cause a person to "trip" or experience false visions, smells, and sounds for hours. Sensations may be confused and feelings may change rapidly. Music may appear as colors and colors as flavors or odors. Some people say these experiences are exciting; others say they are nightmares. Those having a "bad trip" may take dangerous or irrational actions to escape from this imaginary situation. In addition to these affects, LSD can cause nausea, vomiting, and misinterpretations of time and distance. Some people experience flashbacks of LSD's effects days, weeks, and years after the original trip. An overdose of LSD can result in psychosis, accidental death, and suicide.

Phencyclidine Hydrochloride

Phencyclidine hydrochloride (PCP, Angel Dust, Hog, Superjoint, Busy Bee, Green Tea Leaves, DOA <dead on arrival>) can be in the form of a liquid, capsules, white crystalline powder, or pills. Of the various types of hallucinogens, only PCP has a medical use as a tranquilizer for animals.

PCP interrupts the functions of the neocortex, which is the section of the brain that controls the intellect and keeps instincts in check. The effects of PCP are unpredictable, but users frequently report a sense of distance and alienation from the world and others. Sometimes a user may feel drunk, but at other times the same dose may cause depression, paranoia, hallucinations, and suicidal thoughts. Time and movement are slowed down; muscular coordination worsens; senses are dulled; and speech is blocked and incoherent.

PCP stays in the system for a long time. Chronic users report persistent memory problems and speech difficulties as well as psychological and behavioral changes. Some of these effects may last six months to a year following prolonged daily use. Mood disorders such as depression and anxiety also occur, and users may exhibit paranoid and violent behavior. In fact, many deaths attributed to PCP do not occur from the drug itself, but from accidents, like falling from high places, drowning, or car wrecks, related to the behavior PCP produces. Large doses of PCP can cause convulsions and coma, heart and lung failure, or ruptured blood vessels in the brain. Treatment for an overdose is very difficult and requires hospitalization.

PCP, used as a tranquilizer for animals, can cause frightening hallucinations when used by humans. Abuse can result in seizures, coma, and death or in violent, unpredictable behavior. Some abusers have committed murder and suicide.

Psilocybin (Mushrooms, Shrooms) and Mescaline (Mesc, Buttons, Cactus)

Two other hallucinogens are psilocybin, produced from a type of mushroom, and mescaline, produced from a type of cactus. Similar to other hallucinogens, use of these drugs can cause hallucinations, perception problems, nausea, vomiting, and, in extreme cases, mental illness, suicide, or accidental death. Mescaline effects, while compared to a mild LSD trip, are often accompanied by sweating and severe abdominal cramps. Eating mushrooms poses another danger since many mushrooms look alike and some are poisonous enough to cause death.

Inhalants (Air Blast)

Key Note Term

inhalants – medications or chemicals that are inhaled.

Inhalants are toxic chemicals like glue, freon, nail polish, spray paint, and gasoline that are huffed (sprayed into a cloth and held over the mouth and nose) or bagged (sniffed from a bag, bottle, or can) to achieve a brief, mild euphoria. All of these products contain labels warning against inhaling their fumes because of the hazards involved. Some inhalants used medically are also abused, such as amyl nitrate which relieves heart pain and nitrous oxide which relieves anxiety.

Risks involved with inhaling these chemicals include nausea; dizziness; vomiting; headaches; unconsciousness; pneumonia; permanent brain and nerve damage; bleeding of the brain; eventual liver, brain, and kidney cancer; and death due to heart failure and suffocation. Effects of inhalants are unpredictable and depend on what chemical or chemicals are inhaled and how much. Brain damage and death may result after only one use depending on the inhalants involved.

Ecstasy (xtc, Love Drug)

Ecstasy is a "designer drug" that closely resembles cocaine. It produces euphoria that lasts several hours, heightens pleasure, and may even produce hallucinations in high doses. Ecstasy is taken orally and may cause mood swings, overly friendly behavior, insomnia, anxiety, and nausea. In extreme cases, abuse may result in seizure and death.

Rohypnol (Roofies, Forget Pill, Date-rape Pill)

Rohypnol is used legally as a medical sedative in Europe and Latin America. As a drug of abuse, it is called roofies, forget pill, and date-rape pill. At first, it produces an alcoholic type of high, but then heavy sedation and short-term memory loss that lasts up to eight hours. It earned its reputation as the date-rape pill by being slipped into the drinks of females, who were taken advantage of in a state of sedation brought on by the drug and then unable to remember exactly what happened to them. In addition to the drawback just discussed, dangers of abusing rohypnol include impaired motor skills and slow respiration.

Tobacco

Key Note Term

tobacco – the leaves of cultivated tobacco plants, prepared for use in smoking, chewing, or as snuff.

Many people hold the view that experimentation with or use of **tobacco** is considered normal or acceptable behavior. However, the use of tobacco often progresses to further drug abuses. Accordingly, some experts attach the term "gateway" to this substance. Use of drugs such as cocaine and heroin is unusual in those who have not previously used tobacco.

Tobacco's hazards include cancer and other diseases and can also have ill effects on others. As awareness of these ill effects reaches new heights, more and more Americans are joining forces to fight tobacco abuse every day.

In addition to smoking cigarettes, pipes, or cigars, people who use tobacco products can also do so orally in the forms of chewing tobacco (by placing a wad between the cheek and teeth and sucking on it) and snuff (by placing a pinch between the lower lip and teeth).

Three major components make up tobacco, each having their own ill effects. One such component, tar, causes a variety of cancers and contributes to emphysema and other respiratory problems. For this reason, people often choose to smoke low-tar cigarettes, but even low-tar cigarettes can be unsafe because smokers often smoke more while using these brands. Carbon monoxide, also found in tobacco, restricts the oxygen-carrying capacity of the blood, and can often cause insufficient heart operation. Nicotine, the substance in tobacco believed to cause dependency, is absorbed into the bloodstream, reaching the heart and brain within a few seconds of the onset of smoking.

> ## Note
>
> Nicotine in its pure state is a toxic poison and is used in insecticides.

Some of the diseases associated with long-term tobacco smoking include chronic bronchitis, emphysema, coronary heart disease, and lung cancer. Lung cancer is the leading cause of death among women today. Cigarette smoking is a major independent risk factor for heart attacks (sometimes fatal) in both men and women. Pipe and cigar smokers are more prone to dying from cancer of the mouth and throat than non-smokers. Smoking also reduces the effectiveness of prescription and over-the-counter medications.

> ## Note
>
> Infections, especially pneumonia and acute bronchitis, are twice as common in young children whose parents smoke than children with non-smoking parents.

Although chewing tobacco and snuff are not smoked, they increase the risk of disease and damage to the delicate lining of the mouth and throat. As a result, individuals who use these products are more likely than non-users to develop mouth cancer, throat cancer, and gum disease. Chewing tobacco and snuff can also contribute to heart disease and strokes. The harmful effects of one can of snuff are equal to that of about sixty cigarettes.

Despite the labels required by federal law warning individuals about the hazardous effects of using tobacco products, use continues.

Recent research has indicated that non-smokers who breathe in second-hand smoke (smoke that escapes from the burning end of a cigarette as well as the smoke exhaled by the smoker), can have an increased risk of lung cancer, heart disease, and respiratory disorders. Inhaling second-hand smoke makes the heart beat faster, the blood pressure go up, and the level of carbon monoxide in the blood increase. Smoke from an idling cigarette contains even more tar and nicotine than an inhaled one, in addition to more cadmium, a substance which has been related to hypertension, chronic bronchitis, and emphysema.

As the public becomes more aware of the dangers of inhaling second-hand smoke, the legislation protecting the rights of non-smokers continues to increase. Smoking is increasingly being banned in both public and private places.

The Chemicals in Tobacco Smoke

With each puff on a cigarette, cigar, or pipe, a smoker inhales over 4,000 different chemicals. Of these 4,000 chemicals, at least 1,000 are known to be dangerous. Table 3.1.1 lists some of the harmful chemicals found in cigarette smoke. Among all the dangerous substances, nicotine, tar, and carbon monoxide can be identified as the most deadly ones found in tobacco smoke.

Nicotine and Addiction

The drug in tobacco that may act as a stimulant and cause addiction is **nicotine**. A stimulant is a drug that speeds up the activities of the central nervous system,

Key Note Term

nicotine – the drug in tobacco that may act as a stimulant and cause addiction.

Table 3.1.1: Harmful Chemicals in Tobacco Smoke

acetaldehyde	butylamine	methyl alcohol
acetone	carbon monoxide	methylamine
acetonitrile	dimethylamine	methylfuran
acrolein	dimethyl-nitrosamine	methylnaphthalene
acrylonitrile	ethylamine	nicotine
ammonia	formaldehyde	nitric oxide
aniline	hydrocyanic acid	nitrogen dioxide
benzene	hydrogen cyanide	phenol
benzopyrene	hydrogen sulfide	pyridine
2,3 butadione	methacrolein	toluene

the heart, and other organs. In its pure form, nicotine is one of the strongest poisons known. Taken in large amounts, nicotine can kill people by paralyzing their breathing muscles. Smokers usually take in small amounts of nicotine. However, over several years the effects on the body of much smaller amounts are numerous and severe.

When tobacco is smoked, nicotine enters the lungs, where it is immediately absorbed into the bloodstream. Seconds later, the nicotine reaches the brain. Chemical changes begin to take place. Nicotine causes the heart to beat faster, skin temperature to drop, and blood pressure to rise. Nicotine constricts blood vessels, which cuts down on the blood flow to hands and feet. Beginning smokers usually feel the effects of nicotine poisoning with their first inhalation. These effects include rapid pulse, clammy skin, nausea, dizziness, and tingling in the hands and feet.

The degree of reaction varies from person to person, depending on the person's tolerance to nicotine. The effects of nicotine poisoning stop as soon as tolerance to nicotine develops. Tolerance can develop in new smokers after the second or third cigarette. The smoker begins to experience a "lift," a physical reaction to the chemicals in nicotine. As tolerance builds, however, the user may need more and more tobacco to produce the same feeling. The Surgeon General, the country's highest medical authority, has called nicotine an addicting drug, just like heroin and cocaine.

In a short time, tobacco users develop an addiction to nicotine. A tobacco addict who goes without tobacco for a short time may experience nicotine withdrawal. Nicotine withdrawal is a reaction to the lack of nicotine in the body, which causes symptoms such as headache, irritability, restlessness, increased coughing, nausea, vomiting, a general feeling of illness, and intense cravings for tobacco. Withdrawal effects may begin as soon as two hours after the last cigarette. Physical craving for a cigarette reaches a peak in the first 24 hours.

Tobacco users also suffer psychological withdrawal symptoms when they stop smoking. They feel emotionally and mentally uncomfortable without tobacco. By using tobacco at certain times—when under stress, for example—tobacco users actually condition themselves to rely on tobacco whenever a stressful situation arises. When tobacco users go without tobacco, they may feel unable to handle stress. Many tobacco users begin to depend on tobacco at particular times of the day, such as when they awaken or after they finish a meal. Others begin to depend on tobacco in social or work situations, such as parties or meetings.

Tar

The dark, sticky mixture of chemicals that is formed when tobacco burns is known as tar. Smokers can see evidence of this substance on their fingers and teeth, which turn brown when tar sticks to them. The tar also sticks to the cells of the respiratory system, where it damages the delicate cells that line the respiratory tract. The cells have tiny hair-like structures, or cilia. The cilia beat back and forth and sweep dust and other foreign particles away from the lungs. If the cilia are damaged, foreign particles can enter the lungs, leading to disease.

The tar in tobacco smoke contains hundreds of chemical carcinogens, or cancer-causing agents. Cancer of the lungs, throat, and mouth are caused by the inhalation of tar in tobacco smoke.

Carbon Monoxide

A poisonous, colorless, odorless gas that is found in cigarette smoke is carbon monoxide. You may be familiar with the dangers of carbon monoxide. Deaths that result from leaving a car engine running in a closed area are caused by carbon monoxide poisoning.

Carbon monoxide has a greater attraction for the oxygen-carrying molecules (hemoglobin) in the red blood cells than oxygen does. When carbon monoxide is inhaled, it takes the place of, or displaces, large amounts of oxygen from hemoglobin. The more carbon monoxide present in the blood, the less oxygen in the blood. Carbon monoxide also makes it hard for the oxygen that is left in the blood to get to the muscles and organs. When a person smokes, the heart works harder but accomplishes less. Because their blood contains too little oxygen to function properly, smokers often experience shortness of breath when they are active.

Chemicals in Smokeless Tobacco

Most tobacco users smoke cigarettes, cigars, or pipes. And yet there has been an increase, especially among teenage boys, in the use of smokeless tobacco. Smokeless tobacco is tobacco that is chewed or sniffed through the nose. Some people who use smokeless tobacco think that the products are safe because no smoke is produced or inhaled. What they may not realize is that smokeless tobacco contains many of the same harmful chemicals found in tobacco smoke, including the highly addictive drug nicotine.

There are two different kinds of smokeless tobacco products. Chewing tobacco is poor-quality tobacco leaves mixed with molasses or honey and placed between the cheek and gums. Snuff is finely ground tobacco that may be held between the lower lip and teeth or sniffed through the nose. One can of snuff delivers as much nicotine as 60 cigarettes. The nicotine in chewing tobacco enters the bloodstream through the membranes of the mouth. The nicotine in snuff gets into the body through the membranes of either the mouth or the nose. After it has entered the body, nicotine from smokeless tobacco has the same effects as nicotine from cigarettes.

Conclusion

When drugs are properly used, they can cure illnesses and save lives. When abused, however, drugs and alcohol can destroy lives and cause death. It is important to understand that although people often abuse drugs and alcohol to find happiness and fulfillment, these substances only create more problems and unhappiness. To keep from falling into the trap of drug and alcohol abuse stay smart, strong, and active. Say "no." Recognize the different drugs that are abused in our society and what effect they have on people's health and lives. Understand the dangers of alcohol abuse, not only to the drinker but to family and friends. You can set an example as an informed, drug-free individual.

Lesson Review

1. What are the differences between drug use, misuse, and abuse?
2. List three risks associated with the use of alcohol.
3. Is there any "safe" cigarette? Why or why not?
4. Define the term "gateway".

Chapter 3

Lesson Review

Lesson 2

Critical Decisions about Substances

Key Terms

detoxification program
methadone
normal
stress
therapeutic communities

What You Will Learn to Do

- Respond to substance use and abuse situations

Linked Core Abilities

- Take responsibility for your actions and choices
- Do your share as a good citizen in your school, community, country, and the world

Skills and Knowledge You Will Gain along the Way

- Weigh the external and internal factors that influence decisions about substance abuse
- Apply the F-I-N-D-S Decision Process
- Employ pre-deciding techniques as a substance abuse prevention strategy
- Identify two kinds of intervention - Interpersonal and Enforcement
- Recognize signs of substance abuse

- Describe why people abuse substances and ways to remain drug, alcohol, and tobacco-free
- Identify ways to approach/help someone you suspect has a drug problem

Introduction

Obviously, all drug use is not bad. Drugs taken as prescribed by doctors or as indicated on over-the-counter drug packaging can help prevent and cure illnesses and relieve symptoms of illnesses. When taken under these circumstances and for these reasons, drugs are a useful tool in keeping people healthy. However, drugs should only be a small part of an individual's efforts to maintain wellness, since the best way to stay healthy is to maintain a healthy lifestyle. When people are healthy and feeling well both mentally and physically, they do not require drugs. So why do people misuse and abuse drugs when they do not need them?

Reasons for misusing and abusing drugs all have one thing in common—people depend on drugs to change the way they feel, instead of learning to change themselves or their behaviors to solve their problems or face new challenges. You do not need drugs to have a good time; there are many other longer lasting ways to feel good. You do not need drugs to relieve uncomfortable feelings; many other young people struggle with trouble and challenges much like your own. Even adults are often concerned with the same things you are. Many people, young and old, work to change the things they do not like in their lives and learn to live with those aspects of their lives that they cannot change—all free of drugs. In fact, people who abuse drugs to avoid their problems are not able to solve them.

It is important for you to learn about the effects of drug use, the reasons why drugs are harmful, and ways to resist pressures to try drugs. However, imbedded within the principles of good citizenship, JROTC cadets take this one step further. They also learn about the dangers posed by drugs to help other students avoid them, thus persuading those using drugs to seek help. Involvement in intervention programs can only help to dissolve the drug problem.

How Use Develops

Students are usually first tempted to smoke cigarettes and marijuana and drink alcohol at parties and other social occasions because of peer pressure and curiosity. From there, drug abuse may then progress in stages. These stages are:

1. **Experimental use**
2. **Occasional use**
3. **Regular use**
4. **Multiple drug use**
5. **Total dependency**

This progression of stages is not inevitable; it can be stopped at any stage, although stopping becomes more difficult in later stages. The best way to prevent a problem with drugs is to simply not abuse them in the first place.

Experimental Use

Those who experiment with drugs may be more curious about a drug's effects than the drug's dangers. In the case of certain drugs, however, the dangers of addiction, permanent psychological damage, or physical harm takes only one unlucky experiment. Drugs have different effects on different individuals who have no way of knowing what that effect may be. For some, trying a drug once can result in immediate addiction, serious injury to themselves or others, and even death. Remember, those who are now dependent started with experimentation, and they probably never thought that trying a drug once or twice would become an addiction. The many lives ruined by drugs prove that this can indeed happen.

Occasional Use

For occasional drug users, drugs become a way of having a good time with friends in social situations. At this point, using drugs while alone is still relatively uncommon. Drug use may become the major social activity of the group, so it is very easy for occasional use to turn into a regular habit.

Regular Use

Regular users take drugs to maintain a drugged feeling. Though they may deny it, these users are psychologically dependent on drugs. Drug use has become a regular part of their lifestyle, and although they continue to carry out their daily activities at home, school, or work, they are usually barely making it.

Multiple Drug Use

In many cases, after people try one drug and get comfortable taking it, they are more likely to feel comfortable trying other types of drugs. For example, after many young people give in to pressures to try marijuana, and if they continue to use it regularly, it is likely they will try other drugs as well. Unfortunately, each drug produces different effects, and although users of one drug may know what to expect when they take it, another drug may be much more dangerous and affect them in a very different way.

> **Note**
>
> The chances that a first-time user of cocaine will become addicted are 1 in 6; the chances that a first-time user of crack will become addicted are 1 in 3; and 1 out of 10 drinkers becomes an alcoholic.

Total Dependency

Dependent users rely on drugs physically as well as psychologically and will go to great lengths to get them. Without drugs, they experience severe physical and mental distress. Dependent users all started with experimental drug use. In many cases, as users grow more dependent on drugs, they crave new sensations and may try more than one drug at a time or different ways of taking a drug. Such habits multiply the risks of drug use. For example, people who start injecting drugs risk contracting diseases like AIDS through shared needles.

Determining Who's at Risk

Anyone has the potential to become dependent on substances, but some people seem to be more susceptible than others. Certain times in life may make someone more likely to try drugs for the first time or to use drugs to escape problems. People who are under a great amount of **stress** are more likely to use drugs; adolescence is a time of great stress and drugs are often readily available to young people. Young people who have family problems are more likely to use drugs, and those with low self-esteem run the risk of continuing to use drugs after "just trying" them to deal with peer pressure or bad feelings.

> ### Key Note Term
>
> **stress** – strain or pressure on the body or mind.

> ### Managing Stress
>
> One way to avoid drugs is to manage the stress in your life. There are many methods that you can use to help manage stress, including:
>
> - Run, swim, ride a bike, or engage in some other form of exercise
> - Take a hot shower or bath to relax
> - Consciously relax all the muscles in your body
> - Do deep-breathing exercises
> - Learn to manage your time effectively

The best prevention is simply not to use drugs except as directed for medical reasons and not to drink alcohol until you are of legal age and then only moderately. Children of alcoholics should consider not drinking at all, even when reaching legal age, because their risk of alcoholism is much greater than that of children of non-alcoholics.

Remember, no matter how rough things may get, there are always alternatives to drug abuse, whether it is changing an uncomfortable situation, participating in a healthy activity you enjoy, or seeking counseling for problems you feel you cannot handle alone. While it may seem that drug abuse is very prevalent in the United States, it does not mean that it is normal.

What Is Normal, Anyway?

Key Note Term

normal – according
to a rule or standard
pattern; regular;
usual.

While you may wonder what the term "**normal**" has to do with drugs, deciding what kind of behavior is "normal" in your life has a lot to do with whether or not you abuse drugs. Many young people are very concerned with being normal, which can mean different things in different situations to different people. Behavior that is normal for one person may not be normal for another. What is normal in one group may be considered strange in another.

When you worry about how your clothes and hair look, if you are saying the right things, or if people will laugh at you for certain things, you are concerned with whether other people think you are normal. In fact, worrying about being normal is very normal. Young people, in particular, worry because they are experiencing so many changes in their lives. This acute awareness of "fitting in" usually decreases as you become an adult and gain a better sense of who you are. Your teenage years are a time for learning what is normal for you. It is not an easy process, so give some thought to the type of behavior you believe is normal.

Do not make the mistake of labeling your emotions as good or bad. You may not enjoy feeling angry, sad, or bored, but these are emotions that everyone has. They teach you about yourself. When you abuse drugs to escape these feelings, you are cheating yourself. Uncomfortable feelings are often messages that you need to change something in your life; look at them as feedback on how you think, act, and view your environment. They are for you to analyze and work with. They are normal.

What you consider normal is generally considered normal by your group of friends. You became friends because you have things in common. But what do you do if your friends want you to try drugs? Is it normal behavior to go along with the group? If what is standard for the group is not for you, then it is better for you not to be what the group considers normal.

If you could run faster than all the others in your group, you would not want to slow down just to be normal. The same goes for drugs. If you know that drugs hurt you, why use them to be considered normal? Why slow down with the crowd when you know you can win the race?

Legal Risks of Illegal Drug Use

Before deciding to drink alcohol or abuse drugs, remember that abuse of legal drugs, taking illegal drugs, underage drinking, and driving while intoxicated are all against the law. By endangering their lives and the lives of others, users become a societal problem, often requiring legal punishment. Drug laws vary from state to state, but the general trend throughout the United States is toward stiffer penalties for those convicted of drug possession, drug selling, and alcohol-related car accidents. People convicted of these crimes must pay higher fines and must often spend time in jail. If you think trying drugs might be a fun way to spend some time, think about how much fun you would have spending time in a prison.

Tell-tale Signs of Drug Abuse

As a cadet and leader in the JROTC program, you serve as a role model for other cadets. You send a positive message to your followers about how to successfully function without drugs. You can also help by recognizing signs of problems in other cadets. The following list of symptoms and signs of drug use will help you to determine if someone you know may be using drugs or has a serious drug problem.

- **Changes in attendance, discipline, interests, neatness, and attention**
- **Loss of interest in sports, extracurricular activities, or hobbies**
- **Failing memory**
- **Unusual degree of activity, like excitement, boundless energy, excessive laughter, and excessive talkativeness**
- **Unusual inactivity, like moodiness, depression, drowsiness**
- **Poor physical coordination**
- **Slurred speech**
- **Deterioration of physical appearance and lack of concern for health habits and dress**
- **Loss of appetite and rapid weight loss**
- **Sudden increase in appetite**
- **Unpredictable outbreaks of temper and arguing**
- **Nervousness and irritability**
- **Reduced motivation, self-discipline, and self-esteem**
- **Wearing sunglasses at inappropriate times to conceal the eyes which may be red or have constricted or dilated pupils**
- **Constantly wearing long-sleeved shirts or blouses (to hide needle marks)**
- **Borrowing frequently from others or stealing money (required to purchase drugs)**
- **Chronic dishonesty; such as lying, stealing, or cheating**
- **Appearing frequently in out-of-the way areas; such as closets, storage areas, or rest rooms**
- **Guilty behavior and fear of discovery**
- **Association with known or possible drug sellers or abusers**
- **Not giving straight answers when questioned about activities**
- **Appearance of intoxication but no smell of alcohol, indicating possible use of barbiturates or marijuana**
- **Use of drug-related vocabulary**
- **Possession of pipes, rolling papers, small decongestant bottles, and lighters**
- **Possession of drugs or evidence of drugs, such as peculiar plants, butts, seeds or leaves in ashtrays, or clothing pockets**
- **Odor of drugs and the smell of incense or other "cover-up" scents**

Remember these are just guidelines of which you should be aware. Many of these behaviors or signs can have causes other than drug use. However, if you notice some of these signs in someone, you can be fairly certain that there is some kind of problem; whether related to drugs or not, the person needs help. You can be a part of that help.

Turning the Pressure Off

As a teenager, you have many new pressures in your life, as well as many new challenges and experiences. Along with these new opportunities come added responsibilities. While adjusting to these changes that are a part of becoming an adult, you are constantly making decisions. Sometimes you make good decisions and other times you may make mistakes. Making mistakes is normal in a good way because they are part of the learning process. Of course, nobody likes to make mistakes, so try to analyze each situation beforehand to minimize them.

When it comes to drugs; however, it is extremely important to make the right decision before you make a mistake; making just one wrong choice may be too late. Having to juggle pressures from your family, school, activities, job, and friends may overwhelm you at times. The many new situations and emotions you experience can sometimes seem unbearable with no end in sight. Unfortunately, drugs and people who use them and are willing to share them are readily available with what seems like a quick solution to all your problems.

Pressures from society, your family, friends, and yourself may sometimes make it difficult for you to say no to drugs. Our culture often encourages quick solutions to problems; many people would like to believe that taking a pill could cure all types of problems, but there is no magic pill to make it all better. Pills and other drugs only produce chemical reactions in your mind and body, which in turn create artificial feelings and unhealthy side effects.

Advertising, movies, and television shows often glamorize drug and alcohol abuse. It may appear that all the beautiful, fun people are drinking at a bar or taking a refreshing break with the "crisp, clean" smoke of a cigarette. These types of false messages reinforce the idea of drug abuse as a normal and desirable part of life. You may see your parents drink at parties, you may know students who use drugs, and you may be curious about drugs' effects or tempted to use them to relieve uncomfortable emotions. Though all these situations may make drug abuse attractive to you, the reality of drugs' effects is far from glamorous. The pleasure drugs give is short-lived and unreal. They never solve problems; only you can do that, and you cannot function if drugs are a problem in your life.

Deciding not to take drugs can be a difficult decision when you are faced with pressure to take them. There are ways to avoid drugs in your life. One way is to refuse when someone offers you drugs. To be effective, you can present your personal reasons for not wanting to take drugs. Be honest—do not supply phony reasons. For example, you could say, "No thanks... I want to keep a clear head," or "I don't want to become addicted," or simply "I don't use drugs." To make it clear that you mean what you say, look the person in the eyes when presenting your thoughts about drug abuse.

If the person who is offering you drugs continues to try to persuade you, make a definite action that removes you from the situation. This action should make it clear that you cannot be persuaded to change your mind. For example, you can simply get up and leave or enjoy activities with another group of non-abusing friends.

What you need is a plan of action to cope with all the pressures to abuse drugs. After you decide that you do not want drugs to be a part of your life, you must develop strategies to resist these pressures as well as healthy alternatives to drugs. To handle internal pressures, you can:

- **Accept and analyze your emotions.** If you are feeling something unpleasant, take time to consider the cause of your emotions instead of trying to avoid feeling bad. If you do not address the cause, the uncomfortable feelings will return to bother you. Also, remember that certain amounts of anger, sadness, boredom, and frustration are normal human responses to life that must be accepted.

- **Seek out help when you feel overwhelmed.** Members of your family, teachers, counselors, and friends can help you. There are also many places that offer help for specific problems; such as divorced parents, shyness, alcoholism, or lack of reading skills. You can ask a counselor or instructor at school about them or look in the phone book. If you are willing to make the effort, there are people willing to help you. Seek them out.

- **Find alternatives to drug use.** If your routine is a big yawn, take a look around and see if there is an activity that looks interesting to you. Photography, auto mechanics, painting, chess, drama, singing, playing an instrument, and part-time employment are among the many activities you could do that would add new challenges to an unexciting routine.

  Of even greater importance, these activities pay you back with a real sense of accomplishment and heightened self-esteem as you get better and better at them. Drugs cannot give you these benefits; they can only temporarily produce a false feeling of well-being. In the long run, drugs always take far more than they give and leave the user with nothing but problems.

- **Release excess energy and learn how to relax.** If you cannot sit still in your seat during class, maybe you are not exercising your body enough. Physical activities such as running, walking, biking, tennis, basketball, weight training, martial arts, skiing, and dance, among others, keep your body in shape while relaxing and focusing your mind during mental activities.

  If you have problems relaxing, try the relaxation methods in the chapter on stress, such as meditation, deep breathing, and visualization techniques.

- **Practice patience.** If there is a situation that makes you feel bad, you cannot think of a way to change it, and nothing you do seems to work, what can you do? Wait! You may not like that answer because waiting is difficult, especially for young people. But there will be times in life when the situation is out of your control. This fact is understandably hard for young people to accept. However, change is certain and inevitable. If you wait and stay alert, new solutions and opportunities will become available to you in time. People on drugs never learn this lesson of waiting and miss opportunities to change their lives for the better.

You also need to develop a strategy for resisting external pressures. This strategy can include:

- **Learn how to refuse drugs effectively.** Standing up to peers when they want you to do something that you do not want to do can be very difficult. When you go against the crowd, you risk rejection—and that is scary. However, every time you make a decision to do what is best for you and those you care about, you become a stronger person. You also gain the respect of those people who are your true friends. Your strength and your decisions may even give others the courage to do what is best for them as well. In today's school environment, saying no may not be easy, but it is definitely worth the effort.

   If you do not feel comfortable saying no in a situation, find a way to remove yourself from the scene. Suddenly remembering an appointment or some other excuse can get you away from the situation and give you time to think of another way of handling it next time. The important thing is not to do the drugs.

- **Analyze media and advertising.** Is the image of drugs projected by advertising accurate? Who gains by making products appear glamorous and sophisticated? People who sell products want you to buy them and will use psychological techniques in advertising to create a demand for their goods. Companies that sell beer, cigarettes, and non-drug related products, such as cars, have one main goal—they want your money.

   Your goal is to do what is best for you. Some products that advertising tries to sell you are opposed to that goal. Your defense against advertisements for products that are useless or harmful is the power to read between the lines of the psychological game. Think about the message an ad is giving and decide for yourself whether it is accurate.

If the person who is offering you drugs continues to try to persuade you, make a definite action that removes you from the situation. This action should make it clear that you cannot be persuaded to change your mind. For example, you can simply get up and leave, or enjoy activities with another group of non-abusing friends.

Getting Help

If you decide that the stresses and problems in your life are too much to manage, find someone to help you. Many people are willing to help, but first you must let them know that you need help. Parents, teachers, friends, brothers, sisters, school counselors, school nurses, and members of the clergy are usually available for guidance and support. A second option is to call one of the national hotlines that tell you where to call for drug information and treatment referral in your area. For these numbers, call 1-800-662-HELP.

Alternatives to Drug Use

Turning to drugs to try to feel good or deal with problems is a risky choice. You can get involved in many healthy and constructive activities to lift your mood, feel better about yourself, and deal with the pressures in your life.

Engaging in physical activity is one way to help yourself feel better. Physical activity not only helps improve your mood, but it also relieves the negative effects of stress. Getting enough exercise and getting involved in sports can help you feel energetic, positive, and self-confident.

Helping other people can give you a good feeling about yourself, too. Many social service agencies need volunteers. You could volunteer to read to someone with a visual handicap, make a social visit to an elderly person in a nursing facility, or teach a hobby or sport to a youngster.

Participating in youth groups can help you feel a sense of belonging and connection to others. The members of these groups support one another as each person strives to find his or her place in the world. Youth groups also volunteer to help others in need.

Working at a part-time job not only provides you with spending money, but can also give you a sense of accomplishment and increased self-esteem. Not only can you learn a new skill, but you can meet new friends. Your family, friends, or school counselor may be able to help you find such a job.

Remember that abusing drugs cannot relieve the pressures and problems in life. It can only postpone decision-making and create more problems. Imagine how you would feel if you had to tell lies, hide your physical condition, worry about police, and deal with drug side effects. People who become dependent on drugs spend almost all of their time thinking about drugs, taking drugs, getting the money for drugs, and looking for drugs. Drugs end up controlling their lives. By deciding not to use drugs, you are acting to take control of your life.

Helping Others Avoid Drug Use

It is important for you to learn about the effects of drug use, the reasons why drugs are harmful, and ways to resist pressures to try drugs; however, imbedded within the principles of good citizenship, JROTC cadets take this one step further. They also learn about the dangers posed by drugs to help other students avoid them, thus persuading those using drugs to seek help. Involvement in intervention programs can only help to dissolve the drug problem.

Where to Find Help

If a friend you know is having problems and is considering abusing drugs to relieve the pain, you can be of help just by being there to listen and by affirming your personal decision that drugs are not a good way to deal with problems. In some cases, this may be all that is needed—a caring and strong presence can go a long way as can an informed discussion about what a particular drug can do to the mind and body. There may be other situations, though, which require specific and professional help that you are not prepared to give.

When you realize that someone you know may have a drug problem, there are some choices of action you need to make. Among your choices are:

- **Convince the person to seek help.** Be prepared with the names of people and agencies that can provide help.

- **Tell a responsible adult, such as an instructor or counselor, that you are concerned about the person.** You may be reluctant to do this because it feels like telling on someone; however, especially in cases where you know the person is using life-threatening drugs or participating in dangerous situations, you are really doing this person a favor. Your action may save a life.

- **If you know of someone selling drugs, report the person to an appropriate authority.** People who sell drugs have passed the point of having a personal problem. Drug dealers are hurting others.

Find out what types of help are available at your school and in your community for people with problems. Know the proper procedure for reporting drug-related incidents, and above all, show the cadets whom you lead that you care about their well-being and are willing to help. Your example and your support can have a positive impact on those around you.

Treating Drug Abuse and Addiction

Before drug abusers can be helped, they need to recognize their problem. Unfortunately, this may be difficult for them. Many abusers deny their behavior; others deny the problems that led them to drug abuse. Figure 3.2.1 shows some of the signs of drug abuse. This list may help you recognize a drug abuse problem in a friend or classmate and allow you to convince the abuser that he or she has a drug problem.

After drug abusers recognize their problem, many options are available to them. Options for drug abusers include programs in which people withdraw from the drug under medical care and treatment centers in which abusers learn to live drug-free lives. Programs to help abusers and their families are available. Understanding the underlying cause for the drug abuse and involving family members can restore and reinforce the family's stability.

Figure 3.2.1: Learning to recognize the signs of drug abuse can make a difference.

Signs of Drug Abuse

- Major changes in behavior
- Lying, cheating
- Sudden changes in mood
- Forgetfulness, withdrawn attitude
- New friends who are suspected of abusing drugs
- Loss of memory
- Poor school performance
- Poor coordination
- Changes in appearance
- Slurred speech
- Irresponsible decision-making
- Attention-getting behavior
- Aggressiveness
- Denial of any problems

Many organizations counsel people about drug problems. Community hospitals have clinics or programs that provide low-cost or no-cost/volunteer counseling for teenagers and adults. Local schools and governments also schedule parent meetings, peer group counseling, and drug-free programs.

Exploring Careers: Drug Counselor

A person trying to overcome a drug abuse problem may need assistance from someone outside of his or her circle of family and friends. A drug counselor can help. Drug counselors are trained to help abusers overcome the difficult problem of drug abuse. These counselors also often work with the abuser's family.

Drug counselors work in one-on-one situations, in group situations, in special drug abuse clinics, in hospitals, or for companies with employee drug programs. They also work for telephone hotlines or run private counseling services.

No certification or license is needed for this career, but a drug counselor must have compassion and an ability to gain a client's trust. A high school diploma and training are sufficient to become a drug counselor; however, college and master's degree programs are available.

Detoxification Programs

One type of drug abuse treatment is a **detoxification program**. A detoxification program involves gradual but complete withdrawal from the abused drug. People who enter detoxification programs usually receive medical treatment and supervision in a hospital. Drug abusers may stop taking the drug all at once, or physicians may reduce the drug dosage slowly to avoid painful withdrawal symptoms. Detoxification programs always include counseling to help program participants deal with their abuse and to cope constructively with the problems that led to it and were caused by it.

Therapeutic Communities

Another type of drug abuse treatment are **therapeutic communities**. A therapeutic community is a residential treatment center where drug abusers live and learn to adjust to drug-free lives. Members of therapeutic communities lend support and friendship to each other. Often drug abusers are required to undergo detoxification before becoming a part of the community. Therapeutic communities provide medical advice and counseling to help abusers develop a sense of personal and social worth. The staff of therapeutic communities usually consists of health-care professionals and former drug abusers.

Methadone Maintenance Programs

A third type of drug abuse treatment, called methadone maintenance, helps heroin abusers. **Methadone** is a drug that produces many effects similar to heroin, but does not produce the same "high" that causes heroin addicts to crave the drug. This type of treatment involves substituting methadone for heroin. Small, regular doses of methadone prevent withdrawal symptoms. Methadone treatment is intended to eliminate the desire for heroin.

Key Note Term

detoxification program – a type of program where drug users or addicts can get help withdrawing from substances.

therapeutic communities – usually a residential treatment center for drug abusers and addicts.

methadone – controlled substance that is used in heroin withdrawal; produces some effects similar to heroin, but does not produce a "high."

Methadone can cause dependency. Therefore, a trained professional must carefully monitor treatment and slowly lower the dosage. Long-term methadone use causes side effects such as liver damage. Methadone is not a cure for heroin addiction, but it can be a first step.

Drug Abuse Prevention

There are many ways in which you can become involved in drug abuse prevention. You might be able to volunteer at drug treatment and rehabilitation centers. Look in the phone book under "drug abuse" for information and prevention programs. You may be able to find several local sources for preventive information. There are also toll-free numbers that provide information on drug abuse and prevention.

Many major hospitals have chemical dependency hospitals affiliated with them. These hospitals may offer professional treatment for alcoholism and drug dependency. Some may offer services such as seminars on drug recovery, depression, or anxiety and other individualized programs.

Help or information is available from many private and public agencies, facilities, and people. Drug treatment centers and clinics specialize in treating people with drug problems. Hospitals treat on an in or out-patient basis. Mental health centers can treat people with drug problems by dealing with underlying problems. Public health agencies and social service agencies can give practical advice, make referrals, etc. Halfway houses provide residential treatment for those with drug problems.

If you need help with a cocaine problem, call the help line: 1-800-COCAINE, or volunteer to help others with their drug problems and help to promote prevention programs.

The Office for Substance Abuse Prevention (OSAP) promotes and distributes prevention materials throughout the country. OSAP also supports the National Clearinghouse for Alcohol and Drug Information (NCADI) and the Regional Alcohol and Drug Awareness Resource (RADAR) Network. To learn more about alcohol and other drugs, write or call: National Clearinghouse for Alcohol and Drug Information: Information Services; P.O. Box 2345; Rockville, MD 20847–2345; (301) 468-2600.

Alcohol Abuse Prevention

Alcoholics Anonymous (AA) is a worldwide group of men and women who help each other maintain sobriety and who offer to share their recovery experiences freely with others who may have a drinking problem. The AA program consists basically of "Twelve Steps" designed for personal recovery from alcoholism. The organization functions through almost 73,000 local groups in 114 countries. Several hundred thousand alcoholics have achieved sobriety in AA, but members recognize that their program is not always effective and that some may require professional counseling or treatment.

Look for Alcoholics Anonymous in any telephone directory. In most urban areas, a central AA office can answer your questions or put you in touch with AA members. If AA is not in your local directory, write the General Service Office, P.O. Box 459, Grand Central Station; New York, NY 10163.

Al-Anon is a worldwide organization that offers help to families and friends of alcoholics. Members receive support through a mutual exchange of experiences about how an alcoholic has affected their lives. Alateen is a fellowship of young Al-Anon members, usually teenagers, with someone else's drinking problems affecting their lives. Young people come together to share experiences, strengths, and hopes with each other as they discuss their difficulties. They can also encourage one another to learn effective ways to cope with their problems.

To contact the nearest Al-Anon or Alateen Group, call the local Al-Anon Information Service (Intergroup) in metropolitan areas, or write to Al-Anon Family Group Headquarters; 1600 Corporate Landing Pkwy., Virginia Beach, VA 23454.

There are many other places that people can get help for problems caused by alcohol. They can talk with family, friends, a school counselor, or a doctor. Look in the yellow pages under "alcohol" or "alcoholism." Use referral services and get information provided by the local affiliate of the National Council on Alcoholism (1-800-NCA-CALL). Remember, it is important to seek help and support for people with drinking problems.

At least 22 states have established formal programs for citizen-reporting of drunk drivers. Oregon has a toll-free hotline and a governor who, at one time, displayed a red star on his car for every drunk driver he reported. During 1982 and 1983—the first two years of Oregon's reporting program—tragic fatalities were the lowest in 20 years. Most will agree that everybody has to work together. The government cannot do it alone. In Nebraska, fatalities dropped 26 percent in the first year of its drunk driver-reporting program.

Note

Drinking is the third leading cause of death in the United States—right behind heart disease and cancer.

Call your police department to see if such a program exists in your area. If not, push for one. There are many other organizations working to get drunks off the roads. For specific information on how you can help, send a stamped, self-addressed envelope to: Mothers Against Drunk Drivers (MADD) National Office; 511 E. John Carpenter Frwy., Suite 700; Irving, TX 75062–8187 or call 1-800-438-6233.

"Know When to Say When," which has been in effect since 1983, is a nationwide consumer education campaign developed by Anheuser-Busch that encourages consumers to be responsible when they drink. It aims at morally responsible, law-abiding citizens who only need reminders of their legal and moral obligations to themselves and others. The purpose of the campaign is to help create a climate that strongly discourages "situational abuse." The campaign involves a series of television commercials, a movie, billboards, and newspaper advertisements which remind consumers not to overindulge.

"The Buddy System" is an education campaign aimed at college students and other young adults. It includes a short movie, brochures explaining the program, and posters. The program makes a strong point that friends should be responsible for each other and should help one another avoid drunk driving situations.

Other programs developed to avoid drunk driving situations include free or reduced-price taxi rides home to customers who are unable to drive safely, and designated driver programs. A group designates one person to refrain from drinking so that a safe ride home is available to the other members of the group.

Students Against Driving Drunk (SADD) is a student-run program that works to counteract peer pressure to drink and drive. The founder of SADD, Bob Anastas, suggests that teenagers call their parents if they or their driving friends have been drinking. Anastas has found that such an agreement between parents and teenagers works. Since the founding of SADD in 1981, more than three million students in 6500 high schools in all 50 states have become involved in SADD chapters. The efforts of groups such as SADD are beginning to have an impact.

In 1980, traffic accidents accounted for killing 12,214 Americans ages 16 to 21; in 1983, 9054. In 1980, 49 percent of drivers ages 16 to 21 killed in traffic accidents were legally intoxicated; in 1983, 47 percent. For information about the parent-teenager agreement, or about starting a SADD chapter at your school, send a stamped, self-addressed envelope to SADD; P.O. Box 800; Marlborough, MS 01752 or call 1-800-886-2972.

Each year in the United States, drinking and driving results in costs totaling more than a billion dollars for property damage, insurance, and medical expenses. Drinking and driving accounts for over 500,000 people being injured and more than one million people arrested.

Tobacco Abuse Prevention and Treatment

The very best way to quit smoking is to never start. And although cigarette smokers can drive and function while using tobacco, the facts are that tobacco is still considered an addictive substance and a drug. Even Phillip Morris, one of the largest cigarette manufacturers in the world, has devoted part of their website to the health risks posed by tobacco use (http://www.pmusa.com/health_issues/default.asp).

Quitting smoking is one of the best things that a smoker can do for themselves and the people around them. The benefits include the following.

- **You will live longer and live better.**
- **Quitting will lower your chance of having a heart attack, stroke, or cancer.**

- **If you are pregnant, quitting smoking will improve your chances of having a healthy baby.**

- **The people you live with, especially young children, will be healthier.**

- **You will have extra money to spend on things other than cigarettes.**

There are several methods for quitting smoking, ranging from nicotine patches and gum to just quitting "cold turkey." If you know someone who is serious about quitting, you might suggest that they talk with their family physician about which method seems to be most effective, and follow the doctor's recommendations. Remember: the earlier you quit, the easier it will be.

Contact the following organizations for further information on smoking and how to quit.

American Heart Association

7272 Greenville Avenue

Dallas, TX 75231

(800) AHA-USA1 (242-8721)

American Cancer Society

1599 Clifton Road, NE

Atlanta, GA 30329

(404) 320-3333

American Lung Association

1740 Broadway, 14th Floor

New York, NY 10019

(212) 315-8700

National Cancer Institute

Bethesda, MD 20892

(800) 4-CANCER (422-6237)

Getting More Information

The following is a list of numbers to call if you need more information on what you can do to help.

Hazeldon Educational Materials

1-800-328-9000

Alcohol Hotline

1-800-ALCOHOL

Youth Power (formerly Just Say No)

1-800-258-2766

Dare America (CA)

1-800-223-3273

Center for Substance Abuse Treatment National Hotline

1-800-662-HELP

Conclusion

Now that you have finished this lesson, you have a better understanding of drugs, their effects, their dangers, and the correct role they should play in a person's life. You have also learned the importance of remaining drug-free and ways to avoid the pressures to abuse drugs. Use your knowledge to make your life and the lives of those around you better. You do have the power to control much of the way your life turns out. Set an example—your actions do make a difference in the world.

Become involved as an individual. Talk to your friends and neighbors about drugs. Ask them to join you in your community's attack on drugs. Reach out a helping hand to your community—join the fight against drugs and become a part of the solution. If you feel you need help to be sober and drug-free, try to be brave enough to call the telephone numbers provided in this chapter. If you know someone who needs help, be a true friend and pass these phone numbers along. Your assistance could save a life.

Chapter 3

Lesson Review

Lesson Review

1. Explain the stages of how drug use develops.

2. What do you do to manage stress?

3. What choices do you have if you know someone who is abusing drugs and needs help? Which option would you choose?

4. What does the acronym "AA" stand for? What is it?

Geography and
Earth Science

Unit 5

Chapter 1

Map Skills

Lesson 2

Introduction to Maps

Key Terms

bar scale
contrast
elevation
intermittent
landforms
legend
man-made
marginal information
orient
prominent
relief
terrain
topographic maps

What You Will Learn to Do

- Use map reading skills

Linked Core Abilities

- Apply critical thinking techniques

Skills and Knowledge You Will Gain along the Way

- Identify symbols, colors, and features on standard road maps
- Identify locations on a city and state map
- Communicate directions to specified sites using a city and state map
- Define key words contained in this lesson

Chapter 1

Introduction

Have you ever found yourself on the wrong road or in the wrong neighborhood? If you asked for directions in this situation, were you told, "Go right," or "Turn left"? After following these directions for a few blocks, the question arises, "Turn right . . . where?" These types of situations call for map reading skills.

Knowing how to read and understand maps are valuable skills that can strengthen your awareness of the world around you. Your effective use of maps requires a basic understanding of them, their scales, symbols, and colors. This lesson introduces you to this information and explains how to orient a map by matching manmade or natural features with map symbols.

Maps are in common use throughout the world today. For instance, when a family takes a vacation, a map is used to guide the driver from one city to another. The airline pilot and the sea captain use special charts or maps from which to navigate. Rarely do experienced navigators become lost because they apply their map reading abilities to read, understand, and use maps effectively.

Definition of a Map and Map Reading

A map is a line drawing of a portion of the earth's surface, as seen from above. Obviously any attempt to plot each feature to its exact shape and scale would result in a map too big to read. Therefore, maps are drawn "to scale" with each set measurement on the scale representing a set amount of the earth's surface.

In general, maps provide information about the existence and location of man-made and natural features; show distance, **elevation**, and different types of landforms; and depict man-made and natural features by the use of symbols, lines, colors, and forms or shapes.

There are many different types of maps. However, the most common types are:

- **city or state road maps**
- **geographic maps/atlases**
- **topographic maps**

City or state road maps, also known as tourist maps, provide information on street names, important buildings, route numbers, distance, and transportation centers. In many cases, they include the location of recreational or historical areas, as well.

Geographic maps show an overall view of the mapped area in relation to climate, population, **relief**, and/or vegetation. An atlas is a collection of geographic maps of regions, countries, continents, or the world. These maps are generally not as accurate as city or state maps. And compared to **topographic**

Key Note Term

elevation – height above sea level or the earth's surface.

Key Note Term

relief – the shape of land formations on the earth's surface.

topographic map – a map that shows relief and the position of natural and man-made features.

maps, their accuracy is significantly inferior; therefore, they should be used for general information only.

Topographic maps show **terrain** and **landforms** in a manner which can be measured. They also show the horizontal positions and elevations of these features. Elevation on these maps is normally indicated by vertical contour lines. Topographic maps are the ones most commonly used in the military. Beginning with the next lesson, you will examine topographic maps in detail and will use them throughout the remainder of this unit so that you can begin to understand how to read and use them.

Road Maps

You can compare a map to any piece of equipment—before you use it, you must first read the instructions. Most mapmakers place the instructions (known as the **marginal information**) around the outer edge of a map. All maps are not the same, so it is necessary to read the marginal information carefully every time you use a different map. The following discussion describes and illustrates the most commonly used elements of marginal information found on road maps.

- **Sheet or Map Name.** Whenever possible, a map is named after the most **prominent** cultural or geographic feature in that area (For example, Orlando or the Official Transportation Map for the State of Florida). Although the most prominent feature on the map may be a state or other large geographical region (for example the Mid-Atlantic States), the map sheet normally contains numerous inserts of smaller sections in order to show them in more detail. These inserts can be found around the margin or on the reverse side of the map sheet.

- **Bar Scales. Bar scales** are special rulers used to measure ground distance on a map. Although these scales may vary with each road map, the most common units of measurement are miles and kilometers. Figure 1.2.1 shows an example of a scale used on the Official Transportation Map for the State of Florida.

- **Printing Note.** This note indicates the agency responsible for printing the map. The printing date determines when the map information was obtained, not when the map was printed.

- **Legend.** The **legend** is part of the mapmaker's dictionary. It is a shorthand method of illustrating and identifying mapped features using symbols to show some of the more prominent features on the map. These symbols are not the same on every road map.

Map Symbols

Because all features on a map cannot represent their true position and shape, mapmakers must use symbols to represent these features. These symbols are made to look as closely as possible to the actual features themselves as they are

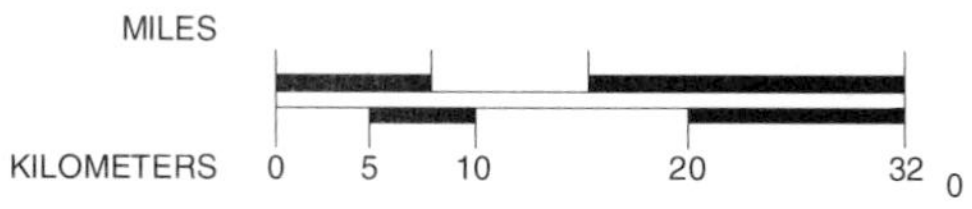

Key Note Term

terrain – a region or tract of land; the character (or topography) of a tract of land.

landform – a natural or man-made feature on the earth's surface.

Key Note Term

marginal information – instructions placed around the outer edge of a map.

prominent – very noticeable or conspicuous; well-known.

bar scale – a ruler used to measure actual ground distances by converting distances on a map.

legend – an explanatory description on a chart, map, or other illustration.

MILES

KILOMETERS   0   5   10   20   32   0

Figure 1.2.1: An example of a bar scale.

seen from above. The legend indicates the meanings of the symbols that are used on a map. A few of the commonly used symbols that you will find on road maps are identified in Figure 1.2.2.

- **Roads:** Indicated by parallel or solid lines. Thickness and color of these symbols indicate the road size.

- **Interchanges:** Indicated by a heavy solid line for major access roads and parallel lines for intersecting secondary roads. Legends also illustrate full, partial, and no access at these interchanges.

- **Railroads:** Commonly shown by single or parallel lines with horizontal tick marks.

- **Buildings:** Symbols for buildings may vary from map to map according to the purpose of the map or building. Schools and churches are commonly represented by a solid square with a flag or cross affixed. Hospitals may be shown by a cross. Universities and colleges may sometimes have a special symbol as a point of interest.

- **Points of Interest:** Indicated by a special marking and its name; for example, a historical marker.

- **Airports:** Normally shown by a picture of an airplane.

- **Water Features:** Normally shown in blue and take the approximate shape of the feature.

Figure 1.2.2: Commonly used map symbols.

- **Special Features:** Significant natural features (forests, recreational areas, national monuments, and so on), military reservations, or Indian reservations are normally highlighted with a specific color and do not have a standard shape. Many road maps also have a chart indicating the services that are available at the recreational areas and parks shown on the map.

You may also find the following symbols on road maps; these can provide helpful information to you when using the map.

- **Route Markers:** Represented by a shield or some other shape containing the number of the road in its center. Although the map may show these route markers with white numbers and/or letters on a black shield or shape, the actual colors of the signs as seen on the highway are indicated in the previous bulleted list.

- **Interstate Highways:** There are a number of interstate highway types, and these are generally shown as:

  - **Principle Routes:** Red, white, and blue signs with one- or two-digit numbers. East-west routes have even numbers (I-4 or I-70), whereas north-south routes have odd numbers (I-5 or I-95).

  - **Loop or Belt Routes:** Red, white, and blue signs with three-digit numbers; the first number is always even (I-295). These routes circle or bypass major cities.

  - **Spur Routes:** Red, white, and blue signs with three-digit numbers; the first number is always odd (I-580). These routes lead into major cities.

  - **Business Routes:** Green signs marking routes from principal, loop, or belt highways that go to or through cities.

- **Boundary Symbols:** Shown as broken or **intermittent** lines, that vary in pattern, to denote different boundaries.

- **Mileage Markers:** Shown between towns and road junctions or between dots with the mileage indicated in red or black. State and regional maps also show long distance mileage between major cities by printing that information in red (with red directional arrows), and centering it between the two cities. An example of this long distance mileage indicator may appear as follows:

TAMPA

199 Miles

320 Kilometers

WEST PALM BEACH

- **Official Highway Mileages:** This chart shows the actual ground mileage between the major cities that are located on the map.

- **City/Street Names:** This information lists alphabetically (wherever space permits on the map—including on the reverse side of it—and printed adjacent to its corresponding feature) the names of cities on state and regional maps and the names of streets on city maps. Beside each city or street listing is a letter/number code (for example, D-9). Along the outer edge of the margin are letters ranging from "A" to "P" (or beyond) and numbers ranging from "1" to "15" (or beyond). Note that the letter "I" is usually omitted so as not to be mistaken for the number "1."

The following example shows how to locate features on a road map using this letter/number code.

Key Note Term

intermittent – alternately stopping and starting; coming at intervals.

Note

For this example, the map sheet will have the letters along the vertical (left and right) edges of the margin and the numbers along the horizontal (top and bottom) edges.

To find the feature at D-9, use a finger on one hand to locate the letter "D"—it should be close to the top left or top right edges of the map. Next, use a finger on your other hand to locate the number "9" across the top or bottom margin. Now, move both fingers in from the margins toward the map. Where they meet is the general location of the feature. Street names may still be hard to find on a cluttered map, but you have narrowed the search to a specific area.

- **Special Traffic Regulations/Traffic Control Devices:** This section contains some of the traffic regulations and/or control devices signs used within the state that may be different from other states within the region.

Note

It is the motorist's responsibility to know the regulations and meanings of all control devices within the region in which he/she is driving. Ignorance is not an acceptable excuse under the law.

Map Colors

Key Note Term

contrast – to show differences when compared.

Colors on a road map provide **contrast** to map features, making them easier to identify. Map symbols are usually printed in different colors with each color identifying a class of features. However, colors may vary from one map to another. When used differently, mapmakers indicate these colors and their uses in the marginal information.

The following describes the basic colors used on most road maps and the features they represent. Occasionally, mapmakers may use other colors to indicate special information.

Key Note Term

man-made – manufactured, created, or constructed by man, rather than formed by nature.

- **Black:** Indicates the majority of **man-made** features: buildings or roads.
- **Blue:** Identifies water features: lakes, swamps, or rivers.
- **Brown:** Identifies elevation and relief features: mountain ranges.
- **Green:** Identifies vegetation: woods, grassland, brush, orchards, or vineyards.
- **Red:** Classifies man-made features: populated areas, main roads, special features, or boundaries on older maps.

Orienting a Map

Finding your way requires the ability to read and interpret a map, compare it to the features on the ground, and move to the desired location. One method of comparing your map to the ground is to **orient** it so that the map symbols fit the location of the features as they appear on the ground. A properly oriented map can also indicate direction; that is, after you have it correctly oriented to the ground, the top of it will usually point toward the north.

The following situation shows you how to orient a map without using a compass.

While participating in a bike rally, Barry traveled off the main road and became lost. He knew for certain he was lost when he came upon the main entrance to North Fork State Park on his right. Across from this entrance was a small bridge which crossed the North Fork River. Because Barry had a route map for this bike rally, he took the following steps to orient it.

1. **Barry determined his location using at least two known points. He chose to use the man-made features of the bridge and the park entrance and the natural feature of the river.**

2. **Next, he located these same features on his map. With the map in a horizontal position, he rotated it until the symbol for the river was pointed in the same direction as (or aligned with) the river in front of him.**

3. **Barry then checked to ensure that the park entrance was correctly aligned with its actual location. From where he was located, the park entrance was on the right side of the road. He checked to see if the map symbol for the park entrance was also on the right side of the road.**

With his map properly oriented, he realized what direction he had to take to rejoin the bike rally.

In many cases, orienting a map may mean turning it upside down or holding it with one of its edges pointing toward you. Holding a map like this may make it harder for you to read street names or other symbols, but it properly aligns the features on the ground with those on the map. After you know where you are (by using the two or more known points discussed in the above story), keep the map oriented until you are at your destination or in an area familiar to you.

The next time you are on a trip to a place where you have never been before, try this method—it works! You will be able to navigate your way to your destination much easier.

Care of Maps

Because you may have to keep a map for a long time, exercise care when using it. Three important considerations in the care of maps are:

- **Properly refold it after each use.**
- **Use a pencil if it becomes necessary to mark on it, so that you can easily erase those marks.**
- **Avoid spilling liquids on it.**

Key Note Term

orient – to align or position oneself (or a map) in relationship to one's surroundings.

Global Positioning System

The Global Positioning System (GPS) is a high-tech worldwide radio-navigation system formed from a network of 24 satellites and their ground stations. GPS provides more precise and efficient methods of surveying and mapmaking. Today, GPS makes it possible to accomplish the same work in a fraction of the time. Mapping is the science of using GPS to pinpoint locations and then create maps of any location in the world, including both natural and man-made features.

Conclusion

Maps permit you to see an area of the earth's surface with the key features of that area properly positioned. They can take the guesswork out of traveling to new locations, preventing wasted time and effort. Therefore, make the most of your trips—know how to read and understand your maps beforehand. Even the best maps are useless if you do not know how to properly use them.

Lesson Review

1. What information do maps provide?
2. Explain what a map's marginal information is.
3. What do the different colors on a map represent?
4. Describe how to orient a map without using a compass.

Citizenship in American History and Government

Unit 6

You the People—Citizenship Skills

Lesson 1

The Preamble

Key Terms

beneficiaries
goals
preamble
responsible parties

What You Will Learn to Do

- Examine the Preamble to the American Constitution

Linked Core Abilities

- Do your share as a good citizen in your school, community, country, and the world

Skills and Knowledge You Will Gain along the Way

- Classify the components of the Preamble to the United States Constitution
- Explain the goals of the Preamble
- Connect the principles of the Preamble to the United States Constitution with your personal values
- Define key words contained in this lesson

Chapter 1

Key Note Term

goals – what one strives to achieve and attain.

beneficiaries – those who benefit.

responsible parties – those who take responsibility to ensure goals are met.

Key Note Term

Preamble – the basic mission statement for the United States Consitution.

The Preamble to the Constitution of the United States establishes the purpose of the Constitution. It served as a "mission statement" for the framers of the Constitution. In this lesson, you analyze the Preamble to determine the **goals**, the **beneficiaries**, and the **responsible parties**.

The U. S. Constitution and the Preamble

The Constitutional Convention of 1787 produced the most enduring written Constitution ever created by human hands. Though the United States existed prior to the ratification of the Constitution, it was a nation held together by the threads of the Articles of Confederation, a sometimes contentious and often ineffectual national government. The men who attended the Constitutional Convention in Philadelphia, usually referred to as the Framers of the Constitution, created a document that was the result of dozens of compromises and shaped by the failures of the Unites States under the Articles as well as the failures of European governments of the time.

The entire Constitution was written by several committees, but the committee most responsible for the final form recognized today is the "Committee of Style and Arrangement." This Committee was tasked with getting all of the articles and clauses into a logical order. On September 10, 1787, the Committee of Style set to work, and two days later, it presented its final draft. Heading the draft was the **Preamble**. Committee members included Alexander Hamilton, William Johnson, Rufus King, James Madison, and Gouverneur Morris. The actual text of the Preamble and of much of the rest of this final draft is usually attributed to Gouverneur Morris.

The Preamble holds in its words the hopes and dreams of the delegates to the convention, a justification for what they had done. Its words are familiar to us today, but the words are not always easy to follow. The Preamble to the United States Constitution reads as follows:

> *We the people of the United States, in order to form a more perfect union, establish justice, insure domestic tranquility, provide for the common defense, promote the general welfare, and secure the blessing of liberty to ourselves and our posterity, do ordain and establish this Constitution for the United States.*

Taking a look at the different parts of the Preamble can help you understand this important start to our Constitution.

We the People of the United States

The Framers were an elite group, among the best and brightest America had to offer at the time. But they knew that they were trying to forge a nation composed not of an elite, but of the common man. This first part of the Preamble speaks to the common man. It puts into writing the notion that the people were creating this Constitution. It was not handed down by a god or by a king; it was created by the people.

in order to form a more perfect union

The Framers were dissatisfied with the United States under the Articles of Confederation, and were striving for something better. The Articles of Confederation had been a grand experiment that had worked well up to a point, but now, less than ten years into that experiment, cracks were showing. The new United States, under this new Constitution, would be more perfect. Not *perfect*, but more perfect.

establish justice

Injustice, unfairness of laws and in trade, was of great concern to the people of 1787. People looked forward to a nation with a level playing field, where courts were established with uniformity and where trade within and outside the borders of the country would be fair and unbiased.

insure domestic tranquility

One of the events that caused the Convention to be held was the revolt of Massachusetts farmers knows as Shays' Rebellion. The taking up of arms by war veterans revolting against the state government was a shock to the system. The keeping of the peace was on everyone's mind, and the maintenance of tranquility at home was a prime concern. The Framers hoped that the new powers given the federal government would prevent any such rebellions in the future.

provide for the common defense

The new nation was fearful of attack from all sides, and no one state was really capable of fending off an attack from land or sea on its own. With a wary eye on Britain and Spain, and ever-watchful for an Indian attack, not one of the United States could go it alone. They needed each other to survive in the harsh world of international politics of the 18th century.

Misspelled words in the Constitution?

The Constitution was written in 1787, in the manner of the day—in other words, it was written by hand. According to the National Archives, the version we are most familiar with today was penned by Jacob Shallus, a clerk for the Pennsylvania State Assembly. In the document itself are several words which are misspelled. Far from the days of spell checkers and easy edits, these misspellings survive in the document today.

At that time, the American spelling of words was inconsistent at best, and several words are spelled in the British manner. These words are "defence," "controul," and "labour." In America, we would today write these words as "defense," "control," and "labor."

Most of the misspellings are in the original document, which was written hastily after the Convention concluded. Aside from one use of British spelling in the Bill of Rights, the amendments are all error-free. The authors of the latter amendments all had the benefit of a standardized American dictionary.

Promote the General Welfare

This, and the next part of the Preamble, are the culmination of everything that came before it–the whole point of having tranquility, justice, and defense was to promote the general welfare–to allow every state and every citizen of those states to benefit from what the government could provide. The framers looked forward to the expansion of land holdings, industry, and investment, and they knew that a strong national government would be the beginning of that.

> ### Note
>
> *Welfare* in today's context also means organized efforts on the part of public or private organizations to benefit the poor, or simply public assistance. This is not the meaning of the word as used in the Constitution.

And Secure the Blessings of Liberty to Ourselves and Our Posterity

Along with the general welfare, the Framers looked forward to the blessings of liberty–something for which they had all fought just a decade before. They wanted to create a nation that would resemble something of a paradise for liberty, as opposed to the tyranny of a monarchy, where citizens could look forward to being free rather than looking out for the interests of a king. And more than for themselves, they wanted to be sure that the future generations of Americans would enjoy the same.

Do Ordain and Establish This Constitution for the United States of America

The final clause of the Preamble is almost anti-climatic, but it is important for a few reasons–it finishes the "We, the people" thought, saying what we the people are actually doing; it gives a name for the document, and it restates the name of the nation adopting the Constitution. That the Constitution is "ordained" reminds us of the higher power involved here–not just of a single person or of a king, but of the people themselves. That it is "established" reminds us that it replaces that which came before–the United States under the Articles.

Components of the Preamble

Table 1.1.1 shows how the components of the Preamble can be broken down into three catagories: the beneficiaries (those who benefit); the goals (what the Preamble sets out to do); and the responsible party (those who are responsible for attaining the goals).

Table 1.1.1: Components of the Preamble

beneficiary	goals	responsible party
to ourselves and our posterity	promote the general welfare	we the people of the United States
	establish justice	
	provide for the common defense	
	in order to form a more perfect union	
	do ordain and establish this constitution for the United States of America	
	and secure the blessing of liberty	

Conclusion

The Preamble is the "mission statement" to the document known as the United States Constitution. It lays the framework for this ever-changing and growing roadmap for our democratic society. This lesson examined the various parts of the Preamble, and explained the beneficiaries, the goals, and the responsible parties of this document.

Chapter 1

Lesson Review

1. Define what is meant by the beneficiaries, the goals, and the responsible parties regarding the Preamble.

2. Choose one component of the Preamble and discuss it.

3. Why was the Preamble written?

4. Who wrote the Preamble?

Lesson Review

Lesson 2

Citizenship Skills

Key Terms

balance
cooperation
fairness
patience
respect
strength
self-improvement

What You Will Learn to Do

- Hypothesize what our country would be like without the seven citizenship skills

Linked Core Abilities

- Do your share as a good citizen in your school, community, country, and the world

Skills and Knowledge You Will Gain along the Way

- Define the seven *You the People* citizenship skills

- Relate the seven *You the People* citizenship skills to the Preamble of the Constitution

- Explain the relationship between the citizenship skills and effective teamwork

- Define key words contained in this lesson

Chapter 1

Introduction

The Preamble to the United States Constitution sets the stage for the success of our nation. Individual values, which are also important to the success of our nation, are inferred from the Preamble and are known as Citizenship Skills in the Cadet Citizenship Training Program. These Citizenship Skills are basic human values envisioned by the Founding Fathers when they drafted the Constitution. This lesson explores the relationship between the values described in the Preamble and the seven Citizenship Skills to which you will be introduced.

You the People Educational Programs are designed to train Americans to make their nation truly a country of the people, by the people, and for the people.

Within this overall mission, the *Cadet Citizenship Training Program* is designed to help cadets:

- **Better understand the development of the United States system of government**
- **Learn the mechanics of how government works, in the United States, through hands-on exercises and experiences**
- **Develop interpersonal skills that will assist them throughout their personal and professional lives**

The primary teaching tool for this training program is the Citizen Action Group Process. The purpose of this group is to help cadets become effective citizens, able to guide the governmental activity in their school, town, state, and country as the Founders of the United States of America envisioned.

After completing this course, cadets will be better educated and trained to effectively participate in their local, state, and federal governments by voting and by other means (for example, attending meetings, communicating effectively with representatives, and invoking change in their community).

You the Citizen

The Declaration of Independence established the ideals upon which this nation is based: freedom, equality, and unity. These ideals provide our country with a common theme.

The Constitution was written so that every American citizen is given equal opportunity to pursue these ideals. Only by exercising our rights as citizens, can we enhance our governmental ideals of freedom, equality, and unity.

After you have registered to vote, you hold the highest office in America. You are the one who elects the representatives who go to Washington, D.C. and administer the government. It is your tax money that those representatives decide how to spend.

The Constitution specifies that the people rule the American government. American citizens, on paper, hold the ultimate power in this nation. While it appears that the President holds the highest office in this nation, as American citizens—we do. The President works for us.

How will you use your power as a registered voter? Do you care about this responsibility? Will you vote regularly? In what other ways (in addition to voting) will you participate?

Your answers to these questions will determine what kind of life you will have as well as what quality of life you will pass to your children and your children's children.

How can you become a more effective citizen of this country? The best way is to educate yourself.

The *You the People* text is organized into two main sections, each with corresponding exercises and classroom activities:

- **Citizenship Skill Development. To become an effective citizen you must develop certain skills or values that were well known to the Founders of our nation. Most of us have forgotten or have never learned these skills. This section provides an overview of the skills.**

- **Citizen Action Group Process. This section forms the core of the You the People Educational Series: a pro-active group process known as the Citizen Action Group Process. This process may be the future of democracy in America. Several types of these groups are already developing through grassroots organizations in many communities across the nation, perhaps even your own. In this section, you will get a chance to practice being a member of a Citizen Action Group, and address issues that may concern you or others in your school. With this knowledge and experience, you can then decide how you want to participate at the next level—in your own communities.**

This lesson introduces you to Citizenship Skill Development.

Citizenship Skill Development

As you learned in the previous lesson, the Preamble to the United States Constitution sets the stage for the success of our nation. Individual values, which are also important to the success of our nation, are inferred from the Preamble and are known as citizenship skills in this Cadet Citizenship Training Program. These citizenship skills are basic human values the Founding Fathers envisioned when they drafted the Constitution.

> ### The Preamble to the United States Constitution
>
> We the people of the United States, in order to form a more perfect union, establish justice, insure domestic tranquility, provide for the common defense, promote the general welfare, and secure the blessing of liberty to ourselves and our posterity, do ordain and establish this Constitution for the United States of America.

Our government is based upon seven main citizenship skills. These individual skills are also interdependent; that is, to practice one skill you will need to use the others as well.

The Seven Citizenship Skills

Skill 1   Cooperation—"We the people," not we the individuals; work together as a group.

Skill 2   Patience—A "more" perfect union; take progressive steps towards a better situation.

Skill 3   Fairness—"Establish justice;" consider the common good as well as individual desires.

Skill 4   Respect—"Insure domestic tranquility;" accept your fellow citizens.

Skill 5   Strength—"Provide for the common defense;" stand up for what is right, denounce what is wrong, and admit your mistakes.

Skill 6   Self-improvement—"Promote the general welfare;" seek knowledge and skills.

Skill 7   Balance—"Secure the blessing of liberty to ourselves and our posterity;" support our nation's ideals (freedom, equality, and unity) by harmonizing or compromising solutions to our problems.

Skill 1: Cooperation

The Preamble to the Constitution states "We the people," not we the individuals. The premise here is that we can rule more effectively if we cooperate as a group to solve problems. In some instances, this might mean looking out for the common goals of the group at the expense of personal desires.

Cooperation involves thinking, as a group with each person trying to help the group in whatever way is best given the time and circumstances involved. Properly done, cooperative efforts can be more efficient and more successful than individual efforts. To accomplish this; however, people need an attitude of working together to achieve a common goal.

For example, a new student joined a science class that was undertaking a major research project to monitor the water quality of a nearby river. The instructor asked the class to include this new student in their project. Because she was not trained in collecting and recording water quality samples, an easy solution would have been to assign her a minor role. However, a group of students

Key Note Term

cooperation – the art of working together as a group towards a common goal. Cooperation is shown in an attitude of group awareness and willingness to help each other reach a common goal.

offered to spend their own time, after school, to train her. They knew their project would be enhanced if they had another trained sampler who could collect valid samples from an additional location along the river.

The students' efforts are an example of a cooperative attitude. They did this extra work to help the overall purpose of the class research project.

Cooperation does not mean; however, we give up our beliefs and opinions for the good of the group or support a poor idea. Instead, cooperation uses individual talents to obtain the very best group results.

It follows the popular saying: The whole is greater than the sum of the parts. When we cooperate using everyone's best talents, the group is more powerful than all the individual efforts.

Cooperation is an important citizenship skill because any nation of, by, and for the people must work together. If we can truly govern ourselves, we have to be willing to subordinate some of our individual desires so that the whole (our country) operates efficiently and effectively.

Cooperation is an active skill based upon a common purpose and common goals to achieve that purpose. The students in the example above were aware of the common purpose of the research project (to collect valid data) and recognized this purpose could be enhanced if they had another trained person taking samples from an additional location. Their actions were in support of this purpose.

Cooperation is important to achieving the rights promised to us in the Declaration of Independence (life, liberty, and the pursuit of happiness). Cooperation also supports peaceful coexistence. Cooperation means, among other things, helping others to see your point of view or helping them to clarify their own point of view. Without cooperation, humans break down into bickering, small groups, constantly fighting each other, as many societies have done all too often. Sometimes, cooperation is necessary for survival.

For example, geese fly in a "V" formation for a specific reason. Scientists have found that each goose receives uplift from the one in front. By flying this way, geese extend their flying distances by more than 70 percent. Whenever a goose falls out of formation, it quickly feels the drag of flying alone and joins the formation again. The honks from behind encourage the leader to maintain the pace. When the leader is tired, it moves to the rear and a goose near the front takes over. If a goose lands for a rest or is injured, two or three from the flock will land with it and wait until the tired goose is able to fly again or dies; then they will fly together in a smaller "V" formation until they catch up with a larger flock. The flock depends on each goose cooperating and working together.

Skill 2: Patience

The Founding Fathers' goal was to form a more perfect union. The Articles of Confederation were not working well at the time and the Founders wanted to improve this design of government in the Constitution. In so doing, they were working toward a more perfect situation in our government.

The **patience** citizenship skill illustrates this idea of progressing toward a more perfect situation. Patience is knowing when it is best to wait, when it is best to act, and how much action one should take based on the circumstances. It is both an active and a passive skill.

Key Note Term

patience – the skill of knowing the proper timing for acting on an idea or decision.

One example of the use of patience in our nation's history is the signing of the Declaration of Independence. Why was the Declaration signed in 1776? Why not after the Stamp Acts or the Boston Massacre?

The Founding Fathers had been preparing for independence for some years before 1776. Committees of Correspondence had been formed, ammunition and weapons were being stockpiled, and political discussions were ongoing.

These preparations helped the independence movement. The Founders knew that independence from England would probably mean war. War required soldiers and the new colonies did not have a draft. Anti-English sentiment had to be widespread among the people, not just the political leaders of that time. Enough American colonists had to feel so strongly about their freedom that they would fight for it.

The Founders' preparations encouraged the anti-English feelings in 1776. Before this time the Founders were unsure if enough American colonists were ready to fight. Waiting until after 1776 provided too many unknowns. The English oppressions might lessen, thereby reducing the colonists' strong desire for freedom, or English oppressions might escalate, making the colonists' desire for freedom even stronger.

Therefore, the Founders felt the time was "ripe" for declaring independence in 1776 and they acted accordingly. They were successful because they used the patience citizenship skill effectively.

Patience is not just waiting for something it is knowing when is the right time to act. In other words, patience is knowing when to act and when to wait. You have probably been told sometime in your life to be patient, to wait. Practicing the patience citizenship skill means waiting for something, as the Founders did when they waited for the right time to declare independence from England.

Patience is one of the most difficult skills to practice. Sometimes we do not like to wait because we have been programmed by our culture to receive instant gratification. In addition, sometimes we like to "tune out" the world and watch it go by. In both cases, we are not using the patience citizenship skill effectively.

Skill 3: Fairness

Establishing justice, which is what the citizenship skill of fairness is about, involves balancing individual desires with the common good. This is a tricky balance to maintain and why we have a unique Supreme Court. Our justice system is based on following the spirit of the law. In turn, the laws are based on the ideals of the Declaration of Independence.

Key Note Term

fairness – the act of tempering individual desires with the needs of society as a whole.

We elect representatives and judges (in most cases) who then create and execute the laws of our country. A sense of **fairness** within ourselves is important if we are to pick the right people to make and enforce these laws.

The United States' ideal of "equality" is a good illustration of the fairness citizenship skill. Under our Constitution, we citizens are encouraged to grow as individuals, but we must also promote equality so that all people have an equal opportunity to grow as well.

The method our government has chosen to promote equality has some inherent conflicts. Similar to most methods, there are two ways of looking at the promotion of equality: Do we promote individual opportunity, or do we focus on bringing everyone up to the same level? In other words, do we look at the "form" of a person (their race, religion, economic status) or do we look at both the "form" and "substance" (how much education a person has, how qualified a person is for the job, and so on) when promoting opportunity?

One way equality can be achieved is if there is a balance between form and substance, allowing equal opportunity while maintaining objective standards for promotion—balancing individual desires against the common good for the nation as a whole. That is where fairness comes in.

Fairness means we constantly measure our individual desires against what is in the best interest of others and the majority of people around us.

Skill 4: Respect

The Preamble to the Constitution states "...insure domestic tranquility. . . ." This can be a challenge in a diverse country like the United States. This nation has a wide mix of cultures, races, and religions. We have achieved togetherness within this diversity because we have common ideals. The Constitution and the Declaration of Independence are based upon our common ideals of freedom, equality, and unity.

To work toward these ideals, our nation must learn to accept and incorporate the various differences in our society. To do otherwise is to resort to fighting wars over these differences.

Key Note Term

respect – accepting the differences in others and honoring those differences.

Our institutions and laws are designed to ensure, as much as possible, that our government works together so that we rule as one unified body. To be unified, however, we must recognize each other as being equal and deserving of **respect**.

Think of respect as having acceptance of others, not necessarily, love for each other. Nice though it may be, loving everyone is difficult to achieve. We all evaluate others. The difference is how we act on these evaluations. That is where respect comes in.

Respect is a critical citizenship skill for any nation with our ideals (freedom, equality, and unity). If we can respect each other with all our differences, we will feel secure enough to state our ideas and opinions to each other. Everyone's opinion matters and deserves to be heard no matter how much we may disagree with it.

Respect is especially important to the Citizen Action Group Process introduced in this Cadet Citizenship Training Program. Without it, this group process might be stymied or dominated by one person or a group of persons. Respect allows cooperative communication to take place.

As you practice the respect citizenship skill, you may need to evaluate those around you based on their skills rather than on any personal or preconceived judgments. Respect for each other encourages participation, and participation is needed to keep our country alive. Participation is also vital to the Citizen Action Group Process.

Skill 5: Strength

The Preamble included the need for common defense, which refers to national **strength**. To be strong nationally, we must have a nation of citizens with strong convictions.

The strength citizenship skill involves the ability to stand up for what you believe (based on factual evidence and/or your values) even in the face of strong opposition. Strength is the main skill in the drug awareness program, D.A.R.E.

Strength is saying "no" when you mean "no" and "yes" when you mean, "yes." Strength is a skill that challenges all of us.

We humans, it seems, are born with a "fear of rejection" (among other fears) written on our birth certificates. Students and adults alike all want to be accepted and liked by others. In addition, it is precisely the fear of not being accepted that keeps us from standing up for what we believe in. We are afraid if we say something others disagree with, they will not like us.

Consequently we tend to do one of two things: either we say nothing or we go along with our friends even when we do not agree. This is the working definition of peer pressure. We want our friends to like us. This is human.

We are not using the strength citizenship skill when we buckle under to peer pressure that ultimately hurts others and ourselves. We can be so afraid of "making waves" we will do what the group wants even if we do not believe in it. To the extreme, this can become dangerous. In political terms, it can lead to a dictatorship.

Germany had a democratic government in the 1920's, but by the 1930's, it was ruled by a dictator who imprisoned and executed millions of men, women, and children simply because of their race, religion, or disability. What happened? Part of it was unwillingness for people to denounce what was wrong. Unfortunately, there are countless other examples like this throughout history.

For our government to succeed, we need a nation composed of people willing to stand up for what they believe in and to denounce what is wrong.

Stand by your beliefs. Do not be afraid to say what you think, even if it might be construed as uncooperative. If you do it in a way that honors those who are listening, you will not come across as uncooperative.

Try also to be strong enough to allow others the same freedom—to have and hold their own beliefs. The greatest strength in many cases is the strength to admit when you have made a mistake.

For example, suppose you have told a joke you think is funny to someone who felt insulted by your joke. This joke poked fun at a particular ethnic group. You find out that this person belongs to that ethnic group. It takes great strength to admit that you were wrong—your joke was in poor taste.

> **Key Note Term**
>
> **strength** – the willingness of citizens to stand up for what they believe in, to denounce what's wrong, and to admit when they've made a mistake.

Skill 6: Self-Improvement

"Promoting the general welfare", as the Preamble states, gives all of us the freedom to learn and work as we want. The Founding Fathers hoped that this would create a prosperous nation; however, for our nation to be prosperous, we have to be willing to improve ourselves.

Self-improvement is the skill of educating and training yourself so that you can be the best at whatever you do. We tend to be a nation of achievers because most of us have had to work hard to be where we are today. In essence, this is part of our national personality. Thus, most of us want to be the best we can be at whatever we attempt; to pursue perfection without being perfectionists.

As humans, we are imperfect. We make mistakes. Mistakes and failures are part of self-improvement. Without mistakes, we might never know where we need to improve. Being a perfectionist means being intolerant of mistakes. Although some of us tend to be perfectionists, this can be counter to the self-improvement citizenship skill.

Thomas Edison tried over 2,500 times before he was successful at inventing the light bulb. Each time he failed, he learned something that helped him on the next try.

That is what self-improvement is all about—looking at weaknesses and discovering where to improve. Weakness can be another term for challenges or obstacles. Self-improvement involves the willingness to overcome obstacles even in the face of hardships. It is looking at obstacles as opportunities for growth rather than as stopping places.

Our country gives everyone an equal chance for education through our public school system. This relates to the citizenship skill of self-improvement. Our country must have educated citizens to elect good representatives and participate in running the government.

The "American Dream" of becoming or doing what you want is also based on this self-improvement skill. If you want to change your career and/or go to college at age 40, you have the freedom in this country to make that choice.

Self-improvement means looking at everything you do, whether it is cleaning a toilet or writing a novel, and doing the very best you can at that task. To do this, you may need more education or training, or you may have to overcome some obstacles.

For example, if you want to be good at competitive sports you not only have to practice to become better, you also have to overcome the obstacle of losing some games or matches and learn from those losses. From this learning, you can become a more effective player.

Likewise, if you want to make good decisions on community or school issues, you need to educate yourself about those issues. Be willing to make some mistakes (such as bad decisions), learn from those mistakes, and be willing to overcome the obstacle of interacting with others who might think differently than you.

Because self-improvement takes courage and perseverance (strength and patience citizenship skills), it can only be practiced when there is an overall ideal or purpose in mind.

Key Note Term

self-improvement – a desire to continually learn new skills and improve on others so that citizens can better serve themselves and those around them.

The Declaration of Independence provided the overriding ideals for our country (freedom, equality, and unity). When we use the self-improvement skill as a citizen, we are helping our country work toward these ideals.

Skill 7: Balance

To secure the blessings of liberty (as mentioned in the Preamble), our nation must continue to follow the ideals of the Declaration of Independence. The key to following these ideals is to work through problems until we find the best solution for all involved. This requires **balance**—both nationally and individually.

Our nation, indeed our world, is made up of different people with differing ideas and ways. Throughout history, many wars have been fought over differences. To eliminate war, the world must find another way of resolving differences. That is where the citizenship skill of balance comes in.

Balance is accepting that there are at least two sides to every issue, each with some truth. There is not a wrong and a right viewpoint, even though one might appear better initially. All sides can have some merit. All viewpoints can have some errors as well.

Balance plays a win/win game where both sides benefit from the process. Winning and losing are for debates and football games. Thus, in some ways, practicing the skill of balance can be contrary to everything we have been taught.

The skill of practicing balance involves using either compromise or harmony to achieve an agreement that works. The two are very different. Harmony means combining the best qualities of all sides and coming up with an entirely different but better solution that meets all sides' needs. Sometimes this is called a win/win solution.

Compromise, on the other hand, is a solution in which each side gives a little to come to a common ground. This can also be win/win if each side does not give up too much.

Probably the best example of using balance in history was the development of the Constitution. Both harmony and compromise were used in the drafting of this document. Take look at each of these, respectively.

Two strong factions had differing opinions about the balance of power in our government. Some Founders wanted the states to hold the primary power of the nation; others wanted the majority of power to be held by a federal government.

Both sides had valid points. To harmonize the two factions, the Founders came up with a third solution that satisfied both sides of the argument—sovereign state governments supplemented by a federal government that was given great power but only in certain specific areas such as foreign affairs, defense, and interstate trade. The federal government was also given the power to resolve differences between states if the states alone could not resolve them. All other powers not specifically wielded by the federal government were reserved for the states.

This design was based on the dual-sovereignty theme of the Native American Iroquois Council of Governments. For hundreds of years before our nation was formed, the Iroquois used a form of government that combined five separate

> **Key Note Term**
>
> **balance** – the understanding that there is more than one side to every issue, and having the ability to come to an agreement and resolve differences by using either compromising or harmonizing solutions.

nations— Mohawk, Onondaga, Seneca, Oneida, and Cayuga into one overall League of Nations.

Each nation elected representatives called sachems. Sachems held meetings (called councils) to discuss issues that concerned the internal affairs of each nation. Periodically the sachems from all five nations would meet together in a Grand Council to discuss issues that affected all five nations such as war, peace, treaties, and new members to the Grand Council.

Benjamin Franklin became intimately familiar with the Iroquois government because of his job as a diplomat for Pennsylvania and as a scholar of Native American literature. He was able to persuade the Founders to copy the Iroquois system in many ways. The most important way was the design of state governments with an overall federal government.

The Founders were able to design a system of government that satisfied the needs of both sovereign states and a federal government—a win/win solution.

The debate between state or federal control of power continues in Congress to this day. Control of power was really challenged in the Civil War, but the design envisioned by the Iroquois and used by the Founders works because it uses balance as a key element.

Another agreement that was needed, as part of the Constitution, is known as The Great Compromise. This agreement obviously used compromise as a way to achieve balance. Large states wanted representation based on population, but small states were afraid the heavily-populated states would dominate. Therefore, both a Senate and House were formed in our Congress.

Both sides had to give up something—the heavily populated states had to relinquish their power in the Senate and the sparsely populated states had to relinquish their power in the House.

You are probably more familiar with the use of compromise as a way to achieve agreement, but do not rule out using harmony. A whole new solution can be used that solves the problem for both sides.

One place to practice balance is when reading or hearing news reports. Political campaigns have shown how influential the news media can be. Before we make up our minds on an issue, we need to look at more than one news source to understand all sides. From this balanced knowledge, we are better able to see compromising or harmonizing solutions.

Conclusion

From the signing of the U. S. Constitution to present day, the seven citizenship skills have played a major part in shaping and developing our country. The Preamble set the groundwork for the ideals of this nation, and also created a guide to what good citizenship should be.

Chapter 1

Lesson Review

Lesson Review

1. List the seven citizenship skills.
2. Choose two of the skills and explain how they can work together.
3. How do the seven citizenship skills relate to the Preamble of the Constitution?
4. Explain how self-improvement can make you a better citizen.

Lesson 3

Small Group Meetings

Chapter 1

Key Terms

agenda
consensus
decision-making
ground rules
simple majority
small group leader
small group meeting
timekeeper

What You Will Learn to Do

- Use the small group meeting process in decision-making situations

Linked Core Abilities

- Do your share as a good citizen in your school, community, country, and the world

Skills and Knowledge You Will Gain along the Way

- Compare simple majority and consensus decision-making processes
- Explain the impact of the small group meeting agenda
- Describe each You the People ground rule
- Identify the small group meeting roles
- Explain the small group meeting process
- Design a process for the role rotations
- Define key words contained in this lesson

Introduction

Citizens participate in two types of Citizen Action Group meetings: small group meetings that are covered in this lesson, and representative group sessions that are discussed in the next lesson. In this lesson, you examine the purpose and process of small group meetings, from choosing a meeting leader to presenting the meeting **agenda**. You will also practice using the seven citizenship skills as you participate in small group meetings.

Key Note Term

agenda – a list of tasks or a schedule to be followed.

Note

Before the first small group meeting, it is recommended that you view the You the People Video. It is a three part series on citizenship.

The video also contains segments that refer to the separation between church and state. Please review the following sidebar for one perspective on that topic.

Small Group Meeting

A **small group meeting** is a gathering of about five to nine cadets who use a process to discuss and decide issues (selected by you and/or your instructor). The overall purpose of these groups is to teach you how to become an effective citizen and how to guide the governmental activity in your school, town, state, and as the Founders of the United States of America envisioned. In practical terms, the small group meeting gives your group a forum to apply and practice the citizenship skills.

Your instructor has preselected the members of your small group. Barring any unforeseen consequences (such as students moving away), members within your small group should not change.

One of the first things you will do as a group is to come up with a name or number for your group. Deciding and agreeing on this name or number may be the first opportunity you have to practice the citizenship skills as a group. This name or number will be used to identify your particular group when you meet with other small groups.

Key Note Term

small group meeting – one of two types of Citizen Action groups where a small group of five to nine persons meets periodically to discuss and decide on various issues and actions.

Choosing a Group Leader

After you have a group name or number, select your first group leader. A group leader runs a small group meeting. Every member of your group will have the chance to be a group leader. Ask a volunteer to be your first **small group leader**. If no one volunteers, your instructor will select a leader. This leadership role rotates around the small group with each meeting.

Key Note Term

small group leader – leads a small group meeting.

Group Leader Responsibilities

As a small group leader, you are responsible for conducting the small group meeting. You learn the skills necessary to be a group leader as you conduct a meeting. The first few meetings you lead may be difficult, but that is also part of the learning process. Your responsibilities include:

1. **Prepare in advance.** Read over your worksheets and notes from the last meeting. Know what the old issues are. Write or type out an agenda and give it to the other group members before the small group meeting (at least two days before if possible). If this is the first small group meeting, your instructor will have an agenda prepared for you.

2. **Start your meeting on time.** Even if not all your group members are present, begin your meeting; otherwise, you will be hard-pressed to finish on time. If you start on time, group members are more likely to be punctual.

3. **Distribute optional blank worksheets (group worksheet and decision making worksheet).** Members of your group can decide whether or not to use these worksheets. Your instructor may also have guidance for you pertaining to these worksheets.

4. **Keep the group focused on the agenda.** Keep the group focused on the agenda by assigning someone in the group to be the **timekeeper.** When it is time to move to the next agenda item, the timekeeper will notify you. Quickly bring the discussion to a close and move on.

5. **Distribute action assignments to all small group members.** Make sure that you come up with specific assignments for each group member before your meeting is adjourned. Do not let one or two group members end up doing all the work.

Being a group leader is a challenging job, but it is a great opportunity for self-improvement.

Small Group Meeting Process

Learning how to work together with other cadets and make real decisions on issues that affect all of you is a process; however, the process of making a decision will be as important as the final decision itself.

As you participate in these groups, you will find the need to develop group skills. The following section covers these skills that will come in handy when working in small groups.

Group Skill 1: Reaching a Simple Majority

Most of us are familiar with the skill of reaching a **simple majority**. It is the "show of hands" voting process. To have a simple majority, more than half of the votes must be in favor of a certain option. Your group can decide what to do with an issue using this voting process.

Key Note Term

timekeeper – an individual who keeps track of the time at a small group meeting.

Key Note Term

simple majority – a show of hands in the voting process.

As an issue is raised, you will ask for a vote to see what to do with it (do we act on it, do we research it more, or do we drop it because we're not interested enough). After you have brainstormed ideas on how to act on an issue or research it further, you will also call for a vote to determine which idea to select.

The following shows an example of how a simple majority works.

Simple Majority Example

A member of your group has raised the issue of reducing the voting age from eighteen to sixteen years of age. As a group, you must first decide what you want to do with this idea.

There are seven members in your group and you call for a vote to decide: Do you research it further? Do you drop it? Or do you act on it? The vote is:

- **Research it further: 5**
- **Drop it: 2**
- **Act on it: 0**

More than half of the group supports exploring the issue further; however, if the vote were 2, 3, 2, you would not have a majority because more than half of your group (that is, four or more) was not in favor of one option. You would then have to continue discussing the issue until your group came up with a simple majority in favor of one option. They could decide to delay discussing the issue until a later meeting where it might be easier to come to a majority (sometimes called "tabling" the issue).

For now, assume your group agrees by a majority that this issue needs further research. You brainstorm ways to research it further, and two ideas are thrown out for the group to consider:

- **Find out what the voting age is in other democratic countries.**
- **Take a survey of your school to see if other students your age are interested in having the voting age reduced to sixteen.**

You call for another vote to see what your group wants to do:

1. **Find out voting age in other countries: 0**
2. **Take a poll of other students: 1**
3. **Do both 1 and 2: 5**
4. **Do neither 1 or 2: 1**

By a majority, your group has decided to research both options.

After a week, members from your group who were assigned the tasks of exploring this issue give their reports. (Cadets who are practicing the cooperation citizenship skill may have found out more than they were asked.) Your group discusses the results—there is little interest in lowering the voting age among your peers. Your group votes on what to do now: act on this issue or drop it. The vote is:

- **Act on Issue: 3**
- **Drop Issue: 4**

By a majority, albeit a slim one, your group can now drop the issue if the entire group consents to the process it took to reach this decision. Consensus is the next skill you need to learn.

Group Skill 2: Reaching a Consensus

Consensus is coming to general acceptance on an issue. Consensus is a vital group skill. Without it, your groups may not function. Instead, meetings may become squabbling matches and arguments.

The key to consensus comes from the word "consent." It can be more a passive skill than an active one. Consensus is the skill of perhaps not agreeing with the decision the group made, but accepting it because the process used by the group allowed your needs and opinions to be heard and acknowledged.

Consensus is more of a feeling than an action. You consent to the group's decision and thus you ultimately support it, or not actively oppose it, even though it is not your idea of a great choice.

As a group, you will use the skill of reaching a consensus to evaluate the process your group went through to make a decision. In essence, you will determine whether the seven citizenship skills discussed in the previous lesson were sufficiently practiced by your group in reaching decisions. This is not to imply your group used the citizenship skills perfectly, but that your group did the best they could. Thus you can live with the decision you made together.

Consensus is critically important because the real test of whether we can govern ourselves is if we can work together toward our country's ideals of freedom, equality, and unity.

One of the best ways to come to a consensus is to practice the seven citizenship skills. If you feel your group successfully used the seven citizenship skills to reach a decision, your group is working together and exercising the power envisioned by the Founders when they drafted the Constitution.

Conversely, if you do not feel your group used the citizenship skills successfully, if you or another member of your group was not heard or given respect, or if your group was uncooperative, you can decide not to consent to the process after a decision has been made.

You have power when you do this because then you can veto the decision. This power must be used wisely; however, or the **decision-making** process breaks down.

The following shows an example of how your group might reach a consensus on the decision making process.

Key Note Term

consensus – a process by which everyone in a group accepts a decision. It is not necessary for everyone to agree to the decision to reach a consensus, but that everyone accepts the decision or the manner in which it was made, and will not oppose or undermine the results.

Key Note Term

decision-making – the process through which a decision is made.

Consensus Example

Continuing with the example discussed under the simple majority example, imagine your group decided, because of little interest, to drop the idea of trying to reduce the voting age from eighteen to sixteen. Also assume you were the one who raised the issue in the first place.

Now you are evaluating your group's performance at the end of the meeting. You feel that there were members of your group who ridiculed your idea, calling it stupid and foolish. Their behaviors were out of line and disrespectful, in your opinion.

Consequently, you feel your group did not follow the seven citizenship skills as best they could, and you do not consent to the group's decision process. Therefore, at the end of the meeting, you stand up and say, "I veto the decision," and give your reasons. Your group will now delay the decision and discuss it further at the next group meeting. In this instance a consensus was not reached.

A "veto" should be rarely used—only when a decision is reached with obvious and blatant disregard for the seven citizenship skills. It is important that every group member knows that he or she can use the "veto." It is also important that members learn to use it wisely—in other words, veto only when absolutely necessary.

The strength citizenship skill gives you the courage to be honest and indicate when you think your group did not work together. It serves no one, especially the group, if you remain silent when the purpose is to learn more about working together according to the seven citizenship skills.

Now imagine that you did raise the voting age issue, and your group listened to your thoughts and ideas without judging or ridiculing them. Your group went through the decision process considering this issue as objectively as possible and still decided to drop it after researching it further and finding little student support.

In this instance, as you evaluate your group's performance at the end of the meeting, you admit the seven citizenship skills were adequately addressed during the handling of this issue even though the final decision didn't go your way. Thus, you feel the decision was arrived at satisfactorily and so does the rest of your group. This is when a consensus is reached.

By now, you should understand why the process itself is as important as the final decision. Before you begin an actual small group meeting, there are a few ground rules to cover.

Group Skill 3: Following the Ground Rules

Rules are necessary to maintain fairness (Citizenship Skill 3) and give each participant an equal chance. Rules of conduct ensure the ideals of our nation (freedom, equality, and unity) are fulfilled for our citizens.

For this reason small group meetings have rules to ensure that everyone has an equal chance to participate fully and the group works together. The following are 13 **ground rules** to keep in mind during your small group meetings.

Key Note Term

ground rules - rules to ensure that everyone has an equal chance to participate fully and the group works together.

- **Ground Rule 1:** Each group meeting will start and end on time. Group members need to be punctual.

- **Ground Rule 2:** A group leader will run each group meeting. This job will rotate among all group members so that everyone will have an opportunity to be a group leader. The group leader will be responsible for facilitating the group discussion, making sure everyone follows the ground rules, and for keeping the group on track and on time. He/she may assign someone else in the group to monitor the time.

- **Ground Rule 3:** Each group member will be conscious of the seven citizenship skills as well as the group skills of reaching a simple majority, reaching a consensus, and following the ground rules during all meetings. If group members start to label, judge, or blame other group members for problems, the group will review the seven citizenship skills again and find out why there are difficulties in the group.

- **Ground Rule 4:** At the end of each group meeting, each individual will evaluate the group's performance as well as his or her own individual performance.

- **Ground Rule 5:** Personal topics will be left out of group discussions. These groups are not meant to be therapy groups.

- **Ground Rule 6:** If a group member gets angry or emotional, he or she will be asked to leave the group for 5 to 15 minutes to cool off (the timing is up to the group leader and/or instructor, if necessary), but he or she must agree to return to the group after the cooling-off period.

- **Ground Rule 7:** Each group member will be allowed time to speak if he/she desires; however, shouting or screaming will not be allowed. The group leader (or instructor, if necessary) may ask a shouting participant to leave the room to cool-off. The group leader will also make sure that each member has voiced her or his views and participated in the process. An issue cannot be decided upon unless everyone in the group has spoken or has openly chosen not to speak.

- **Ground Rule 8:** An issue can be "tabled" by a simple majority of those present, if the following occur:

  - A person is absent from a meeting.

  - The right people are not there to make a decision.

  - The group just cannot come to a simple majority for any reason (such as the need to take a break from a highly emotional topic or the need to further research a topic). This issue will then be delayed for discussion at a later meeting.

- **Ground Rule 9:** The person, who vetoes a decision, will verbalize their reasons to the rest of the group. The issue will then be discussed at the citizenship skill portion of the following meeting.

- **Ground Rule 10:** An issue can only be discussed in a total of four meetings (counting the first meeting it was brought up) unless agreed to otherwise by your group (see next ground rule).

- **Ground Rule 11:** Any change in the group process will be approved by a simple majority vote of at least 75 percent of the group. For example, if an issue has been overdone and your group wants to stop discussing it before the normal limit (four meetings), 75 percent or more of your group must vote in favor of dropping the issue. If your group wants to continue discussing an issue past the four-meeting limit, 75 percent or more of your group must vote in favor of this.

- **Ground Rule 12:** Your group will agree to meet and work together as long as determined by your instructor.

- **Ground Rule 13:** Discussions within any group meetings are confidential. That is, each group member must agree to not discuss group topics outside the group meetings unless the entire group approves.

Helpful Hints for Running a Small Group Meeting

As the leader of a small group, there are a few hints that might make your job easier and more fulfilling. These hints include:

1. **To keep the group discussion on track, use gentle reminders such as:**

   - "Can we get back on the subject?"

   - "Maria has a good point, let's listen to her and not talk among ourselves."

   - "If we stay on the subject, we will finish on time."

2. **Do not worry if you do not know all the answers. You do not have to be the most knowledgeable one in the group. Your job is just to keep the discussion moving and on track.**

3. **You might have group members who do not like to talk in the group. If you haven't heard from a group member, ask them for their thoughts, ideas, or opinions with specific questions like:**

   - "Chad, what do you think of Mary's idea to hold an assembly on citizenship skills?"

   - "Belize, do you like the idea of having a senior litter pick-up day?"

   - "Will, what's the best way you can see for us to present our opinions to the city council when they decide on the town's curfew?"

4. **Avoid having one person talk all the time. Keep everyone's discussion brief so that all group members have an equal chance to talk. Tell each group member that he or she will have two minutes to talk and that the timekeeper will monitor the time. Then move on to the next person. If there is time at the end, you can come back to that person again.**

5. **You might have group members who want to help others with personal problems (such as parent and boyfriend/girlfriend issues). Gently remind those group members that this type of discussion must take place outside the group meeting after class and then get back on track. Keep personal problems out of the group discussion.**

6. **If you have a group member who seems to know a lot about a certain subject, he or she may monopolize the entire discussion. Acknowledge this person for his or her knowledge and then when time is up, move on to the next person. Your group can use this person as a resource for finding out more information on a certain issue. Be careful, though, of making this your only source. All issues have more than one side to them.**

7. **Group members will want to talk among themselves. Eliminate side talking by calling attention to it such as: "Mandela and Leo, could you share your ideas with the group?"**

8. You may have members of your group competing for your job. Simply remind them that they had their turn or that their turn is coming. Ask them to help you out with this difficult job by letting you do it your way. Also, remind them that making mistakes is the only way you will learn. Perhaps they will show respect for your strong and weak points as a result. If you really have trouble, ask your instructor for help.

9. If you have uncooperative members, remind them of the ground rule stating that they can walk out of the room to cool off, but emphasize that they must return to the group. If their behavior persists, ask them to leave the room to cool off. Get your instructor's help if necessary.

10. If group members start to label, judge, or blame other group members for problems, talk within the group about the respect citizenship skill.

11. When asking questions of your group members, wait a few seconds for the answers. Be patient. Give others in your group time to think about their answers.

12. Finally, if you have major problems in the group you cannot resolve, ask your instructor for help.

Small Group Meeting Agenda

The Small Group Meeting flow chart, as seen in Figure 1.3.1, shows the general small group meeting process. Through a systematic process, an issue is brought up, discussed, and decided upon.

At first, your group might struggle with this process. Anytime we try something new (like a new sport for instance), it takes practice to excel at it. The same is true for this small group meeting. Have fun experimenting with this group process. Focus on the process itself and observe yourself and other group members.

Detailed Small Group Meeting Agenda

This section discusses what happens in each portion of a small group meeting. The small group leader is responsible for conducting the meeting and ensuring that each portion is accomplished.

1. **Administrative Business:** Read the group purpose: The purpose of these groups is to help us become effective citizens, able to guide and/or monitor the governmental activity in our school, town, state, and country. Take attendance. Name those group members who had homework and what they will be discussing later in the meeting (this will help those people get prepared). Schedule the next meeting. Pick the next group leader.

2. **Citizenship Skills Discussion:** Spend a moment in silence. Ask group members to close their eyes and visualize themselves practicing the citizenship skills during this group's session. Talk about homework (usually an individual assignment working on a specific citizenship skill, like patience, at home, work, and school). Bring up next skill and open it up to brief discussion. Distribute and explain citizenship skill homework (which your instructor will give you). Discuss any issues that were vetoed in the previous meeting to see if there are simple solutions to the problems or if they should be discussed again under old

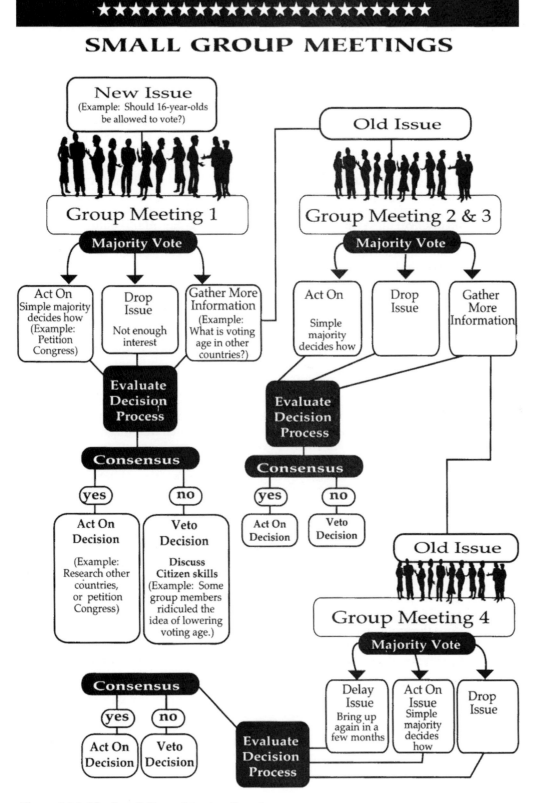

SMALL GROUP MEETINGS

Figure 1.3.1: The Small Group Meeting flow chart.

issues. Focus your group's discussion on the use of citizenship skills and not on the various slants to the issue itself (this discussion occurs under Old Issues following).

3. **Old Issues:** Ask for reports on assignments. For example: Maria says, "I spoke with Mr. Dean, and he's open to having an assembly on citizenship skills if we give him an outline of what we would cover." Be sure that an issue is fully discussed but not overly so. Ensure everyone's participation and do not let one person dominate the discussion. Ask the group if there is enough information to act on this issue. If there is, call for a vote to decide on a course of action. If there is not enough information, ask group members for ideas on research assignments. For example, "Mike, can you and Maria brainstorm a rough outline for a citizenship skills assembly and present it to us at the next meeting?" Finally, if any issues cannot be resolved at this time (as will be the case with sensitive and highly emotional issues), delay the issue until the next meeting (when it will be first on the agenda under old issues). An issue can only be discussed in a total of four meetings (including the first meeting it was mentioned) unless agreed to otherwise by your group. At this point, discuss any issue decisions that were vetoed to see if there are new grounds for agreement. Your group can also vote to drop an issue by a simple majority or to "table" it for later discussion, also by a simple majority.

4. **New Issues:** Ask the group members to bring up any new issues. Discuss each new issue briefly so you can decide to research it further, act on it, or drop it. Use a majority vote to decide what to do with this issue. If an issue cannot be decided on, it will be discussed under Old Issues at the next meeting. Occasionally, you will have issues with relatively simple resolutions. You can choose at this meeting to use a majority vote to handle these issues if there is not significant opposition within your group.

5. **Evaluation:** Spend a few minutes evaluating yourself and the group as a whole. The purpose of this evaluation session is for everyone to think about how well they participated in the group and how well they exhibited the citizenship skills. Except for the veto (which is stated), this evaluation process is anonymous. Use the group and individual evaluation forms for this purpose. Any poor ratings on the group's performance will be discussed at the next meeting's Citizenship Skills Discussion, but the decision will still be in force. This is where the group decides whether or not a decision was arrived at properly, using the consensus approach. If even one member is not satisfied and openly vetoes the decision, the problem becomes the first topic under the next meeting's Citizenship Skills Discussion. The decision remains vetoed until this discussion is completed and a new vote is taken. With time, you and your group will become familiar with the importance of this evaluation process. Remember also if this process becomes overly obstructive your group can vote to change it by a 75 percent or more majority.

6. **Action Assignments:** Assign tasks to each member of your group based on decisions the group made under Old or New Issues and consented to under the Evaluation discussion. For example, Joshua is assigned to arrange a meeting with the principal and assistant principal and go over the outline for the citizenship skill assembly. Jae is the next leader. Bernadette will attend the student government meeting and take notes. Tanya will do some research on an issue the group decided to continue.

7. **Closeout Details:** Take time to tie up any unfinished business—do group members have anything further to say? Remind people of their assignments for the coming week. Remind all group members of the next meeting and the name of the new group leader. Adjourn on time.

Quick Overview of the Small Group Meeting Agenda

1. Administrative Business
2. Citizenship Skills Discussion
3. Old Issues
4. New Issues
5. Evaluation
6. Action Assignments
7. Close-out Details

Conclusion

As with any process, there are rules and guidelines for holding and attending small group meetings. These rules and guidelines keep the meeting on track and enable those attending to know what's coming up in the current meeting as well as what's expected of them in the next meeting. Small group meetings are headed by a group leader, and that leader will change to another member of the group each time a meeting is held. All seven Citizenship Skills should be practiced at each small group meeting.

Lesson Review

1. How is the small group meeting leader chosen, and what are the roles of the leader?
2. Choose one of the seven Citizenship Skills and explain how it pertains to small group meetings.
3. What are the three group skills that should be practiced at each meeting?
4. Explain what is meant by an action assignment.

Chapter 1

Lesson Review

Lesson 4

Representative Group Session

Key Terms

representative group session
representative group session agenda
small group representatives

What You Will Learn to Do

- Participate in a Representative Group Session

Linked Core Abilities

- Do your share as a good citizen in your school, community, country, and the world

Skills and Knowledge You Will Gain along the Way

- Identify the responsibilities of a small group representative
- Explain the impact of the representative group session agenda
- Describe the representative group session process
- Define key words contained in this lesson

Introduction

This lesson introduces you to representative group sessions, one of two types of Citizen Action Groups. A **representative group session** occurs when all the small groups merge into a larger assembly or class to discuss an all-class or all-school position on a specific issue. Representatives are elected from each small group. These representatives then hold a meeting, which is observed by all the small groups.

The purpose of the representative group session is twofold. In the beginning, these representative sessions are simply training sessions in which you will be addressing hypothetical issues, such as gun control or the United States' policy with China. These first few training sessions will help you become familiar with the representative process in general.

After you are familiar with the representative process, the second purpose of the representative group session is to address issues that need far-reaching action and cooperation from your class or school as a whole. Your **small group representatives** will be discussing and deciding on issues (such as a school-wide parking problem) and then coming up with action steps to resolve these issues.

This process can be expanded to the next level—to your school district—where small group representatives from other schools using the Student Citizenship Training Program, gather together in larger representative sessions. Thus, the representative group session mirrors the current representative process of our local, state, and federal governments.

Before a representative session can be held; however, your small group needs to elect a representative. The procedure to elect a representative from your small group differs somewhat from the way you have elected class representatives for your school government.

Key Note Term

representative group session – One of two types of Citizen Action Groups in which small groups elect representatives to discuss and decide on issues in front of a class or other gathering.

small group representatives – a member of a small group who is elected to represent the group at the Representative Group Session.

Selecting a Representative

Learning how to select an effective representative will not only help your small group, but will also help you select better representatives for your student government. When you are eligible to vote, this exercise will help you support the best person for political office.

To understand how to select the best representative, you can revisit the time when our government was being formed and look at the selection of George Washington as the Chairman of the Constitutional Convention.

He was the most obvious choice for Chairman, but not because of his knowledge of government. Almost all the Founders were better educated and knew more about the workings of a government than George Washington. However,

Washington had a complementary set of skills that perfectly suited him as the chosen representative for the people in this new government.

Foremost, Washington had demonstrated his strength and leadership in the American Revolutionary War. Moreover, he had proven himself trustworthy over time. He was open-minded, able to look at both sides of an issue, and make wise decisions. His cooperation skills were well developed and he always treated others with the utmost fairness and respect.

In essence, George Washington was the best at the citizenship skills you have learned so far. That is why he was the best choice as a representative.

When you choose your own representative, whether it is for this representative group session, your student government, city mayor, council member, or even the President of the United States, you begin by analyzing this person's grasp and practice of seven citizenship skills: cooperation, patience, fairness, respect, strength, self-improvement, and balance. You also look for a person who is trustworthy, intelligent, wise, and who acts calmly under pressure. In other words, a person similar to George Washington.

Knowledge of the issues is a good trait for a representative to have, but it is not as important as these other skills. Any interested person can always learn about the issues. What helps is a person competent in the seven citizenship skills.

Recognize also that your small group's ability to pick a representative will be measured by the quality of the representative you pick. The other small groups will assume you have picked a worthy representative when she/he goes to the front of the class. Your other classmates will take what that person says as being representative of your small group's feelings and decisions, so choose wisely.

How to Select a Representative

There are three ways that you can select a representative for your small group. These steps include:

- **Ask cadets to volunteer if they are interested in becoming a small group representative. If no one volunteers, ask your instructor to select someone.**

- **Rate each potential candidate (hopefully you have more than one choice) on the representative rating sheet. Interviewing your prospective choices is a good way to gain more knowledge about them. Watching a debate between your choices (in a student or political election if these are held) also will give you information on a person's citizenship skills.**

- **Hold an election for those in your small group who are interested in being a representative. Each group member votes for only one representative (usually the one who rated the best on the representative rating sheet). Write that person's name on a piece of paper and pass it to the group leader. The leader adds up the votes and the person with the most votes is your small group's representative. Your small group can choose to keep this representative for any period (a month, two months, semester, or year) or to elect a new representative at each representative group session.**

Representative Group Session Agenda

If you are not an elected as the small group representative, you will merely observe this representative group session and then discuss it with your small group afterwards. Your instructor will give all the small groups the same issue to discuss. During the representative group session, your small group representatives will attempt to reach a class decision on the issue through a majority vote.

Detailed Representative Group Session Agenda

Similar to the small group meeting agenda, a **representative group session agenda** is necessary to keep the session on track. This agenda includes the following.

Key Note Term

representative group session agenda – a list of tasks or a schedule to be followed during a Representative Group Session.

1. **Small Group Meeting:** Meet as a small group. Discuss the issue given to you by your instructor or decided upon by your class. Take a majority vote on what your group agrees is the best course of action for this issue. Elect your representative, if you have not already done so. Brief your representative on the thoughts and feelings of your small group.

2. **Representative Issue Discussion:** Small group representatives meet together in the presence of small groups and discuss the issue. Make sure each small group representative has had an opportunity to speak. Use a majority vote between the representatives to decide what to do with the issue. Call for a vote from the representatives to decide on a course of action (research it further, act on it, or drop it). If there is not enough information, decide what research is needed. If any issues cannot be resolved this time (as may be the case with sensitive and highly emotional issues), delay the issue until the next representative group session or ask your instructor for guidance. The issue also can be returned to the small groups for further research and/or discussion.

3. **Large Discussion (Class-wide, School-wide, or Larger):** With your instructor, discuss the results of the representative session with all the small groups (in the first few training sessions only). Did your small group representative present your group's ideas effectively and correctly? How was the conduct and quality of the representatives themselves? How well did the representative group session function? Were the seven citizenship skills used in the representatives' meeting?

4. **Action Steps:** Representatives then decide on the action steps needed to put their decision into effect. They will assign tasks to other students. These tasks might be as simple as writing a letter to the appropriate person(s) (congressmen/women, school board) or arranging a meeting between your principal and a few of your small group representatives. If you do not have enough data to make a decision on your topic, your action step might be to find out more information on this issue.

5. **Small Group Evaluation:** During the first few training representative group sessions, you will break into your small groups and fill out a group evaluation form to evaluate the representative process. Did your group's representative follow the citizenship skills while participating in the representative group session? Did your small group do a good job of selecting a representative? How well did the representative process work? Any problems that come up during this evaluation step will be used for discussion at your next small group meeting.

6. **Homework Assignments:** If desired by your instructor, cadets (including small group representatives) are assigned various tasks determined by the representatives.

> **Quick Overview of the Representative Group Session Agenda**
>
> 1. Small Group Meeting
> 2. Representative Issue Discussion
> 3. Large Discussion
> 4. Action Steps
> 5. Small Group Evaluation
> 6. Homework Assignments

Small Group Representative Responsibilities

Your duties and responsibilities as a small group representative include the following:

1. **Communicate accurately and effectively to the rest of the representatives your small group's majority feelings and opinions, not necessarily your own opinions and feelings.**

2. **Address other small group representatives as "the honorable representative from Group _____ (group's name or number)" rather than by name when he or she is participating in the representative group session.**

3. **Participate fully in the representative session by speaking when addressed and by ensuring the other representatives have heard your small group's ideas.**

4. **Be conscious of the seven citizenship skills and use them throughout the representative group session.**

5. **Work cooperatively with other representatives to reach a majority decision by the end of the representative session. (This decision does not necessarily have to be an action step.)**

6. **Contribute ideas and research needs to the other representatives. Help assign research or action steps to small group members.**

Evaluation

After your small group or representative group session has concluded a meeting, each member of your small group will be given time to evaluate the group's participation, especially the way the group arrived at certain decisions.

The primary purpose of this evaluation procedure is to evaluate your group's grasp of the citizenship and group skills and the Citizen Action Group Process itself. This evaluation process may be the most important learning you will take with you from this course. That is why this phase is so critical.

Take time to fill out the evaluation forms during each small group meeting or the first few training representative group sessions. After you have filled them out, your small group will discuss the results. If you do not reach a consensus that each decision was arrived at properly using the seven citizenship skills (that is, one person stands up and vetoes the decision), then that decision is vetoed and no action is taken. This problem is then discussed under the Citizenship Skills Discussion of your next small group meeting.

If; however, your small group agrees the decision was arrived at properly, you are free to go ahead and act on that decision.

After you understand the evaluation procedure, begin your first small group meeting or your first representative group session. After you have worked through two or three issues in a representative group session and understand how the representative process works, you will understand how our government currently works and how you can be more effective in getting your ideas and issues heard by your representatives (for example, by working in Citizen Action Groups and having your representative present issues to your school, city, state, or federal government representatives).

This is the process upon which our government was founded, and it is the way we make our government continue to work and improve. The process itself is as important as reaching decisions. Enjoy the learning in this Citizen Action Group Process. Take time to honestly evaluate yourself and your group and then look for areas where your representative can improve.

Conclusion

A representative group session takes place when many small groups combine into a larger group to share information about a specific issue. Representatives are elected from each small group, and these representatives then hold a meeting that is observed by all of the small groups. The representative reports back to the small group and discusses what was decided at the representative group session, and what action steps need to be taken.

Chapter 1

Lesson Review

Lesson Review

1. **What are the ways you can select a representative from your small group? What do you think is important when choosing a representative?**

2. **What is the main purpose of a representative group session?**

3. **What are the responsibilities of a small group representative?**

4. **Discuss why the evaluation step after a meeting is so important. What types of things would you evaluate?**

Lesson 5

Introduction to Chief Justice®

Chapter 1

Key Terms

Chief Justice
cross examine
deliberations
forum
judge
jury
jury foreman
law firm
opening statements
trials
verdict

What You Will Learn to Do

- Explore the Chief Justice® process for debating constitutional and contemporary issue

Linked Core Abilities

- Do your share as a good citizen in your school, community, country, and the world
- Apply critical thinking techniques

Skills and Knowledge You Will Gain along the Way

- Examine the purpose of the Chief Justice® game
- Explore the rules of the Chief Justice® game
- Identify how to render a verdict in a case
- Define key words contained in this lesson

Introduction

Chief Justice® is an educational game designed to give the cadets an appreciation of the United States Constitution and of our democratic form or government. The complete game contains 100 critical thinking questions that incorporate today's most important moral and ethical issues. The following five questions have been selected to be used by the U.S. Army Junior ROTC program for their curriculum.

- **Should The Ten Commandments be posted in classrooms in all public elementary and secondary schools?**

- **Should public school students be allowed to voluntarily participate in prayer before school sponsored sporting events?**

- **Should the news media be allowed to disclose the name of a felony suspect before a trial?**

- **Should post-conviction DNA testing be a right granted upon request to all inmates in state and federal prison?**

- **Should rap groups be allowed to include lyrics in their music, which advocate physical violence against law enforcement officers?**

Chief Justice

Chief Justice® is a game designed to engage the participants in a variety of debates on constitutional and contemporary issues. The purpose of the game is to:

- **Design a forum within which people, who hold opinions about various constitutional and contemporary issues, can come together and discuss those issues in an organized and effective manner.**

- **Encourage each participant to give careful thought and consideration to his or her own views affecting our society and to express those thoughts in a meaningful and contemplative way.**

- **Create a game in which each participant is motivated to learn and appreciate the United States Constitution.**

- **Discover new ways of looking at constitutional issues and learn from other participants who may be able to share new insights on these issues.**

- **Introduce a game that requires each player to use critical thinking skills.**

- **Entertain the participants while at the same time create an environment for learning.**

- **Create a purpose for the players to extensively research their topics by using various search engines on the Internet.**

- **Provide a forum in which players can develop their public speaking skills in a debate format.**

- **Provide a forum that teaches ethics and values by using the United States Constitution as a moral compass.**

- **Provide an opportunity for cooperative learning to take place.**

Key Note Term

forum – a place or opportunity for open discussion and participation.

Introduction to Chief Justice

This country was founded on basic democratic principles which from time to time come under attack from misguided and uninformed forces that reside not only outside our borders, but too often live among us. These forces pose a threat to our survival not because they have a better system to impose upon us but because quite often we do not understand and appreciate the liberties we currently enjoy. Democracy is a concept for which we own no copyright. We can cherish it, share it and proudly display it to those in the darkness of ignorance and in doing so remain free or we can do nothing and watch it gradually fade away.

We the people are at our best when those of us who understand the true value of democracy fear that it is about to be lost. We have in the past come together as a mighty nation to stand tall against those who would deprive us of it. Over the past two centuries Americans have willingly chosen to lay down their lives on many battlefields to uphold the freedoms they so cherished. Now we face a great challenge in our country. The time has come again for a new generation of Americans to step forward and bravely answer the call.

Chief Justice provides an exciting new way to inform our young people of the value of the civil liberties we currently enjoy and the dangers of losing them. Students are asked to research constitutional and contemporary issues, investigate their own conscience about those issues, give voice to it in a debate format and then organize themselves and move into the community to affect positive change. Chief Justice provides an exciting forum for the discussion of key ethical and moral issues. It gives your students a compelling reason to explore and appreciate the Constitution. Chief Justice can be a very valuable addition to a government or civics class, a character education program, a citizenship program, a speech and debate class, a leadership training program or courses in service learning.

Game Contents

Nearly all games have various pieces for the players to use. Chief Justice is no exception. This game contains:

- **A game poster depicting the U. S. Supreme Court with six steps leading up to the court house. Each step is labeled and represents a career path for an aspiring law student from law school to the top step of Supreme Court, and ultimately Chief Justice of the United States.**

- **A list of one hundred game questions, for one hundred courtroom trials to be held in a classroom setting focusing on various constitutional and contemporary issues.**

- **A supply of colored marker pins to identify where various teams are on the game poster during the course of the game. (Not available to Army JROTC at this time.)**

- **A copy of the U. S. Constitution.**

- **Game instructions and a suggested lesson plan for playing Chief Justice® in your class.**

- **A rubric to inform cadets of the method of grading to be used, and a guideline for the teacher to determine how to measure the cadets performance in order to issue an appropriate grade.**

Rules of the Game

Game rules are important. Without rules, it would be hard to determine if players are playing fairly or if the winner actually won. The following sections detail the rules of the Chief Justice® game.

Setting

This game is most appropriate in a classroom setting, but could be played in any forum where people choose to gather on an ongoing basis and debate constitutional and contemporary issues.

Number of Players

It is necessary that the participants be divided into small groups which are considered "law firms"; two players in each law firm. If you have an odd number of people playing, it is allowable to have a law firm with three players participating. An unlimited number of people can participate in this game as jurors. The number of players participating as attorneys will depend on the size of the class and time constraints.

The Jury

A **jury** can be composed of any number of people who are not the attorneys in the present case. In a classroom situation, the remaining cadets not involved in the case are the jury. These people listen to the opening statements presented by the attorneys, the cross examination and the closing arguments, and then privately deliberate the case and deliver a verdict.

Selection of a Judge

A **judge** is selected at the beginning of the game to keep order and have the players follow the rules of the game. In a classroom setting, this job normally would fall to the teacher.

Duties of the Judge

As in a real courtroom, the judge has specific duties. In the Chief Justice® game, the duties of the judge include the following.

1. **The first duty of the judge is to determine the players in each law firm. This can be done in a number of different ways; however, it is recommended in a classroom setting that the cadets be allowed to choose their partners. Each law firm should include two attorneys; if there is an odd number of cadets in the class, some law firms may be made up of three attorneys.**

Key Note Term

jury – a select group of individuals chosen to listen and render a verdict in a court case.

judge – a high-ranking court officer who supervises and give a decision on an action or court case.

Key Note Term

law firm – a group of lawyers.

Key Note Term

trials – examinations of facts and law in a court of law.

2. Next, each cadet should read carefully the rules to the game and the rubric which will serve as a guideline for the grading process. The **trials** are expected to be held on a periodic basis over the course of a semester, or perhaps the school year, with trial dates scheduled on a weekly basis or as time allows. A consistent pattern of scheduled trials works best. For example, every Tuesday could be used for the purpose of the courtroom trials. (Army JROTC will have five trials.)

3. The law firms are then directed to select a case from the first 20 questions listed in the Chief Justice® booklets. After the first series of trials have been concluded, the next set of questions, 21 through 40, would be used for the second set of trials and so forth until the 100 questions have been explored, and each law firm has had five chances to win a case and move up to the top step of Supreme Court on the game poster. (Army JROTC will have five trials.)

4. At the start of each series of trials it is necessary to determine which cases are to be heard. The judge will call two law firms to come forward with their one selection and on the flip of a coin will determine which of the two cases chosen by each law firm will be heard. The team winning the coin toss not only gets to have their case heard, but gets to choose the side of the argument they wish to defend. The law firm that loses the toss will have to take the opposing view of that case and argue that side as effectively as possible. Good attorneys can argue either side of any case brought before them as will happen in the practice of law. This process will continue until all law firms have come forward and all the cases to be tried have been determined.

5. In a classroom situation, it is important to allow sufficient time for the law firms to research their cases and schedule court dates for sometime in the future. A minimum of two weeks might be necessary before the first case is heard. Following cases would be scheduled on an ongoing basis over the course of the following weeks as time permits. Cadets should be encouraged to use the Internet as an excellent source to gain material for their arguments.

Key Note Term

opening statements – statements that state the opinion of one side in the beginning of a court case.

cross examine – to question the witness or opposing side.

6. During the day of the trial, the judge will call the attorneys to the front of the room where a sufficient number of chairs have been placed to seat them. It is recommended that a podium be placed between the two law firms, if one is available, and other props such as a gavel or a judge's robe (black choir robe) might be used to add authenticity to the setting.

7. The judge will then call for the opening statements from each side, starting with an attorney representing the proponent's side of the question, to be considered. For example: If the issue to be debated is "Should minors under the age of 18, who commit first degree murder, be given the death penalty?", the side arguing for giving the death penalty would go first.

8. The attorneys are allowed to use their three-page written reports as reference, but they should engage the jury with direct eye contact and not read the report word for word. They should be prepared to speak on the issue and only occasionally use the prepared text for assistance.

9. Only one attorney from each side is allowed to give **opening statements** and should be limited to five minutes for this phase of the trial.

10. After the opening statements, the attorneys are allowed to **cross examine** each other. The law firm taking the opposing side of the issue would go first. In the example above that would be the side arguing against the death penalty for minors. Each side would be allowed up to five minutes each to cross examine the opposing law firm and to try to expose weaknesses in their arguments.

11. Closing arguments are then given by the attorney who did not give the opening statements. Five minutes are allowed for each side and the law firm opposing

the question would begin. In this case, the side against the death penalty would give their closing arguments first and the proponents would present last.

12. At the end of the closing arguments, the judge (teacher) would collect the three page research material used by the attorneys and ask the attorneys to wait just outside the classroom with the door closed. The teacher will later administer a grade for their work based on the rubric provided.

Jury Deliberation

When the attorneys have given their closing arguments, it's time for the jury to begin their work. The steps for jury deliberation are:

1. The jurors (the remaining cadets in the class) then pick a **jury foreman.** This should not take much time and it is acceptable to have someone volunteer or have the judge, who is still sitting in the room, select someone to expedite this process. The foreman will take an initial vote on the case by reading the question to the jury and recording the number of jurors who raise their hands for the death penalty for minors and those who are against it.

2. The jurors are then asked by the foreman to comment on their positions regarding the case and try to influence the other jurors to vote with their side. The foreman is expected to keep order during this phase and to allow all jurors an opportunity to share their views on the case in an appropriate way. It is important to have selected a responsible cadet who can carry out these duties.

3. The foreman must conclude the **deliberations** and reach a final **verdict** by simple majority vote with at least five minutes remaining in the class. The verdict is kept secret and the attorneys are now asked to reenter the courtroom and take their seats at the front of the room.

4. The judge will then bang the gavel and call the courtroom to order. The foreman will stand and will be asked by the judge if the jury has reached a verdict. After answering in the affirmative, the foreman will then be asked to announce the verdict. The foreman will then announce the verdict.

5. The judge will then move the winning team's colored marking pin up one step on the Chief Justice poster which has been hung on the bulletin board somewhere in the classroom. The judge will declare, "The court is now adjourned." (Poster not available to Army JROTC at this time.)

The highest honor at the end of the game is to become **Chief Justice.** The game will come to an end when one law firm has reached the level of Supreme Court. The cadets are then asked to confirm a Chief Justice by secret ballot. Only one of the attorneys who has reached the level of Supreme Court will become Chief Justice. The Chief Justice should be chosen on the basis of his or her depth of knowledge of constitutional law, the amount of research of the various case laws used during the trials, and the degree of articulate persuasion of those moral and ethical principles the attorney has shared during the course of the game.

The final duty of the judge is to announce the name of the Chief Justice to the class and allow that cadet to move the colored marking pin representing his or her winning law firm to the star on the Chief Justice poster. Applause is very appropriate at this time.

Key Note Term

jury foreman – a person who conducts the jury deliberation and speaks for the jury.

deliberations – a period of time given to a jury to discuss and determine a ruling in a case.

verdict – the decision rendered by a judge or jury in a court case.

Chief Justice – the highest honor at the end of the game is to become Chief Justice. The game will come to an end when one law form has reached the level of Supreme Court. The cadets are them asked to confirm a Chief Justice by secret ballot.

Time Frame to Conclude the Game

This game is designed to be played in a variety of time frames that suit a course curriculum or the schedule of any club or organization that wishes to provide a forum to debate current moral and legal issues. The time allocated for the Army JROTC program is five hours, one hour for each trial to be heard on a weekly basis.

Conclusion

It is believed, by the author of this game, that in most cases the collective wisdom of the majority of the people will determine the "right answer" given enough research, serious contemplation, and open debate on any ethical or moral issue before them. Democracy works because "We the People" have inherent within us the collective wisdom and ability to govern ourselves. In this game cadets not only research what existing laws are relative to the questions before them, but also are asked to decide for themselves what the laws should be.

Chief Justice® is designed on the positive assumption that enlightened citizens are very capable of deciding what the laws should be. It is then the duty of all enlightened citizens to become actively engaged in the democratic process to ensure that our freedom is preserved.

The cadets are strongly encouraged to read the U.S. Constitution and interpret this historic document as a guide to finding the answers to as many questions as possible in this game.

Chapter 1

Lesson Review

1. What do Chief Justice® players learn about the U.S. Constitution? What is the purpose of the game?
2. What are five duties of the judge?
3. Explain the steps for jury deliberations.
4. How does a player get to be Chief Justice?

Lesson Review

Foundations of the American Political System

								Declaration of Independence (1776)			
							Glorious	English Bill	Virginia Declaration of Rights (1776)		
Mayflower		English Petition	Massachusetts Body of Liberties (1641)				Revolution	of Rights	First Continental Congress (1774)		
Compact (1620)		of Right (1628)	The Law and Liberties (1648)				(1688)	(1689)	The Stamp Act (1765)		
1610s	**1620s**	**1630s**	**1640s**	**1650s**	**1660s**	**1670s**	**1680s**	**1740s**	**1750s**	**1760s**	**1770s**
	Virginia House of	First colonial printing			Bacon's Rebellion		First newspaper		Britain defeats France in		
	Burgesses, colonies' first	press (1639)			against the governor		published in the		the Seven Years War (1763)		
	representative assembly				of Virginia (1676)		colonies (1690)				
	(1619)										

Lesson 1

Our Natural Rights

Chapter 2

Key Terms

cantons
civil rights
consent
constitutional government
democracy
equal protection
higher (fundamental) law
human nature
law of nature
legitimate
limited government
natural rights
political rights
private domain
republic
right of revolution
social contract
state of nature
unalienable (inalienable)
unlimited government

What You Will Learn to Do

● Examine how the Founders' ideas of government were to protect natural rights of citizens

Linked Core Abilities

● Communicate using verbal, non-verbal, visual, and written techniques

● Apply critical thinking techniques

Skills and Knowledge You Will Gain along the Way

- Describe how and why the natural rights philosophers used an imaginary state of nature to think about the basic problems of governments

- Explain some of the basic ideas of the natural rights philosophy, including state of nature, law of nature, natural rights, social contract and consent

- Explain that the purpose of government based on the natural rights philosophy is to preserve our natural rights to life, liberty and property

- Describe how the natural rights philosophy uses the concepts of consent and social contract to explain the formation of government

- Describe the influence of the natural rights philosophy on the Founders

- Explain the concepts of constitution and constitutional government

- Explain the essential characteristics of constitutional government that differentiate them from autocratic or dictatorial governments

- Explain the essential characteristics of a constitution or higher law

- Explain how the Founders' fear of abuse of power by government may have motivated them to establish a constitutional government

- Define key words contained in this lesson

Introduction

Natural rights philosophers such as John Locke explored ideas about the laws of nature and natural rights of all people. This lesson explores how the Founders ideas of government supported Locke's philosophy of natural rights. Through discussion and reflection activities, you will compare how Locke's definition and philosophy are similar or different to the natural rights protected by our government today.

What Would Life Be Like in a State of Nature?

What Is the Natural Rights Philosophy?

We hold these Truths to be self-evident, that all Men are created equal, that they are endowed by their Creator with certain unalienable Rights, that among these are Life, Liberty, and the Pursuit of Happiness—That to secure these Rights; Governments are instituted among Men, deriving their just Powers from the Consent of the Governed, that whenever any Form of Government becomes destructive of these Ends, it is the Right of the People to alter or to abolish it, and to institute new Government....

Declaration of Independence, 1776

Reprinted from *We the People: The Citizen and the Constitution,* published by the Center for Civic Education.

This excerpt from the Declaration of Independence includes some of the most important philosophical ideas underlying our form of government. They are ideas that had been familiar to almost everyone in the American colonies long before the Revolutionary War.

These ideas had been preached in churches, written in pamphlets, and debated in public and private. They had been developed and refined by political philosophers such as the Englishman John Locke (1632–1704) and others. Locke was the most important influence on the thinking of the Founders at the time of the Revolution. Locke's political philosophy is often called the **natural rights philosophy.**

The natural rights philosophy is based on imagining what life would be like if there were no government. Locke and others called this imaginary situation a **state of nature.** By this, Locke did not necessarily mean people living in a wilderness. A state of nature is a condition in which there is no government. For example, even with the existence of the United Nations, international relations between countries today operate in a state of nature. There is no superior power that can act effectively as a government over these individual states.

Thinking about what life would be like if there were no government was very useful to philosophers such as Locke in answering questions like these:

- **What is human nature? That is, what traits of personality and character, if any, do all human beings have in common? For example, are all people selfish or do they tend to care for the good of others?**
- **What should be the purpose of government?**
- **How do the people running a government get the right to govern?**
- **How should a government be organized?**
- **What kinds of government should be respected and supported?**
- **What kinds of government should be resisted and fought?**

The natural rights philosophers' answers to these questions provided the foundation for many arguments the Founders made to explain and justify their decision to separate from Britain. They also used these ideas in writing state constitutions after the Revolutionary War and later in writing the Constitution of the United States and the Bill of Rights.

Critical Thinking Exercise
Taking the Position of a Political Philosopher

To understand the natural rights philosophy, you should try to answer the questions it addresses. Some important questions are included in the following exercise. Your class should be divided into small discussion groups. The members of your group may not all agree on the answers. It is important to know that at various times in history, people have had very different views on these matters.

Imagine that all the students in your school were transported to a place with enough natural resources for you to live well, but where no one had lived before. When you arrive, you have no means of communicating with people in other parts of the world. With this imaginary situation in mind, answer the following questions. Discuss your answers, and then compare your answers with those of John Locke, in the next section.

1. **Upon arrival would there be any government or laws to control how you lived, what rights or freedoms you exercised, or what property you had? Why?**

2. **Would anyone have the right to govern you? Would you have the right to govern anyone else? Why?**

3. **Would you have any rights? What would they be?**

4. **What might people who were stronger or smarter than others try to do? Why?**

5. **What might the weaker or less sophisticated people try to do? Why?**

6. **What might life be like for everyone?**

How do your answers compare with those of John Locke?

Your answers may be similar to those developed by John Locke or they may differ. In this lesson we are focusing on understanding Locke's answers because they were widely shared by Americans living during the 1700s. They also played a very important role in the development of our government.

1. **Locke believed that there were rules in a state of nature. He called these rules natural law or the law of nature. He said, "The state of nature has a law of nature to govern it which obliges every one... No one ought to harm another in his life, health, liberty, or possessions..."**

   They were "the Laws of Nature and of Nature's God," as Thomas Jefferson called them in the Declaration of Independence. Jefferson believed they were laws made by a Supreme Being for the benefit of human beings.

According to Locke, how is personal property protected in a state of nature?

Locke believed that most people understood this law of nature through the use of their reason and followed it because their consciences obliged them to do so. Not all humans were reasonable or good, however. There might even be disagreement about what the "laws of nature" were. If there were no government, there would be no one with the right to interpret or enforce these laws.

According to Locke, there would be no government because a government cannot exist until it has been created. A **legitimate** government cannot exist until the people have given their **consent** to be ruled by it. Thomas Jefferson included this idea in the Declaration when he wrote that "Governments are instituted among men, deriving their just powers from the consent of the governed...."

2. No one would have the right to govern you, nor would you have the right to govern anyone else. According to Locke, the only way anyone gets the right to govern anyone else is if that person gives his or her consent. If the people to be governed have not consented to the creation of a government, there is no legitimate government.

3. Using his reason to determine what rights were provided for by the law of nature, Locke asked himself: "What are the things that all people always need and seek, no matter what they believe, no matter when or where they live?" His answer identified the following rights:

   • **Life.** People want to survive and they want their lives to be as free as possible from threats to their security.

   • **Liberty.** People want to be as free as possible from the domination of others, to be able to make their own decisions, and to live as they please.

   • **Property.** People want the freedom to work and gain economic goods such as land, houses, tools, and money, which are necessary to survival.

   These rights were called **natural rights** and you would have the right to defend them if other people threatened to take them away.

4. Locke believed that people are basically reasonable and sociable, but they are also self- interested. Since the only security people would have for the protec-

Why did Locke believe it was necessary for people to create governments?

tion of their natural rights would be their own strength or cunning, people who were stronger or smarter would often try to take away the life, liberty, and property of the weak.

5. Weaker or less sophisticated people might try to protect themselves by joining together against the strong.

6. Since there would be no laws that everybody agreed upon, and no government to enforce them, everybody's rights would be very insecure.

What do you think?

1. Give examples of problems that might arise when one individual's rights to life, liberty, and property conflict with those of other individuals. What considerations might be used to resolve these conflicts?

2. Should some rights be given more protection than other rights? Why? Give examples.

3. The natural rights philosophy claims that government is based on consent. How do we give our consent and how do we withdraw it?

4. Many people today believe that the rights to life, liberty, and property include the right to public education and health care. Would the founders have agreed? Do you agree? Why?

What is the significance of Locke's definition of the natural rights to life, liberty, and property?

References to "human rights," "political and economic rights," "student rights," "consumer rights," "parental rights," and other terms using the word appear in the news every day. "Rights" is a word you are already familiar with. We have become so accustomed to the word, we don't often think about what it means.

A **right** may be described as a claim to have or obtain something, or to act in a way that is justified on legal or moral grounds. For example, you might claim the right to practice your own religion and justify it by appealing to the First Amendment of the Constitution. This is not, of course, the only justification you could give.

In describing the concept of **natural rights,** philosophers like John Locke were making a bold, new departure from previous uses of the term rights. Before the time of Locke and the other natural rights philosophers, the concept of rights had been applied in a very limited and selective way. More often than not, rights were considered special privileges, enjoyed only by certain groups, classes, or nations of people. They were exclusive rights, not enjoyed by those outside the group.

The natural rights philosophers disagreed with this interpretation. They believed that people's opportunities should not be limited by the situation or group into which they were born. These philosophers regarded the individual, rather than the class or group, as the most important social unit. They saw society as a collection of individuals, all of whom shared the same right to pursue his or her own welfare.

Locke, for example, defined natural rights in terms of life, liberty, and property because he considered them to be the essence of humanity. They are what make us human beings and what define our purpose in life. They are inclusive rights, belonging to every human being. These rights Locke also considered to be

unalienable, the word that Jefferson used in the Declaration. This means they are so much a part of human nature that they cannot be taken away or given up. "The sacred rights of mankind," said another Founder, Alexander Hamilton, "are written, as with a sun beam in the whole volume of human nature, by the hand of the Divinity itself, and can never be erased or obscured by mortal power."

Governments and societies based on the natural rights philosophy guarantee specific rights to preserve our natural rights. Under the U.S. Constitution, for example, you possess **civil rights,** securing such things as freedom of conscience and privacy, and protecting you from unfair discrimination by government or others. You also possess certain **political rights,** like the right to vote or run for office, which give you control over your government. Such civil and political rights serve to protect natural rights to life, liberty, and property.

Why are political rights necessary to protect our natural rights?

What did Locke mean by the "social contract"?

In an ideal state of nature, the law of nature would prevail. No one would have the right to interfere with your life and your freedom to acquire and hold property. Locke, however, realized that because not all human beings were rational or good, there would always be people who would try to violate your rights. Since there would not be any government, you and others would have to defend your rights on your own. The result would be that in the state of nature, your rights and their enjoyment would be insecure. You would be in constant danger of losing them.

For Locke and the other natural rights philosophers, the great problem was to find a way to protect each person's natural rights so that all persons could enjoy them and live at peace with one another. Locke said that the best way to solve this problem in the state of nature is for each individual to agree with others to create and live under a government and give it the power to make and enforce laws. This kind of agreement is called the **social contract.**

As in all contracts, to get something, you must give up something. In the social contract everyone promises to give up the absolute right to do anything he or she has the right to do in a state of nature. In return, everyone receives the security that can be provided by a government. Each person consents to obey the limits placed upon him or her by the laws created by the government. Everyone gains the security of knowing that his or her rights to life, liberty, and property are protected.

Government, then, is the better alternative to an imperfect state of nature where some people will not obey the laws of nature. Government's purpose is to protect those natural rights that the individual cannot effectively secure in a state of nature.

What do you think?

1. **If the purpose of government is to provide security for the rights to life, liberty, and property, under what circumstances, if any, should government be able to limit these rights?**

2. **What criteria should be used to determine when, if ever, government should be able to limit an individual's liberty to:**

   - **Believe as he or she wishes**

   - **Practice his or her beliefs**

   - **Use his or her property**

   - **Associate with whomever he or she wishes**

3. **Imagine yourself living in a community where all order and authority have broken down. Violent lawlessness is widespread. Do you think any government is better than none? Explain your answer.**

4. **It has been said that since people are not equal in their intelligence and character, it is unjust for everyone to have the same rights. Do you agree? Be prepared to defend your answer.**

How Does Government Secure Natural Rights?

Critical Thinking Exercise

Examining Government Protection of the Basic Rights of the People

Suppose you are not satisfied with living in a state of nature. You and others agree to enter into a social contract and a government to protect your natural rights. You must decide what kind of government you want and then establish it. Locke, Jefferson, and others knew that this is not an easy task. Throughout history governments have deprived people of their rights more often than they have protected them. Your problem is to design and establish the kind of government that will do what you want it to do, that is, protect your natural rights. This also means providing **equal protection** for the rights of everyone.

You and everyone else in your imaginary state of nature have agreed to live under a government. There are questions you must answer in deciding what kind of government to create. Your teacher will divide the class into small groups to discuss your answers. Then compare your answers with those of John Locke and explain why you agree or disagree with Locke.

1. **What in your opinion is the main purpose of government?**

2. **How should government get the authority or right to make laws telling people what they can and cannot do?**

3. **What should the people have the right to do if their government does not serve the purposes for which it was created? Why should they have this right?**

How do your answers compare with those of John Locke?

1. **Locke and other natural rights philosophers said that the purpose of government is to protect natural rights. Thomas Jefferson agreed and in the Declaration of Independence argued that the protection of rights is the main purpose of government.**

2. **Another of Locke's ideas that Jefferson stated in the Declaration of Independence is that government gets its right to govern from the consent of the people. Its powers are delegated to it by the governed.**

   People give their consent in several ways. People can give explicit consent by:

   • **Agreeing to the contract that establishes the society whose members then establish the government and choose its officers**

   • **Joining a society that already is established**

   People give implicit consent, also called tacit consent, by accepting the laws and services of the government and nation of their birth.

3. **Locke believed that since the people give the power to the government, they have the right to take it away if the government is not serving the purposes for**

Reprinted from *We the People: The Citizen and the Constitution,* published by the Center for Civic Education.

Under what circumstances would Locke agree that people have the right to take up arms against an established government?

which it was established. They can then create a new government. Locke argued and the Founders agreed that if a government fails to protect the people's rights, the people have a right of revolution.

Who is to judge if a government has failed? Locke and the Founders said that the people have the right to make that decision. This position is in the following words from the Declaration of Independence: "Whenever any Form of Government becomes destructive of these Ends, it is the Right of the People to alter or abolish it, and to institute new Government . . ."

Revolution, however, is an extreme way in which to deal with bad government. Government should be designed or organized to limit its powers in order to protect individual rights and thus reduce the need for such extreme measures.

How do Americans express consent to their government?

The Americans who ratified our Constitution in 1787 gave explicit consent to their new government. So did the many immigrants who came to America to seek a better life. Those who are born here have implied their consent by remaining in this country and living under its laws.

Every native-born American, as he or she grows up, has the choice of seeking the citizenship of another country. By remaining in this country, accepting its laws, and enjoying its benefits, you imply your consent to be governed by your federal, state, and local governments. You also affirm your consent every time you take the Pledge of Allegiance, participate in an election, or engage in other civic actions.

What is constitutional government?

Limited governments have established and respected restraints on their powers, restraints such as laws and free and periodic elections. The opposite is **unlimited government,** in which those who govern are free to use their power as they choose, unrestrained by laws or elections. Tyranny, autocracy, dictatorship, and totalitarianism are other words to describe unlimited government.

What form of government was best suited to prevent the abuse of power in the newly independent states of America? From their reading of both history and the natural rights philosophers, the Founders believed that any government that served its proper ends would have to be a limited or constitutional government.

In a **constitutional government,** the powers of the person or group controlling the government are limited by a set of laws and customs called a constitution.

What is a constitution?

A constitution is a set of customs, traditions, rules, and laws that sets forth the basic way a government is organized and operated. Most constitutions are in writing, some are partly written and partly unwritten, and some are not written at all.

Notice that according to this definition of the word, every nation has a constitution. Good governments and bad governments may have constitutions. Some of the worst governments have constitutions that include lists of the basic rights of their citizens. The former Soviet Union had one of the longest and most elaborate constitutions in history, but in reality its citizens enjoyed few of the rights guaranteed by it.

If you study the constitution of a government, you will be able to answer the following questions about the relationship between the government and its citizens:

- **What are the purposes of government?**
- **How is the government organized?**
- **How is the government supposed to go about doing its business?**
- **Who is considered to be a citizen?**
- **Are the citizens supposed to have any power or control over their government? If so, how is it to be exercised?**
- **What rights and responsibilities, if any, are the citizens supposed to have?**

It is very important to understand that having a constitution does not mean that a nation has a constitutional government. If a constitution provides for the unlimited exercise of political power—by one, few, or even many—such a constitution would not be the basis of a constitutional government. If a constitution provides that the government's power is to be limited, but it does not include ways to enforce those limitations, it is not the basis of a constitutional government. In a constitutional government the constitution is a form of **higher** or **fundamental law** that must be obeyed by everyone, including those in power.

How did the Founders characterize higher law?

According to the Founders, a constitution or higher law should have the following characteristics:

- **It sets forth the basic rights of citizens to life, liberty, and property.**
- **It establishes the responsibility of the government to protect those rights.**

How does the principle of private domain protect you from government interference?

- It establishes the principle of a **private domain**—which means that there are areas of citizens' lives that are no business of the government and in which the government cannot interfere.

- It establishes limitations on how those in government may use their powers with regard to:

  - Citizens' rights and responsibilities

  - The distribution of resources

  - The control of conflict

- It can only be changed with the widespread consent of the citizens, and according to established and well-known procedures. This distinguishes the higher law from the ordinary law that governments regularly create and enforce.

What do you think?

1. One of the purposes of the limitations imposed by constitutional government is to check the power of the majority. How can this be justified in a political system that is supposed to be democratic?

2. What are the major advantages, in your judgment, of limited government? What are the most serious disadvantages?

3. Are there advantages to unlimited government? If so, what are they?

How does a constitutional government protect natural rights?

Constitutional government assures the rights of its citizens in two ways:

- It establishes limits on the power of the government to prevent it from violating natural rights.

- It states that the government should be organized and its power distributed in such a way as to increase the possibility that those limitations will be effective.

The first is a purely **legal protection** of a citizen's freedom. The next is an **organizational protection,** having to do with the way in which government operates.

How can constitutional governments be organized to prevent the abuse of power?

In constitutional governments, powers are usually distributed and shared among several branches of government. This distribution and sharing of power makes it less likely that any one branch can abuse or misuse its powers. It is also less likely that any group will gain so much power that it can ignore the limitations placed on it by the constitution.

To prevent our government from abusing its powers, the Framers provided for distribution and sharing of powers among three branches of the national government. Each branch has primary responsibility for certain functions, but each branch also shares these functions and powers with the other branches. For example,

- **The Congress may pass laws, but the president may veto them.**
- **The president nominates certain government officials, but the Senate must approve them.**
- **The Congress may pass laws, but the Supreme Court may declare them unconstitutional.**

It is this system of distributed and shared powers that provides the basis for **checks and balances.** Although each branch of the government has its own special powers, many of these powers are "checked" because they are shared with the other groups.

Does a system of checks and balances guarantee that power will not be abused?

Legislative

Judicial

Executive

The complicated ways in which constitutional governments are organized often mean that it takes them a long time to get things done. It may seem strange, but this "inefficiency" was seen by the Framers as an advantage. They thought that these difficulties would help to prevent the abuse of power and make it more likely that when a decision was finally made, it would be a good one.

Critical Thinking Exercise

Examining Why the Founders Feared the Abuse of Power by Government

Given their knowledge of history and their experiences with the British government, it is not surprising that the Founders greatly feared the possible abuse of the powers of government. For example, read the following selections from some of their writings. Then discuss with the class your answers to the questions that follow.

> *Give all power to the many, they will oppress the few. Give all power to the few, they will oppress the many.*
>
> Alexander Hamilton, 1787

> *There are two passions which have a powerful influence on the affairs of men. These are ambition and avarice; the love of power and the love of money.*
>
> *Benjamin Franklin, 1787*

> *From the nature of man, we may be sure that those who have power in their hands...will always, when they can...increase it.*
>
> George Mason, 1787

1. **Explain the view of human nature expressed in each of these quotations.**

2. **If you agreed with the views of human nature expressed in the quotations, what kind of safeguards to prevent the abuse of power would you include in your government?**

3. **Do you think the Founders' fear of government is as valid today as it was in the 1700s? Explain your answer.**

What kinds of governments maybe constitutional governments?

The Founders knew that constitutional government can take many forms. It is possible to have a constitutional government with one ruler, a group of rulers, or rule by the people as a whole, so long as those in power obey the limitations placed on them by the "higher law" of the constitution. Historically, constitutional governments have included monarchies, republics, democracies, and various combinations of these forms of government.

History has shown, however, that problems inevitably arise when a constitutional government is ruled by one person or a small group of people. If all power is given to a select few, it is difficult to ensure that they will obey the limitations placed on them by a constitution. The rulers in such nations would control the armed forces and law enforcement agencies. How could citizens force the rulers to obey their constitution?

Monarchy—rule by a king or queen—was by far the most common form of government in the eighteenth century. The Founders preferred a form of government more broadly representative of the interests of the whole nation.

What alternative models of government could the Founders choose from?

The most obvious alternative to monarchy was a **republic,** a model of government with which the Founders were familiar through their knowledge of ancient history. The Founders admired the republics of ancient Greece and Rome. They also had studied more recent examples of **republican governments,** such as the Italian **city-states** of the Renaissance and the **cantons** of Switzerland.

The Founders differed among themselves about exactly what a republican government was. In general it meant a form of government:

- **Devoted to promoting the public good, the** *res publicae,* **which is Latin for "thing of the people"**
- **In which political authority was shared by all or most of the citizens rather than held by a hereditary monarch**
- **Whose political authority was exercised through the community's chosen representatives in government**

Today we view republican and democratic government as almost the same thing. The United States, we believe, is both a republic and a democracy. The Founders, however, drew a sharp distinction between the two forms of government.

Democracy had traditionally meant a form of government in which ultimate authority was based on the will of the majority.

This majority usually consisted of those classes in the community that had the greatest number of people—it came from the Greek *demos,* meaning people. These classes tended to be the poorer people.

In its purest form, democracy also meant a government in which members participated directly in their own governance instead of through representatives.

The Founders were familiar with democratic institutions. For generations, local government in many of the colonies tended to be democratic in nature. The New England "town meeting" is one example. Based on their reading of history and their own experience, however, the Founders were concerned about democracy as a model for state or national government. Their preference for the republican as opposed to the democratic model of government influenced the framing of the Constitution.

What do you think?

1. **How would you organize a government so it would be fairly easy to remove and replace officials who were not doing a good job?**

2. **What might happen in a government where there was no agreed-on or peaceful means for removing officials? Give a recent example to support your answer.**

3. How did the Founders describe the difference between republican and democratic forms of government? Why do you think the Framers of the Constitution favored the former rather than the latter?

Reviewing and Using the Lesson

1. Explain what is meant by each of the following ideas from the Declaration of Independence:

   - all men are created equal
   - people have certain rights that are unalienable
   - unalienable rights include rights to life, liberty, and the pursuit of happiness
   - governments are created to secure these rights
   - Governments derive their just powers from the consent of the governed
   - People have the right to alter or abolish their government if it becomes destructive of the purposes for which it was created

2. What is meant by "the law of nature" or "natural law"? How did Locke try to establish or figure out what limitations it imposed on human conduct?

3. How did Locke use the idea of a "state of nature" to try to establish or figure out what the purpose of government should be?

4. What was Locke's view of human nature? How did it influence his ideas about what type of government is best?

5. What is meant by the term "social contract"? How is it connected to the idea that government derives its authority from the consent of the governed?

6. Do research to find out about the Mayflower Compact. Explain what it was, why it was created, and how it shows the connection between "social contracts" and the idea that government should be based on consent.

7. How would you explain the difference between a limited government and an unlimited government? Do you think the difference is important? Why or why not?

8. In theory, the government of the United States gets its authority from the consent of the people. What evidence can you identify to show that people actually do consent to be governed by the United States government?

9. What is meant by the claim that the people have a "right of revolution"? What arguments can you make to support the claim that such a right does or does not exist?

10. What is a constitution? What is the difference between a constitution that establishes a constitutional government, and a constitution that does not?

11. Why did the Framers organize the government into separate branches with shared and divided powers? What are some examples of the ways in which governmental power is divided and shared? Why is this sometimes called a system of "checks and balances"?

12. Do research to find out about a country whose written constitution failed to protect the rights of the people. Why did the written constitution fail to establish a constitutional government in that country? What essential things were missing?

Lesson 2

Developing Republican Government

Key Terms

Age of Enlightenment
capitalism
Christendom
civic virtue
classical republicanism
common good
established religion
factions
hierarchical
Judeo-Christian
Middle Ages
mixed government
nation-state
papacy
Providence
public and private morality
Reformation
Renaissance
representative democracy
secular governments

What You Will Learn to Do

- Trace how the American ideas of individual rights developed

Linked Core Abilities

- Communicate using verbal, non-verbal, visual, and written techniques
- Apply critical thinking techniques

Chapter 2

Skills and Knowledge You Will Gain along the Way

- Examine how the ideas of classical republicanism influenced the Founders' ideas of what kind of government they wanted

- Distinguish between classical republicanism and the natural rights philosophy

- Recognize how the ideas of Judeo-Christian tradition, the Middle Ages, the Renaissance, the Reformation and the rise of nation-state and capitalism supported the founders' thinking about natural rights and classical republicanism

- Explore how James Madison refined the ideas of classical republicanism to meet the needs of the new Americans

- Define key words contained in this lesson

Introduction

The Founders were influenced by many ancient thoughts and ideas. From the Roman perspectives of classical government to the Judeo-Christian traditions of moral obligation, our government began to shape into what Americans experience and enjoy as privilege today. In this lesson you explore how the ancient world influenced republican government and how modern ideas of individual rights developed.

What Did the Founders Learn about Republican Government from the Ancient World?

What Ideas about Government Did the Founders Find in Classical Republicanism?

Most of the public buildings and monuments in Washington, D.C., and state capitols across the nation are built in the "classical" style. This architectural tradition symbolizes our nation's indebtedness to the world of ancient Greece and Rome, especially to their ideas about government.

The Founders had studied the history of the classical periods of ancient Greece and Rome. The society that had the greatest influence on their ideas was that of the Roman Republic, which lasted for almost 500 years—509 B.C. to 27 B.C. Many philosophers and historians believed the Roman Republic had provided Roman citizens with the most liberty under government that the world had ever known. It also was believed widely that the Roman Republic promoted the **common good,** that is, what was best for the entire society. The theory based on this form of society became known as **classical republicanism.**

Reprinted from *We the People: The Citizen and the Constitution,* published by the Center for Civic Education.

Classical republicanism is a theory that the best kind of society is one that promotes the common good instead of the interests of only one class of citizens. In a classical republic, citizens and their government are supposed to work cooperatively to achieve the common good rather than their own personal or selfish interests. The Roman Republic was thought to be one of the best examples of this type of society. Americans in the eighteenth century shared the view that citizens should work to promote the common good. They also believed that the type of government and society most likely to promote the common good was only possible if the society and its citizens shared the following characteristics:

- **Civic virtue**
- **Moral education**
- **Small, uniform communities**

Civic virtue. The classical republics demanded that their citizens have a high degree of civic virtue. A person with civic virtue was one who set aside personal interests to promote the common good. Today we might describe this as "public spiritedness."

Citizens were expected to participate fully in their government to promote the common good. They were not to be left free to devote themselves only to their personal interests. They were discouraged from spending much time doing such things as making money or caring for their families. They also were discouraged from traveling or reading and thinking about things that had nothing to do with their government. If citizens had the freedom to do such things, it was feared, they might stop being reliable and fully dedicated to the common good.

To make sure citizens participated in their government, the classical republics often drastically limited individual rights. There was little concern with protecting an individual's privacy, freedom of conscience or religion, or non-political speech or expression.

Certain rights, however, were necessary for citizens to participate in governing themselves. These were political rights, such as the right to vote, to express ideas and opinions about government, and to serve in public office.

Moral education. People who believed in classical republicanism were convinced that civic virtue is not something that comes automatically to people. Citizens must be taught to be virtuous by moral education based on a civic religion consisting of gods, goddesses, and their rituals.

Classical republicans believed that young citizens must be raised in a manner that develops the right habits. They should learn to admire the people with civic virtue described in literature, poetry, and music. The Founders themselves admired such heroes of antiquity as the Roman patriot and orator Cato and the citizen soldier Cincinnatus. The Founders believed they were examples of civic virtue whom Americans should emulate. His fellow Americans admired George Washington as a modern-day Cincinnatus because he sacrificed his private pursuits in order to lead the nation in war and peace. George Washington was often called "our Cincinnatus" because his fellow citizens believed he was an example of the civic virtue that all citizens should possess.

According to classical republicans, children, as well as adults, should be encouraged—partly by the belief in a watchful god or gods—to practice virtues, such as generosity, courage, self-control, and fairness. They should learn the importance of taking part in political debate and military service. The whole community must closely supervise the upbringing of the next generation of citizens and be attentive to how individuals behave in their daily lives.

Small, uniform communities. Classical republicans believed that a republican government would only work in a small community. A small community is necessary if people are to know and care for each other and their common good. In addition, the people must be very much alike. A great degree of diversity should not be tolerated. They did not believe, for example, that people should be very different in their wealth, religious or moral beliefs, or ways of life.

Classical republicans believed that if people differed greatly, they would divide into **factions** or interest groups, rather than work together for the common good. To prevent this, citizens should be encouraged, by education and example, to avoid the development of great differences in their ownership of property, religion, and way of life. To prevent diversity in religious beliefs and lifestyles, they believed the community should have one official, **established religion** and one set of family and moral standards to which all must conform.

Great inequalities of wealth led inevitably to corruption as well as to factions or interest groups. Individuals would be more concerned with their own interest rather than the interest of the community. Their fear of great economic inequality and the corrupting effect of luxury led the classical republicans to be wary of money-making and economic growth. Such economic growth, they thought, gave rise to the great economic inequality which was inconsistent with the goals of republicanism.

Why did classical republicans believe that republican government could only work in small, uniform communities?

What do you think?

1. Identify someone living today who you think shows civic virtue. Explain the reason for your choice.

2. What did classical republicans think should be the goal of education? Do you agree? Why or why not?

3. What civic virtues are important for young people to have today and why?

4. What similarities and differences are there between your ideas about rights and those of the classical world?

Critical Thinking Exercise

Understanding the Differences Between the Natural Rights Philosophy and Classical Republicanism

You may work individually, with a study partner, or in small groups to develop responses to the following questions. Be prepared to share your answers with the class.

1. The classical republican idea of civic virtue conflicted with the Founders' belief in natural rights and their understanding of human nature as defined by John Locke. Create a chart, similar to the example below, that illustrates the differences between natural rights and classical republicanism. In completing your chart, you may need to review some of the ideas presented in Chapter Two, Lesson 1.

Natural Rights Philosophy	Classical Republicanism
1. Stressed the rights of the individual to life, liberty, and property	1. Stressed promoting the common good above the rights of the individual
2.	2.
3.	3.

2. Suppose you were among the Founders chosen to participate in drafting a constitution. How might you reconcile these differences between natural rights and classical republicanism? Which ideas would you choose to emphasize? Why?

3. What problems might you encounter in transferring some of the ideas of classical republicanism to American society? How might you solve these problems?

How did the Founders think a government should be organized to promote the common good?

In addition to the example of the ancient Roman Republic, the Founders also learned about republican government from writers of their own time. One of the most important of these was the Baron de Montesquieu (1689–1755), a French writer who was widely admired by Americans.

Montesquieu advocated a system that **divided** and **balanced** the power of government among the classes. This, he believed, was the best way to ensure that the government would not be dominated by a single social class and would be able to enhance the common good.

He admired the Roman Republic as a representative government that combined elements of three basic types of government: monarchy, aristocracy, and democracy. Since all classes shared power, this type of government seemed best for serving the common good.

Even though Britain was a monarchy, Montesquieu admired the British constitution. He believed it embodied the idea of a **mixed government,** in which power was divided among different classes in British society.

What were some problems in transferring the ideas of classical republicanism to eighteenth-century America?

In some respects, the Founders were uncritical admirers of the ancient world, most especially the Roman Republic. They were inclined to exaggerate the degree to which these states represented the interests of the whole community rather than just the interests of the upper classes. They also overlooked the fact that the ancient republics depended on the institution of slavery. Their admiration for classical republicanism was based on a somewhat idealized version of antiquity.

The Founders were aware of the difficulty in transplanting ideals of classical republicanism to the newly independent American states. They differed concerning the degree to which these ideals could be adopted. The classical republicanism of the ancient world only flourished in small, uniform communities.

The following expectations of classical republicanism posed several problems for the founders of the new American nation:

- **caring for each other and the common good in small communities**
- **believing that people must be very much alike**
- **supervising citizens to avoid the development of great differences among them in their ownership of property, religion, and way of life**
- **believing that great economic inequality is destructive of the common good**
- **having one official "established" religion and one set of family and moral standards which everyone would follow**

How was a political ideal based on small, tightly knit communities to be applied to a new country as large as the young United States, which represented people of different cultural backgrounds, economic conditions, and religious beliefs?

The classical republican idea of civic virtue conflicted with the Founders' belief in natural rights and with their understanding of human nature as defined by Locke and the other natural rights philosophers. The natural rights philosophy considered the rights of the individual to be primary in importance. The state existed to serve the interests of the individual, instead of the other way around. In classical republicanism, the rights of the community as a whole came first.

Americans of the founding era seemed more representative of human nature as described by the natural rights philosophers than the ideal expected by the civic virtue of the classical republicanism. They and their ancestors had come to the new land to take advantage of the opportunities it offered. Such restless, diverse, and ambitious people were ill-suited for the ideals of self-sacrifice and conformity of classical republicanism.

How did James Madison refine the ideas of classical republicanism?

James Madison was one of the most important Founders responsible for creating the U.S. Constitution. He has been called "the Father of the Constitution." He was very influential in translating the ideas of classical republicanism in such a way as to make them practical in the new American republic.

Madison defined the difference between democracies and republics in the following way:

- **In a democracy, the people administer the government themselves. These "direct democracies" must be confined to small communities like the ancient city-states of Greece.**

- **In a republic, the people's representatives administer the government, allowing it to be extended over a much larger area.**

Madison believed, therefore, that America could and should have a republican form of government. Laws would be made and administered by representatives elected by the people. Madison also accepted certain principles of democracy. He insisted that members of government should be elected by a large number of the people, rather than by a small number or a specially favored group. Such a form of government was a democracy in the sense that it derived its authority— its right to govern—from the people as a whole. Madison's new definition of a republican government, therefore, also could be defined as a **representative democracy.** In this way the two classical ideas of republic and democracy were adapted to the new form of government created by the Founders.

How did the Founders adapt the ideal of civic virtue to the American republic?

Like the other Founders, Madison understood the importance of informed and public-spirited citizens to this new government. He had to modify the classic definition of civic virtue to make it practical in the very different conditions of America. He accepted the natural rights philosophers' view of human nature—people were motivated primarily by self-interest. He believed that the pursuit of self-interest could in its own way further the common good. For example, a statesman's desire for fame and admiration from others would lead him to practice civic virtue. The common good could be served by each individual pursuing his or her economic self-interest. Each would contribute to the general prosperity.

Madison also realized that as people pursue their own interests they sometimes act against the interests of others and against the common good. Any sound government had to make allowances for this. As Madison said, if all people were angels, there would be no need for government. He argued for a government that would encourage people to act as good republican citizens possessing the quality of civic virtue. At the same time, this government would guard against the consequences if they did not. This is why Madison favored a constitution that limited government by the following methods:

- **Separation of powers**
- **A system of checks and balances**

The American adaptation of the principles of classical republicanism was, then, a sort of compromise. The Founders created a form of government they called **republican,** even though it was different from the models of republicanism in the ancient world.

They believed that it was important for citizens to possess civic virtue. Civic virtue could not be relied upon, however. Therefore, the proper structure provided by a system of representation with separation of powers and checks and balances also was necessary to protect the common good.

What do you think?

1. **Under a republican form of government, if elected officials hold views of the common good contrary to those of their constituents, what do you think the officials should do? Why?**

2. **Should a member of Congress vote against anti-smoking legislation intended to protect the health of the general population if it would hurt the economy of his or her state and put people out of work in that state?**

3. **To what extent do you think the common good in today's American society depends on the classical republican ideal of civic virtue and to what extent on the natural rights philosophy idea of each individual pursuing his or her own self-interest? Cite examples to support your case.**

How Did Modern Ideas of Individual Rights Develop?

How Did the Judeo-Christian Heritage Contribute to the Founders' Understanding of Human Rights?

The Founders were heirs to another legacy of antiquity, as important in its own way as that of the Greeks and Romans. They belonged to a religious tradition thousands of years old: Judeo- Christianity. Though of different faiths within this tradition, most of the Founders had grown up in a religious environment. From early childhood, they were familiar with the teachings of the Bible.

Reprinted from *We the People: The Citizen and the Constitution,* published by the Center for Civic Education.

The **Judeo-Christian** world view holds that the world was created and is governed by one God. Humanity occupies a special place in that creation. Each human being is created in God's image and each possesses an immortal soul. For many, the striving for salvation through obedience to God's divine law is of prime importance.

Some Founders were critical of organized religion and skeptical of certain religious doctrines. Most believed in a Supreme Being and in that Supreme Being's interest in humanity and affairs of the world. Above all, they were convinced of the importance of each person obeying the moral code that they believed was given by that Supreme Being.

As you know, the Declaration of Independence acknowledges the "Creator" who "endowed men with certain unalienable rights." The Founders often spoke of **"Providence"** to suggest their belief in God's interest and involvement in the affairs of the world. During the writing of the Constitution in the summer of 1787, Benjamin Franklin encouraged his fellow delegates by declaring his conviction that "God governs in the affairs of men."

Whatever their particular religious backgrounds, the Founders believed strongly in the importance of the moral principles of Judeo-Christianity to benefit the common good. Judeo-Christian morality was different from the Greek and Roman ideals of civic virtue. Instead of **public morality,** these principles emphasized **private morality** as expressed in biblical teachings such as the Ten Commandments and the Sermon on the Mount. To classical republican virtues—courage, moderation, and wisdom—Judeo-Christianity added other moral qualities, such as love and benevolence toward others.

To achieve what was best for society as a whole, the Founders thought that each person's moral principles and behavior should be based on both classical and Judeo-Christian virtues. They felt that the practice of religion would help people live according to such moral standards.

Their religious faith also strengthened the Founders' belief in the ideals of justice and liberty. The Bible stories of the struggle of the Hebrews against oppression and tyranny helped to inspire the American Revolution. These words from the Book of Leviticus are inscribed on the Liberty Bell in Philadelphia: "Proclaim liberty throughout all the land unto all the inhabitants thereof."

Finally, the teachings of Judeo-Christianity also helped to develop the Founders' appreciation of individual rights. Classical republicanism put the good of the state and community above that of the separate interests of the individuals who belonged to it.

The Judeo-Christian view of the individual and his or her place in the world was different. Its teachings stressed the dignity and worth of each human being. It was believed that each person possessed an individual soul. Therefore, the individual assumed a new importance in people's thinking about society and government. Much in the Founders' commitment to liberty and individual rights sprang from their belief in the rightness of such ideals.

What were the concepts of the individual and society during the Middle Ages?

Christianity spread rapidly in the centuries following the death of Jesus and eventually became the predominant faith within the Roman Empire. The Roman Empire collapsed in the fifth-century A.D., but Christianity survived to shape European society in the centuries that followed. This period, from the fifth-century to the fourteenth, we call the **Middle Ages**—the period that lies between antiquity and modern times.

Medieval society was based on the ideas of unity, social harmony, and other-worldliness. The European people of the Middle Ages saw themselves united in a single society called **Christendom.** Their spiritual leader was the Pope in Rome. The Popes enjoyed great authority and respect throughout Europe. There were no nations at this time to compete for people's loyalty. Most people thought of themselves in terms of only two allegiances: to their own local community and to the great unity of Christendom with one "universal" or "catholic" church presiding over it.

Medieval ideas about society also reflected the harmony that was thought to exist between each individual and the whole of society. Society was sometimes compared to a body, in which some parts were more important than others but all parts were necessary for the good of the whole. The parts were dependent on each other.

- **Society was divided into different classes and groups such as royalty, nobility, clergy, tradesmen, craftsmen, and peasants. Each class or group had certain rights and responsibilities.**

- **Society was hierarchical, that is, groups and classes were ranked from the most important at the top to the least important at the bottom. There was no equality between groups and classes.**

- **Each individual's role in society was defined by his or her role in one of these groups. A person had little chance of leaving the group into which he or she had been born.**

Why did the Popes and the church attain such important status in the Middle Ages?

- Any rights and duties a person had were usually spoken of in terms of the group to which that person belonged. There was no concept of "natural" or "universal" rights belonging to all people. Rights were seen as privileges or "liberties" belonging to particular groups in society. Members of the group enjoyed its "rights." There were few individual rights.

Medieval society was also other-worldly in its interests and activities. Christianity taught that the primary purpose of this life was to achieve salvation after death in another spiritual eternal life. The most important institutions of the Middle Ages, including churches and monasteries, were devoted to this end. Whatever else people achieved in their lives was secondary.

Economic life in the Middle Ages was based on subsistence agriculture. Most people lived on small farms or manors, producing enough food for the inhabitants to live on. There were few towns or cities. Travel was limited. Most people spent their entire lives within a few miles of the place where they were born. The few economic markets were tightly regulated by the nobility.

What do you think?

1. What is meant by the rights of groups as opposed to the rights of individuals?

2. What are the advantages and disadvantages of viewing rights as being possessed by individuals rather than groups?

3. Give some contemporary examples of claims for group rights. What arguments can you make for and against these claims?

4. Should certain individuals in our society be given special rights and privileges because they are members of a particular social group?

How did the Renaissance contribute to the development of individual rights?

During the medieval period, people did not strive to make "progress." That is, they did not believe that they could make things better for themselves and their children through hard work or individual initiative. Despite these attitudes, medieval cities did develop and prosper. Commerce began to flourish, cities grew, people started to travel more. **Nation-states** began to form. The invention of modern printing methods increased communication and knowledge.

The most important outcome of these changes was the **Renaissance.** The term Renaissance means "re-birth." It describes a rebirth or revival of intellectual life that began in Italy around the fourteenth century and spread throughout Europe. This new interest was inspired by the rediscovery of ancient Greek and Roman history, literature, and art, with a view of the world and humanity that was very different from that of medieval Christianity.

Instead of focusing only on other-worldly matters and the quest for salvation, people took an interest in the world around them. They directed their energy toward the possibilities of human achievement in this life rather than the life to come. They expanded their knowledge and began to develop new ideas about the world. Their art and architecture glorified the beauty of the human body; their literature and philosophy explored all aspects of human nature and human creativity.

During the Renaissance people began to accept the idea of progress and historical change. In many areas of life, greater importance was placed on the individual than on the class or group into which that individual had been born. People believed they could work to improve their positions in society. The new emphasis on individual opportunity led to an increased interest in the rights of individuals. This interest contributed to a reexamination of the individual's relationship to religious institutions and governments.

How did the Protestant Reformation advance the cause of individual rights?

The Protestant Reformation was a powerful stimulus to modern individualism. The **Reformation** was a religious reform movement that began in the early sixteenth century in western Europe. It resulted in new ideas about religion, individual rights, and government. Like the Renaissance, the Reformation was a rebirth and rediscovery of certain things. Supporters of the Reformation believed they were returning to the original principles of Christianity.

Medieval society in western Europe had been dominated by the Church of Rome. Religious reformers, studying the Bible and other ancient religious texts, began to challenge the doctrines, traditions, and practices of the Church of Rome. They believed that the medieval church had become corrupt and had lost sight of the original truths of Christianity. Some critics attempted to reform the church from within, but many Protestant reformers, like Martin Luther and John Calvin, established their own churches with the help of **secular governments.**

The Reformation was aided by the invention of the printing press. Books that formerly were scarce now became more available. The Bible was the most important of these books. For centuries the Bible had been printed only in Latin, which few people other than priests could read. Medieval Christians relied on the Church to interpret the word of God for them. During the Reformation, however, Bibles were printed in English, German, French, Italian, and Spanish. Individuals were encouraged to read the Bible in their native language to determine for themselves what it meant. Being able to read the Bible for oneself encouraged greater freedom of conscience.

Protestant religious doctrine emphasized the direct relationship between each individual believer and God. The result was to reduce the importance of the church and to increase the importance of the individual. All individuals were seen as equal in the eyes of God. Each person is to be respected and held accountable by God as an individual.

The spirit of free inquiry and individual conscience inspired by the Reformation contributed to the development of modern individualism. It also ultimately posed a threat to all established institutions and authority. Some religious reformers soon began to question the authority of the Protestant churches and the governments that supported them. In England, for example, reformers attacked the Church of England for not being Protestant enough. They were called Puritans because they wanted to "purify" the church. Some reformers sought to reform the established church. Others decided to separate from it. Many American colonies were originally settled by people seeking freedom to worship in their own way and new forms of government that would allow this.

What caused the rise of modern nation-states?

The modern nation-state's development was speeded by the forces of change created by the Renaissance and Reformation. There were no nations, as we understand that word today, during the Middle Ages. The power of kings and princes did not reach very far. Power was exercised locally by authorities who usually inherited their power. In theory, at least, all secular governments were subservient to the Church of Rome. They had little authority over church officials and institutions in their territories.

Toward the end of the Middle Ages many of these secular governments were expanding and consolidating their power into independent states. The Reformation helped this development by challenging the Church of Rome. Some states, like England, broke free from the Church of Rome and created their own national churches. Others remained loyal to the **papacy** but reduced the authority of the Church of Rome within their territory.

The rise of the modern nation-state was very important to the development of modern ideas about government and rights. People began to think of themselves as citizens of a particular state or country, with public rights and duties. Political thought began to focus on the question of what kind of government would be best for these states.

The modern nation-state also brought with it national legal systems and representative institutions of government.

What was the new economic system of capitalism?

Among the forces that helped to break up medieval society and pave the way for the Renaissance was the increase in commercial trade and its expansion over greater distances. Eventually, this growth produced a new economic system called **capitalism.** Capitalism is an economic system in which:

- **The means of producing and distributing goods are privately owned and operated for profit in competitive markets**
- **Production and distribution are not controlled by the government**

Under capitalism people gained more freedom to choose their occupations, start their own businesses, and own property. People had more control over their lives than had been possible in the Middle Ages.

People were able to pay more attention to their private interests than to the common good. They were encouraged to work to gain property and improve their positions in society. As a result, political and economic power shifted to a newly developed middle class of successful citizens.

What do you think?

1. **Why do you think Americans in the eighteenth century were so receptive to the new ideas that developed out of the Renaissance and Reformation?**

2. **With the development of capitalism, people began to view the individual differently than they had in antiquity or during the Middle Ages. What was this different view and why did it come about?**

3. **How were the rise of the nation-state and capitalism related to individualism? What effect did they have on the common good?**

How did the Renaissance and Reformation contribute to the growth of individual rights?

The Renaissance and Reformation produced a greater emphasis on the importance of the individual than had existed in the Middle Ages or in classical Greece and Rome. The ideas and opinions of individuals were valued. As the Renaissance emphasized individual activity and creativity, the followers of the Protestant Reformation emphasized the relationship between the individual believer and God. The rise of nation-states stimulated new thought about government and rights. Capitalism translated this new spirit into economic opportunity. More individuals could compete on an equal footing and hope to improve their place in society.

Critical Thinking Exercise
Understanding the Effects of the Renaissance and Reformation on Ideas about Rights

Your teacher will ask you to work in small groups of four or five students to examine how the ideas of the Judeo-Christian tradition, the Middle Ages, the Renaissance, the Reformation, and the rise of the nation-state and capitalism supported the Founders' thinking about natural rights and classical republicanism.

1. **Suppose that you lived in the American colonies during the eighteenth century. Like the Founders, you firmly believe in the ideas of the natural rights philosophers concerning individual rights and the purpose of government. You also believe in classical republican ideas of civic virtue and the common good. Examine what you have learned in this lesson about the Judeo-Christian tradition, the Middle Ages, the Renaissance, the Reformation, and the rise of the nation state and capitalism. Create a chart that illustrates which ideas prevalent during these historical periods influenced your thinking about the importance of the individual, individual rights, and the common good.**

2. **Were there any ideas prevalent during one of these periods which you, as a believer in natural rights and classical republicanism, do not agree with? What are these ideas? Why do you disagree with them?**

3. **Do you think the ideas about the importance of the individual, individual rights, and the common good that emerged during these historical periods have influenced your thinking about the nature and purpose of government? If so, explain how.**

What do you think?

1. **If the ideas about rights that prevailed during the Middle Ages were dominant today, how would they affect your life?**

2. **What conflicts arise in a society that emphasizes both the importance of individual rights and of the common good? What evidence, if any, do you see of such conflicts in your own experiences?**

3. **It has been said: "Each Protestant becomes his own Pope when he has a Bible in his hands." What does this mean? How did the religious revival of the Reformation contribute to modern ideas about individual rights? To constitutional government?**

How did increased interest in scientific study relate to the development of the natural rights philosophy?

What was the Age of Enlightenment?

The natural rights philosophy was a product of what is sometimes called the **Age of Enlightenment.** The Enlightenment was an intellectual movement of the late seventeenth and eighteenth centuries that celebrated human reason and sought to realize its potential in all areas of human endeavor. The Age of Enlightenment is also called the Age of Reason.

The worldly interests inspired by the Renaissance stimulated natural science—the study of the natural world and the laws that govern it. This new interest also was encouraged by commercial expansion and voyages of discovery beyond Europe. These voyages brought new knowledge about the natural world and about other cultures.

One advocate of scientific discovery, the English philosopher Francis Bacon, believed in the power of human reason and observation not only to understand nature, but also to control it for humanity's own purposes. "The end of scientific study," he said, "is the enlarging of the bounds of human empire, to the effecting of all things possible." The discoveries of scientists like Copernicus, Galileo, and Newton seemed to confirm Bacon's faith.

Eventually this spirit of scientific discovery was applied to human nature and society as well. During the Enlightenment people began to apply the method of scientific thinking to the study of society and politics.

The American Founders belonged to the Age of Enlightenment. They believed in the powers of reason and observation to understand the workings of governmental and societal institutions. They thought these powers also would be a guide in ways to improve institutions. With such faith and self-confidence, the Framers of our Constitution thought they could create a new order of government during one summer's deliberations in Philadelphia.

Reviewing and using the lesson

1. What is meant by "the common good"? Give an example of a rule or law that you think promotes the common good.

2. What is meant by the term "civic virtue"? Give an example of a situation in which someone is expected to show civic virtue.

3. What did classical republicans believe the purpose of government should be? What essential characteristics should a society and its citizens possess in order for a classical republican form of government to work? Why would these characteristics be important? How could these characteristics be established or maintained?

4. Why might small, uniform communities be more likely to foster civic virtue than large, diverse communities?

5. How would you describe the differences between the natural rights philosophy and classical republicanism?

6. How did James Madison adapt the ideals of classical republicanism to the large, diverse group of colonies that became the United States? How did he try to compensate or make up for the possible lack of civic virtue in the people?

7. What is the difference between a democracy and a republic? What aspects of the government of the United States suggest it is a democracy? What aspects suggest it is a republic?

8. Do research to find out more about the political philosophy of Baron de Montesquieu. What did he admire about mixed governments? What influence did his ideas have on the Founders?

9. How would you describe the difference between the classical republican idea of civic virtue and Judeo-Christian ideas of morality?

10. How did the Judeo-Christian heritage contribute to the Founders' understanding of human rights?

11. What features of society in the Middle Ages contributed to the view that rights belonged to groups, rather than to individuals?

12. How did the Renaissance contribute to modern ideas about rights? How did the Protestant Reformation contribute to modern ideas about rights? How did the rise of nation-states contribute? How did the economic system of capitalism contribute?

13. Why was the invention of the printing press important in promoting the spirit of individualism?

14. What was the "Age of Enlightenment" and why is it sometimes called the "Age of Reason"?

15. Working with a group of classmates, prepare and perform a skit that shows how ideas about rights during the Middle Ages were different from modern ideas about rights. Think about what the advantages and disadvantages of the view that prevailed during the Middle Ages might be, and find a way to present these advantages and disadvantages in your skit.

Lesson 3

British Origins of American Constitutionalism

Key Terms

American Constitutionalism
burgesses
charters
common law
contracts
due process of law
Magna Carta
manorialism
monarch
parliamentary government
realm
rights of Englishman
rule of law
tenets
vassal

What You Will Learn to Do

- Show how the Founders built on the principles of British representative government

Linked Core Abilities

- Communicate using verbal, non-verbal, visual, and written techniques
- Apply critical thinking techniques

Skills and Knowledge You Will Gain along the Way

- Examine how the nature of the British constitution emerged from struggles between royalty, nobility and the church

- Identify how parliamentary government changed and began to represent the interests of all people

- Identify how the constitutional principles from the English Bill of Rights impacted the U.S. Bill of Rights

- Defend a position on the importance of specific rights such as habeas corpus and trial by jury and on what limitations, if any, should be placed on them

- Define key words contained in this lesson

Introduction

The American colonial period lasted for 150 years. The Founders were loyal subjects of the British crown and were proud to enjoy the rights of Englishmen as protected by the English constitution. The Founders were greatly impacted by the English form of government, which ultimately influenced the creation of United States Constitution. In this lesson you explore how the establishment of representative government in British history influenced the Founders and helped establish some of our most important constitutional rights today.

What Were the British Origins of American Constitutionalism?

How Did English Government Begin?

For several centuries after the fall of the Roman Empire, England was divided among a number of tribes, each ruled by its own leader or "king." These early kings were selected by councils of advisers because they were the strongest and most powerful members of their tribes. For many years these tribes were at war with each other. Eventually all the tribes of England became united under one king. Christianity increased the authority of kingship by teaching that kings were "anointed by God" and that all the people governed by the king were **subject** to his rule—which is why they were called "subjects."

England was too large for one person to rule because quick and efficient means of communication and travel did not exist. Most kings had to let people in local areas tend to their own affairs according to customs that had developed over the years.

What was feudalism?

A major change in the way England was ruled took place on October 14, 1066, when William the Conqueror, the leader of the Normans (from Normandy, France), invaded England and defeated King Harold at the Battle of Hastings. William introduced the new system of feudalism to control the conquered land.

Reprinted from *We the People: The Citizen and the Constitution*, published by the Center for Civic Education.

How did feudalism change the way people were governed?

Feudalism is not easy to define because it varied greatly in different times and different places. Generally, feudalism was a form of political organization in which a lord gave land to other men in return for their personal allegiance and for military and other service. The men who received land from the lord were known as his **vassals**—they served their lord and were entitled to be protected by him.

Feudalism is important to the development of constitutional government because of its ideas about **contracts.** Feudal government depended on a series of agreements or contracts between lords and vassals. Each contract included mutual rights and responsibilities. Thus, feudalism introduced the idea of government based on a contract—those in power pledged to respect the rights of the people who gave them allegiance.

The basis of this feudal system was land use. Parcels of land were divided into self-contained farms or **manors.** Peasants were legally required to remain on the land and in that sense were part of the property enjoyed by the owner or "lord" of the land. Even peasants, however, enjoyed certain customary rights on the manor. For this reason, the system of **manorialism** as well as feudalism helped to develop ideas about the fundamental rights of Englishmen.

What do we mean by the "rights of Englishmen"?

The **rights of Englishmen** had been established slowly over centuries of British history. They were certain basic rights that all subjects of the English **monarch**—king or queen—were believed to have. They were fundamental in the sense that they could not be changed or violated.

The Founders began their lives as loyal subjects of the British Crown, proud to enjoy the rights of Englishmen. This privilege, they believed, set them apart from the other peoples of the world.

Centuries of respect gave these rights a special status. They included:

- **The right to a trial by jury**
- **Security in one's home from unlawful entry**
- **No taxation without consent**

The historical sources of these rights are **custom** and **law.** They were confirmed by **royal charters** and became part of English **common law.** The common law consists of the accumulated legal opinions of judges explaining their decisions in specific court cases. These decisions provide guidelines or precedents for later judgments. The English common law provides the historical foundation of our American legal system.

What is the British constitution?

Unlike the U.S. Constitution, the British constitution did not exist before the creation of a government. The constitution of Great Britain is not a single written document. Instead it is made up of the common law, acts of Parliament, and political customs and traditions.

Three great historical documents are important in the development of the British constitution and the rights of the British people. These are the Magna Carta (1215), the Petition of Right (1628), and the English Bill of Rights (1689).

These documents were written during times of great conflict. Much of English history is the story of a bloody struggle for power between the most important groups in society. These groups were the royalty, nobility, and the clergy. By the thirteenth century, the struggle was mainly between royalty and the **Parliament.** Parliament was originally a council of nobles created to advise the monarch. It soon became the branch of government that represented the most powerful groups in the kingdom.

For hundreds of years, Parliament and the monarch struggled for power. During these conflicts, English subjects were jailed, tortured, and executed. Kings and queens defeated in battle were imprisoned and beheaded. Because of these conflicts, several important legal documents were written that limited the power of the monarch in order to protect the rights of other groups. These documents were important not only in English history, but they also had a great influence on the Founders. One of the most important of these documents is described below.

What was the Magna Carta and why is it important to us?

The first great landmark of British constitutionalism and one of the great **charters** of human liberty originated as a quarrel between a feudal lord and his vassals. One of William the Conqueror's successors, King John, tried to take back some rights and powers of his barons. This was the title of nobility given to principal vassals. The result was a war between the barons and their king, a war that the barons won.

With the support of the church and others, the barons, in June 1215, forced John to sign the **Magna Carta**—Great Charter—confirming certain traditional rights and, by implication, promising not to violate them again. Most of the rights in question were feudal privileges, enjoyed only by the feudal nobility.

The **tenets**—principles or doctrines—of the Magna Carta were very important in the later development of constitutional government:

Government should be based on the rule of law. The Magna Carta was perhaps the most important early example of a written statement of law limiting the power of a ruler. It expresses the idea of limited government by requiring the king to govern according to established rules of law. The Magna Carta, for example, states that no free man could be imprisoned or punished "except by the lawful judgment of his peers and by the law of the land." "Judgment of his peers" did not originally mean trial by jury as we understand it. This statement, however, did explain the principle of **due process of law**, whereby no government could take action against those it governed except by settled and generally agreed on procedures and rules.

Certain basic rights may not be denied by government. In limiting the power of the king, the Magna Carta also expressed the idea that established rights of the governed could not be violated. Most of the rights guaranteed in the Magna Carta belonged only to the feudal nobility. The Magna Carta did, however, secure some rights for others in English society. The king, for example, promised to respect the "ancient liberties and free customs" of London and other towns.

Government should be based on an agreement or contract between the ruler and the people to be ruled. The agreement in the Magna Carta was between the king and a very limited number of his subjects. It did not include the majority of the English people. It did, however, express the feudal principle of drawing up an agreement between parties as a basis for legitimate government. Government by contract meant that if either side broke the agreement, that agreement would no longer be valid.

Later generations also would discover in the Magna Carta the seeds of other important constitutional principles. For example, the American colonists found in King John's promise not to levy certain feudal taxes without the consent of "our common counsel of the kingdom" the principle of no taxation without representation and consent.

Critical Thinking Exercise
Analyzing and Evaluating Specific Rights

People have fought and died to establish such rights as those described in this lesson. It is often difficult, however, to understand their importance from merely reading about them. By examining specific rights more closely and discussing your opinions about them, you may be able to gain a greater appreciation of their meaning and importance. Let's examine more closely some of the provisions of the Magna Carta.

Two parts of the Magna Carta, Articles 39 and 40, contain some of the most important principles of modern constitutionalism. Working in small groups, read and discuss these provisions. Then develop responses to the questions that follow. Be prepared to explain your answers to the class.

> Article 39: *No freeman shall be taken or imprisoned or disseised [dispossessed] or banished or in any way destroyed, nor will We proceed against or prosecute him, except by the lawful judgment of his peers and by the law of the land*

> Article 40: *To no one will we sell, to none will we refuse or delay,...justice.*

1. **What rights are listed in Articles 39 and 40?**

2. **How do these rights limit the power of the king?**

3. **Why would the English nobles want to place such limits on the power of the king?**

4. **What values and interests are protected by these statements?**

5. **What events in the United States or other nations can you identify in which one or more of the above rights have been upheld or violated?**

What do you think?

1. **In what ways might the rights in Articles 39 and 40 be relevant to you today?**

2. **Do you think the declaration of these rights alone is enough to protect individuals from unfair and unreasonable treatment by their government? Why or why not?**

3. **At Runnymede in England, where King John signed the Magna Carta, there are three monuments. One is a tribute to U.S. President John Kennedy. Another is the Magna Carta national memorial erected by the American Bar Association. In addition there is one honoring the Commonwealth airmen who died in World War II. Why do you think the Magna Carta might be especially important to Americans?**

Did the Magna Carta protect the rights of all Englishmen? Why?

How Did Representative Government Begin in England?

How did parliamentary government in England begin?

The Magna Carta brought the law to bear against a law-breaking king. It did not, however, solve the problem of how to make sure the king would continue to comply with the law. The Magna Carta gave King John's barons the right to go to war with him if he broke their agreement. Going to war, however, was not a satisfactory basis for assuring responsible government. A better way began to develop in the century following the Magna Carta.

In the feudal system English kings relied on councils to advise them in the task of governing. The councils came to be called **parliaments,** from the French word *parler,* to speak. At first these councils of advisers included only the leading nobles and clergy of the **realm.** Gradually, the number of members and the role of these councils expanded to more effectively represent the interests of the different parts of the realm.

In the fourteenth century these parliaments divided into two parts or houses: the **House of Lords**—representing the interests of the feudal nobility and major churchmen; the **House of Commons**—representing not the common people as we understand that term, but rather people who were not nobility but who still possessed wealth and stature in the kingdom. The Commons included knights, who represented the shires or counties of the kingdom, and **burgesses,** wealthy merchants and craftsmen, who represented the cities and towns of England.

Parliament developed as a representative institution of government because the kings of England found it an effective way to raise money from their subjects. They also found it an efficient way to make important laws. Henry VIII, for example, used the authority of Parliament to break away from the Church of Rome and to establish the Church of England. English subjects found Parliament to be an effective way to voice their grievances to their monarch and also to limit or check his or her power.

How did the struggles between the English kings and their subjects develop the British constitution?

Eventually, Parliament became so important to English government that it was capable of challenging the king's ability to act without its support. The struggle for ultimate power in England's government came to a head in the seventeenth century, when the Stuart kings and their Parliaments quarreled over a variety of issues, including money, religion, and foreign policy. At the heart of these struggles was a key constitutional issue:

- **Did the king have the authority or prerogative to act independently of established law and parliamentary consent?**

OR

- **Must the king govern through Parliament and accept the ultimate supremacy of Parliamentary law?**

On the outcome of this struggle, which included a bloody civil war, the execution of one king, Charles I, and the overthrow of another, James II, depended the future of British—and American—constitutional government.

What was the Petition of Right?

The constitutional struggles of seventeenth-century England included several important events. One of these events produced a constitutional document almost as important as the Magna Carta: the **Petition of Right** of 1628. Pressed for money, King Charles I sought to raise funds without the consent of Parliament. He also tried to force this money from his subjects through illegal pressures. For example, he required subjects to "quarter" or house soldiers in their homes.

In 1628 Parliament forced Charles to consent to the Petition of Right, which confirmed that taxes could only be raised with the consent of Parliament. It also guaranteed English subjects other rights, including a prohibition against requiring people to quarter soldiers in their homes. The Petition of Right thus strengthened the idea that English subjects enjoyed certain fundamental rights that no government could violate.

What was the connection between the Petition of Right and the Magna Carta?

One parliamentary leader in favor of the Petition of Right was the famous jurist Sir Edward Coke, who was greatly admired by the Founders. Coke championed the

How did the Petition of Right of 1628 strengthen the principle of constitutional government?

rights of Englishmen. He believed that the Magna Carta was not only a victory for feudal privilege but also a confirmation of the fundamental rights belonging to all Englishmen, rights that had existed since time immemorial. The Petition of Right, he believed, was, like the Magna Carta, a confirmation of these ancient rights.

Why is habeas corpus such an important right?

Another important milestone in this constitutional struggle was the **Habeas Corpus Act** of 1678, in which Parliament gained from English monarchs the right of their subjects to a legal document called a **writ of habeas corpus.** The Latin phrase *habeas corpus* means to "have the body." A writ of habeas corpus orders the government to deliver a person it has arrested to a court of law and explain why that person has been arrested and held. If the government cannot produce evidence to show that the arrested person may have broken the law, the person must be set free.

The English subject's right to a writ of habeas corpus may have existed in English law even before the Magna Carta. Its guarantee was also one of the provisions of the Petition of Right. English monarchs, however, had for centuries ignored this guarantee by using unlawful arrest and prolonged imprisonment without trial as weapons against their subjects.

Critical Thinking Exercise

Evaluating the Importance of the Rights to Habeas Corpus and Trial By Jury

The following exercise asks you to examine the rights of habeas corpus and trial by jury. Your class should be divided into two groups, one group will read selection 1 and the other selection 2. Then each group will answer the questions that accompany their selection. Discuss your reading with the entire class.

Group 1: Habeas corpus. The writ of habeas corpus has been called the "Great Writ of Liberty." One constitutional scholar called it "the greatest guarantee of human freedom ever devised by man." Let's examine why this right was thought to be so fundamental.

Suppose you were arrested and imprisoned by the Queen of England. Although you have the right to be tried by the law of the land, the queen's jailers keep you in prison. They refuse to bring you before a court to be charged with a crime and tried.

How could the right to a writ of habeas corpus protect you from such treatment? How could the jailers be forced to bring you into a court of law for a fair hearing?

Suppose you had a family member, a friend, or a lawyer who knew you had been arrested and were being kept in prison. That person could go to court and ask the judge to issue a writ of habeas corpus. This writ would be an order by the judge to your jailer to bring you, that is your "body," to court and present evidence that you have broken the law. If there is evidence, you would be held for trial. If there is no evidence, you would be set free.

Examining the right

1. **What limits does the right to a writ of habeas corpus place on the power of the monarch?**

2. **Why would the English Parliament want to place such limits on the power of the monarch?**

3. **What arguments can you make for this right today?**

4. **What examples of situations in the United States or other nations can you identify that uphold or violate this right?**

5. **Under what conditions, if any, do you think this right should be limited?**

Group 2: Trial by jury. The right to a trial by a jury of one's peers is one of the oldest and most important of the fundamental rights of Englishmen. It has become an essential right in a free society.

Suppose you were arrested and imprisoned by the English king. A judge, appointed and paid by the king, has examined the evidence against you and decided you should be tried for breaking the law.

The English constitution guarantees you the right to be tried by a jury of your peers. This means that a group of people from your community will listen to the evidence the king's prosecutor has against you. They also will hear your side of the story. The jury has the authority to decide if you are guilty or innocent of breaking the law. Its verdict must be unanimous to find you guilty. Jurors also have the power to find you not guilty even if you have broken the law if they think the law in question is unfair.

Examining the right

1. **What limits does the right to a trial by jury place upon the power of the monarch?**

Why is the right to a writ of habeas corpus so important in protecting the rights of a person accused of crimes?

2. **Why would the English Parliament want to place such limits on the power of the monarch?**

3. **What relation does the right to a trial by jury have to the separation of powers and checks and balances?**

4. **What arguments can you make for this right?**

5. **Under what conditions if any, do you think this right should be limited?**

What led to the English Bill of Rights of 1689?

The struggle between the monarch and Parliament came to a head in a bloodless revolution known as the **Glorious Revolution** of 1688. King James II was overthrown and forced to flee the country. The king's son-in-law, Prince William of Orange, and his followers had suspected James II of trying to make Roman Catholicism the established religion in England and of resorting to various illegal acts to accomplish this.

In the **Revolution Settlement** that followed the Glorious Revolution, Prince William and his wife, Mary, succeeded to the throne. A condition of their succession, however, was that they agree to a **Declaration of Rights**. The Declaration was then enacted into law by Parliament as the **English Bill of Rights**. It became the cornerstone of the Revolution Settlement and of England's constitution.

What protections did the English Bill of Rights include?

The English Bill of Rights was a practical and specific document rather than a statement of general constitutional principles. Its primary objective was to make sure that what James II had tried to do would never happen again. It limited the power of the monarch by placing the dominant power of government in Parliament and providing for the security of the Church of England against any attempts at counter-revolution by James or his descendants on behalf of Roman Catholicism.

The English Bill of Rights includes many ideas about rights and government that were later included in our Declaration of Independence, Constitution, and Bill of Rights. In addition to limiting the monarch's power to act without the consent of Parliament, it provides for such traditional rights of Englishmen as trial by jury, prohibition of cruel and unusual punishments, the right to petition the government, and the right to bear arms for personal defense—a right, however, granted only to Protestants.

The English Bill of Rights does not provide for freedom of religion. Nor does it guarantee freedom of the press or freedom of speech outside Parliament. An Act of Toleration, however, passed shortly after the Glorious Revolution, gave freedom of worship to Protestant dissenters. Though not included in the act, Roman Catholics were thereafter generally left alone to practice their faith. The government also expanded freedom of the press by repealing the act that allowed censorship of printed material.

How does the English Bill of Rights differ from the U.S. Bill of Rights?

The English Bill of Rights differs from the U.S. Bill of Rights in several important respects. The former was ratified by Parliament and could be changed by Parliament. The U.S. Bill of Rights was ratified by the people and could only be changed with their consent through the amending process of the Constitution.

The English Bill of Rights was intended primarily to limit the power of the monarch and increase the power of Parliament. The U.S. Bill of Rights was intended to prohibit the federal government from violating the individual rights of all people and to protect the rights of minorities.

The Glorious Revolution and the English Bill of Rights, however, express several important constitutional principles that influenced our Constitution and Bill of Rights. These were

- **Rule of law.** The English Bill of Rights restated the old idea that legitimate government must be according to the rule of law. Both government and the governed must obey the laws of the land.

- **Parliamentary supremacy.** The Glorious Revolution finally settled the question of supremacy in the English government. While retaining important executive powers, the monarch must govern through Parliament. Parliamentary law was the highest law in the land.

- **Government by contract and consent.** By over-throwing a monarch who broke the law and by declaring respect for the English Bill of Rights as a condition for his successors, the Glorious Revolution confirmed the idea that government is based on a contract between the rulers and those who are ruled.

What do you think?

1. In what ways did the British documents about rights reinforce the major ideas found in the Magna Carta? In what ways did they expand upon these ideas?

2. How are the ideas in the Magna Carta, the Petition of Right, and the English Bill of Rights related to the natural rights philosophy?

3. Why might an understanding of British history have led the Founders to want to protect the right of religious freedom and dissent?

Why did Montesquieu admire the British constitution?

Many Europeans admired the British constitution in the eighteenth century. They were impressed by the degree of liberty enjoyed by British subjects and by

How did the Glorious Revolution of 1688 and the resulting English Bill of Rights change the balance of power between the monarch and Parliament?

the growing power and wealth of the British Empire. One admirer of the British constitution was the French philosopher Montesquieu, whose writings on classical republicanism we discussed earlier. His interpretation of the British constitution had a great influence on the Founders.

Montesquieu admired what he believed to be the "mixed" nature of the British constitution, which included the best of monarchy—the king or queen, aristocracy—the House of Lords, and democracy—the House of Commons. This constitution was, he believed, a modern example of the classical republican model of government. Montesquieu also saw in the British constitution the principle of separation of powers in government, whereby the executive, legislative, and judicial powers are independent of each other.

To some extent, however, Montesquieu misinterpreted how the British constitution worked. It was not as "mixed" in its composition as he believed. Both the House of Lords and House of Commons in the eighteenth century were predominantly aristocratic. Moreover, the three branches of government were not fully separated. The monarch through his or her ministers took an active part in the affairs of Parliament. English judges also were considered part of the executive branch.

The British constitution as secured by the Glorious Revolution did, however, create a **balance of power** between the monarch and the two houses of Parliament. Judges were granted independence from both the monarch and Parliament to interpret the law fairly. This balance of power was a first step toward the idea of separation of powers and checks and balances in our Constitution.

Reviewing and Using the lesson

1. What is meant by the "rights of Englishmen"? How were these rights established?

2. What is the common law? How does it develop?

3. What was feudalism and how did it contribute to the development of constitutional government?

4. What is the Magna Carta? How was it created? How did it contribute to the development of constitutional government?

5. What ideas in the U.S. Constitution or in your state constitution can you trace back to the Magna Carta?

6. How would you describe the evolution of parliamentary government in England?

7. Among the key events in the struggle for power between the Crown and Parliament were the Petition of Right of 1628, the Habeas Corpus Act of 1678, and the Glorious Revolution of 1688. Describe how each of these contributed to the development of constitutional government in England.

8. How does the English Bill of Rights differ from the U. S. Bill of Rights?

9. In recent years proposals have been made to limit or restrict the right to habeas corpus. Do research to find out about these proposals. What concerns are they intended to address? What arguments have been made for an against these proposals? Given what you have learned in this lesson about the importance of writ of habeas corpus, what do you think of these proposals?

Lesson 4

Colonial Government–Basic Rights and Constitutional Government

Key Terms

Boston Massacre
Boston Tea Party
Committees of Correspondence
constituents
convenant
Declaration of Independence
established religion
First Continental Congress
Fundamental Orders of Connecticut
governors
indentured servant
Intolerable Acts
legislatures
magistrates
Massachusetts Body of Liberties
Mayflower Compact
Minutemen
primogeniture
Quartering Act
Seven Years War
Sons of Liberty
sovereignty
Stamp Act Congress
suffrage
Tea Act
The Laws and Liberties
writs of assistance

What You Will Learn to Do

- Form an opinion about how the Declaration of Independence reflects your ideas about the purpose of government and protection of individual rights

Chapter 2

Linked Core Abilities

- Communicate using verbal, non-verbal, visual, and written techniques
- Apply critical thinking techniques

Skills and Knowledge You Will Gain Along the Way

- Explain how differences between colonial America and Europe affected the Founders' beliefs about government and individual rights
- Consider how you, as a citizen today, would view the limitation of many rights to white, male, property owners
- Show how the Declaration of Independence justified the arguments for separation of the colonies from Great Britain
- Examine what the Declaration of Independence says about the purpose of government and protection of individual rights
- Define key words contained in this lesson

Introduction

In this lesson you consider why the American colonists who founded your country decided to seek independence from England. You examine how the Founders carefully crafted the Declaration of Independence to summarize their reasons for seeking independence and to lay the groundwork that would give us a government that would better protect our rights. Finally, you have an opportunity to judge if the rights the American colonists worked to protect measure up to today's equal rights expectations.

What Basic Ideas about Rights and Constitutional Government Did Colonial Americans Have?

How Did the Colonial Settlement of America Inspire New Experiments in Constitutional Government?

Almost half of our history as a people—over 150 years—took place before we gained our independence in 1776. This history had a great influence on the Founders.

The many thousands of immigrants in the seventeenth and early eighteenth centuries came to America for various reasons. The most common were eco-

Reprinted from *We the People: The Citizen and the Constitution,* published by the Center for Civic Education.

nomic and religious. The English colonists brought with them English customs, laws, and ideas about good government. They were separated from England, however, by 3,000 miles of ocean. Consequently, the colonists soon discovered that they would have to improvise, adapt old ideas, and develop new ones if they were to survive.

In some respects, the settlement of America meant a return to a state of nature as later described by the natural rights philosophers. This new experience required new political solutions. One of our country's oldest and most famous charters, the **Mayflower Compact**, was a **covenant** or social contract, to which the Pilgrims agreed prior to landing in Plymouth, Massachusetts, in 1620. The Compact established a civil body authorized to make laws and appoint officers.

What was unique about the American experience?

The special conditions of an undeveloped land profoundly affected economic, social, and political life in colonial America. Land was cheap and readily available. People available to till this land or perform other jobs in colonial society were always in short supply.

Cheap land and the great demand for workers meant that most American colonists had far greater opportunities to get ahead and achieve prosperity than most people in Europe. While some became very wealthy, others failed, creating a class of American poor. But the great majority realized at least a moderate prosperity that was beyond their reach in Europe. Almost any white man with ambition could gain the fifty acres of land required as a qualification to vote in most colonies.

There was no nobility whose social and economic status was protected by law. In Great Britain laws prohibited the sale and distribution of property attached to a noble title; it had to be handed down to eldest sons—the right of **primogeniture.** Since economic and political power was based on this property, generations of noble families had a privileged status in English government and society.

It is true that those people who came from educated British families or those with great personal wealth had an advantage over those who arrived in the colonies almost penniless and unknown. But wealth and family name did not mean automatic success in a land without a rigid class system; and the lack of these advantages rarely held back for long those with ambition. The carpenter and brick mason, for example, enjoyed modest social status in England. The constant demand for new buildings in America, however, allowed such craftsmen to earn a living equal to many of their social "superiors." A well-born gentleman from Europe who considered hard work or manual labor beneath him might have a difficult time surviving in the colonies.

Thus, there was greater equality among Americans than among Europeans in their economic, social, and political life. While some upper class Americans might not have liked this situation, equality of opportunity and the chance to better one's position in life became fundamental ideals in the American experience. In this land of almost unlimited opportunity, one of a candlemaker's 17 children, Benjamin Franklin, could rise to become a great inventor, statesman, and diplomat. An English corset-maker's son, Thomas Paine, could become a famous writer on behalf of the American Revolution. Alexander Hamilton, the illegitimate son of poor parents, could become the first Secretary of the Treasury of the newly formed United States.

Critical Thinking Exercise

Examining an Original Document about Colonial Life

In the mid-eighteenth century a colonial farmer, Philip Taylor, wrote about his life on the border of what today is the state of Vermont. Read what he wrote and then be prepared to discuss your answers to the questions that follow.

> *We now have a comfortable dwelling and two acres of ground planted with potatoes, Indian corn, melon, etc. I have 2 hogs, 1 ewe and a lamb; cows in the spring were as high as 33 dollars, but no doubt I shall have 1 by fall.*
>
> *I am living in God's noble and free soil, neither am I slave to others...I have now been on American soil for two and a half years and I have not been compelled to pay for the privilege of living. Neither is my cap worn out from lifting it in the presence of gentlemen.*

1. **What was it that Philip Taylor liked about life in America?**

2. **What rights did he enjoy? How are they related to the ideas of the natural rights philosophers? Do you enjoy these rights today?**

3. **Given what you know of Philip Taylor's experiences, explain why he would be more or less likely to favor laws that:**

   - **Guarantee each individual the right to be secure in his property**

   - **Limit an individual's right to buy and sell goods to anyone he or she chooses**

   - **Give people certain rights because they are wealthy or from a certain family background or group**

What basic ideas of constitutional government did the colonial governments use?

The colonies were originally founded by charters or grants given to private groups or individuals. These charters and grants said little about what form of local government the colonies should have. As a result the colonies developed their own forms of government, and America became a fertile ground for constitution making. The colonies depended more on written constitutional arrangements than was the case in England, whose own unwritten constitution represented centuries of evolution.

In creating such limited government, the colonists tried to protect themselves not only from abuse of power by the English government in London, but also from abuses by colonial governments themselves. The first governments of many of the colonies lacked constitutional restraints that were later seen as essential. Some of the early colonial governments persecuted those who refused to conform to the **established religion.** Resistance to religious persecution in the colonies became an important stimulus to the advancement of constitutional ideas and institutions.

There are many stories of religious dissenters who were persecuted in these early years. Anne Hutchinson, a brilliant and talented woman, arrived in Massachusetts in 1634 with her husband and seven children. She gained great respect as a midwife, healer, and spiritual counselor. Before long she began preaching a theory of salvation that was contrary to the official Puritan beliefs. Not only was she a dissenter but as a woman she was particularly offensive to the male leaders of the community. Brought to trial, she was cast out of the colony as "a heathen and a leper."

Hutchinson fled Massachusetts to Rhode Island where religious dissenters were tolerated. It was the first colony to grant freedom of conscience to everyone. The Charter of 1663 provided that "noe person...shall bee any wise molested, punished, disquieted, or called in question, for any differences of opinione in matters of religion." Jews, Quakers, Catholics, and others not welcomed elsewhere found a haven in Rhode Island.

Others were inspired by constitutional values early on. The first colonial constitution was the **Fundamental Orders of Connecticut,** created in 1639 by three town settlements along the Connecticut River. Deriving its authority from all free men living in these towns, this constitution established a central legislative body for making laws. The other colonies would adopt constitutional arrangements of their own in the years that followed.

Some of these experiments were successful. Others failed or had to be revised many times before they became practical. The forms of colonial government varied somewhat from colony to colony. They all, however, shared certain basic constitutional principles. These principles generally reflected the influence of England but in some ways they differed. The ideas of British constitutionalism embodied in the governments of the British colonies follow.

Why is it important to protect the right to dissent?

Fundamental rights. The colonists were concerned foremost with protecting those fundamental rights they believed they had brought with them from England. At first these basic rights were seen as the ancient and fundamental rights of Englishmen. These basic rights were later described as the rights of all men. They were defined by the natural rights philosophers as the natural rights to life, liberty, and property.

Rule of law. In order to protect their fundamental rights, the colonists insisted on the creation of a government of laws, in which those responsible for making and enforcing the laws could not exercise arbitrary power as had been the case in some of the first colonial governments. The colonial constitutions also included the idea that the English law was higher law and was superior to any laws the colonial governments might make.

Separation of powers. To a greater extent than in the British government, colonial governments provided for a separation of powers among the three branches of government. In colonial governments the three branches tended to be more independent of each other. Separation of powers was evident in the following ways:

- **An executive branch. Governors** **were responsible for carrying out and enforcing law. In most of the colonies by the time of the American Revolution, the governors were chosen either by the monarch or the proprietors. Only in Connecticut and Rhode Island were the governors elected by those men in the colonies who were allowed to vote.**

- **A legislative branch. All the colonies had legislatures that were responsible for making laws. All but Pennsylvania were similar to the Parliament in Britain with an "upper house" like the House of Lords and a "lower house" like the House of Commons. Members of the upper house were either appointed by the governor or elected by the most wealthy property owners of the colony. The lower house was elected by all the men in the colony who owned a certain amount of property. Pennsylvania was an exception; it had only one house. More independent of the executive branch than the British Parliament, the colonial legislatures would eventually become the strongest of the three branches of government.**

- **A judicial branch. This branch was made up of judges called magistrates who were usually appointed by the governor. Their responsibility was to handle conflicts over the laws and to preside at trials of those accused of breaking the law. They also were responsible for making sure the colonies were being governed in a way that was consistent with English law and tradition.**

Checks and balances. Power was separated and in some cases shared among these branches, so that the use of power by one branch could be **checked** by that of another. That is, the power of one branch could be opposed and therefore limited by the power of another branch.

The powers of the **governors** were checked because they could not

- **collect taxes without the consent of the legislature**

- **imprison people without a trial by a magistrate**

- **set their own salaries**

The **legislatures'** powers were checked by

- reliance on the governor to enforce the laws that they passed
- the power of the judges to make sure they did not make laws that violated those of England
- the veto power held in some colonies by the governor

The powers of the **judges** were checked by

- their being appointed by the governor
- the governor or legislature having the power to remove them if their decisions seemed inappropriate
- their reliance on the governor to enforce their decisions
- the basic right of every Englishman to a trial by a jury of his peers from the community

Representative government and the right to vote. One of the most important constitutional developments during the colonial period was the growth of representative institutions in government. Representative government began soon after the first colonies were established. The first representative assembly was held in Virginia as early as 1619. The right of colonists to elect representatives was seen as a way to

- reduce the possibility that members of government would violate the people's rights
- make sure that at least a part of the government could be counted on to respond to the needs and interests of the people, or at least of those people who had the right to vote. It also established firmly the principle that those governed could not be taxed without their consent or that of their representatives.

Why did colonial governments become more representative than Britain's?

Like their English counterparts, the American colonists believed that the security of life and liberty depended on the security of property. Thus, property had to be protected. This explains why in the colonies as well as England there was a property requirement for the enjoyment of political rights like voting. If one of the purposes of government was to protect property, it seemed reasonable to limit **suffrage**—the right to vote-to those who possessed at least a small amount of property.

Fifty acres was the usual requirement for voting in the colonies. Since land was easily acquired in America, the body of eligible voters was proportionally larger than in England and the colonial legislatures were accordingly more representative. The economic opportunities in America meant that a larger proportion of colonial society enjoyed political rights than was the case in England.

There were other important differences between elections to the colonial legislatures and those to Parliament. More colonial elections offered the voters a choice of candidates. The colonial legislators were elected more frequently than members of Parliament, who usually faced reelection only once in seven years.

Unlike their British counterparts, colonial legislators usually came from the districts they represented and were considered to be the agents of their **constituents'** interests. By the time of the Revolution, members of the British Parliament, on the other hand, were said to be representative of the interests of the nation as a whole. The colonists were considered part of the British nation. Therefore, the British argued, the colonies were represented in Parliament.

What basic rights did most Americans enjoy?

The royal charter that established the Jamestown colony in Virginia in 1607 declared that

> [T]he persons that shall dwell within the colony shall have all Liberties as if they had been abiding and born within this our realm of England or any other of our said dominions.

Similar guarantees were included in the royal charters establishing Massachusetts, Maryland, and other colonies. Such guarantees echoed the ideals of the Magna Carta—that all Englishmen, wherever they went, enjoyed certain fundamental rights, which needed to be confirmed from time to time in official documents.

This tradition became a fundamental part of American constitutionalism and led eventually to the U.S. Bill of Rights. The first of the colonial charters of rights was the **Massachusetts Body of Liberties,** adopted in 1641. This charter secured the rule of law and protection of basic rights of persons living in that colony against any abuse of power by the colony's magistrates. In some respects this document was America's first bill of rights.

Why did more people in America enjoy the right to vote than in England?

No man shall be arrested, restrayned, banished nor anywayes punished...unless by vertue of some express laws of the country warranting the same.

The Body of Liberties guaranteed trial by jury, free elections, and the right of free men to own property. It also made it illegal for government to take property away without fair compensation. It prohibited forced self-incrimination as well as cruel and unusual punishment, rights that later were incorporated into the U.S. Bill of Rights. Though it limited suffrage in Massachusetts, the Body of Liberties granted nonvoters certain political rights, including the right of petition, which was to become part of the First Amendment.

Similar chartered guarantees of basic rights were later passed in other colonies. In addition to such guarantees as freedom from illegal arrest, trial by jury, and no taxation without consent, Pennsylvania's first constitution provided for freedom of conscience. By the eighteenth century all of America's colonies had come to acknowledge this basic right, though in some colonies full enjoyment of political rights remained restricted to those belonging to the established religion in the colony.

Most of these charters guaranteed rights that were familiar to English law. Sometimes they went even further than English law. The Massachusetts Body of Liberties, for example, was followed seven years later by an even more comprehensive code of laws, called **The Laws and Liberties** (1648). This code abolished the laws of primogeniture. It also provided more humane treatment of convicted criminals and debtors and simplified the judicial process.

What do you think?

1. **Did the colonists enjoy a greater degree of representation in their local governments than British citizens had in Parliament? Why or why not?**

2. **Why were voting rights limited to men of property in the colonies and England despite the belief in representative government?**

3. **In what ways did the colonists' experience with limited self-rule for over 150 years affect their ideas about government?**

Did all Americans enjoy these rights?

Not all Americans, however, enjoyed the rights that had been secured in the colonial constitutions. In some colonies the right to vote or hold office remained restricted to male Protestants, in others it was restricted to those who belonged to the established state religion.

Women were denied political rights. Colonial laws limited their ability to own property and manage their own legal and personal affairs. Although laws varied in different colonies, women usually had the legal status of underage children. When they married, they lost most of their legal identity to their husbands. According to English law,

The husband and wife, are one person...the very being or legal existence of the woman is suspended during the marriage.

There were also in the colonies a large number of **indentured servants,** most of them white, who were little better than slaves while they completed their period of service.

The most glaring example of the violation of rights was the permanent enslavement of Africans, which had become well established in the American colonies by the eighteenth century. Slaves, who made up twenty per cent of the population at the time of the Revolution, were treated as property and thus denied their basic human rights. Much of the prosperity enjoyed by colonial Americans came from slave labor.

The contradiction between the colonists' demands for liberty and their continued tolerance of slavery was often noted by the British at the time of the American Revolution. As one English observer asked, "How is it that we hear the loudest yelps for liberty among the drivers of negroes?" The Reverend Samuel Hopkins criticized his fellow Americans for "making a vain parade of being advocates for the liberties of mankind, while...you at the same time are continuing this lawless, cruel, inhuman, and abominable practice of enslaving your fellow creatures."

Critical Thinking Exercise
Evaluating the Institution of Slavery by Using the Natural Rights Philosophy

Twenty percent (700,000) of the 3,500,000 people living in the colonies in 1776 were enslaved Africans. Slavery flourished in the plantation economy of the southern colonies, but existed elsewhere and was legally recognized throughout the colonies. New York City had a significant slave population, as did New England.

There was some opposition to slavery among the population of free citizens as well as among the slaves themselves. Some opponents sought its peaceful abolition; others were willing to use violent or illegal means.

1. **How might the natural rights philosophy be used to oppose slavery in the colonies?**

2. **How might the supporters of slavery also have appealed to the natural rights philosophy to justify their cause?**

3. **Is slavery compatible with the natural rights philosophy? Explain.**

How did the colonial experience prepare Americans for independence?

By the time Americans became independent, they had acquired more than 150 years of experience in self-government at the local level. Such self-government had become necessary because of the colonies' distance from the government in England. This long experience in self-government would become invaluable in building a new nation.

The colonists had adapted the governmental institutions and constitutional principles inherited from England to meet their own special needs. They had created colonial constitutions that embodied such important principles as the rule of law and a separation of powers between the executive, legislative, and

DESCRIPTION OF A SLAVE SHIP.

How does this diagram of a typical slave transport vessel show the inhumanity of the slave trade?

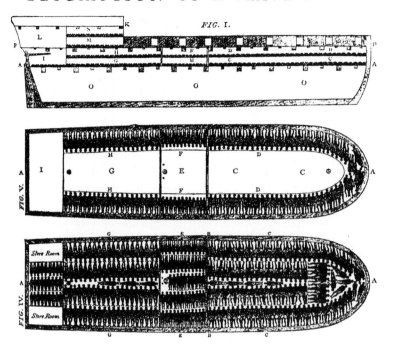

judicial functions of government, thus limiting the power of government through checks and balances.

Perhaps most important to America's future were the legacies of strong representative government and written guarantees of basic rights. As they developed, colonial legislatures became more representative and independent than the British Parliament. Colonial charters guaranteeing fundamental rights became treasured reminders of the colonists' constitutional inheritance. Together, these two traditions of representative government and written guarantees of rights would provide a basis for the American Revolution.

What do you think?

1. **In what ways were eighteenth-century American and British societies similar or dissimilar in terms of the rights of individual liberty, equality of opportunity, and property?**

2. **What effect did colonial experiences have on the Founders' views about rights and government?**

3. **In what ways were liberty and opportunity for women and minorities restricted because of limited property rights in eighteenth-century America?**

4. **Do you think the same degree of social and economic opportunity exists for immigrants to America today? What has remained the same? What has changed?**

Reprinted from *We the People: The Citizen and the Constitution,* published by the Center for Civic Education.

Why Did the American Colonists Want to Free Themselves from Britain? What Basic Ideas about Government Did the Founders Put in the Declaration of Independence?

What was Britain's new policy toward the colonies?

After 1763, several factors caused the British to exert more control over the American colonies than in the previous 150 years. Britain had incurred large debts in its great victory over the French in the **Seven Years War** of 1756–1763. In North America this war was known as the French and Indian War. The British government was under heavy pressure to reduce taxes at home. To the British ministers this meant the American colonists paying a fair share of the war debt.

Between the end of the war in 1763 and the Declaration of Independence in 1776, Britain tried to increase control of the colonies. To reduce tensions with the Native Americans, the British government passed a law forbidding the colonists from settling in the western territories. To raise revenue, the government increased control of trade and customs duties. The **Stamp Act** of 1765 introduced a new kind of tax on the colonists by imposing duties on stamps needed for official documents. To the British these measures seemed reasonable and moderate, but they had a common flaw. They lacked a fundamental principle of the natural rights philosophy-the consent of the governed.

Why did the colonists resist British control?

Generations of colonists had grown used to very little interference from the British government in their affairs. The new policies meant a change in these conditions. Although some colonists accepted the new measures, many others resisted. New trade restrictions and taxes meant some colonists would lose money. Perhaps more important, the new regulations challenged their belief in representative government. Locke had said,

What basic rights are violated when the government orders private citizens to "quarter" soldiers?

*...the supreme power cannot take from any man any part of his property with-
out his own consent..., that is, the consent of the majority, given it either by
themselves or their representatives chosen by them.*

The colonists believed that each man had a natural right to life, liberty, and
property. Consequently, they thought that tax laws should only be passed in
their own colonial legislatures, in which they were represented. "No taxation
without representation" had become an established belief of settlers in the
American colonies.

Colonists calling themselves the **Sons of Liberty** rioted against the Stamp Act.
Representatives from the colonies met in the **Stamp Act Congress** to organize
resistance—the first such gathering in American history. The British government's response created new grievances. For example, the **Quartering Act** of
1765 forced the colonists to shelter British soldiers in their homes. To the
colonists this violated a basic guarantee of the Petition of Right.

Writs of assistance gave government officials new powers to search and seize
colonial property. Colonists charged with various crimes were transported to
England for trials that were frequently delayed.

The **Boston Massacre** of 1770 helped convince many Americans that the British
government was prepared to use military and arbitrary rule to force the
colonists into obedience. The **Tea Act** of 1773 reasserted the right of Parliament
to tax the colonists and led to the **Boston Tea Party.** The British government
responded angrily with what were called the **Intolerable Acts,** closing Boston
harbor to all trade. These measures attacked representative government in
Massachusetts by giving more power to the royal governor, limiting town meetings, weakening the court system, and authorizing a massive occupation of the
colony by British troops.

Critical Thinking Exercise
Identifying Violations of Rights

Each of the following situations is based on the experiences of colonists in
America. Each has at least one British violation of a right that Americans
thought they should have. If you had been an American colonist at the time,
what rights would you claim on the basis of such experiences?

1. **Your name is Mary Strong. You have lived in Charlestown most of your life and
   have strong feelings about how Massachusetts is being governed. Whenever you
   speak your mind freely, you find yourself arrested and put in an iron device
   that fits over your head like a mask to prevent you from talking.**

2. **Your name is Elsbeth Merrill. While you were baking bread this afternoon and
   awaiting the return of your husband, an agent of the king arrived to inform you
   that you must shelter four British soldiers in your home.**

3. **Your name is Lemuel Adams and you have a warehouse full of goods near
   Boston Harbor. The king's magistrate gives British officials a writ of assistance
   that enables them to search all homes, stores, and warehouses by the harbor to
   look for evidence of smuggling.**

Should publishers be prohibited from printing criticisms of government leaders? Why? Why not?

4. **Your name is James Otis. You represent colonists who have been imprisoned and are being denied their right to a trial by a jury from their own communities. You argue that to deny their traditional rights as British subjects is illegal because it violates the principles of the British constitution. The royal magistrate denies your request and sends the prisoners to England for trial.**

5. **Your name is William Bradford. You have been arrested and your printing press in Philadelphia destroyed for printing an article criticizing the deputy governor. In the article you said the governor was like "a large cocker spaniel about five foot five."**

How did the colonists organize to resist British control?

Committees of Correspondence were formed to publicize colonial opposition and coordinate resistance throughout the colonies. In the fall of 1774, twelve of the thirteen colonies sent representatives to a meeting in Philadelphia to decide on the best response to the actions of the British government. The meeting was the **First Continental Congress.** Its members agreed to impose their own ban on trade with Great Britain in an attempt to force the British government to change its policies toward the colonies. British officials, however, considered that decision an act of irresponsible defiance of authority and ordered the arrest of some leading colonists in Massachusetts.

By this time many of the more radical colonists, especially in New England, were beginning to prepare for war against Great Britain. They believed it was the right of the people to overthrow any government that no longer protected their rights. The colonists formed civilian militia of **Minutemen,** supposedly ready at a minute's notice to respond to the British attack that everyone expected.

On April 19, 1775, British troops tried to march to Concord, Massachusetts, where they had heard that the Minutemen had hidden arms and ammunition. The colonists were alerted by Paul Revere and William Dawes who rode through the countryside warning people that the British were about to attack. On that day, at the towns of Lexington and Concord, war broke out between the colonies and Great Britain—the "shot heard around the world" had been fired.

What was the purpose of the Declaration of Independence?

With Americans fighting the British, Richard Henry Lee of Virginia introduced a resolution in the Continental Congress on June 7, 1776, that called for a declaration of independence.

The **Declaration of Independence** was drafted by Thomas Jefferson. The Declaration announced the final, momentous step in the colonies' resistance to the British government. It renounced that government's sovereignty over them.

Every state, no matter what its form of government or constitution, must have an authority beyond which there is no appeal. **Sovereignty** means that supreme authority in a state.

Sovereignty in Britain rests in the British Parliament. Parliament can, as some have said, "do anything but make a man a woman." It could, if it wished, repeal the English Bill of Rights or the remaining guarantees of Magna Carta, or in other ways change Britain's unwritten constitution. Parliament would not likely use its sovereign power in such ways because of respect for the unwritten constitution by its members and by the British people as a whole.

Rebellion against the sovereignty of a government to which the colonists and generations of their forbears had sworn allegiance was a serious matter. Members of the Continental Congress believed it important to justify this action to other nations, to win both sympathy and active support.

What were the main ideas and arguments of the Declaration?

The Declaration of Independence is the best summary available of the colonists' ideas about government and their complaints about British rule. It does not make an appeal on behalf of the king's loyal subjects to the fundamental "rights of Englishmen." The Declaration renounces the monarchy itself and appeals to those natural rights common to all men and women everywhere. It identifies sovereignty with the people.

The complete text of the Declaration of Independence is in the Reference Section. These are its most important ideas and arguments:

1. **The rights of the people are based on natural law, that is a higher law than laws made by men. Its existence is "self-evident." It is given by God and is "unalienable." Neither constitutions nor governments can violate this higher law. If a government violates the law and deprives the people of their rights, they have the right to change that government or abolish it and form a new government.**

2. **A compact or agreement existed between the colonists and the king. By the terms of this compact, the colonists consented to be governed by the king—deriving his "just powers from the consent of the Governed"—so long as he protected their rights to "life, liberty, and the pursuit of happiness."**

3. "Whenever any form of government becomes destructive of those Ends" for which government is created, it is the right of the people to "alter or abolish it" and to create a new government that will serve those ends.

4. The king had violated the compact by repeatedly acting with Parliament to deprive the colonists of those rights he was supposed to protect. These violations and other abuses of power, the Declaration argued, suggest the creation of an "absolute Tyranny" over the colonies by a "Tyrant" who is "unfit to be the Ruler of a free People." He is accused of:

   - Seeking to destroy the authority of the colonial legislatures by dissolving some and refusing to approve the laws passed by others

   - Obstructing the administration of justice by refusing to approve laws for support of the colonial judiciary and making judges dependent on his will alone

   - Keeping standing armies among the people in time of peace without the approval of the colonial legislatures

   - Quartering soldiers among the civilian population

   - Imposing taxes without consent

   - Depriving colonists of the right to trial by jury

   - Attacking the colonial charters, abolishing laws, and changing fundamentally the constitutions of colonial governments.

5. The colonists therefore had the right to withdraw their consent to be governed by the king of Great Britain and to establish their own government as "Free and Independent States…absolved from all allegiance to the British Crown."

What impact did the experience of the American Revolution have on American constitutionalism?

During the first years of independence, the grievances that had persuaded the American colonists to seek independence had an effect on how Americans shaped their state and national governments. The abuses of power by the British government made them distrustful of strong central government and strong executive power. The violation of such fundamental rights as:

- Freedom of speech and assembly
- Trial by jury
- Security from illegal search and seizure of property, and
- Protection from military rule

convinced them to secure these rights by formal declarations in the new state constitutions and eventually in the U.S. Constitution.

What do you think?

1. The Declaration of Independence states that people have a right to abolish their government. Under what circumstances, if any, do you think such an action is justified? Would the Founders agree?

2. Would the Declaration of Independence justify a state leaving the union if a majority of its citizens wished to do so? Why or why not?

3. What was the intended audience for the Declaration of Independence? Does this focus explain the Declaration of Independence's appeal to "natural rights" instead of to "rights of Englishmen"?

Reviewing and using the lesson

1. What was the Mayflower Compact? Why was it drafted? How does it reflect the idea that government should be based on consent?

2. How would you describe the economic, social, and political conditions of life in colonial America? How were these conditions important in the development of American ideas about government?

3. What basic features of English constitutionalism were found in the governments of the colonies?

4. Why was the right to vote in the colonies limited to those who owned a certain amount of property? Why were colonial governments nevertheless more representative than the British government?

5. What examples can you identify of written guarantees of basic rights in colonial America? How were these written guarantees important in the development of Americans' ideas about government?

6. Do research to find out more about the controversies over slavery that existed in colonial America. What arguments were made to abolish it? What arguments were made to justify it? What actions were taken by people on each side of the issue to achieve their goals?

7. How would you describe British policies toward the colonies before the 1750s? How did these policies change in the 1760s and 1770s?

8. What were the colonists' objections to the new British policies? What rights did the colonists claim the policies violated?

9. How would you explain the term "sovereignty"? What was the conflict between Great Britain and the colonies over sovereignty? How was this conflict resolved?

10. What are the basic ideas and arguments set forth in the Declaration of Independence? Why was it written?

11. Imagine that you are a merchant, a farmer, a craftsman, or a royal official living in one of the American colonies in 1776. People all around are talking about fighting for independence from Great Britain; some are in favor and some are opposed. Write a speech, a letter to the editor, or a short skit expressing your views on this important issue. Be sure to explain the reasons for your position.

Lesson 5

State Constitutions

Key Terms

absolute veto
higher law
legislative supremacy
override
political guarantees
popular sovereignty
procedural guarantees of due process
representation
social contract
state declarations of rights
veto
Virginia Declaration of Rights

What You Will Learn to Do

- Examine how state constitutions support protection of individual rights

Linked Core Abilities

- Communicate using verbal, non-verbal, visual, and written techniques
- Apply critical thinking techniques

Skills and Knowledge You Will Gain along the Way

- Explain the purpose of the state declarations of rights
- Explain the value of checks and balances
- Compare the early state constitutions and current state constitutions
- Define key words contained in this lesson

Chapter 2

Introduction

Our Founders designed their state governments to protect the rights of individuals and to help the common good. In this lesson you examine how the basic ideas about government and rights were included in state constitutions.

What Basic Ideas about Government Did the State Constitutions Include? How Did the New States Protect Rights?

Why Were the Colonies Returned to a "State of Nature"?

In terms of the natural rights philosophy, the American Revolution returned the colonists to a state of nature. The old colonial governments under the authority of the British ceased to exist. New governments would have to be created. Soon after the Revolutionary War started in 1775, the 13 states began to develop their own written constitutions. Never before had so many new governments been created using the basic ideas of the natural rights philosophy, republicanism, and constitutional government.

What six basic ideas did the state constitutions include?

The experiments of the new American states in constitution-making provided the Framers with valuable experience that later greatly influenced their writing of the Constitution of the United States. The following basic ideas were included in these state constitutions:

- **higher law and natural rights**
- **social contract**
- **popular sovereignty**
- **representation and the right to vote**
- **legislative supremacy**
- **checks and balances**

Higher law and natural rights. Every state constitution was considered a **higher law** and was based on the idea that the purpose of government was to preserve and protect citizens' natural rights to life, liberty, and property.

Reprinted from *We the People: The Citizen and the Constitution,* published by the Center for Civic Education.

Social contract. Each state constitution also made it clear that its government was formed as a result of a **social contract**—an agreement among its people to create a government to protect their natural rights.

Popular sovereignty. In all the new state constitutions sovereign authority existed in the people. The authority to govern was delegated to the government by the sovereign people.

Representation and the right to vote. One of the most significant characteristics about each state constitution was the importance it placed on **representation** of the people in their government. All the state constitutions created legislatures that were composed of elected representatives of the people. Most of these constitutions required annual elections to their legislatures.

Some state constitutions gave the right to vote for representatives to all white male taxpayers. In most states, this right was limited to people who owned a specified amount of property, as it had been when the states were colonies. Since property was relatively easy to acquire in America, about 70 percent of adult white males could vote.

In seven states, free African Americans and Native Americans could vote if they met the property requirements. In New Jersey, the vote was given to "all inhabitants...of full age, who were worth fifty pounds" and who met a twelve-month residency requirement. Under these rules, both women and free African Americans were able to vote until 1807, when the law in New Jersey was rewritten to exclude women. Twelve states specifically denied women the right to vote by inserting the word "male" in their constitutions.

Legislative supremacy. Legislative supremacy means a government in which most of the power is given to the legislature. Most state constitutions relied on a strong legislature and majority rule to protect the rights of citizens. This reliance continued a development that had begun in the colonial period when the legislatures had become strong.

All the state constitutions included some separation of powers. This reflected the former colonists' distrust of executive power which they believed had been abused under British rule.

The belief in legislative supremacy was based on the following:

- The **legislative branch** of government, composed of representatives who are elected by the voters and vulnerable to removal by the voters, is the most democratic branch of government. Therefore, in a government based on popular sovereignty it is considered the safest branch in which to place the most power and the most likely to protect the rights of citizens and promote their welfare.

- The **executive branch** should not be trusted with much power because it is not easily controlled by the people. You may remember that the colonists' greatest problems with the British government had been with its executive branch-the king's ministers and the royal governors in the colonies.

- The colonists also distrusted the **judicial branch**—the king's magistrates—who tried them for breaking British law.

The following examples of a preference for legislative supremacy can be found in the state constitutions:

- **The constitutions of most of the new states provided for executive branches but made them dependent on the legislatures. Pennsylvania's new constitution eliminated the office of governor altogether and replaced it with a twelve-man council. In other states, legislatures were given the power to select the governor or to control his salary.**

- **Governors were allowed to stay in office for only one year. This limit was an attempt to make sure that the governor would not have time to gain much power while in office.**

- **Appointments made by a governor had to be approved by the legislature.**

- **Governors in most of the state constitutions were almost totally excluded from the process of law- making, which the legislatures kept to themselves. In all the states, the governor no longer had an absolute veto over legislation. He could still refuse to approve a proposed law in some states, but the legislatures in those states could override his veto by passing the proposed law again.**

- **State legislatures exercised influence over the judiciary through control of salaries and length of tenure.**

Checks and balances. Although the powers in the state governments were **unbalanced** in favor of strong legislatures, there were some **checks** provided by their state constitutions. Most of these checks existed within the legislatures themselves. For example, in every state except Pennsylvania and Georgia, the legislature was divided into two houses, just as was the case in the British Parliament. Since most important decisions had to be made by both houses, each had a way to check the power of the other house. Unlike Parliament and the colonial governments, however, both houses of the new state legislatures were made up of representatives elected by the people. The voters could check the legislators' power by electing new representatives to both houses if they did not like the way the government worked.

Critical Thinking Exercise
Evaluating Legislative Supremacy

John Locke and the natural rights philosophers believed that in a representative government the legislative branch should be supreme because it was the branch closest to the people and it reflected most accurately the people's wishes. The legislative branch was, therefore, less likely to violate the people's rights.

Most of the state constitutions accepted this argument and heavily weighted the balance of power in favor of their legislatures.

1. **What are the advantages and disadvantages of legislative supremacy?**

2. **Do you agree with Locke's argument presented above?**

3. **Does the legislative branch necessarily reflect the people's wishes?**

4. How might the people's wishes pose a threat to basic rights?

5. Describe what a government might be like in which the executive or judicial branch was supreme.

How was the Massachusetts constitution different?

In 1780, Massachusetts became the last state to ratify a new constitution. Written principally by John Adams, the Massachusetts constitution was different from those of the other states. In addition to relying on popular representation as a means of preventing the abuse of power, it used a system of separation of powers and checks and balances. It gave government more effective checks on the powers of the state's legislature.

Since the Massachusetts constitution is more similar to the present Constitution of the United States than the other state constitutions, it is worth looking at in some detail. The following are some important characteristics of the Massachusetts constitution.

A strong executive branch. Under the Massachusetts constitution, the governor was elected by the people. The writers of this constitution believed that because the governor would be elected by the people, it would be safe to trust him with greater power so that he would be able to protect their rights and welfare.

To enable the governor to be more independent of the legislature and to allow him to check the legislature's use of power, the Massachusetts constitution contained the following provisions:

- **The governor's salary was fixed and could not be changed by the legislature.**

How did the Massachusetts constitution differ from those of the other states? Why did the Massachusetts constitution provide for a strong executive branch?

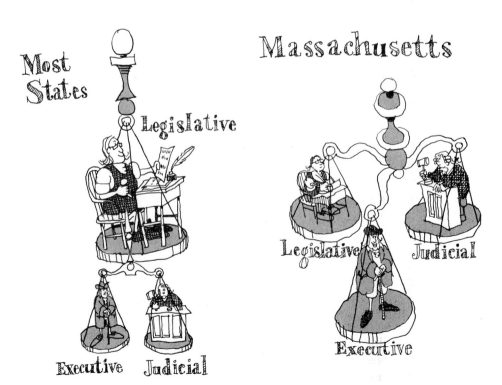

- **The governor had the power to veto laws made by the legislature, and his veto could only be overridden by a two-thirds vote of the legislature.**

- **The governor could appoint officials to the executive branch and judges to the judicial branch.**

Representation of different groups in society. Several other parts of the Massachusetts constitution show how that government was organized more like the British model of government than were those of the other states. This state constitution separated powers among the different classes in society to prevent one group from dominating the others. The Massachusetts constitution divided the people of the state into groups based on their wealth since there was no royalty or nobility.

- **Only people with a large amount of property could elect the governor.**

- **People with slightly less property could vote to elect members of the upper house of the state legislature.**

- **People with the minimum amount of property that qualified them to vote could vote for members of the lower house.**

Thus, the Massachusetts state constitution expressed the classical republican ideal of mixed government. Consequently, it provided for more balance among the powers of the different branches of government. It did not make the legislature the most powerful branch as did the other state constitutions. This approach reveals different beliefs about the best ways to prevent the abuse of power by members of government.

The constitutions of the other states were based primarily on the idea that representation of the people in a strong state legislature was the best way to protect their rights. They reflected a basic trust in political power held directly by a majority of the people.

The Massachusetts constitution reflected a more skeptical view of human nature and of unchecked power held by any group in society. It was based on the idea that representation, separation of powers, and checks and balances were all essential for the protection of the rights of the people.

What do you think?

1. **Which branch of government do you think is most responsive to the will of the people? Should that branch have more power than the other two branches? Why or why not?**

2. **In what ways was the Massachusetts constitution a forerunner of the U.S. Constitution?**

What were the state declarations of rights?

None of the state constitutions, however, relied entirely on the form of their governments to protect individual liberties. Most of them began with a **declaration of rights.** By doing this, they indicated that the citizens to be governed by these new constitutions possessed certain basic rights that existed prior to government and that no constitution or government could take away.

Americans in the colonial era attached great importance to guarantees of basic rights. Although the lists of rights differed somewhat from state to state, they were all based on the idea that people have certain inherent rights that must be protected. It was only after safeguarding these rights at the very start that the authors of these constitutions believed it proper to form state governments.

Taken together, the rights protected in the state declarations included all the fundamental rights guaranteed today in our Bill of Rights. By looking at these declarations and how they were developed, we can learn a great deal about how we came to have the rights we enjoy today under both our state and federal constitutions.

What important ideas are in the Virginia Declaration of Rights?

On June 12, 1776, Virginia became the first state to adopt a declaration of rights, almost a month before the colonies declared their independence from Great Britain. The **Virginia Declaration of Rights** helped convince other colonies to vote for independence and influenced Thomas Jefferson's writing of the Declaration of Independence itself.

The Virginia Declaration was written primarily by George Mason (1725–1792), who later opposed the ratification of the U.S. Constitution because it did not include a bill of rights. In writing Virginia's own bill of rights, Mason relied heavily on the writings of John Locke. He also was influenced by the ideas of classical republicanism and by the American colonial experience.

The Virginia Declaration of Rights stated:

- **That all power is derived from and kept by the people.**

- **That all men are by nature equally free and independent, and have certain inherent rights, of which, when they enter into a state of society, they cannot, by any compact, deprive or divest their posterity; namely, the enjoyment of life and liberty, with the means of acquiring and possessing property, and pursuing and obtaining happiness and safety.**

- **The government is, or ought to be, instituted for the common benefit, protection, and security of the people. If a government does not serve these purposes, the people have an unalienable right to alter or abolish it.**

The Virginia Declaration also included many of the rights we enjoy today under both our state and federal bills of rights, such as the right to trial by jury, protection against forced self-incrimination and cruel and unusual punishments, freedom of the press, and the free exercise of religious beliefs. Concerning the right to religious freedom it stated:

> *That religion, or the duty we owe to our Creator, and the manner of discharging it, can be directed only by reason and conviction, not by force or violence; and therefore, all men are equally entitled to the free exercise of religion, according to the dictates of conscience.*

The Virginia Declaration ended with a statement based on the ideas of classical republicanism about civic virtue and religious values:

No free government, or the blessings of liberty, can be preserved to any people but by a firm adherence to justice, moderation, temperance, frugality, and virtue. . . . it is the mutual duty of all to practice Christian forbearance, love, and charity, towards each other.

The framers of the Virginia Declaration believed that listing rights and establishing a constitutional government were not enough to guarantee people their freedom. They argued that each individual must accept the responsibility to live according to certain moral principles and ideals.

It is important to note that the Virginia Declaration omitted some important rights found in other state declarations and later made part of the U.S. Constitution.

Critical Thinking Exercise
Examining Historical Documents

Work with a study partner to complete the following exercise.

1. **Refer to the Virginia Declaration of Rights in the Reference Section to this text. Identify specific examples of the following basic ideas:**

Natural rights	**Classical republicanism**
• social contract	• civic virtue
• individual rights	• common welfare
• limited government	• political rights

2. **Which historical experiences of the colonists seemed to have the greatest influences on the authors of the state declarations?**

3. **Why do you think that, generally, state constitutions protected rights first and then created governments with limited powers?**

What rights were protected by the other states?

Most states adopted declarations or bills of rights that resembled Virginia's. The few that did not have such declarations included guarantees of certain rights in the main body of their constitutions. Like Virginia's, the other states' declarations began with statements about natural rights, popular sovereignty, and the purposes of government. Some declarations also included the idea that civic virtue and a commitment to certain moral and religious principles were essential to preserving freedom.

Other states' declarations varied in the rights they chose to include or leave out. Most included such **political guarantees** as:

- **The right to vote**
- **Free and frequent elections**
- **Freedom of speech and of the press**
- **The right to petition the government**
- **No taxation without representation**

They all included important **procedural guarantees of due process** such as:

- **The rights to counsel and trial by jury**
- **Protection from illegal search and seizure**
- **Protection from forced self-incrimination, excessive bail and fines, and cruel and unusual punishment**

Most of the state declarations, including Virginia's, expressed a fear of military tyranny by condemning professional standing armies in time of peace and the quartering of troops in civilian homes. Many endorsed the idea of "well regulated" civilian militia and the right to bear arms.

Vermont took its commitment to natural rights literally by becoming the first state to outlaw the institution of slavery.

In what ways were the state declarations different from the U.S. Bill of Rights?

The state declarations of rights would have a great influence on the later drafting and adoption of the U.S. Bill of Rights. Many states drew from their own declarations to propose the rights that should be included in the federal version. The principal writer of the U.S. Bill of Rights, James Madison of Virginia, was strongly influenced by his own state's Declaration of Rights.

The state declarations, however, differed from the U.S. Bill of Rights in many ways. They resemble more the Declaration of Independence. They were written as preambles to the state constitutions to establish the moral and philosophical foundations of the state governments. They describe the purpose of government and set forth the principles of the natural rights philosophy and classical republicanism.

How did the state constitutions balance fear of military tyranny with recognition of a need for defense?

How did independence create a need for a national government?

Problem 1. Fear of a strong national government. Once the war against Great Britain had started, each state was like a separate nation with its own constitution and government. To the people, their state was their "country" and all eligible voters could have a voice in government. They could elect members of their communities to represent their interests in their state legislatures. The government was close enough to most citizens so they could even participate in some of its activities.

The Founders agreed they needed a central government, but they were afraid of making one that was too strong. Americans believed that the British government had deprived people of their rights, including their right to be represented in government. They thought this was likely to happen with any central government that was both powerful and far away. Consequently, they were convinced that government should be close to the people so they could control it and make certain that it did not violate their rights. Finally, their study of history and political philosophy lead them to believe that republican government could only succeed in small communities where people shared common ideas and beliefs.

Why did the Founders create a weak national government?

Solution: **Create a weak national government.** The Founders finally arrived at a solution to this problem—they created a weak national government. The government created by the Articles of Confederation was just a central legislature, the Confederation Congress. There were no executive or judicial branches. While Congress could establish courts for certain limited purposes, most legal disputes were handled in state courts. Moreover, Article II states,

> *Each state retains its sovereignty, freedoms, and independence, and every Power, jurisdiction, and right, which is not by this confederation expressly delegated to the United States, in Congress assembled.*

The Articles of Confederation left most of the powers of government with the states; the national government had little power over the states and their citizens. For example:

- **The Confederation Congress did not have any authority over any person in any state. Only the state governments had authority over their citizens.**

- **Congress did not have the power to collect taxes from the states or from the people directly. It could only request money from the state governments, which were supposed to raise the money from their citizens.**

- **Congress did not have the power to regulate trade among the various states.**

Problem 2. **Fear that some states would dominate others in the national government.** The leaders in each state wanted to make sure that the new national government would be organized in a way that would not threaten their state's interests. As a result, the most important disagreement was about how states would vote in Congress. Would each state have one vote, or would states with greater population or wealth be given more votes than others? Decisions in the Congress would be made by majority vote. Some leaders were afraid that the majority would use its power for its own interest at the expense of those who were in the minority.

Solution: **Give each state one vote.** The solution to this problem was to give each state one vote in the Confederation Congress regardless of its population. The Articles also provided, however, that on important matters—for example whether to declare war—nine states would have to agree. This way the seven smaller states could not outvote the six larger states.

Critical Thinking Exercise

Examining the Advantages and Disadvantages of the Articles of Confederation

Work with a study partner, or in small groups, to complete the following exercise.

1. **Read the following excerpts from the Articles of Confederation.**

2. **For each excerpt create a list of advantages to the states and/or to the national government resulting from the Article.**

3. **Create a second list of the disadvantages to the states and/or to the national government resulting from the Article.**

4. **When you finish, compare your lists and be prepared to share your ideas with the class.**

Articles of Confederation

Article II. Each State retains its sovereignty, freedom and independence, and every power...which is not by the Confederation expressly delegated to the United States, in Congress assembled.

Article V. No State shall be represented in Congress by less than two, nor more than seven members.... In determining questions in the United States, in Congress assembled, each State shall have one vote.

Article VIII. All charges of war, and all other expenses that shall be incurred for the common defense or general welfare...shall be defrayed out of a common treasury, which shall be supplied by the several States, in proportion to the value of all land within each State. . . . The taxes for paying that proportion shall be laid and levied by the authority and direction of the Legislatures of the several States. . . .

Article IX. The United States in Congress assembled shall also be the last resort on appeal in all disputes and differences...between two or more States....

Article IX. The United States in Congress assembled shall also have the sole and exclusive right and power of regulating the alloy and value of coin struck by their own authority, or by that of the respective States....

Article XIII. ...nor shall any alteration at any time hereafter be made in any of [these articles]; unless such alteration be agreed to in a Congress of the United States, and be afterwards confirmed by the Legislatures of every state.

What were weaknesses in the Articles of Confederation?

On March 1, 1781, Maryland became the last state to ratify the Articles. Maryland had wanted western lands to be under the control of Congress, not of individual states. Not until New York, Connecticut, and Virginia surrendered their western claims did Maryland ratify the Articles.

You have seen how the people of the states attempted to deal with their fear of a strong national government—they created a national government that had very limited power. This reflected their belief that power that is not given is power that cannot be misused.

The limitations of the Articles of Confederation and the difficulties that arose under them led to the decision to develop our present Constitution. These limitations are described below.

1. **No money and no power to get it.** Congress had no power to tax. All it could do was request that state governments pay certain amounts to support the costs of the national government.

This system did not work. Congress had borrowed most of the money it needed to pay for the Revolutionary War from Americans and foreigners, but had no way to pay its debts. The state governments and many of the people living in the states were also deeply in debt after the war. Therefore, when Congress requested $10 million from the states to pay for the costs of fighting the war, the states paid only $1.5 million.

How was Congress's ability to govern hurt by not being able to collect taxes from the states?

2. No power over the state governments and their citizens. Congress did not have the power to make laws regulating the behavior of citizens or the states or to force state governments or their citizens to do anything. The citizens could be governed only by their own state governments. This meant that if members of a state government or citizens within a state disobeyed a resolution, recommendation, or request made by the national government, there was no way the national government could make them obey. The Articles clearly stated that each state kept its "sovereignty, freedom, and independence."

The national government's inability to make state governments and their citizens live up to treaties it had made led to a serious situation. Not all of the colonists had been in favor of the Revolutionary War; some had remained loyal to Great Britain. Thousands of these people, called **loyalists,** still lived in the United States. When the war was over, the national government signed a peace treaty with Great Britain called the Treaty of Paris. It was intended in part to protect loyalists' rights and ensure that they were treated fairly. Some of these loyalists owned property in the states and some had loaned money to other citizens.

Some state governments refused to respect this treaty. They often made it difficult for loyalists to collect the money owed to them by other citizens. In some cases the states had confiscated the loyalists' property during the war. The national government had no power to force the state governments to respect the property rights of the loyalists or to force individual citizens to pay back money owed to the loyalists. Thus, the national government was powerless to live up to its promise to the British government to protect the rights of these citizens.

3. Unenforceable trade agreements. Although Congress had the power to make agreements with foreign nations, it did not have the power to make state governments live up to these agreements. This raised another difficulty. Some citizens imported goods from other nations and then refused to pay for them. Not surprisingly, people in foreign countries became reluctant to trade with people in the United States. In addition, when Great Britain recognized how weak Congress was in controlling foreign trade, it closed the West Indies to American commerce. As a result, many Americans lost money because they were unable to sell their goods to people in other nations. Others were not able to buy goods from abroad.

4. Unfair competition among the states. Congress had no power to make laws regulating trade among the states. As a result, some states levied taxes on goods passing through them to other states. For example, both New York and Pennsylvania taxed goods going to New Jersey which was compared to "a keg tapped at both ends."

Such activities prevented efficient and productive trade across state lines. It also worsened the economy, which was still recovering from the devastation of the war.

5. Threats to citizens' right to property. Many people believed that one of the most serious problems in the United States during the 1780s was the failure of the state governments to protect their citizens' property rights. In most states the government was controlled by the legislative branch, composed of representatives elected by a majority of the people.

People with common interests formed **factions.** These factions sometimes formed majorities in the state legislatures. James Madison defined a faction as a group of people that seeks to promote its own interests above the interests of other individuals or groups. These groups were accused of making laws that benefited themselves at the expense of the minority and of the common good. For example, they passed laws that canceled debts and that confiscated the property of loyalists. They created paper money causing inflation that benefited debtors at the expense of their creditors.

People hurt by such laws argued that their property was not being protected by their state governments. They claimed that the state governments were being used by one class of people to deny the rights of others.

Some people argued that these problems were the result of too much democracy in the state governments. They claimed that representative government with **majority rule** did not adequately protect the natural rights of individual citizens or the common good. They argued that majority rule, when the majority pursued its own selfish interests at the expense of the rights of others, was just another form of tyranny, every bit as dangerous as that of an uncontrolled king.

What do you think?

1. **The Articles of Confederation demonstrated a distrust of a strong national government. What were the historical and philosophical reasons for this distrust?**

2. **What were the positive and negative consequences of a weak national government?**

3. **Why do you think the smaller states were satisfied with government under the Articles of Confederation?**

4. **Many people today continue to distrust the federal government. In your opinion, is such distrust justified? Explain your position.**

How did Shays' Rebellion sow the seeds of change?

Many people realized that the Articles of Confederation were weak, but it took a dramatic event to convince them of the need for a stronger national government. In 1786, a group of several hundred angry farmers in Massachusetts gathered under the leadership of Daniel Shays. Their intent was to attack the state government.

The farmers had serious economic problems. Those who could not pay their debts lost their homes and their farms. Some were sent to prison. Discontent arose among the people and mobs prevented the courts from selling the property of those who could not pay their debts.

Shays and his men needed weapons for their rebellion. They tried to capture the arsenal at Springfield, Massachusetts, where arms were kept for the state militia. Although Shays' men were defeated, their rebellion frightened many property owners who feared similar problems might arise in their states.

The fears raised by such conflicts as **Shays' Rebellion,** combined with difficulties of raising revenues and regulating foreign trade, convinced a growing number of people to strengthen the national government. George Washington was one of these people. He wrote to James Madison saying, "We are either a united people or we are not. If the former, let us act as a nation. If we are not, let us no longer act a farce by pretending to it."

What were the achievements of the first national government?

Although the national government under the Articles of Confederation left much to be desired, it did accomplish a number of important things. The Revolutionary War was conducted under this government and, through the efforts of its diplomats, it secured recognition of American independence by European governments.

Perhaps the most lasting achievement of the Confederation government was the **Northwest Ordinance** of 1787, which defined the Northwest Territory and created a plan for its government. The ordinance provided for the transition from territory to statehood for what would become five states north of the Ohio River and east of the Mississippi. The ordinance saw to it that the states provided for education by setting aside land for that purpose, and also stated that slavery would be forever prohibited from those lands.

The Confederation Congress could make these regulations for the Northwest Territory because it had complete control over it. Yet Congress had not the slightest control over enforcing its own treaties in the 13 states. By 1787, many

How did problems that arose in the Northwest Territory demonstrate the weaknesses of the new national government?

people had agreed that the power of Congress needed to be adjusted, because such a situation could not last. The first steps then were taken to create a stronger national government.

Reviewing and using the lesson

1. Why did the Articles of Confederation fail to provide for an executive and a judicial branch of government? How did the Articles of Confederation deal with fears that some states would dominate others in the national government?

2. What were some of the weaknesses of the Articles of Confederation? What were some of the achievements of the national government under the Articles of Confederation?

3. What was Shays' Rebellion? Why did it occur? What was its historical importance?

4. What is a "faction"? Why did some Founders consider factions to be a threat to natural rights?

5. Compare the government under the Articles of Confederation with one of the contemporary confederations of nations, e.g., the United Nations, the European Union, the Organization of American States, or the Organization of African States.

Lesson 2

Creating Our Constitution

Key Terms

delegates
equal representation
executive
federal system
Framers
House of Representatives
judicial
legislative
Philadelphia Convention
proportional representation
ratification
Senate
Virginia Plan

What You Will Learn to Do

- Explain how the Philadelphia Convention and the Virginia Plan helped create the Constitution

Linked Core Abilities

- Communicate using verbal, non-verbal, visual, and written techniques
- Apply critical thinking techniques

Skills and Knowledge You Will Gain along the Way

- Describe the steps leading to the calling of the Philadelphia Convention and the initial purpose of the Convention

Chpater 3

- Describe the characteristics of the Framers who attended the Convention
- Describe the Framers' agreement on how to conduct the business of the Convention
- Defend positions on how the constitution should be developed—by Congress or by a special national convention
- Describe the basic elements of the Virginia Plan and the New Jersey Plan and the differences between them
- Relate the elements of the Virginia and New Jersey Plans to the basic ideas of government such as natural rights, republican government, and constitutional government
- Explain the reasons for the disagreements among the delegates regarding representation
- Evaluate the advantages and disadvantages of the Virginia and New Jersey Plans for a national government
- Explain why the Virginia Plan was used as the basis for the new Constitution rather than the New Jersey Plan
- Define key words contained in this lesson

Introduction

The second U.S. Constitution was written at a convention held in Philadelphia in 1787. Both the New Jersey and the Virginia delegates to the convention submitted plans to organize the new national government. In this lesson, you learn how the Philadelphia Convention came to be, the major issues that were discussed and debated, and the role that the New Jersey and Virginia plans played in creating the Constitution.

Who Attended the Philadelphia Convention? What Did They Agree to Do?

What Attempts Were Made to Solve the Problems of the Articles of Confederation?

Many political leaders, including Alexander Hamilton and James Madison, were dissatisfied with the government under the Articles of Confederation. They claimed the government was inadequate for meeting the problems of the United States.

A number of prominent leaders suggested holding a meeting of representatives of all the states. This idea of holding a special meeting or convention to discuss constitutional changes, instead of using the legislature, was an American inven-

Reprinted from *We the People: The Citizen and the Constitution,* published by the Center for Civic Education.

tion. Most of the early state constitutions had been written by state legislatures. In 1780, Massachusetts became the first state to hold a constitutional convention. By 1786, Madison and other leaders decided that if a convention could be used successfully in a state, it was worth trying at the national level.

In 1786, a meeting to discuss commercial problems was held in Annapolis, Maryland. Only five states sent representatives. Disappointed at the low turnout, Hamilton, Madison, and others wrote a report asking Congress to call a meeting in Philadelphia to suggest ways to change the Articles of Confederation to strengthen the national government. Congress did so after a delay of several months. **Delegates** to the Philadelphia Convention were authorized only to propose amendments to the Articles, not to develop an entirely new constitution which is exactly what they did.

Critical Thinking Exercise
Evaluating Alternative Political Strategies

Suppose you wanted to develop a plan to change the Constitution of the United States. Your class should be divided into two groups. Each group should adopt one of the positions. Be prepared to present and defend your assigned position.

Group 1. Position: The plan to change the Constitution should be developed by Congress and then submitted to state governments for approval.

Group 2. Position: The plan to change the Constitution should be developed at a special national convention of delegates from the states selected by their legislatures and then submitted to the people of their state for approval.

Who attended the Philadelphia Convention?

Fifty-five delegates attended the meeting that later became known as the **Philadelphia** or **Constitutional Convention.** This group of men are now often called the **Framers** of the Constitution. Most of the delegates were fairly young; the average age was 42. About three-fourths of them had served in Congress. Most were prominent in their states, and some had played important parts in the Revolution. Some were wealthy, but most were not. A French diplomat in America at the time said that the Framers "without being rich are all in easy circumstances."

Contemporary observers were impressed by the quality of the delegates to the Philadelphia Convention. Another French diplomat stationed in America observed that never before, "even in Europe," had there been "an assembly more respectable for talents, knowledge, disinterestedness, and patriotism." From Paris, Thomas Jefferson wrote to John Adams in London that the convention "is an assembly of demigods."

We should remember, however, that some of the Framers were men of modest abilities or questionable motives. Probably the most balanced view of the men at Philadelphia has been given by Max Farrand, a historian, who wrote: "Great men there were, it is true, but the convention as a whole was composed of men such as would be appointed to a similar gathering at the present time: professional men, business men, and gentlemen of leisure; patriotic statesmen and clever, scheming politicians; some trained by experience and study for the task before them; and others utterly unfit. It was essentially a representative body."

Most of the Framers' stories are worth telling in detail, but here we are limited to introducing you to those who were the most important. We also will mention some leaders who did not attend the convention but who played a part in the establishment of our constitutional government.

George Washington. George Washington was probably the most respected and honored man in the country. During the Revolutionary War, he had left Mount Vernon, his Virginia plantation, to lead the American army to victory over the British. When the war was over, Washington returned to private life. Although convinced of the necessity for a strong national government, he was not interested in holding public office.

At first Washington refused the invitation to attend the convention. He later agreed to be a delegate from Virginia, fearing that if he did not attend, people might think he had lost his faith in republican government. Washington was unanimously elected president of the convention, though he was not active in the debates. His presence and support of the Constitution, together with the widespread assumption that he would be the nation's first president, were essential to the Constitution's **ratification** by the states.

James Madison. Of all the Framers, James Madison probably had the greatest influence on the organization of the national government. Born in 1751, Madison was one of the youngest of the revolutionary leaders, but by 1787 his talents had long been recognized and admired. In 1776, at the age of 25, Madison had been elected to the Virginia convention, where he was named to a committee to frame the state constitution. There, he first displayed his lifelong commitment to freedom of religion. Madison was instrumental in persuading **George Mason,** author of the Virginia Bill of Rights, to change the clause that guaranteed "toleration" of religion to one that secured its "free exercise."

As a leader in Virginia politics and a member of the Confederation Congress, Madison was active in the 1780s in support of a stronger national government. His influence at the convention was great, in part because he brought with him a plan he had already developed for creating a new national government—the **Virginia Plan.** After much debate over alternatives, this plan was used as the basis for discussion on improving the government.

Had it not been for Madison, we probably would not know much about what happened during the convention. The Framers had decided to keep the discussions a secret, although delegates were free to take notes. Madison attended nearly every session and kept careful notes. Much of what we know today about what happened in the convention is based on his records.

After the convention, Madison collaborated with **Alexander Hamilton** and **John Jay** to write a defense of the new Constitution. This defense was a series of 85 articles written for newspapers in New York. In 1788, the articles were collected in a book called *The Federalist*. The articles urged citizens of New York to vote for delegates to the state ratifying convention who were favorable to the Constitution. *The Federalist* is probably the most important work written on the basic principles and ideas underlying our constitutional government.

What other important delegates attended?

In addition to Washington and Madison, the delegates included many other prominent men. **Benjamin Franklin** was 81 and in poor health, but because he was internationally respected, his mere presence lent an aura of wisdom to the convention. **Alexander Hamilton,** although one of the strongest supporters of a strong national government, was outvoted within his own state delegation and left in frustration before the convention was half over. He returned for a few days and he signed the completed document in September. Hamilton played a major role in the struggle over ratification, as a principal author of *The Federalist* and as the leader of pro-Constitution forces in New York. **James Wilson,** although not as well known as Madison or Hamilton, was also a major influence in shaping the theory of the Constitution. Later, Wilson would lead the Federalist forces in Pennsylvania, and in 1789 President Washington appointed him a justice of the Supreme Court.

Besides Madison and Wilson, the delegate who spoke most frequently at the convention was **Gouverneur Morris** of Pennsylvania. **Edmund Randolph,** who as Governor of Virginia was officially the head of the Virginia delegation, introduced the Virginia Plan into the convention. Randolph, however, refused to sign the completed document. **Roger Sherman** of Connecticut was instrumental in forging the "Connecticut Compromise" on representation in Congress. **George Mason,** author of the Virginia Bill of Rights, believed that the national constitution also should contain explicit guarantees of fundamental rights. Like Randolph, he did not sign the Constitution. **Elbridge Gerry,** who also refused to sign the Constitution, later led the forces against ratification in Massachusetts. Later still, he served as vice president under President James Madison.

What important Founders did not attend the convention?

There also were some important political leaders who did not attend the Constitutional Convention.

Thomas Jefferson was in Paris as U.S. ambassador to France. **John Adams,** who was serving as U.S. ambassador to Great Britain, was recognized as a leading American political thinker. Adams had been a principal architect of the Massachusetts constitution of 1780. The first volume of his *Defence of the Constitutions of Government of the United States of America* had also appeared in early 1787.

Patrick Henry, the revolutionary leader, refused to attend the convention. He was against the development of a strong national government and was suspicious of what might happen at the convention. He supposedly said later that he had "smelt a rat."

Other leaders not present at Philadelphia included **John Hancock, Samuel Adams,** and **Richard Henry Lee.** Besides these prominent individuals, one state—Rhode Island—refused to be represented at the convention.

What do you think?

1. **In what ways were the Framers representative of the American people in 1787? In what ways were they not?**

   a. **What criteria would you use to select a group of people to draft a constitution today?**

   b. **Explain any advantages and disadvantages that might result from using your criteria to select people to write a constitution compared with the group of Framers who actually wrote our Constitution.**

   c. **Are there any groups whose interests you feel do not need to be represented? Why or why not?**

2. **Would you agree with Thomas Jefferson's characterization of the Philadelphia Convention as an "assembly of demigods"? Explain your answer.**

What happened when the convention began?

By Friday, May 25, 1787, eleven days after the convention was scheduled to begin, delegations from a majority of the states were present in Philadelphia. George Washington was unanimously elected president of the convention, and a committee was appointed to draw up the rules for the meeting.

Once the rules were agreed on, the convention got to work. Almost immediately, the Framers decided to ignore their instructions from Congress to limit their work to amending the Articles of Confederation. Instead, they voted to work on the development of an entirely new constitution.

The Framers decided that what was said in the convention should be kept secret. There were two reasons for this:

Why did the delegates to the Constitutional Convention decide to keep their deliberations secret?

- The Framers wanted to develop the best constitution they could. This required a free exchange of ideas. They were afraid that if their debates were made public, many of the delegates would not feel free to express their real opinions.

- The Framers thought the new constitution would have a greater chance of being accepted if people did not know about the arguments that went on while it was being created.

The Framers agreed that each state would have one vote at the convention, even though their delegations varied in size. They also agreed that a member could not be absent from the convention without permission if it would deprive a state of its vote. In addition, they adopted a rule making it possible to reconsider issues freely. This way no decision had to be made permanent until the entire plan was completed.

What do you think?

1. Were the members of the convention right to ignore their original instructions? Why?

2. Should the debates at the Constitutional Convention have been open to the public? Why?

Why Did the Framers Use the Virginia Plan to Create the Constitution?

What was the Virginia Plan?

Many delegates came to Philadelphia convinced that the defects of the Articles were so serious it would be better not to use them as a starting point. One of these was James Madison. Before the convention, he already had drafted a plan for a new national government, which came to be called the **Virginia Plan.** While they waited for the other state delegations to arrive, the Virginia delegates had agreed to put Madison's plan forward as a basis for the convention's discussions.

The most important thing to know about the Virginia Plan is that it proposed a strong national government. Under the Articles of Confederation, the national government could act only on the states, not on the people directly. For example, the national government could request money, but only the states had the authority to raise that money through taxes.

Under the Virginia Plan, the national government would have the power to make and enforce its own laws, and to collect its own taxes. Each citizen would be governed under the authority of two governments, the national government and a state government. Both governments would get their authority from the people. The existence of two governments, national and state, each given a certain amount of authority, is what we now call a **federal system.** In addition, the Virginia Plan recommended the following:

Reprinted from *We the People: The Citizen and the Constitution,* published by the Center for Civic Education.

- Three branches—**legislative, executive, and judicial**—would compose the national government. The legislative branch would be more powerful than the other branches because, among other things, it would have the power to select people to serve in the executive and judicial branches.

- The national legislature, Congress, was to have two houses. A **House of Representatives** would be elected directly by the people of each state. A **Senate** would be elected by the members of the House of Representatives from lists of persons nominated by the legislature of each state.

- The number of representatives from each state in both the House and the Senate would be based on the size of its population or the amount of its contribution to the federal treasury. This system of **proportional representation** meant that states with larger populations would have more representatives in the legislature than states with smaller populations.

The Virginia Plan gave the legislative branch of the national government the following powers:

- To make all laws that individual states were not able to make, such as laws regulating trade between two or more states

- To strike down state laws that it considered to be in violation of the national constitution or the national interest

- To call forth the armed forces of the nation against a state, if necessary, to enforce the laws passed by Congress

- To elect people to serve in the executive and judicial branches of government

What do you think?

1. What are the advantages and disadvantages of having two houses of Congress? Explain what position you would take on this question.

2. Why do you suppose the Virginia Plan gave Congress the power to strike down laws made by state legislatures? What arguments could you make for or against giving Congress this power?

3. In what ways does the Virginia Plan correct what the Framers perceived to be weaknesses in the Articles of Confederation?

How did the Framers react to the Virginia Plan?

There was considerable debate among the Framers over the Virginia Plan. In the early weeks of the convention, as specific features of the plan were discussed, a major disagreement over representation became apparent.

- The larger states wanted both houses of the national legislature to be based on proportional representation. They argued that a government that both acted on and represented the people should give equal voting power to equal numbers of people.

- The smaller states wanted **equal representation**—equal voting power for each state. Their position was based on their fear that unless they had an equal voice, as they did under the Articles of Confederation, the larger states would dominate them.

Why were delegates from small states suspicious of the Virginia Plan?

By mid-June this disagreement had created a crisis for the convention. The delegates from the small states, led by **William Paterson** of New Jersey, asked for time to come up with an alternative to the Virginia Plan.

What was the New Jersey Plan?

On June 15, Paterson presented the small states' plan, which has become known as the **New Jersey Plan.** The small states did not wish to create a national government in which they had little power. They argued that the best and safest thing to do would be to keep the framework of the Articles of Confederation, as they had been asked to do. The following are some of the main parts of the plan.

1. **Legislative branch. Congress would have only one house, as in the Confederation, and it would be given the following increased powers:**

   - **Taxes. The national government would be given the power to levy import duties and a stamp tax to raise money for its operations, together with the power to collect money from the states if they refused to pay.**

   - **Trade. Congress would be given the power to regulate trade among the states and with other nations.**

   - **Control over the states. The laws and treaties made by Congress would be considered the supreme law of the land. No state could make laws that were contrary to them.**

2. **Executive branch. This branch would be made up of several persons appointed by Congress. They would have the power to administer national laws, appoint other executive officials, and direct all military operations.**

3. **Judicial branch.** A supreme court would be appointed by the officials of the executive branch. It would have the power to decide cases involving treaties, trade among the states or with other nations, and the collection of taxes.

Critical Thinking Exercise
Developing and Defending Positions

The Virginia and New Jersey Plans each had certain benefits and costs. Understanding these is helpful in making intelligent decisions about which is the better plan. Work in small groups to identify and describe the benefits and costs of each plan and list them on a chart similar to the one below. Select the plan that your group thinks would make a better government. Be prepared to explain and defend the reasons for your decision.

Virginia Plan		New Jersey Plan	
Benefits	Costs	Benefits	Costs

Why was the Virginia Plan used?

The New Jersey Plan continued the system of government existing under the Articles of Confederation. In this system, the national government represented and acted upon the states rather than directly representing and acting upon the people. The New Jersey Plan did contain useful suggestions to solve some weaknesses of the Articles of Confederation. By the time the New Jersey Plan was presented, after two weeks of debate on the Virginia Plan, many delegates had become convinced that the national government needed new powers and a new organization for exercising those powers.

When the vote was taken on June 19, the New Jersey Plan was supported by the delegations from New Jersey and Delaware, by a majority of the New York delegation since Hamilton was always outvoted by his two colleagues, and by half the Maryland delegation. So, the Virginia Plan continued to be the basis for the convention's discussion.

A number of major issues had not been resolved, however. Among them were two potentially explosive ones.

- How should the number of representatives from each state be determined? According to population? Many delegates still argued that each state should have an equal vote, no matter how large or small its population.

- What powers should the national government have?

There were serious disagreements among the delegates. These disagreements were so intense that the convention nearly failed.

Reviewing and using the lesson

1. Why did Congress call for a constitutional convention? What did Congress authorize the delegates to the Philadelphia Convention to do?

2. How would you describe the delegates to the Philadelphia Convention? What prominent political leaders attended?

3. Why did the delegates to the Philadelphia Convention decide to conduct their deliberations in secret?

4. In recent years there have been calls for a constitutional convention. If such a convention were to be held today, what should be the make-up of its members? List the characteristics desirable in members attending a contemporary constitutional convention.

5. Why is it said the delegates to the Philadelphia Convention ignored their instructions?

6. What was the conflict between larger and smaller states over representation in Congress? Which states favored equal representation, and which favored proportional representation? What is the difference between equal and proportional representation?

7. What were the important differences between the Virginia Plan and the New Jersey Plan? Why did the Framers decide to work with the Virginia Plan?

8. Research the history of proportional representation in the United States and explain the changes in how United States senators are now selected.

Balancing the Power

Key Terms

appellate jurisdiction
apportioned
balance of power
bills of attainder
electoral college
electors
enumerated powers
equal [state] representation
executive power
executive departments
ex post facto laws
fugitive slave clause
the Great Compromise
impeach
judicial review
legislative power
necessary and proper clause
original jurisdiction
proportional representation
separated powers
supremacy clause
treason
veto

What You Will Learn to Do

● Categorize the powers granted to the legislative, judicial and executive branches of government

Linked Core Abilities

- Communicate using verbal, non-verbal, visual, and written techniques
- Apply critical thinking techniques

Skills and Knowledge You Will Gain along the Way

- Explain how and why the Framers developed the present system of representation in Congress and the advantages and disadvantages of this system
- Describe how Article 1 of the Constitution delegates explicit powers to the Congress and limits the powers of both the national and state governments
- Describe the "three-fifths clause" and the "fugitive slave clause" and explain what issues they were intended to resolve
- Defend positions on disagreements at the Philadelphia Convention over representation and slavery
- Explain the basic organization of the executive and judicial branches set forth in Articles II and III of the Constitution
- Describe the limitations on the powers of the executive and judicial branches
- Explain why the Framers developed the electoral college as the method for selecting the president
- Defend positions on the influence of the presidency over legislation
- Define key words contained in this lesson

Introduction

The Framers of the Constitution addressed a variety of concerns, issues and problems as they worked to establish the national government. Specific powers were granted and denied to each of the three branches of government: the legislative branch, the executive branch, and the judicial branch. This distribution of power resulted in a balance of power designed to keep any one branch from becoming too powerful. In this lesson you explore how the Framers addressed a variety of issues and concerns facing them as they established the national government and how they distributed power among the three branches of government.

What Powers Were Granted to the Legislative Branch?

How Should the Legislative Branch Be Organized?

After agreeing to use James Madison's Virginia Plan as the starting point for discussion of a new constitution, the Framers still faced two major decisions: they

Reprinted from *We the People: The Citizen and the Constitution,* published by the Center for Civic Education.

had to decide what powers to give the new government and how to organize the new government.

The Framers believed that the most important role would be held by the legislative branch. That is why Article I of the Constitution deals with the legislative branch. The first debates, therefore, were about the duties and powers that should be given to Congress and how it should be organized. The Framers encountered problems in developing Article I that are still being debated today.

What were the disagreements about representation?

Continuing the British and colonial practice of two-house legislatures, every state except Pennsylvania had a legislative branch with two houses. There also was a widespread belief that a two-house legislature would be less likely to violate the people's rights. Each house could serve as a check on the other.

The Virginia Plan's proposal to create a two-house Congress was not controversial. What was controversial in the plan was the principle of **proportional representation.** James Madison, James Wilson, Rufus King, and others who represented states with large populations, thought that the number of members in both houses should be based on the number of people they would represent. They argued that because the new government would operate directly on the people, it was only fair that a state with a larger number of people should have a greater voice, that is, more votes, in the national government.

The delegates from states with smaller populations were afraid that proportional representation would result in a national government dominated by the more populated states. They argued that each state should have the same number of representatives in Congress, **equal representation**. These delegates also were convinced that the people of their states would never approve the Constitution if it did not preserve equality among the states.

On July 2, the Framers voted on whether there should be equal representation in the upper house of Congress. The result was a tie, five states to five, with Georgia divided. Neither side seemed willing to compromise, and delegates began to fear that the convention would end in disagreement and failure.

Then a special committee, composed of one delegate from each state, was formed. This committee was responsible for developing a plan to save the situation. Some supporters of the Virginia Plan, including James Madison and James Wilson, were against giving this responsibility to a committee. Most of the Framers disagreed with them, however, and the committee went to work.

Critical Thinking Exercise
Developing and Defending Plans for Representation

Your class should be divided into committees of about five students each. Each committee should have some students who represent small states and some who represent large states. The task of each committee is as follows:

1. Develop a plan for how many representatives each state should be allowed to send to the Senate and to the House of Representatives. Your committee may decide, of course, that there is no need for a two-house Congress and that a single house will represent the people most effectively.

2. Select a spokesperson to present your committee's plan to the entire class. Then all members of the committee may help to defend its plan against criticisms by members of other committees.

3. Following the presentation of all the plans, each committee may revise its original plan if it wishes.

The entire class should then examine the plans made by all the committees and try to reach agreement on a plan.

Compare the plans of the committees and the final class plan with the plan of the Framers described in the next section.

What was the Great Compromise?

The result of the special committee's work is known as the **Connecticut Compromise** or the **Great Compromise.** The committee adopted a proposal previously suggested by Connecticut delegates Roger Sherman and Oliver Ellsworth. The Great Compromise contained the following ideas:

How did the Connecticut Compromise resolve differences in the Virginia and New Jersey Plans?

- The **House of Representatives** would be elected by the people on the basis of **proportional representation.**

- There would be **equal representation** of each state in the **Senate.** The legislature of each state would select two senators.

- The House of Representatives would be given the power to develop all bills for taxing and government spending. "Direct" taxes would be assigned and divided—**apportioned**—among the states by population. The Senate was limited to either accepting or rejecting these bills, but it could not change them. This provision was later changed to permit the Senate to amend tax bills developed in the House and to develop appropriation bills itself.

As in most compromises, each side gained a little and lost a little. The small states received the equal representation in the Senate that their delegates wanted to protect their interests. Many delegates also believed that a constitution without equal representation of states in at least one house of Congress would not be approved by the smaller states. The large states gave up control of the Senate but kept their control of the House of Representatives. The House was also given important powers regarding taxation and government spending.

How did the Connecticut Compromise resolve differences in the Virginia and New Jersey Plans?

The result was that the more populous states would have more influence over laws to tax the people and over how the money would be spent. The larger states also would pay the larger share of any direct taxes imposed by Congress. The decisions of the House of Representatives, however, always would be subject to the check of the Senate, in which the small states had equal representation.

When the committee presented this compromise to the convention, it was bitterly fought by some members from the larger states, including Madison, Wilson, and Gouverneur Morris. They viewed the idea of state equality in the Senate as a step away from a national government, back toward the system under the Articles of Confederation. Delegates from the small states remained suspicious as well. Two delegates from New York, who had consistently voted with the smaller states, left the convention and did not return. The crisis was over when the compromise passed by one vote.

What do you think?

1. Are there good arguments today in support of continuing to divide Congress into two bodies, a Senate and a House of Representatives? If so, what are they?

2. What contemporary issues do you know about that involve conflict over the fairness of representation in Congress?

3. Why should senators be selected for six years and members of the House of Representatives for only two years? Do you think members of the House of Representatives would more effectively represent their constituents if they could serve longer terms?

What powers did the Constitution give to Congress?

The Framers intended the new government to be a government of **enumerated**—specifically listed—powers. They thought it was important to list the powers of each branch of government so that there would not be any confusion about what they could and could not do.

Most of the powers of Congress are listed in Article I, Section 8 of the Constitution. It includes such important matters as the power

- **To lay and collect taxes**
- **To pay the debts and provide for the common defense and general welfare of the United States**
- **To regulate commerce with foreign nations, and among the several states**
- **To declare war**
- **To raise an army and navy**
- **To coin money**

The Framers also intended the new system to be a government of **separated powers,** or, as political scientist Richard Neustadt has called it, "a government of separated institutions sharing powers."

Each branch of the government is given powers that enable it to check the use of power by the others. In Article I, Congress was given the power

- to **impeach** the president, other executive branch officials, or members of the federal judiciary and remove them from office.

The executive and judicial branches also have checks, or controls, on Congress. The Framers specifically gave Congress the power to make all other laws that are "necessary and proper" for carrying out the enumerated powers. This is called the **necessary and proper clause.**

What power did the national government have over state governments and the people?

One reason the Framers agreed to meet in Philadelphia was their concern about some things that state governments were doing. They believed that some states were undermining Congress's efforts to conduct foreign relations, and they feared that, in others, individual rights might be threatened by the state governments. They also knew that the national government had no power to enforce its decisions. The Framers all agreed they had to create a national government with more power than the government had under the Articles of Confederation. They did not agree, however, about how much power the new national government should have over citizens and the state governments.

The Framers resolved their disagreements by establishing a **national government** with authority to act directly on the people in certain specific areas. The national government no longer would be dependent on the states for income or for law enforcement. The state governments, however, would keep many of the more important powers over people's daily lives. The states would keep their powers over education, family law, property regulations, and most aspects of everyday life. The people would not feel they had surrendered too much power to a distant government.

The Framers included a number of phrases in the Constitution that set forth the powers of the national government. They also included phrases that limited the power of both the national government and state governments. Some of the more important of these are listed below.

1. **Some powers of the national government:**

    -   The **supremacy clause** says that the Constitution and all laws and treaties approved by Congress in exercising its enumerated powers are the supreme law of the land. It also says that judges in state courts must follow the Constitution, or federal laws and treaties, if there is a conflict with state law.

    -   Article I, Section 8 gives Congress power to organize the militia of the states and to set a procedure for calling the militia into national service when needed.

    -   Article IV, Section 3 gives Congress the power to create new states.

    -   Article IV, Section 4 gives the national government the authority to guarantee to each state a **republican** form of government.

    -   Article IV, Section 4 also requires the national government to protect the states from invasion or domestic violence.

2. **Limits on power of the national government (1) the Constitution includes several limitations on the power of the national government:**

    -   Article I, Section 9 prohibits the national government from:
        a. banning the slave trade before 1808
        b. suspending the privilege of the **writ of habeas corpus** except in emergencies
        c. passing any **ex post facto laws,** laws that make an act a crime even though it was legal at the time it was committed
        d. passing any **bills of attainder,** laws that declare a person guilty of a crime and decrees a punishment without a judicial trial
        e. taxing anything exported from a state
        f. taking money from the treasury without an appropriation law
        g. granting titles of nobility

    -   Article III defines the crime of **treason** and prohibits Congress from punishing the descendants of a person convicted of treason.

    -   Article VI prohibits the national government from requiring public officials to hold any particular religious beliefs.

3. **Limits on powers of state governments**

    -   Article I prohibits state governments from:
        a. creating their own money
        b. passing laws that enable people to violate contracts, such as those between creditors and debtors

   c. making ex post facto laws or bills of attainder

   d. entering into treaties with foreign nations or declaring war

   e. granting titles of nobility

- **Article IV prohibits states from:**

   a. unfairly discriminating against citizens of other states

   b. refusing to return fugitives from justice to the states from which they have fled

What issues separated the northern and southern states?

The Great Compromise had settled the disagreement between large and small states over how they would be represented in Congress. Many other issues still had to be resolved. Two of the most critical disagreements were those between the southern and northern states on the issues of slavery and regulation of commerce.

Slavery had been practiced for almost as long as there had been colonies in America. Many Framers were opposed to slavery, and some northern states had begun to take steps toward abolishing it. Still, in the south, slave labor was widely used in producing crops. Slaveholders considered their slaves to be personal property, and wanted to continue using them.

Delegates from the southern states told the convention that their states would not ratify a constitution that denied citizens the right to import and keep slaves. If the Constitution interfered with slavery, North Carolina, South Carolina, and Georgia made it clear that they would not become part of the new nation. Some delegates from the New England states, whose shipping interests profited from the slave trade, were sympathetic to the southern position.

What compromises were made to persuade the southern states to sign the Constitution?

After considerable debate, the Framers agreed on a way to satisfy both northern and southern delegates. This agreement gave Congress the power to regulate

Why did the Framers give constitutional protection to slavery?

commerce between the states, which the northern states wanted. The delegates defeated a southern attempt to require a two-thirds vote of both houses to pass laws regulating commerce. To satisfy the southern states, the Constitution provided that the national government would not interfere with the slave trade earlier than 1808.

The Framers also agreed that each slave would be counted as three-fifths of a person when determining how many representatives a state could send to the House of Representatives. Each slave also would be counted as three-fifths of a person when computing direct taxes. The **fugitive slave clause** of Article IV was another concession to the southern states. It provided that slaves who escaped to other states must be returned to their owners.

Critical Thinking Exercise
Examining Northern and Southern Positions on Slavery

The words "slave" and "slavery" are never used in the Constitution. Although the delegates voted to give constitutional protection to slavery, many of them were not proud of having done so. They considered it to be a necessary evil, at best, and many hoped it would go away by itself, if left alone. As we now know, this protection of slavery almost destroyed the United States.

Work in small groups to develop positions on the following questions from both a northern and southern perspective. Then develop a position on the final question.

1. **What arguments could have been made for or against the Framers' decision to include the value of property, including enslaved Africans, in calculating the number of representatives a state should have? Should property in the form of enslaved Africans have been treated differently from other forms of property?**

2. **Should the settling of fundamental issues, such as whether to allow slavery, have been left up to each state?**

3. **What problems, if any, arise from trying to make judgments about positions that were taken 200 years ago?**

What do you think?

1. **Why did northern delegates, some from states which had abolished slavery, vote for compromises which maintained the institution of slavery? Would you have done the same? Why or why not?**

2. **What disagreements might arise over the interpretation of the clause that says Congress has the power to make all laws necessary and proper for fulfilling its responsibilities as outlined in the Constitution. Why?**

Reprinted from *We the People: The Citizen and the Constitution*, published by the Center for Civic Education.

What Powers Were Granted to the Executive and Judicial Branches?

Why did the Framers want to limit executive power?

The Articles of Confederation did not provide for an executive branch, but the Confederation Congress had found it necessary to create executive officials for specific purposes. The Framers wanted to give the executive branch of the new government enough power and independence to fulfill its responsibilities. They did not, however, want to give the executive any power or independence that could be abused. Americans and Englishmen believed that the king, through the use of bribes and special favors, had been able to control elections and exercise too much influence over Parliament. The British constitution permitted members of Parliament to hold other offices at the same time, and even today members of the executive branch, such as the prime minister, are also members of Parliament. In the eighteenth century, the Crown used its exclusive power to appoint people to office to reward friendly members of Parliament.

The Framers thought these actions upset the proper **balance of power** between the monarch and Parliament. It was the destruction of this balance that Americans referred to when they spoke of the corruption of Parliament by the Crown. They also believed that royal governors had tried to corrupt colonial legislatures in the same way.

This destruction of the proper balance of power among different branches of government, many Americans thought, led to tyranny. Consequently, it is not surprising that, after their experience with the king and his royal governors, the Americans provided for very weak executive branches in most of the state constitutions. This, however, created other difficulties. The weak executives were unable to check the powers of the state legislatures. These legislatures passed laws that, in the opinion of many, violated basic rights, such as the right to property.

The problem that faced the Framers, then, was how to create a system of government with balanced powers. They wanted to strengthen the executive branch without making it so strong that it could destroy the balance of power among the branches and thus endanger the rights of the people.

What basic questions did organizing the executive branch raise?

The Framers had to resolve a number of basic questions in organizing the executive branch. Each question concerned the best way to establish an executive branch strong enough to balance the power of the legislature, but not so powerful it would endanger democratic government.

Single or plural executive. Should there be more than one chief executive? The Framers agreed that there should be a single executive to avoid the possible problem of conflict between two or more leaders of equal power. Some delegates also argued that it would be easier for Congress to keep a watchful eye on a single executive. On the other hand, those who argued for a plural executive claimed that such an executive would be less likely to become tyrannical.

Term of office. How long should the chief executive remain in his position? The convention considered a seven-year term for the president, but many delegates thought seven years too long. The final decision was to set the term of office at four years.

Reelection. Should the executive be eligible for reelection? Under the original proposal for a seven-year term of office, the president would not have been eligible for reelection. When the term was reduced to four years, the Framers decided to allow the president to run again. The Constitution originally set no limit on the number of times a president could be reelected. The Twenty-second Amendment, passed in 1951, however, sets the limit at two terms.

What powers should be given to the president?

The most important question the Framers faced was what the powers of the executive branch would be. The **executive powers** include the responsibilities for:

- **Carrying out and enforcing laws made by Congress**
- **Nominating people for federal offices**
- **Negotiating treaties with other nations**
- **Conducting wars**

In addition, the president is given the power:

- **To pardon people convicted of crimes**
- **To send and receive ambassadors to and from other countries**

Although the Framers thought the executive branch should have enough power to fulfill its responsibilities, they also wanted to be sure it did not have too much power. They limited the powers of both the executive branch and the legislative branch by making them share many of their powers. This was intended to keep the powers balanced and to provide each branch with a way to check the use of power by the other branch. This sharing of powers was accomplished in the following ways:

- **Veto.** The president shares in the **legislative power** through the **veto**. Although the president can veto a bill passed by Congress, the bill can still become a law if two-thirds of both houses of Congress vote to override the veto.

- **Appointments.** The power to appoint executive branch officials and federal judges is shared with Congress. The president has the power to nominate persons to fill those positions, but the Senate has the right to approve or disapprove of the persons nominated. To prevent corruption of Congress, members of Congress are not allowed to hold another federal office.

- **Treaties.** The power to make treaties also is shared. The president has the power to negotiate a treaty with another nation, but the treaty must be approved by a two-thirds vote of the Senate.

- **War.** Although the president is Commander-in-Chief, only Congress has the power to declare war. Congress also controls the money necessary to wage a war. Therefore, the power to declare and wage war also is shared.

Although it includes several important powers, Article II seems short and vague when compared with Article I. It speaks of "executive power" but does not define it. **Executive departments** are mentioned, but there are no provisions for creating them, deciding how many there should be, or how they should operate.

By comparison, Article I included a specific list of "legislative powers" granted by the Constitution. The veto power appears in Article I, Section 7, although the term is not used. Article II, Section 3 states that the president has the duty to suggest legislation. These are examples of the executive sharing the legislative power.

The Constitution also gives Congress the power to **impeach** the president, members of the executive branch, and federal judges. Only the House of Representatives can bring the charges. The Senate holds a trial to determine the official's guilt or innocence. If found guilty by two-thirds of the Senate, the official will be removed from office.

The Framers had some experience with elected executives in the states, yet they could not be sure exactly what the presidency of the United States should be like. Many decisions were left to Congress. The Framers also trusted George Washington, who was almost universally expected to become the first president. They thought that he could be counted on to fill in the Constitution's gaps and set wise examples that would be followed by later presidents.

Critical Thinking Exercise

Identifying the Powers of the President to Influence Legislation

The president has the power to veto bills passed by Congress and the power to recommend to Congress legislation that he considers "necessary and expedient." Answer the following questions. It may be helpful to consider some things that have changed since the Constitution was written.

1. **In what other ways can a president have an influence on legislation being considered in Congress?**

2. **Does the party system give a president more influence in Congress when he is a member of the majority party?**

3. **Has the presence of television increased the power of the presidency and weakened that of Congress?**

How should presidents be selected?

The main alternatives debated by the Framers were to have the president selected **indirectly** or **directly** by a majority vote of the people. Among the indirect methods they considered were selection by

- **Congress**
- **State legislatures**
- **State governors**
- **A temporary group elected for that purpose**

The Framers knew that the group with the power to select the president would have great power over the person who held the office. They were concerned that this power might be used to benefit some people at the expense of others. It might also make it difficult for the president to function properly.

If Congress were given the power to choose the president, then limiting the term of office to a single, long term would be a way to protect the president from being manipulated by Congress in order to get reelected. This is why the Framers also decided that Congress could neither increase nor decrease the president's salary once in office.

If a president were **not** chosen by Congress, then providing for a shorter term of office would make the president more accountable to the people. Reelection then would be the will of the people and the president could run for reelection many times.

The problem was given to a committee to develop a plan that a majority of the Framers would support. The committee's plan was a clever compromise. It did not give any existing group the power to select the president. The plan shows that the Framers did not trust any group—the people, the state legislatures, or Congress— to make the selection. In such a large country, the people could not be personally familiar with the candidates and their qualifications, in the Framers' judgment. The state legislatures and Congress, they thought, might use their power to upset the balance of power between the national and state governments, or between the executive and legislative branches.

Instead, the committee proposed what we now call the **electoral college,** which would have the responsibility of electing the president. The main parts of this plan are described below.

- **The electoral college would be organized once every four years to select a president. After the election, the college would be dissolved.**
- **Each state would select members of the electoral college, called electors.**
- **Each state would have the same number of electors as it had senators and representatives in Congress. The method for choosing electors would be decided on by the state legislature.**
- **Each elector would vote for two people, one of whom had to be a resident of another state. This forced the elector to vote for at least one person who might not represent his particular state's interests.**
- **The person who received the highest number of votes, if it was a majority of the electors, would become president. The person who received the next largest number of votes would become vice president.**
- **If two people received a majority vote, or if no one received a majority vote, then the House of Representatives would select the president by a majority**

vote, with each state having only one vote. In case of a vice-presidential tie, the Senate would select the vice president.

The compromise was eventually approved by the Framers, but only after much debate and revision. Although quite complicated and unusual, it seemed to be the best solution to their problem. There was little doubt in the Framers' minds that George Washington would easily be elected the first president. There was great doubt among the Framers, however, that anyone after Washington could ever get a majority vote in the electoral college. They believed that in almost all future elections the final selection of the president would be made by the House of Representatives.

What do you think?

1. **What arguments can you give to support the use of the electoral college to select the president? Explain why you agree or disagree with these arguments.**

2. **What qualifications do you think a person should have, beyond those already in the Constitution, in order to be president? Do you think these qualifications should be required by law? Why or why not?**

3. **Is it still reasonable to have one person serve as the head of the executive branch? Might it be more reasonable to have two people-one for domestic and one for foreign policy?**

What questions did organizing the judicial branch raise?

A national government, with power to act directly on citizens, needed a system for deciding cases involving its laws. This function could be left to state courts, but then the federal laws might be enforced differently from state to state. The Framers realized that some kind of national courts would be needed, at least to resolve disputes involving federal laws.

A judicial branch also would complete the system of separation of powers. They had fewer problems agreeing on how to organize the judiciary than they had with the other two branches. Many of the Framers were lawyers, and so most of them already agreed about how courts should be organized and what responsibilities and powers they should be given. They also agreed that all criminal trials should be trials by jury. This was a very important check, in their minds, on the power of the government.

The Framers created the **Supreme Court** as the head of the federal judiciary, and gave Congress the power to create lower federal courts. They also reached several other important agreements:

- **Judges should be independent of politics so that they can use their best judgment to decide cases and not be influenced by political pressures.**

- **The best way to make sure that judges would not be influenced by politics was to have them nominated by the president. The president's nomination would need to be ratified by the Senate. The Framers thought that appointing the judges by this method rather than electing them would remove them from the pressures of political influence. In addition, the judges would keep their positions "during good behavior." This meant that they could not be removed from** their positions unless they were impeached and convicted of "treason, bribery, or other high crimes and misdemeanors."

There was also a good deal of agreement about the kinds of powers that the judicial branch should have. The judiciary was given the power to:

- **Decide conflicts between state governments**
- **Decide conflicts that involved the national government**

And finally, they gave the Supreme Court the authority to handle two types of cases. These are:

- **Cases in which the Supreme Court has original jurisdiction.** These are cases which the Constitution says are not to be tried first in a lower court, but which are to go directly to the Supreme Court. Such cases involve a state government, a dispute between state governments, and cases involving ambassadors.
- **Cases which have first been heard in lower courts and which are appealed to the Supreme Court.** These are cases over which the Supreme Court has **appellate jurisdiction.**

What do you think?

1. **What are the advantages and disadvantages of having federal judges appointed, not elected, to serve "during good behavior"?**

2. **Should the composition of the Supreme Court be reflective of the political, economic, racial, ethnic, and gender diversity of our citizenry? Why or why not?**

3. **What role, if any, should public opinion play in the Supreme Court deciding a controversial case?**

4. **It has been argued that the Supreme Court is the least democratic branch of our federal government. What arguments can you give for and against this position?**

Why was the question of judicial review left unanswered?

One important matter not decided by the Framers was whether the Supreme Court should be given the power of **judicial review** over the acts of the executive and legislative branches. To do so would give the judiciary the authority to declare acts of these branches of the national government unconstitutional. This would mean giving one branch the power to ensure that the other branches did not exceed the limitations placed on them by the Constitution. The power to declare that legislative acts had violated their state constitution already had been exercised by the courts in several states.

Some Framers simply assumed that the judiciary would have the power to rule on the constitutionality of laws made by Congress. Nothing specific was decided on this subject at the convention. This assumption; however, is one reason why the delegates rejected a proposal to let the Supreme Court and president act as a committee to review bills passed by Congress and decide if they should become law. The only reference in the Constitution to the general powers of the judiciary is at the beginning of Article III: The "judicial power of the United States, shall be vested in one supreme court.... "

The power of the Supreme Court to declare acts of Congress unconstitutional was clearly established by the Supreme Court itself in 1803.

Reviewing and using the lesson

1. Why did the Framers appoint a special committee to deal with the issue of representation? How was the committee organized?

2. What was the Connecticut Compromise or Great Compromise? How did it resolve the conflict over representation?

3. What is meant by "enumerated powers"? Why did the Framers decide to specifically enumerate the powers granted to Congress?

4. What is the "necessary and proper clause"?

5. What is the "supremacy clause"?

6. How did the Framers deal with the issue of slavery? Why did they choose to take the approach they did?

7. Examine Article I, Section 8 of the Constitution. List any powers of Congress that are not included that you believe should be.

8. What issues did the Framers have to decide regarding the organization of the executive branch of government and how did they resolve these issues?

9. How did the Framers make sure the executive branch would have enough power to fulfill its responsibilities, but not so much power that it could dominate the other branches of government?

10. What is the electoral college and why did the Framers decide to create it?

11. What is the difference between "original jurisdiction" and "appellate jurisdiction"?

12. Why did the Framers provide that judges would be appointed by the president, rather than elected by the people? Why did the Framers provide that judges would keep their positions "during good behavior"?

13. What is meant by the term "judicial review"?

14. The electoral college still elects the president every four years, but it now functions very differently from the way the Framers intended. Do research to find out how the system has changed, and report your findings to the class.

The Bill of Rights

Last state church abolished (1833)		Fourteenth Amendment incorporates the Bill of Rights (1868)		*Barrenblatt v. U.S.* (1959) *NAACP v. Alabama* (1958)	Last religious test for public office abolished (1961) *Mapp v. Ohio* (1961) | *Miranda v. Arizona* (1966)	*Furman v. Georgia* (1972)
1830s	**1840s**	**1850s**	**1860s**	**1950s**	**1960s**	**1970s**
Supreme Court rules that the Bill of Rights applies only to the federal gov't (1833)		First Women's Rights Convention held at Seneca Falls, NY (1848)	First transcontinental railroad completed (1869)	First manned space flight (1961)	President Kennedy assassinated (1963)	Last U.S. troops leave Vietnam (1975)

Lesson 6

Protection of Rights Within the Judicial System

Key Terms

acquitted
bail
capital punishment
cruel and unusual punishment
double jeopardy
felony
indicted
right to counsel

What You Will Learn to Do

- Compare positions on capital punishment to rights protected in the Fifth through Eighth Amendments

Linked Core Abilities

- Do your share as a good citizen in your school, community, country, and the world
- Apply critical thinking techniques

Skills and Knowledge You Will Gain along the Way

- Identify how provisions in the Fifth Amendment protect your rights after arrest
- Explain how the Sixth Amendment is intended to provide fair hearing for accused criminals

- Look at issues and controversies over the Right to Counsel
- Examine historic and current positions pertaining to types of punishment
- Define key words contained in this lesson

Introduction

In this lesson, you examine how provisions of the Fifth through Eighth Amendments protect the rights of people accused of crimes and put on trial. You review the importance and history of each right and learn about the right to counsel and its role in the American judicial system. Additionally, you take a close look at the Supreme Court rules concerning the death penalty and issues involved in allowing capital punishment.

How Do the Fifth through Eighth Amendments Protect Our Rights within the Judicial System?

How do provisions of the Fifth Amendment protect an individual's rights after arrest?

Once a person has been arrested for a crime, the next step is usually to charge the person formally in a judicial proceeding. In the federal system, anyone who is to be tried for a crime must be **indicted** by a grand jury. The military, however is an exception to this rule. A grand jury, unlike a trial jury, does not decide whether someone is innocent or guilty, but instead decides whether there is enough evidence to go to trial. This is an important safeguard, because it ensures that the government cannot bring formal charges against people on the basis of weak evidence, or no evidence. A similar purpose lies behind the **double jeopardy** provision of the Fifth Amendment.

The government cannot wear someone out with repeated charges and trials. Usually, someone who is **acquitted**—found innocent—by a jury may not be tried for that crime again.

What limitations does the Sixth Amendment place on the government?

The Sixth Amendment contains a number of additional procedural rights that are part of due process of law. Almost all the protections of the Sixth Amendment have been incorporated into the Fourteenth Amendment, making them applicable to the states.

Reprinted from *We the People: The Citizen and the Constitution,* published by the Center for Civic Education.

The amendment's provisions are intended to provide a fair hearing in court for persons accused of crimes. Briefly examine each of these provisions before looking at their history and focusing on the right to counsel.

- **Speedy trial.** The federal government cannot hold you in jail for a long period of time without bringing you to trial if you demand that the trial be held as soon as possible.

- **Public trial.** The government cannot try you in secret. Your trial must be open to the public and there must be a public record of the proceedings.

- **Impartial jury.** The government must try you before a jury. It cannot try you before a jury that is prejudiced. For example, if you were on trial for a drug-related crime and jurors admitted to having angry and violent reactions because they had been victims of similar crimes, the jury could not be impartial.

- **Location of the trial.** The government must try you in the state, district or community where the crime was committed. You may, however, have the right to have the trial moved if you can show that the community is prejudiced.

- **Information on charges.** The government cannot arrest you and hold you for trial without telling you why it is doing so. Government lawyers also must present in open court enough evidence to justify holding you for trial.

- **Confronting witnesses.** You and your lawyer have the right to confront and cross-examine all witnesses against you. The government cannot present the testimony of secret witnesses who do not appear in court against you.

- **Favorable witnesses.** The government cannot prevent you from presenting witnesses who might testify for you. In fact, if such witnesses do not want to testify and you want them to, the court must force them to appear.

- **Assistance of counsel.** The government cannot prevent you from having a lawyer defend you from the time you are named as a suspect. If you are charged with a serious crime and cannot afford a lawyer, the government must provide one free of charge.

What is the importance of the right to counsel?

The American criminal justice system is an adversary system as opposed to the inquisitorial system used in some other countries. In an adversary system there are two sides that present their positions before an impartial third party—a jury, a judge, or both. The prosecuting attorney presents the government's side; the defense attorney presents arguments for the accused person.

The complexity of our adversary system requires the use of lawyers to represent defendants. Even well-educated people and many lawyers who do not specialize in criminal law, are not competent to conduct an adequate defense in today's courts.

In the twentieth century, the Supreme Court and Congress have extended the right to counsel to people to whom it had not been provided in the past. This right is now interpreted to guarantee:

- That every person accused of a **felony**—a major crime—may have a lawyer
- Those too poor to afford to hire a lawyer will have one appointed by the court

The right also has been extended by decisions in such cases as *Miranda v. Arizona* (1966) to apply not only to criminal trials, but to other critical stages in the criminal justice process, such as questioning of suspects by police.

Critical Thinking Exercise
Examining Current Controversies about the Right to Counsel

A number of issues are currently raised regarding the right to counsel. Two of the most frequently mentioned are discussed below. Read about these issues and develop positions on the questions they raise.

1. **The right to effective counsel. Wealthy people can afford to hire lawyers of their choice; usually the poor must accept the lawyers assigned to them. Lawyers serving the poor may be excellent, but often they are overworked and do not have sufficient time or the resources to prepare the best defense possible.**

    Question: How can the government provide effective counsel to represent the poor? If a poor person is represented ineffectively by a lawyer and found guilty, should this be the basis for a retrial? Explain your position.

2. **Limiting the right to counsel for poor defendants. The law requires that poor defendants be provided counsel at public expense. Counsel may be attorneys from the community selected by judges to defend the poor. They may also be volunteers or public defenders employed by the government. Sometimes poor defendants appeal their cases numerous times, costing the taxpayers millions of dollars each year.**

    Question: Should some limit be placed on how many times or under what circumstances poor people should be provided this assistance? Explain your position.

How are the rights of the Sixth Amendment enforced?

Suppose you are tried in a criminal court, found guilty, and imprisoned. You believe that one or more of your Sixth Amendment rights have been violated by the government during your trial. For example, suppose you believe that the jury was prejudiced against you.

The right to appeal your case to a higher court is available to you if you can show that your constitutional rights have been violated. Each state has a system of appellate courts, and so does the federal government, with the Supreme Court being the highest court of appeals in the nation. If, after reviewing the trial record, an appellate court decides the trial has been unfair, it can overturn the lower court's verdict. If that happens, the prosecution can usually choose whether or not to retry the case.

What limitations does the Eighth Amendment place on the government?

The Eighth Amendment protects people accused of crimes and awaiting trial, and people found guilty of crimes. Its protections, incorporated by the Fourteenth Amendment, limit the powers of the judicial and legislative branches of federal and state government in the following ways:

- **Limitations on the judiciary.** Judges usually have the power to decide whether a person arrested for a crime should be held in jail or set free on bail while awaiting trial. They also have the right to decide how much bail should be required. This amendment says that judges cannot require excessive bail.

- **Limitations of the legislature.** Congress and state legislatures establish the range of punishments for breaking laws. This amendment says legislatures cannot pass laws that impose excessive fines or inflict **cruel and unusual punishments.** The power of judges and juries to decide punishments is limited by the laws passed by the legislatures that, in turn, are limited by the Eighth Amendment.

Critical Thinking Exercise
Examining Early Positions on Punishment

The French philosopher Montesquieu greatly influenced Americans' views on law and punishment. Below is a quotation from his writings followed by an excerpt from a letter by Thomas Jefferson. Read the selections and answer the questions that follow.

> *Experience shows that in countries remarkable for the leniency of their laws the spirit of the inhabitants is as much affected by slight penalties as in other countries by severer punishments.... Mankind must not be governed with too much severity...if we inquire into the cause of all human corruptions, we shall find that they proceed from the impunity [exemption from punishment] of criminals, and not from the moderation of punishments.... It is [also] an essential point, that there should be a certain proportion in punishments.... It is a great abuse amongst us to condemn to the same punishment a person that only robs on the highway and another who robs and murders.*
>
> Baron de Montesquieu, "Of the Power of Punishments," *The Spirit of the Laws*, 1748

> *The fantastical idea of virtue and the public good being sufficient security to the state against the commission of crimes, which you say you have heard insisted on by some, I assure you was never mine. It is only the sanguinary [bloodthirsty] hue of our penal laws which I meant to object to. Punishments I know are necessary, and I would provide them, strict and inflexible, but proportioned to the crime.... Let mercy be the character of the law-giver, but let the judge be a mere machine. The mercies of the law will be dispensed equally and impartially to every description of men.*
>
> Thomas Jefferson to Edmund Pendleton, August 26, 1776

1. **What position does Montesquieu take on the effects of lenient and severe punishments?**

2. **What does Montesquieu say is a major cause of crime?**

3. **In what ways do Montesquieu and Jefferson appear to be in agreement?**

4. **What idea is expressed in Jefferson's statement that is not in Montesquieu's?**

5. **Do you agree or disagree with the positions stated by Montesquieu and Jefferson? Explain your position.**

What are the purposes of the Eighth Amendment rights?

The right to be free on bail pending trial. Although persons accused of crimes have the right to a speedy trial after they have been arrested, there are usually delays while both the prosecution and defense prepare for trial. Since a person is presumed innocent until proven guilty, one might argue that suspects should go free until the time of their trial. Not all suspects can be trusted to appear in court when they are supposed to. Some suspects may be dangerous, and it is reasonable to think that those accused of crimes for which there are severe penalties might not appear.

The government's main responsibility in this regard is to make sure suspects appear in court to be tried. This may be accomplished by

- **keeping suspects in jail while awaiting trial, or**

- **having them place bail—money or property—in the hands of the government to ensure that they will appear in court rather than forfeit it**

The right to bail allows suspects to be free while preparing their defense, which is often difficult to do from jail. It also avoids punishing suspects by holding them in jail before they are found guilty or innocent.

This is particularly important for innocent persons who would otherwise suffer unfair punishment while awaiting trial. The sentencing of persons found guilty takes into account how much time they have spent in jail awaiting trial.

Problems arising from the implementation of the right to bail include the following:

- **Unfair treatment of the poor.** Wealthy people can afford bail; the poor often cannot. Therefore, the poor are more likely to remain in jail awaiting trial, lose income, and not be able to do as much to prepare for their defense.

How does the right to bail help protect an accused person's due process right?

- **Punishment of innocent poor.** Poor people who are innocent and cannot afford bail are kept in jail and then released after their trial. This means that innocent people are punished by imprisonment and rarely compensated for the time they have lost or the wrongs done to them.

- **Increased chances of conviction and more severe sentences.** Studies have shown that being held in jail prior to a trial seems to have a negative influence on judges and juries. It results in a greater possibility of convicting such people of crimes and giving them more severe sentences.

One remedy for the inequitable aspects of the bail system is to release defendants without bail on their own recognizance, that is, on their promise to return to court for trial. This procedure is being used more and more when defendants have families or other ties to the community that would make it unlikely they would flee. It is used when a suspect's release would not seem to present a danger to the community.

The right to be free from excessive fines. The purpose of this provision is to require courts to levy fines that are reasonable in relation to whatever crime has been committed. If a fine was extremely high in proportion to the seriousness of the crime, a person could claim the excessive fine violates his or her rights under the Eighth Amendment.

The right to be free from cruel and unusual punishment. This right is based on the belief that the law should treat even the most horrible criminal with dignity. Punishments should not violate society's standards of decency.

The question raised by this right is to determine what is meant by the terms "cruel" and "unusual." What the Framers meant by "cruel and unusual punishments" is not at all clear. Part of the problem is that what is considered cruel and unusual has changed over the years. The most difficult issues, however, have been raised by the issue of the death penalty.

What is the history of capital punishment in the United States?

Capital punishment has been used in the United States from colonial times to the present, and the Supreme Court has never held that it is prohibited by the Eighth Amendment. The Constitution appears to accept the legitimacy of the death penalty. Both the Fifth and Fourteenth Amendments forbid the government to deprive someone of "life" without due process of law. These clauses seem to suggest that if due process is provided, people may be deprived of their lives by the government.

At one time, execution was the automatic penalty for murder or other serious crimes. By the early twentieth century, most states developed laws that allowed juries a choice between the death penalty and other forms of punishment. In most states, however, the juries were not given much guidance in making these decisions. This policy of allowing juries **unguided discretion** was common until 1972.

What is the basis of opposition to the death penalty?

Executions of murderers and rapists were common in the United States until the 1960s when moral and political opposition developed because of a number of factors:

- **Information on how the death penalty was chosen revealed that juries often acted randomly and capriciously in deciding who should be executed and who should not.**
- **Studies showed that the race of the defendant and the victim appeared to be the most important factors in whether a jury inflicted the death penalty.**
- **Studies did not confirm the belief that capital punishment deterred crime.**
- **Often, the cost of capital punishment, considering appeals, is more expensive than sentencing a person to life in prison without parole.**

What issues are involved in allowing capital punishment?

Studies indicating unfairness in the imposition of the death penalty led to widespread debate and increasing opposition to its use. Courts and legislatures faced growing pressure to develop clear, reasonable, and fair standards to be used by juries in making their decisions.

Since 1972 the Supreme Court and legislatures have been attempting to develop such standards. This process resulted from a decision made by the Court in the case of *Furman v. Georgia* (1972). In that case, a five-to-four majority struck down a statute giving juries unguided discretion in the imposition of the death penalty.

The *Furman* decision did not result in the prohibition of the death penalty. The majority argued that while the death penalty was constitutional, state laws permitting unguided discretion were unconstitutional. The result of this decision was that all executions in the United States were suspended. State legislatures were faced with the task of developing new laws with standards to avoid the arbitrary and discriminatory imposition of the death penalty, which was characteristic of the past.

Some states attempted to solve the problem by going back to the practice of automatic death penalties for certain serious crimes. Others developed new **guided discretion** laws. These laws called for juries or judges to decide whether to impose life or death sentences at a hearing held for this purpose after the trial in which a person was found guilty.

In 1976, the Supreme Court heard five cases on the new state laws. It upheld the new practice of guided discretion and declared that the automatic sentencing law was unconstitutional. Thus, the Court upheld the constitutionality of the death penalty once again. No clear standards were set to implement the policy of guided discretion, however. As a result, the courts have been flooded with appeals of death penalty sentences claiming that unfair standards have been used.

Recent studies have found that, despite the efforts of state legislatures and the courts to develop fair and reasonable standards, the system may still result in inconsistent and racially biased sentences. Murderers of whites are far more likely to be sentenced to death than murderers of blacks. Such studies have given new impetus to the question of the constitutionality of the death penalty.

It is important to note that whether or not the Supreme Court says the Constitution prohibits the death penalty is an altogether different issue from the question of whether or not society ought to execute individuals who have committed certain kinds of crimes. Even if the death penalty is constitutional, states are free to abolish it. It is quite possible to argue that while the Constitution does not prevent the government from imposing the death penalty, the government should not use it.

What is the relationship of procedural justice and a republican form of government?

The Framers had personal experience with arbitrary government. They understood that rights would not be secure if the government had an unlimited ability to investigate people, accuse them of crimes, and hold them in jail or punish them in some other way. They also understood that republican or popular governments were capable of acting just as arbitrarily as monarchies. Thus the Framers addressed the Bill of Rights to all three branches of the federal government.

The Framers set out a careful process by which the innocence or guilt of a person could be decided. It is important to remember that procedural due process is designed to protect the innocent. In doing their job, they also can be used as "loopholes" by those who are guilty. Many have argued that this is a small price to pay for the protection we often take for granted. Above all, they argue, it is a reminder of our commitment to the idea that the actions of the government must be limited by the rule of law.

Reviewing and using the lesson

1. What are some of the procedural rights contained in the Sixth Amendment? How do these rights help guarantee a fair trial for people accused of crimes?

2. How would you explain the right to counsel? Why is this right important in an adversary system of justice?

3. What is "bail"? Why are people charged with crimes allowed to remain free on bail before trial?

4. How would you explain the Eighth Amendment right to be free from "cruel and unusual punishment"?

5. What is "capital punishment"? What arguments have been made to limit or abolish it?

6. The United States imprisons more people than any other nation. Yet, our crime rate remains very high. Do research and find alternative forms of punishment or programs that we, as a society, should explore to reduce the crime rate.

Lesson 7

Military Justice System

Key Terms

admissible
admonition
Article 15
censure
coerced
general, special, and summary court-martials
UCMJ

What You Will Learn to Do

• Justify the differences between the military and civilian justice systems

Linked Core Abilities

• Communicate using verbal, non-verbal, visual, and written techniques
• Apply critical thinking techniques

Skills and Knowledge You Will Gain along the Way

• Identify the four factors that determine whether a crime is service-connected
• Identify the rights of an accused person under the military justice system
• Explain the procedures for administering and imposing non-judicial punishment under Article 15 of the UCMJ
• Differentiate between the three levels of court-martial as they pertain to court composition and the types of cases heard by each level
• Define key words contained in this lesson

Chapter 6

Introduction

Military personnel do not have the same basic national rights and freedoms as civilians. For the armed forces to function efficiently, military personnel must give up some of their personal liberties and conform to military standards. Although most of them do not have a problem with the strict discipline of military life, the issue of basic rights becomes extremely important in a military court of law, especially because many of the military justice procedures are different from those used in civilian (federal and state) courts.

The Uniform Code of Military Justice (UCMJ)

The Uniform Code of Military Justice (**UCMJ**) is the basis of all military law in the United States Armed Forces. It describes all of the procedures that should be followed when a member of the armed forces is accused of committing a military offense. In addition, it protects the accused by listing their rights and ensuring that they receive a fair trial. The purpose of the UCMJ is to recognize the different needs of the military while still ensuring justice for all military personnel.

History of the UCMJ

Until 1951, the U.S. Army and Navy had their own court-martial systems. The Army Articles of War dated back to the Revolutionary War; they were borrowed from the British Articles of War with very few changes. Congress occasionally revised the Articles over the years, but the military justice system remained basically the same through World War II.

Under the Articles of War, the commander who initiated a court-martial had almost complete control over the outcome of the trial. The commander brought the charges, appointed officers to the court, and reviewed the proceedings, verdict, and sentence—all without approval from anyone with higher authority.

After World War II, there were many public objections to the military justice system. Congress responded to the complaints by carefully reviewing the Articles of War. The result of this effort was the UCMJ, which introduced several major reforms. These reforms brought military justice closer to civilian justice.

- **First, the UCMJ established a U.S. Court of Military Appeals composed of three civilian judges appointed for 15-year terms by the President (with the consent of the Senate).**
- **The UCMJ also provided for a law officer, similar to a judge, who would ensure a fair and orderly trial.**

Key Note Term

UCMJ (Uniform Code of Military Justice) – the basis for all military law in the U. S. Armed Forces; established by Congress in 1951.

- A third major reform provided by the UCMJ was that enlisted personnel could sit as members of the court if the accused was an enlisted person.

Since 1951, the Court of Military Appeals has undergone several changes. There are now five civilian judges who each serve for 15-year terms. A chief judge serves for five years and is succeeded by the next senior judge on the court. Additionally, in 1994, the name of the court was changed to the U.S. Court of Appeals for the Armed Forces.

Types of Military Offenses

Before 1969, all soldiers accused of crimes could be court-martialed simply because of their military status. However, the Supreme Court case of *O'Callahan v. Parker* limited the use of courts-martial to "service-connected" offenses. Factors that determine whether an offense is service-connected include the relationship of the offense to military duties, the presence of a threat to military personnel, abuse of military status or the location of the crime on a military base. Except in a few cases, a soldier can only be court-martialed if the offense in some way affects the military or its personnel.

One exception is a drug-related offense. Because an immediate, serious threat to the military is inherent in drugs, a drug offense is service-connected even if it occurs off-base. Violations of federal or state laws are another exception to the "service-connected" rule. According to Article 134 of the UCMJ, a soldier who violates a federal or state law can be court-martialed and can be tried by a federal or state court for the same offense.

Rights of the Accused

Even though the military justice system functions differently from the civilian justice system, the accused still has similar rights:

- **The right to a speedy trial**
- **The right against self-incrimination**
- **The right to counsel**
- **The right of due process**

Speedy Trial

An accused soldier must be brought to trial within 120 days after receiving notice of the charge. If the soldier is confined, the period is 90 days. A trial must occur within these time limits, or the charges will be dismissed.

The government is accountable for the time required to process a case and must explain any delays. Some delays are acceptable, as long as the government can show special circumstances that caused the delay.

Self-incrimination

The Fifth Amendment to the Constitution and Article 31 of the UCMJ protect soldiers against **coerced** statements. As in civilian arrests or questioning, the accused must receive a Miranda warning. For any statement to be used in a court-martial, the statement must be voluntary. If the prosecutor cannot prove that a military person's admission to an offense was voluntary, the statement cannot be used. In addition, any evidence that comes from a coerced statement will not be considered valid.

Counsel

Similar to civilians, military personnel have the right to consult a lawyer both before and during questioning. The accused may have a civilian lawyer, a military lawyer, or both. A civilian lawyer is at the military person's expense, but a military lawyer is free.

Due Process

If the government obtains evidence by using unlawful methods, the evidence cannot be used. For example, obtaining evidence by pumping a suspect's stomach or taking a urine sample is a violation of due process; however, a suspect can be required to step in plaster molds of footprints, make a handwriting sample, or submit to fingerprinting.

Searches and Seizures

The Fourth Amendment of the Constitution protects all citizens, including soldiers, against unreasonable searches and seizures; however, a "reasonable" search in the military may not be considered "reasonable" in civilian life. Before most civilian searches can begin, a judge must issue a search warrant based on a probable cause to search.

In the military, a commander can authorize a search without obtaining a warrant as long as there is probable cause. Although the commander can authorize the search orally, a written authorization stating the reasons for the search is preferred. Whether the authorization is oral or written, the commander must specify the place to be searched and the items to be seized; then, the commander cannot conduct the search personally. He or she can be present at the time of the search, but someone else must actually conduct it (such as the Military Police).

Commanders have the right and duty to inspect their troops to make sure they are prepared to accomplish the unit's mission. Inspections are not the same as searches. During an inspection, the commander looks at the overall status of the unit and does not focus attention on any particular person. A search, on the other hand, singles out individuals and looks for particular evidence.

Key Note Term

coerced – the act, process, or power of forcing someone to act or think in a given manner, such as by using force or threats as a form of control.

Key Note Term

admissible – capable of being allowed or accepted (as in a court of law); worthy of being admitted.

Article 15 – the least severe and most commonly used punitive measure for minor military offenses. Though called non-judicial punishment, the accused's company or battalion commander (who usually imposes non-judicial punishment) act in a quasi-judicial capacity.

If a commander finds illegal drugs, weapons, or other incriminating evidence during a routine inspection, the evidence is **admissible** in a court-martial. However, commanders cannot conduct a search under the pretense of an inspection. Any evidence seized during an unlawful inspection cannot be used in a trial.

Nonjudicial Punishment-Article 15 of the UCMJ

All commanders may impose non-judicial punishment under **Article 15** of the UCMJ on members within their command for offenses they consider to be minor; however, they also have the option of referring the matter to their immediate commander when a higher form of punishment may be more suitable for the offense committed. As one would expect, field grade officers have more punishment power than do company grade officers.

Because the decision to administer discipline under Article 15 is a personal responsibility of each commander, a commander's superior cannot specify when to use an Article 15 or what the punishment should be. However, a superior can withhold or limit a subordinate commander's authority to impose Article 15 punishment.

All commanders can impose any combination of up to four different types of punishment under Article 15. Again, this decision is a personal responsibility made by the commander based on the nature of the offense (after the commander has made a thorough investigation of the incident), prior record of the individual, recommendations made on the individual's behalf by other personnel, and so on.

Key Note Term

censure – an opinion or judgment that criticizes or condemns sternly.

admonition – cautionary advice or criticism for a fault; a mild censure.

- **Censure, admonition**, or reprimand. These types of punishment are generally in the form of an oral or written warning; however, if the offense is repeated, a harsher punishment may occur.
- **Loss of liberty.** Military personnel can be punished by correctional custody, arrest in quarters, extra duty, or restriction.
- **Forfeiture of pay.** Military personnel can lose a portion of their basic pay, sea pay, or foreign duty pay for a specified period of time.
- **Reduction in grade.** This punishment is the most severe non-judicial punishment. It affects the rate of pay and results in a loss of privileges and responsibilities.

Service Members' Options

When non-judicial punishment is being considered against a member of the Armed Forces, that individual has the right to:

- Consult with a judge advocate or other legal expert after receipt of the charges from the commander.
- Request an open hearing, which would be held in an informal and non-adversarial way.

- **Have a spokesperson present at the hearing.**

- **Have witnesses testify on his or her behalf at the hearing.**

- **Present evidence.**

- **Demand a court-martial instead of accepting punishment under Article 15; if this happens, the Article 15 proceedings stop and the commander decides whether to bring court-martial charges against that person.**

Military personnel who are punished under Article 15 have the right to appeal the punishment. The appeal first goes to the officer who imposed the punishment; then, if disapproved, to the next higher authority. Either officer may suspend or reduce the punishment.

Court-Martial Proceedings

Whenever possible, commanders use Article 15 punishment to avoid the time and expense of a court-martial; however, serious crimes require formal proceedings and the more severe punishment that accompanies a court-martial. There are three levels of courts-martial that handle cases ranging from relatively minor offenses to capital crimes. The levels, from lowest to highest are **summary, special,** and **general court martial**.

Summary Court-Martial

The summary court-martial is designed to discipline enlisted personnel who commit relatively minor offenses. The court is composed of one commissioned officer who acts as a judge, jury, and counsel for both sides. In a summary court-martial, the accused is not entitled to a detailed military counsel (although the accused is entitled to consult with military counsel prior to the court-martial); however, this person may be represented by a civilian attorney at no expense to the government.

No accused may be tried by a summary court-martial if he or she objects; however, the case may then be referred to a higher court.

Because the summary court-martial handles only minor offenses, its punishments are similar to Article 15 punishment. The maximum punishments allowed for a summary court-martial for enlisted personnel in the pay grades of E-1 to E-4 are forfeiture of two-thirds of one month's pay; confinement for one month, hard labor without confinement for 45 days, or restriction for two months; and/or reduction to the lowest enlisted grade. Enlisted personnel in the grades of E-5 to E-9 may be reduced only one grade and may not be confined or placed in hard labor without confinement. Officers cannot be tried by a summary court-martial.

Key Note Term

summary court martial – the lowest level of trial courts in the military justice system, which provides for the disposition of minor offenses under a simple procedure when nonpunitive measures and punishment are inappropriate or ineffective. It may try only enlisted personnel; its punishment is less severe for senior enlisted personnel; and it does not have the authority to impose a dishonorable discharge of any kind.

Key Note Term

special court martial – the intermediate level of trial courts in the military justice system, which tries offenses not punishable by death; if convened by a general court-martial convening authority and a punitive discharge is specifically authorized, it has the authority to impose a bad-conduct discharge to enlisted members. It does not have the authority to dismiss or confine commissioned officers.

general court martial – the highest level of trial courts in the military justice system, which tries the most serious kinds of cases with authority to impose a dishonorable discharge or capital punishment.

Special Court-Martial

A special court-martial may try any offense not punishable by death. The special court may consist of at least three members and a military judge or a military judge alone if the accused so requests and the judge grants the request. The accused has the right to be represented by a military lawyer or a civilian lawyer at no expense to the government. An accused enlisted member can also request that the court consist of one-third enlisted personnel.

A special court-martial can order a maximum punishment of confinement for six months, forfeiture of two-thirds of a month's pay for six months, and reduction to the lowest enlisted grade. If a punitive discharge is specifically authorized, a special court-martial can impose a bad-conduct discharge on enlisted members in addition to the other punishments. Although officers can be tried by a special court-martial, they cannot be confined or dismissed.

General Court-Martial

The highest level of trial courts in the military justice system is the general court-martial. General courts try military personnel for the most serious crimes, such as treason and murder. A general officer ordinarily convenes a general court-martial, and each case must have a formal pre-trial investigation.

A general court-martial usually consists of a military judge and at least five members. Except in a capital case, the accused may request that the court consist of a military judge alone. The rules regarding composition of the court and the accused's attorney rights are generally the same for a special court-martial. A general court-martial can impose a dishonorable discharge, dismissal, confinement for life or a lesser term, forfeiture of all pay and allowances, and in capital cases, death.

Court-Martial Appeals

Following a trial, the convening authority has the sole power and responsibility to approve that part of the findings and sentence that he/she finds correct in law and in fact. The convening authority may also approve or set aside, in whole or in part, the findings of guilty and the sentence, but may not change not guilty findings to guilty or increase the severity of the adjudged sentence.

All courts-martial are reviewed by an attorney for legal sufficiency. Findings from a general court-martial or a special court-martial which imposed a bad-conduct discharge are sent to the Court of Military Review for a formal appeal after the convening authority has taken action. Some convictions may also be appealed to the U.S. Court of Appeals for the Armed Forces. This court's jurisdiction is worldwide, but it encompasses only questions of law arising from trials by court-martial where:

- **A death sentence is imposed**
- **A case is certified for review by the Judge Advocate General**
- **The accused, who faces a severe sentence, petitions and shows good cause for further review**

The Supreme Court has jurisdiction to review decisions of the U.S. Court of Appeals for the Armed Forces and of military appellate courts in which the U.S. has taken an appeal from rulings by military judges during trials by court-martial.

Case Studies: A Comparison

How does military justice compare to federal justice? Would a case involving a civilian accused of a crime be handled in the same way if a military person were accused of the same crime, or vise versa? The best way to answer these questions is to compare the two systems; therefore, the remainder of this lesson presents three case studies for you to examine. Be prepared to discuss your views about them or to write your views in your journal.

Article 15 for Insubordination

The duty roster read, "Private Breck—cleaning detail." When Cathy Breck reported to her platoon sergeant, SFC Lancaster, he told her, "Your assignment is to clean the extra rifles before the inspection."

"But I already cleaned my rifle," Private Breck protested. "I shouldn't have to clean the rifles that I didn't even fire."

"It is your turn on the duty roster," replied SFC Lancaster. "I don't want to hear any more complaints. Report to the arms room."

"Well, I didn't make those rifles dirty, so I'm not going to clean them," responded Breck.

"Private Breck, this unit can't function properly with this kind of insubordination. If you refuse to complete this assignment, I'll have no choice but to recommend you for an Article 15. This incident will go on your record."

Private Breck still refused to perform her duty and the company commander administered her an Article 15. She was restricted for 15 days, required to forfeit one-third of her pay for one month, and directed to clean all the rifles as well as the entire arms room. She appealed the punishment, but the company commander stuck with the original decision and the battalion commander did not grant her appeal.

United States v. Garwood

PFC Robert R. Garwood did not return from the Vietnam War until 1979, 14 years after he had been taken a prisoner of war (POW) by the North Vietnamese. Major Thomas Hamilton conducted an investigation of this incident while Garwood was assigned to Camp Lejeune, NC. Hamilton discovered that Garwood had accepted a position in the North Vietnamese Army, acted as a guard for other American prisoners, worked as a questioner for the Vietnamese Communists, struck an American without reason, and encouraged Americans to throw down their weapons and refuse to fight. In February of 1980, Hamilton recommended that Garwood be court-martialed on the charges of:

Soliciting an act of misbehavior before the enemy (authorized a maximum punishment of ten years confinement at hard labor)

Unauthorized absence without leave (this charge was combined with Charge #3)

Desertion in time of war (authorized the maximum punishment: the death penalty, confinement at hard labor for life, total forfeiture of pay and allowances, reduction to the lowest enlisted grade, and/or dishonorable discharge)

Collaborating with the enemy (authorized the same punishment as Charge #3)

Maltreatment of prisoners of war (authorized the maximum punishment, but not the death penalty)

Although Major Hamilton recommended that the death penalty not be precluded as a punishment and that while the alleged offenses were serious in nature, it was his opinion this case be referred as a non-capital offense—unless the ordering officer considered the death penalty to be appropriate punishment if adjudged. Major Hamilton further recommended that if the case was referred as non-capital, then the maximum punishment would be limited to confinement to hard labor for life, forfeiture of all pay and allowances, reduction to the lowest enlisted grade, and/or dishonorable discharge.

After a thorough review, Brigadier General David Barker ordered a general court-martial for Garwood as a non-capital case.

In the only prosecuted case of this kind arising from the Vietnam War, Garwood was found guilty on February 5, 1981 of collaborating with the enemy while a POW in Vietnam in 1967. Because Garwood had presumably been a captive of the North Vietnamese from 1965 to 1979, the court did not sentence him to prison. Instead, he was reduced in rank and given a dishonorable discharge.

Schenck v. United States

Charles R. Schenck was a civilian who opposed the United States' involvement in World War I. In 1917, he mailed pamphlets to thousands of young men, urging them to refuse the draft. According to the Espionage Act of 1917, it was illegal to interfere with the war effort. A U.S. District Court convicted Schenck for his actions.

Schenck's lawyers appealed his case to the Supreme Court, stating that the Espionage Act violated Schenck's First Amendment right to freedom of speech. The Court unanimously decided that what a person has the right to say during peacetime is different from what a person can say when the nation is at war. According to this Court, Schenck's words presented a "clear and present danger" to the U.S., and his acts were not protected by the Constitution.

Conclusion

Before and during World War II, the Army and Navy had separate disciplinary codes, but the creation of the Air Force after that war led to the enactment of a criminal law system that would be uniformly applied by all the services. Since Congress enacted the Uniform Code of Military Justice (UCMJ) in 1951, it has become the basis for the criminal law system for the military. Over the years since its creation, the UCMJ has evolved to the extent that it now balances the need to maintain discipline in the armed forces while giving military members who are accused of crimes rights that closely parallel those of accused persons in the civilian sector.

Lesson Review

1. **What is the UCMJ? Explain its purpose.**

2. **In a military justice system, what are the rights of the accused?**

3. **Explain the three types of court-martial proceedings.**

4. **What is Article 15? What does it provide?**

Chapter 6

Lesson Review

Citizen Roles in American Democracy

United Nations founded (1945)		Universal Declaration of Human Rights (1948)			
FDR delivers "Four Freedoms" speech (1941)		European Convention on Human Rights (1950)	Griswold v. Connecticut (1965)	Voting Rights Act (1975)	Berlin Wall falls (1989)
1930s	**1940s**	**1950s**	**1960s**	**1970s**	**1980s**
First female senator elected (1932)	U.S. tests world's first atomic bomb (1945)	First African American major league baseball player (1947)	First commercial nuclear power plant opens (1957)	Watergate burglars arrested (1972)	First female Supreme Court Justice (1981)	Equal Rights Amendment is defeated (1982)

Lesson 1

Roles of Citizens

Key Terms

civility
civil rights
common good
commonwealth
empowerment
enlightened self-interest
greatest happiness of the greatest number
melting pot
nation of nations
naturalized citizen
orthodoxy
political action
political rights
resident alien
social action
spirit of association

What You Will Learn to Do

- Determine your role as a citizen of a constitutional democracy

Linked Core Abilities

- Communicate using verbal, non-verbal, visual, and written techniques

- Do your share as a good citizen in your school, community, country, and the world

Skills and Knowledge You Will Gain along the Way

- Explain the relationship between self-interest and the common good

- Describe the differences between citizens and resident aliens

- Explain how citizenship in a constitutional democracy differs from citizenship in a totalitarian state
- Explain how citizens can exercise their rights and responsibilities in a constitutional democracy
- Define key words contained in this lesson

Introduction

In this lesson you examine the American citizenship and its relationship to the natural rights philosophy, republicanism, and constitutional democracy. You also examine the characteristics of effective citizenship, explore the rights and responsibilities of citizenship, and determine the qualities citizens need to develop to become effective citizens in our society.

What Does It Mean to Be a Citizen?

How have Americans thought of citizenship?

From its beginnings, America was strongly influenced by the ideals of classical republicanism. The early American colonies of the seventeenth century were political communities in which civic virtue could be exercised. Many of these colonies were called **commonwealths,** a word that meant something like a republic, that is, self-governing communities of equals whose members were expected to help serve the good of all. In the Mayflower Compact, the Pilgrims declared their intent to "covenant and combine themselves together into a civil body politic."

The American Founders admired the civic virtue of the ancients and the classical models of republican government. They also were influenced by the natural rights philosophy of John Locke. The natural rights philosophy conflicted in several important ways with the ideals of classical republicanism. Instead of the common good, it stressed the importance of individual rights and self-interest. Society and government, according to Locke, were established to protect the rights of the individual. Human communities did not exist for their own sake, but rather to protect the individuals belonging to them, each of whom is free to pursue his or her own interest so long as it does not interfere with the interests of others.

The Founders were influenced by both these theories of government. They had to compromise in adapting this intellectual inheritance to the conditions in America. They established a limited government of checks and balances that allowed civic virtue to flourish, but also could prevent abuses of self-interest when it did not.

The Founders realized that the classical republicanism of the ancient city states could not be easily adapted to a country as large and diverse as America. They also recognized that republican self-government required a greater measure of

Reprinted from *We the People: The Citizen and the Constitution,* published by the Center for Civic Education.

civic virtue than did other forms of government. Civic virtue, therefore, was essential. But how was civic virtue to be promoted in this new experiment in republican self-government?

In general, the Founders looked to two solutions: religion and education. The Founders themselves had different religious beliefs. Many were wary of the dangers that religious **orthodoxy** posed to individual freedom. At the same time, however, they acknowledged the value of organized religion in promoting virtue. Virtuous behavior, which enabled people to control their passions, would produce upright, responsible citizens.

The second solution that the Founders recognized was the importance of education to good citizenship. For the American experiment in republican self-government to succeed, each of its citizens had to be schooled in the ideals and principles upon which that experiment was based. Formal schooling, together with a free press, became a priority in the early years of the new republic. Public or "common schools" developed rapidly to prepare Americans not only as workers in a growing economy, but also as citizens committed to the principles of self-government. As nineteenth-century American educator Horace Mann observed, "schoolhouses are the republican line of fortifications."

How did Tocqueville connect good citizenship with self-interest in the American democracy?

Alexis de Tocqueville was a young French aristocrat who visited the United States in the 1830s, at a time when the spirit of Jacksonian democracy was helping to bring about greater equality and more widespread participation in the nation's political life. He was curious about and impressed by America's experiment in democracy and how well it worked. After finishing his tour of the United States, he recorded his impressions in a very influential book, *Democracy in America*.

Tocqueville found much to admire and criticize as he traveled the country. Though impressed by the equality of opportunity in the American democracy, he wondered how a society so devoted to materialism and the pursuit of individual self-interest could produce the civic spirit needed for self-government.

He believed the answer was to be found in the qualities he admired in American democracy: traditions of local self-government and habits of free association.

The New England townships were tiny models of classical republicanism, where the habits of citizenship were developed. Tocqueville observed that a citizen of one of these American towns

takes part in every affair of the place; he practices the act of government in the small sphere within his reach...and collects clear practical notions on the nature of his duties and the extent of his rights.

This tradition of local self-government also encouraged voluntary association. Nothing so impressed de Tocqueville about America as the fondness American citizens had for banding together to address problems of common interest. While Europeans would prefer to let government address all public problems, Americans preferred to do it themselves, as citizens. This **spirit of association** remains a distinctive characteristic of American society today.

Such traditions of local self-government and habits of free association, Tocqueville concluded, provided a way for teaching citizenship in the American democracy. He wrote,

The most powerful and perhaps the only means that we still possess of interesting men in the welfare of their country is to make them participate in the government. At the present time civic zeal seems to be inseparable from the exercise of political rights.

Like the Founders, Tocqueville realized that the civic virtue of the ancients was not practical in the United States. Democratic citizenship, he believed, would have to depend on something else. He did not believe there had to be a contradiction between self-interest and civic-mindedness. In a land of equality and widespread participation in political life, each citizen could see a connection between self-interest and the common good. American citizens are willing to devote themselves to public ends, Tocqueville believed, because they realize that the fulfillment of their private ambitions depends in large part on the success of the democratic society. Good citizenship for Tocqueville, therefore, was nothing other than **enlightened self-interest.**

What do you think?

1. **Some people claim that the best way to achieve the common good is for each person to work for his or her self-interest. Do you agree? Why or why not?**

2. **The common good is a principle originally practiced in relatively small and homogeneous societies. Do you think there is a common good in a nation as large and diverse as the Unites States? Why or why not?**

3. **What should voters do if their representative votes for a bill that is good for the entire country but damages their particular interest?**

Who is a citizen?

In our country, anyone who is born in the United States, or is born to citizens of the United States, is a citizen. The term used for noncitizens who legally reside in the United States is **resident aliens.** By satisfying certain requirements, resident aliens may become **naturalized citizens.**

Both resident aliens and citizens who live in the United States must obey the laws of the United States. They also receive the protection of those laws. Resident aliens are guaranteed most of the rights possessed by citizens. If they are tried in a court of law, for example, they are guaranteed the same rights to due process that are provided for citizens in the Constitution.

There are two important rights, however, that citizens have and aliens do not: the rights to vote and to hold public office. Possessing these rights, many people have argued, is what distinguishes the citizen from the noncitizen. Some people also argue that in possessing these important rights, citizens also have special responsibilities toward their country that noncitizens do not.

Critical Thinking Exercise

Evaluating, Taking, and Defending a Position on Extending the Right to Vote for School Board Members to Resident Aliens

Your class should be divided into four groups—two for the issue and two against. Each group should choose a spokesperson to present the group's views to the class. Groups on the same side of the issue should compare ideas and not make duplicate points. After the four presentations are made the class should vote on whether to pass the proposed legislation.

In some communities in our nation, there is growing interest in extending to resident aliens the right to vote in local school board elections. Proponents of such a law argue that resident aliens pay state and local taxes to support public education and that all taxpayers should have a representative voice influencing policies that directly affect them or their children. In addition, resident aliens have met all the criteria for being in this country legally. Opponents argue that because resident aliens are not citizens, they lack a long-term interest in the welfare of the community, and granting them voting rights in school board elections blurs the distinction between rights of citizens and noncitizens. It is the first step, they argue, in the demise of meaningful citizenship.

1. **Do you think that resident aliens who must pay taxes and obey the government's laws should have a voice in local government by being permitted to vote? Why or why not?**

2. **Do you think that resident aliens should have the right to serve as elected members of local government?**

3. **What political obligations or responsibilities should resident aliens or noncitizens have? Explain your position.**

How has the American ideal of citizenship adapted itself to an increasingly diverse society?

From its beginnings, America has been what the poet Walt Whitman called a **"nation of nations,"** peopled by millions of immigrants of different races, religions, languages, and ethnic backgrounds. One of the greatest challenges to the American experiment in republican government has been to form a common bond out of such diversity. That common bond is provided by the ideal of American citizenship and a commitment to the Constitution and its ideals and principles. Though they could not foresee how diverse the immigration to this country would become, many of the Founders recognized that the new country would continue to take in people of different origins. For them, becoming an American was primarily a matter of allegiance to the political ideals of the new land. In the early nineteenth century, Congress established five years as the minimum time required for immigrants to learn these ideals and to become naturalized citizens.

As George Washington told the members of the Touro Synagogue of Newport, Rhode Island, in 1790,

Happily, the government of the United States that gives to bigotry no sanction, to persecution no assistance, requires only that they who live under its protection should demean themselves as good citizens in giving it their effectual support.

For Washington and other Founders, good citizenship meant responsible conduct and acceptance of the nation's political principles.

For much of our nation's history, becoming an American meant something more. It represented a fresh start, a new beginning, leaving the injustices and prejudices of the old world behind.

"What then is this American, this new man?" asked Crevecoeur, the eighteenth-century French immigrant to America. Americans, Crevecoeur believed, had left the values and lifestyles of their different origins behind to become "a new race of men." Perhaps the most famous metaphor for this ideal of Americanization was expressed by Israel Zangwell in his 1908 play, *The Melting Pot,* "America is God's crucible, the great **melting pot** where all the races of men are melting and reforming."

Has America been a melting pot? Not entirely. Throughout our history the assimilation of different people into a new American identity has been only partially successful in achieving the classical republican ideal of a common culture. Many immigrants to the new land were reluctant to give up the heritages they brought with them. They were proud of both their "Americaness" and the cultural inheritance they carried to the New World.

As a nation of immigrants we have come to appreciate the benefits of the great mixture of heritages transplanted to America. They have enriched American life in many ways. The diversity of the nation's cultural inheritance also has placed a heavy responsibility on our ideal of citizenship. The unity of American society depends very largely on the ability of that ideal—the civic culture all Americans, whatever their particular origins, share in common—to hold us together as a nation. Throughout our history there has been tension between the diversity of backgrounds and the common ideal of citizenship. The need to balance unity with diversity remains a challenging goal for your generation.

Critical Thinking Exercise

Evaluating the Relationship Between the Ideals of Classical Republicanism and Contemporary American Citizenship

Some observers of American society today are worried about the future health of America's experiment in self-government. They believe we have inherited too much of the self-interest of the natural rights philosophy and not enough of the public spirit of classical republicanism. These critics see contemporary America as a fragmented society, in which individuals are preoccupied with the pursuit of economic self-interest. Some feel that government is disconnected from people's lives. Americans see fewer opportunities to exercise their responsibilities as citizens than they did in the past.

Some critics believe a return to the principles of classical republicanism is the solution to this problem. The nation's schools, they say, should improve civics education, and our democratic institutions must create new ways to involve citizens in public affairs.

Work in small groups to develop positions on the following questions. Be prepared to present and defend your positions before the class.

1. **Do you think the observations in the exercise about contemporary American society are accurate? Explain your position.**

2. **Do you think the classical republican sense of community is possible in American society today? What forces work against it? What resources might encourage its development?**

3. **What ways can you think of to involve citizens in public affairs? What reforms would you propose to the political process? To the Constitution? To our education system?**

How Do We Use Our Citizenship?

How do citizens in a constitutional democracy differ from those in a dictatorship or totalitarian state?

Citizenship has meant different things at different times in history and in different places. Totalitarian states and dictatorships also refer to those they govern as citizens—though they may lack the rights and responsibilities associated with American citizenship. Your role as a citizen of a constitutional democracy differs in fundamental respects from the role of a citizen living under unlimited or arbitrary government. While passive obedience and unquestioning loyalty are demanded by unlimited regimes, the citizen of a constitutional democracy is expected to be a critical and participating member of the political community. Citizens of constitutional democracies should have a reasoned loyalty and obedience to law not based on unquestioning deference to authority.

Criticism of one's government may carry with it a right, and perhaps even a duty, to disobey laws you believe are unjust laws—the civil rights movement provides a contemporary example.

What do you think?

1. **Is civil disobedience ever a justified form of political participation? Give two examples to support your position.**

2. **Under what circumstances do you think a citizen in a representative democracy has a right to violate a law? Explain your position.**

3. **What would be a proper response of the government to someone, who for reasons of conscience, breaks a law?**

4. **Do you agree with Thomas Jefferson that "a little rebellion" now and then is healthy for the political system? If so, what form might a little rebellion take?**

Reprinted from *We the People: The Citizen and the Constitution,* published by the Center for Civic Education.

Figure 7.1.1: Is it possible to generate reasoned loyalty and obedience in a system that demands unquestioned deference to authority? Why?

What types of rights and responsibilities do citizens have?

As you consider the rights of citizenship, it is important to distinguish between civil rights and political rights.

- **Civil rights** protect us in our private lives from the arbitrary and unfair actions of government.
- **Political rights** allow us to participate in our own governance.

Since noncitizens living in this country are granted the same civil rights that citizens enjoy, political rights are to a large extent what define our status as citizens. You must be a citizen to exercise the rights to vote or serve in government.

Many of our rights suggest a corresponding obligation. In exercising our rights as individuals, we must respect other citizens' use of those same rights. Some obligations are legal, imposed by laws commonly agreed upon. For example, we have an obligation to obey the law, including those laws that require us to pay taxes, serve on juries, and meet the other responsibilities that help government operate.

Most of us would agree that we also have certain moral obligations as citizens. For example, some argue we have a duty, as well as a right, to vote. Even though the law no longer requires American citizens to perform military service, many Americans believe it is a duty to defend one's country or to assist it in other emergencies.

What do you think

1. How does Voltaire's statement "I may detest what you say, but will defend to the death your right to say it," relate to the responsibilities of citizenship?

2. Why is it important to speak up for the rights of others even if your own rights are not endangered?

Why should we try to be effective citizens?

The natural rights philosophy and classical republicanism provide different answers to this question.

The natural rights philosophy emphasizes the elective nature of citizenship. Each citizen has a choice whether to remain a citizen of the United States. Each citizen possesses certain natural rights and it is the primary purpose of government to protect these rights. In choosing a government to protect these rights, citizens follow their self-interest in making sure that government does its job. We pay attention to how well the people we choose to govern us are doing their jobs. We participate as citizens, therefore, to ensure that government complies with its contractual obligations to us as individuals.

The classical republican philosophy, on the other hand, emphasizes our obligation to the society into which we were born or naturalized. Classical republicanism emphasizes the **common good** and the obligation of each citizen to serve the good of the whole community. Citizenship requires that we put this general good before our own self-interest, especially when the two conflict.

In practice, of course, the American civic tradition includes both concepts of citizenship. One of the enduring challenges you face as a citizen is sorting out for yourself the conflict between them in many different situations.

Critical Thinking Exercise

Reconciling the Common Good and Individual Self-Interest

Your class will be divided into small groups to discuss the issue of conflict between the good of the whole society and individual self-interest. Discuss and take a position on the questions at the end of the exercise. Be prepared to share your opinions with the class.

The conflict between the common good and self-interest is not the only problem you face as citizens. Sometimes it is difficult to determine what the common good or your own self-interest actually is. In some situations the common good may be quite clear as, for example, the need to protect the community from criminals, foreign enemies, and air pollution. In other situations, however, citizens strongly disagree about what the common good is and what policies are needed to serve it. For example, some would argue that laws strictly limiting human activity in environmentally sensitive areas are necessary to preserve the future well-being of our natural resources. Others claim that such restrictive policies can endanger the economy and may violate property rights.

It is not always easy to know how our individual interests are served. What may appear to be self-interest in the short-run might not be in our best long-term interest. Some aspects of this problem are raised in the following questions.

1. Is the common good **the greatest happiness of the greatest number?** If so, what does that phrase mean? Should the measurement of the greatest number be a minimum of 51 percent or should the percentage be higher? What would be the danger in determining the common good according to this principle?

2. Is the common good the goals that all people in the nation share? If so, how do we find out what those goals are?

3. If you find that you and your fellow citizens cannot agree on what the common good is, should you just pursue your own interests and forget about what is good for all? What alternatives might there be?

What do we need to understand to become effective citizens in a constitutional democracy?

However defined, the effective use of rights and responsibilities in a constitutional democracy requires certain beliefs, commitments, and skills. They can be described as follows:

Civic values. These express our most fundamental beliefs about the purpose of government within a society and the goals that we expect a government to achieve. They are ideals expressed or implied in some of the nation's founding documents, including the Declaration of Independence and the Preamble to the Constitution. They include such ideals as the dignity of the individual, equality, and justice. Though we as citizens might disagree about the meaning and relative importance of each specific value, we share a broad agreement about their significance in defining the ultimate ends of the society we have established.

Civic principles. These can be defined as those principles of government that best enable society to realize its civic values. Included among these essential principles would be the rule of law, popular sovereignty, and freedom of expression. Such principles define our commitment to constitutional government and democracy.

Civic skills. These describe the abilities we need as individuals to help realize civic values and make civic principles work. To be effective citizens we must have knowledge of our government's history and how it operates. We also must develop our intellectual abilities: analytical skills for the solving of problems, and communication skills to express our opinions and understand the opinions of others.

Civic dispositions. Effective citizenship is not possible if we do not adopt those dispositions or qualities of behavior that sustain a civic culture in a free society. Such a culture depends on tolerance, fairness, a respect for the opinions of others, and a commitment to truth. The word **civility** suggests the decency and integrity that are essential to a constitutional democracy.

What do you think?

1. What do you consider to be the principle obligations of good citizenship?

2. Does civic responsibility imply that citizens not only obey laws, but report law-breakers to the authorities? For example, if you saw a friend shoplifting, are you morally obligated to report him or her?

3. What arguments can you make to convince a friend or classmate to become a more active citizen?

4. What means should a good citizens use to promote his or her own social and political views?

What do we mean by empowerment?

By developing an informed commitment to the values, principles, and dispositions of our civic culture and by acquiring the knowledge and skills necessary to play a role in it, we become "empowered" as citizens. **Empowerment** is a word we sometimes use today to describe the ability to "make one's voice heard" in public affairs. With empowerment, each of us knows that we have the potential to be effective as citizens when the need and opportunity arise.

You have more empowerment than you may realize. In 1991, at the time our country was celebrating the 200th anniversary of the Bill of Rights, a group of high school students in North Carolina discovered that their state had never ratified the Twenty-fourth Amendment, which abolished the poll tax and other taxes that had been used to discriminate against African Americans. As a project, the students investigated the legal requirements for ratification. They then petitioned the North Carolina state legislature to formally ratify the amendment. The students visited the state capitol and lobbied their legislators. After the legislature complied, the students carried the official notice of ratification to Washington, D.C., where they presented it to the Archivist of the United States. Through this school project, the students demonstrated their empowerment as citizens.

How do we learn to become effective citizens?

Citizenship in a free society is not always easy. Freedom requires us to live as self-reliant individuals, to think for ourselves, to solve our own problems, to cope with uncertainty and change, and to assist and respect others.

Citizens are made, not born. Like the ancient Greeks and Romans, the Founders placed great importance on the role of education in preparing each generation for citizenship. Your education will help provide you with the knowledge and skills to function effectively as citizens of a constitutional democracy. Practical experience has been as important as formal schooling in preparing Americans for citizenship. Americans learn the skills of citizenship through the many opportunities to participate in public affairs.

We begin the process of learning to be citizens in early childhood. At home and in the classroom, we begin to think for ourselves, to express our own opinions, and to respect the opinions of others. Through such activities as student government, school projects, sports, and community and club activities, we begin to acquire the skills of teamwork, organization, and debate. In short, many of the qualities that we need for citizenship begin to develop early in our lives.

How do we exercise our rights and responsibilities as citizens?

In dealing with the problems of our communities and the nation, we have different possibilities. We may engage in **social action** or we may engage in **political action.** We may, of course, choose to engage in both. For example, in dealing with the problems of crime in the community, we might join a neighborhood watch. Alternatively, we might organize other members of the community to present the problem to the city council in an effort to get more police officers on the streets. The first is an example of social action, the second an example of political action. These two courses of action are not mutually exclusive. We might decide to engage in both at the same time.

One of the issues we must decide as citizens is how a particular problem is most effectively solved. The decision we make depends on our analysis of the problem, our estimate of the possible solutions, and our own values. Making these decisions lies at the heart of the practice of responsible citizenship.

Critical Thinking Exercise

Examining the Responsibilities of Citizenship and Deciding on How They Can Be Fulfilled

In contemporary urban and rural America, violence by and against young people is receiving increased social and political attention, as well as daily coverage on television and in newspapers. Statistically, the incidence of youth violence has not increased during the last decade, the deadliness of it has. More young people carry guns or other weapons and use them as a means of settling disputes or intimidating others.

1. **What responsibilities, if any, do you as a citizen have to promote sound political and social policies designed to decrease or prevent the problem of violence?**

2. **What social actions can you, as a citizen of your school and community, become involved in to help prevent the problem?**

3. **What political actions can you become involved in?**

4. **What values and interests do you think are important for you as a citizen to promote in connection with prevention of violence by and against young people?**

Reviewing and using the lesson

1. **How would you explain the term "commonwealth"?**

2. **How did the Founders expect to promote civic virtue in a country as large and diverse as the United States?**

3. **How would you explain the term "enlightened self-interest"?**

4. **What is the difference between citizens and resident aliens? What rights and responsibilities do both citizens and resident aliens have? What rights and responsibilities do citizens have that resident aliens do not?**

5. **Given the diversity of American society, what provides a common bond to us as Americans?**

6. **Write an editorial on the role of citizens in a constitutional democracy based on the following quotation from Adlai Stevenson: "As citizens of this democracy, you are the rulers and the ruled, the lawgivers and the law abiding, the beginning and the end."**

7. **How would you describe the role of citizens in a constitutional democracy?**

8. **How might a classical republican explain the duty to be an active citizen? How might a natural rights philosopher explain this duty?**

9. **How would you define the "common good"? Why might people seek to promote the common good instead of their own interests?**

10. **What are civic values, civic principles, civic skills, and civic dispositions?**

11. **How would you explain the difference between "social action" and "political action"?**

Lesson 2

New Citizenship and Constitutional Issues

Key Terms

broad construction
cosmopolitan
E Pluribus Unum
electronic city-state
emanations
existence
futurists
global village
implied
international
judicial activism
judicial restraint
life
penumbras
plebiscite
strict construction
telecommunications
teledemocracy
unenumerated rights

What You Will Learn to Do

- Predict how increased diversity, technological changes, closer international relationships, and current constitutional issues are likely to affect your life as an American citizen over the next 10 years

Linked Core Abilities

- Communicate using verbal, non-verbal, visual, and written techniques
- Do your share as a good citizen in your school, community, country, and the world

Chapter 7

Skills and Knowledge You Will Gain along the Way

- Describe developments taking place in the world that have the potential to have an impact on the future of American citizenship

- Explain the impact of increased diversity in society on the political system

- Describe the potential impact of increasingly sophisticated technology on representative democracy

- Explain how changes in the complexity of American society create new constitutional issues

- Describe the basic elements of the Virginia Plan and the New Jersey Plan and the differences between them

- Describe constitutional issues currently being raised in American society

- Explain the reasons for the disagreements among the delegates regarding representation

- Describe unenumerated rights and the controversies raised by the Ninth Amendment

- Define key words contained in this lesson

Introduction

In this lesson you explore three trends that may impact citizenship in the future: the increasing diversity of American society; the impact of modern technology; and America's growing interdependence with the rest of the world. In addition, you examine some constitutional issues facing the United States. Finally, you predict how these issues and trends might affect your life as an American citizen over the next ten years.

How May Citizenship Change in the Nation's Third Century?

What are some developments now taking place in the world that will likely affect the future of American citizenship?

Three developments promise to shape the future of American citizenship in important ways:

- **the increasing diversity of American society**

- **the impact of modern technology, especially the computer and electronic telecommunications**

- **America's growing interdependence with the rest of the world**

Reprinted from *We the People: The Citizen and the Constitution,* published by the Center for Civic Education.

How is diversity in American society creating new challenges for the ideal of American citizenship?

You know how Americans have adapted the idea of citizenship to a nation of immigrants, people from many lands and cultures, bound together by a commitment to a common set of political values. The American ideal of *E Pluribus Unum*—Out of Many, One—has usually been able to balance the benefits of a diverse society with the unifying influence of a common civic culture. One of the major challenges you face as an American citizen is to sustain that balance in a society that is becoming far more diverse and complex.

America in the founding era was a nation of 3.5 million inhabitants—3 million free whites and half a million enslaved Africans. Most of the white population were northern European in ancestry. The young republic also was overwhelmingly Protestant. Today America is a microcosm of the world. It has become one of the most ethnically diverse countries on earth. You may see evidence of this diversity in your school. More than 100 languages are spoken by students in the Los Angeles school district. The results of recent immigration to this country have been dramatic. Of the 14 million immigrants since 1965, 85 percent have come from non-European countries. During the 1980s, immigrants to the United States came from 164 different lands. By the turn of the century, one in every four Americans will be either Hispanic, African American, or Asian. By the year 2030, one-half of the country's population will belong to one minority group or another. In a sense, there will no longer be a traditional majority group. In 1995 only 15 percent of Americans identify themselves as descendants of British immigrants, who once comprised a large majority of the population. The faces of "We the People" have changed considerably in the course of 200 years and will continue to change during your lifetime.

What consequences will the change toward a more diverse society have for us as citizens?

Americans today disagree about the answers to this question. To some the diversity brought about by recent immigration is no different from what has happened throughout American history. The mix of people has strengthened American society and reaffirmed our commitment to ideals that are the property of all humanity, not a particular ethnic group. As with their predecessors, most recent immigrants have adapted to American society, enriching the nation's economic life, culture, and educational institutions.

Others worry that there are limits to how much diversity the country can absorb without losing the common bonds that unite us. They fear that in an increasingly diverse society, self-interests may prevail over the common good. A challenge for your generation as for all previous generations is balancing the *unum* with the *pluribus* in America.

What do you think?

1. What advantages does our political system gain from diversity of people and ideas? What might be some disadvantages?

2. When does diversity become an issue in a free society? Is there such a thing as too much diversity? What effects—good or bad—do you think groups and "cliques" have on the life of your school community?

3. Do you agree with Woodrow Wilson that "a man who thinks of himself as belonging to a particular group in America has not yet become an American?" Why or why not?

4. What obligations, if any, do you think you should have as a citizen toward people who hold social, religious, or political beliefs with which you strongly disagree? Explain your position.

How is citizenship being changed by modern technology?

Modern technology has expanded the possibilities for participatory citizenship. Audio and video teleconferencing has become a familiar way for citizens to discuss issues of common concern. So has talk radio. Some state legislatures have begun to use such telecommunications on a regular basis as a way of staying in touch with their constituents. Advocacy groups of all kinds use the internet, databases, and electronic mail to inform and organize their members.

Some **futurists**—theorists who consider possibilities for the future based on current information and trends-see revolutionary implications in this technology. They envision the possibility of a **teledemocracy** in the years ahead. This term means a new version of direct democracy, where citizens can participate to a much greater extent in the affairs of government with less reliance on their elected representatives.

National **plebiscites** also have become a practical option. By use of on-line computerized voting, each citizen could register his or her views on particular issues, with the results instantly tabulated. "Going to the polls" could become an outmoded custom. Citizens could exercise their political rights from a computer work station at home or in public facilities like libraries or the post office.

The Framers believed that classical republicanism in its purest form was impractical in a country as large and diverse as the American republic. Some people believe that teledemocracy overcomes many of these impracticalities. The computer makes possible an **electronic city-state** in which citizens scattered across the country can join together to participate more effectively in public affairs.

Whatever its potential implications, the computer is forcing us to reexamine the most basic principles and institutions in our constitutional democracy.

Critical Thinking Exercise

Role Playing James Madison in the Third Century of Government Under the Constitution

Imagine, for a moment, that you are James Madison, brought back to life in the year 2000. What would be your assessment of teledemocracy and the electronic city-state? To help develop your position answer the following questions.

1. What are the dangers of direct democracy? Why did the Framers of the Constitution distrust it? Why did they prefer representative democracy instead?

2. To what extent is "public opinion" synonymous with the "will of the people"?

3. What should be the role of political leadership in a democracy? To what extent should leaders influence and to what extent should they be influenced by popular opinion? Can government in a democracy be too much in touch with the sentiments of the people?

4. In what ways is computer technology a threat to individual liberty as well as a tool on its behalf?

5. What expectations does teledemocracy place on citizens? To what extent are those expectations realistic?

6. The advancements of technology show us what we have the capability of doing, not what we necessarily have to do or should do. What other considerations about citizenship and civic culture might argue against the creation of teledemocracy?

How is internationalism affecting American citizenship?

One important consequence of the communications revolution has been America's increased interaction and interdependence with the rest of the world. Issues of national importance in the United States have an impact beyond our borders. Conversely, events and developments elsewhere in the world are becoming more significant in the lives of American citizens.

The achievements of modern technology are turning the world into a **global village,** with shared cultural, economic, and environmental concerns. National corporations have become international. Economic decisions made in Tokyo or London affect the things Americans buy and the jobs they seek. Environmental concerns also transcend national boundaries. Entertainment—music, sports, and film—command worldwide markets. The culture that we live in is becoming **cosmopolitan,** that is, belonging to the whole world.

The movement of people, as well as information, has helped bring about global interdependence. Improved transportation has been a key factor in increased immigration to the United States. People go where there is economic opportunity and they can go more easily and much farther than in the past. The movement of people across national borders will continue to increase. Such migrations help to reduce cultural and other differences that have historically divided nations. They also create new problems for governments which have the responsibility for providing for the well-being of citizens and other residents.

Citizenship in modern history has been defined largely in terms of nation-states. The idea of being a citizen, however, developed in many different political contexts throughout history, from tiny city-states to large empires. In the American experience, citizenship has changed in its patterns of allegiance and loyalty. Before the Civil War, many Americans would have defined their citizenship in terms of loyalty to their respective states rather than to the United States.

Although national citizenship is likely to remain fundamentally important in the future, the issues confronting American citizens are increasingly **international.** Issues of economic competition, the environment, and the movement of peoples around the world require an awareness of political associations that are larger in scope than the nation-state.

What do you think?

1. In *The Federalist* essays Madison argued that two conditions would help to prevent a tyranny of the majority in America. One was the diversity of interests in the new nation. The other was geographic distance making it difficult for these different interests to combine. As you evaluate the significant changes now taking place in American society, do you think the threat of such a democratic tyranny has increased or decreased? What trends may have increased the danger? What trends decreased it?

2. In his observations about American democracy, Tocqueville warned of the danger of individual isolation in a society where everyone was equal. Democracy, he said, "throws [each individual] back forever upon himself alone and threatens in the end to confine him entirely within the solitude of his own heart." Has computer technology made such individual isolation more or less likely today? Explain your answer.

3. What advantages might be offered by world citizenship? What disadvantages? Do you think that world citizenship will be possible in your lifetime?

What Are Some Constitutional Issues Facing United States Citizens in the Nation's Third Century?

Why has the Constitution been changed so infrequently?

Some critics believe the system of government created by the Framers for the world of the eighteenth century has proven itself unsuited for the more complex, faster-paced world of the twenty-first century. Others, however, respond by noting that any system that has managed to adapt itself to the changes of 200 years deserves the benefit of the doubt. Tampering with the Constitution, they say, should always err on the side of caution.

Americans have never been reluctant to tinker with the Constitution. More than 10,000 constitutional amendments have been introduced; but only 33 have been approved by Congress and submitted to the states for ratification; and only 27 of these have been adopted. Changing the Constitution has proven to be difficult, which is what the Framers intended when they outlined the requirements for amendment in Article V. After all, it took two centuries for the Twenty-seventh Amendment to the Constitution to be adopted.

The Framers wanted the Constitution to remain the nation's fundamental law, not to be confused, as a result of frequent changes, with ordinary laws and regulations. Because it has proven difficult to amend, the Constitution remains one of the oldest and shortest written constitutions, with a total of 7,591 words.

Reprinted from *We the People: The Citizen and the Constitution*, published by the Center for Civic Education.

What are some constitutional rights issues being raised by changes in American society?

Progress and change have created new issues for the Constitution. Their complexity challenges the nation's historic commitment to resolve its problems through constitutional means. Among the issues likely to be important in the years ahead are the following:

- **Group rights**
- **Right to life and death**
- **Right to privacy**
- **Rights of the individual and providing for the common good**
- **Rights of citizens and rights of resident aliens**

Group rights. America's increasingly pluralistic society and the nation's ongoing commitment to equality have forced Americans to recognize the differences that exist between groups. How far should constitutional guarantees go, for example, in providing for favored treatment of historically excluded groups? In a multilingual society to what extent should the government be obliged to provide ballots, income tax returns, and other government forms in languages other than English?

Right to life and death. The accomplishments of modern science in sustaining life before full-term pregnancy and into old age have made our society reexamine both the legal and ethical meaning of life itself. To some, high tech life support systems have created a distinction between **life** and **existence.** When does life begin? When does it end? Does an individual have a right to take his or her own life? Does an individual have the right to assist someone else's suicide?

Right to privacy. Electronic communications pose new potential threats to individual privacy. Federal, state, and local governments now keep vast computer databases on individual citizens. In the computer age, to what extent do the constitutional protections of personal "papers and effects" under the Fourth Amendment extend beyond one's home into these government files? Who has access to these records and for what purposes?

Moreover, Fourth Amendment protections do not apply to the actions of the private sector of our society. Corporations, hospitals, and other private agencies also keep computer records. Both private and public institutions can invade the privacy of individuals through "electronic snooping"—using video cameras, audio "bugs", and microwave technology to spy on individuals. The constitutional limitations on such activity have yet to be developed.

Rights of the individual and providing for the common good. The enduring tension between these two conflicting values in our constitutional democracy is being tested once again by environmental and other issues in modern society. How will our constitutional arrangements balance the rights of the individual to property and pursuit of happiness with the responsibility to provide for the general good of the larger society by guaranteeing such things as clean air and the preservation of natural habitats? Controversies surrounding the protection of old-growth forests, preservation of the spotted owl, and the effects of cigarette smoking exemplify this tension.

Right of citizens and rights of resident aliens. The increasing movement of peoples across national borders is likely to raise new constitutional issues regarding the meaning of citizenship and the status of aliens in the United States. Aliens enjoy many of the civil rights that the Constitution accords to "persons" as distinguished from citizens. These include most provisions of the Bill of Rights and freedom from arbitrary discrimination. Aliens are subject to the laws of the United States and must pay taxes. If immigration continues in future years new issues are likely to arise regarding the rights of both citizens and aliens under our Constitution.

What are unenumerated rights?

The perplexing constitutional issues of modern life have not only prompted reinterpretations of well established rights, they also have given new importance to a largely unexplored frontier of our Constitution: **unenumerated rights.** Unenumerated rights are rights possessed by every American that are not listed or enumerated in the Constitution. They are unspecified rights.

One of the principal objections to a federal bill of rights was that such a document could not possibly list all the rights of the people. Leaving some rights unlisted, or unenumerated, might imply that they did not exist. Omission also could be interpreted to mean that such rights, even if they did exist, were not important.

It was probably as a result of these concerns that the Ninth Amendment was included in the Bill of Rights. It says,

> *The enumeration in the Constitution of certain rights shall not be construed to deny or disparage others retained by the people.*

The Ninth Amendment embodies that great principle that can be traced back through the history of constitutional government to the Magna Carta—the principle that there exist certain fundamental rights that we take for granted, not just those rights that happen to be specified in a particular document. Justice William O. Douglas stated,

> *It well may be that guarantees which must be written are less secure than those so embedded in the hearts of men that they need not be written.*

What do you think?

1. **Which of the changes taking place in contemporary American society do you think is likely to present the greatest challenge to constitutional rights in the years ahead?**

2. **Which do you think might require a constitutional amendment? Explain your position.**

Who should have the power to identify unenumerated rights?

Who should decide what is an unenumerated right protected by the Constitution? There are differences of opinion on how this question should be answered. At issue is a basic principle of constitutional government that requires the powers of all the agencies of government be limited by law.

The Supreme Court has the power according to the principle of judicial review to decide whether a legislative act or executive order violates a right protected by the Constitution. This task is difficult enough with issues involving rights explicitly listed in the Constitution, such as the rights to a writ of habeas corpus or protection against unlawful entry by the authorities. The task becomes even more difficult when the issue involves unenumerated rights. What standard, if any, can justices use to avoid reading their own prejudices into the Constitution?

Critics of judicial power have claimed that anyone can find any right they want through a subjective interpretation of the Constitution. These critics often refer to the language of the majority opinion in *Griswold v. Connecticut* (1965), written by Justice Douglas. The case involved a Connecticut law that prohibited the use of contraceptives in all circumstances. A physician had been arrested for giving information on contraception to a married couple.

Douglas's opinion claimed that the Connecticut law violated the right of marital privacy. This right is not specifically referred to anywhere in the Constitution. In his opinion, however, Douglas argued that the right was protected by **"penumbras, formed by emanations"** from other enumerated rights, specifically those in the First, Third, Fourth, and Fifth Amendments. By this, he meant that some provisions of the Bill of Rights **implied** a right to marital privacy. In terms of his colorful metaphor, unenumerated rights were to be found in the shadows cast by the light of enumerated rights.

Should judges be given the freedom to decide what rights are to be discovered in the shadows of the Constitution's emanations? Some critics believe that to allow such latitude gives the Court almost unlimited power, not only to interpret the law but by doing so to create new law.

There has been, and will continue to be, disagreement about the role judges should play in a constitutional democracy. There is disagreement about how the Constitution should be interpreted, with some believing in a **strict construction,** adhering as closely as possible to the original intent of the Framers. Others believe in **broad construction,** giving judges considerable leeway in applying the words of the Constitution to the circumstances of a changing world.

There also is disagreement about the degree to which judges should intercede in the activities of the legislative and executive branches. Some believe in a philosophy of **judicial restraint,** that places strong limitations on the discretionary powers of judges and relies instead on the political process to influence legislators to pass laws that protect rights. In the words of former Chief Justice Warren Burger,

In a democratic society, legislatures, not courts, are constituted to respond to the will, and consequently the moral values, of the people.

Others have argued for **judicial activism** by pointing out that the nation's courts, as watchdogs of the Constitution, have always had a special role to play in the identification, definition, and protection of individual rights.

It was an advocate of judicial activism and broad construction, Justice William J. Brennan, who said,

> *We current Justices read the Constitution in the only way we can, as Twentieth Century Americans. We look to the history of the time of framing and to the intervening history of interpretation. The ultimate question must be, what do the words of the text mean for our time? For the genius of the Constitution rests not in any static meaning it might have had in a world that is dead and gone, but in the adaptability of its great principles to cope with current problems and current needs.*

In a sense, what Justice Brennan said applies to every citizen called on to make sense of the Constitution—we cannot escape altogether the context and perspective of our own time. The challenge, as always, will be to apply the principles of the Constitution to changing circumstances without losing its basic principles in the process.

Reviewing and using the lesson

1. **How would you describe the challenges and opportunities created by the increasing diversity of American society?**

2. **How might modern technology expand the opportunities for direct participation by citizens in self-government?**

3. **In what ways has America become increasingly interdependent with the rest of the world? What might be some consequences of this interdependence?**

4. **Locate newspaper and magazine articles about DNA research and the impact of genetic fingerprinting on privacy and due process rights. Report your findings to the class.**

5. **How would you explain the fact that thousands of constitutional amendments have been proposed, but only 27 have been adopted?**

6. **What are "enumerated rights"? Why have Supreme Court decisions protecting unenumerated rights been controversial?**

7. **How would you describe "strict construction" and "broad construction" of the Constitution?**

8. **What is meant by "judicial restraint"? What is meant by "judicial activism"? What arguments have been made in support of these two approaches to fulfilling the responsibilities of being a judge?**

9. **Examine the following U.S. Supreme Court cases regarding the right to travel in the United States and abroad: *Crandall v. Nevada,* 73 U.S. 35 (1869); *Kent v. Dulles,* 357 U.S. 16 (1958); *Aptheher v. Secretary of State,* 378 U.S. 500 (1964); and *Regan v. Wald,* 468 U.S. 222 (1984).**

Lesson 3

Constitutionalism and Other Countries

Key Terms

civil and political rights
European Convention of Human Rights
federalism
Four Freedoms
human rights
independent judiciary
negative rights
positive rights
prime minister
rights of solidarity
social and economic rights
United Nations
Universal Declaration of Human Rights

Chapter 7

What You Will Learn to Do

- Illustrate similarities and differences between the American view of human rights and the views held by other constitutional governments

Linked Core Abilities

- Communicate using verbal, non-verbal, visual, and written techniques
- Do your share as a good citizen in your school, community, country, and the world

Skills and Knowledge You Will Gain along the Way

- Describe the influence of American ideas about government and individual rights have had on other nations of the world

- Describe how constitutional democracy in other nations differs from constitutional democracy in the United States

- Describe the differences between the Bill of Rights and the Universal Declaration of Human Rights and between negative and positive rights

- Defend positions on what rights, if any, in the Universal Declaration of Human Rights should be established in the United States

- Define key words contained in this lesson

Introduction

Constitutionalism is often examined primarily within the context of the American experience. By itself this perspective is too narrow, especially in today's world. In this lesson you look at other traditions of constitutional government and at the many experiments in constitutionalism now taking place in the world. You examine the historical impact of American constitutionalism on other countries and compare the American view of human rights with the views held by the international community.

What Can American Citizens Learn about Constitutionalism from Other Countries?

What has been the influence of American ideals about government and human rights on the rest of the world?

America's constitutional ideals are perhaps this country's greatest contribution to the world. Few historic documents have had the impact of the Declaration of Independence and the U.S. Constitution, whose words have been copied and paraphrased in numerous other charters of freedom.

The American republic, product of the world's first democratic revolution, influenced many other countries during the first decades of its existence. The French Revolution of 1789 was inspired by the American Revolution and the French Constitution of 1791 copied many elements from America's first state constitutions. The world's second-oldest written constitution, the Polish Constitution of 1791, also was influenced by the American example. When Latin American countries won their independence from Spain in the early nineteenth century, they looked to the U.S. Constitution as a model for republican government. In 1825 the first demands for constitutional government in Russia, though unsuccessful, were inspired by American ideals.

The influence of American constitutionalism has expanded in this century because of the position of the United States as a world power. During the American occupation of Japan and Germany after World War II, a committee of Ameri-

Reprinted from *We the People: The Citizen and the Constitution*, published by the Center for Civic Education.

cans drafted the Japanese Constitution of 1947, and similarly, the new German Constitution of 1949 incorporated elements from the American model.

As the United States celebrated the bicentennial of its Constitution in 1987-1991, other nations were writing new chapters in the history of constitutional government. The 1980s and early 1990s saw the collapse of Soviet Communism and the emergence of democratic governments in Eastern Europe. In 1989 students in China staged a challenge to totalitarian government. These dramatic developments could signal the beginning of a new era of constitutionalism with important implications for American citizens.

There has been renewed interest in the heritage of American ideals in the aftermath of the Cold War, as many former Communist states have begun to experiment with their own forms of constitutionalism. Some of the most eloquent tributes to our Constitution's bicentennial were expressed by the leaders of these newly independent countries. The president of Czechoslovakia, Vaclav Havel, remarked in a speech before the U.S. Congress in 1990,

> *Wasn't it the best minds of your country...who wrote your famous Declaration of Independence, your Bill of Human Rights, and your Constitution?... Those great documents...inspire us all; they inspire us despite the fact that they are over 200 years old. They inspire us to be citizens.*

What elements of American constitutionalism have been most widely adopted by other countries?

As the world's first written framework of national government, the U.S. Constitution established an important precedent. Nearly all countries today either have or are in the process of drafting written constitutions. Totalitarian systems also felt it necessary to produce written constitutions, although in no way did they restrict the real exercise of power. The process by which the U.S. Constitution was drafted and adopted also established a precedent—the use of constitutional conventions and popular ratifications.

Key principles of the U.S. Constitution were spread throughout the world by *The Federalist,* America's greatest contribution to political thought. Many of these principles have been adopted in other constitutions.

Perhaps the most widely admired and imitated feature of the U.S. Constitution, after the Bill of Rights, has been the establishment of an **independent judiciary.** An inviolate—secure from outside influence—judicial branch acts as the watchdog of the Constitution and prevents the executive and legislative branches of government from disregarding it. The judicial branch helps to ensure that the words of the Constitution will be obeyed by the government.

Another aspect of American constitutionalism that is of great interest in the world today is **federalism.** By combining a central government with a large measure of autonomy for the states the Framers were able to solve the problem of how to establish effective national and local governments in a large country. America's federal system has interested the former Communist states of Eastern Europe, where decades of centralized control all but destroyed local government. Federalism also has influenced the democracies of Western Europe in their creation of a European union.

What do you think?

1. What responsibilities, if any, do Americans have to promote representative democracy and constitutional government in other nations? Explain your reasoning.

2. What responsibilities, if any, do Americans have to promote respect for human rights in other nations? Explain your position.

How have other constitutional democracies differed from the American model?

The U.S. Constitution, however, is not the world's only source of ideas about constitutional democracy. Nations have looked to other traditions and to their own particular circumstances and historical legacies to find a form of constitutionalism that will be effective for them. However much we value our own political ideals and institutions, we must realize that they cannot always be transplanted.

Some elements in the U.S. Constitution have been adopted by other nations only with substantial modification; other elements have been rejected altogether in favor of different constitutional models. For example, the office of the presidency was another of the great innovations of the Framers. It was their solution to the need for a strong executive to replace a monarchy. Elected independently of the legislature, the president possesses those powers described in the Constitution itself.

The title of "President" to describe the constitutional chief executive has been widely adopted since that time, though usually not with the same powers and responsibilities U.S. presidents have. Because of their own historical experiences, many countries have been fearful of a strong executive. Freed from Communist dictatorships, the countries in the former Soviet bloc have provided for weak executives in their new constitutional arrangements, much like some of the first state constitutions in this country.

Perhaps the most distinguishing characteristic of the American system of government has been its separation and sharing of powers among three co-equal branches. Few other constitutional democracies, however, use that system today. Its critics consider our arrangement of divided powers inefficient and undemocratic. Most of the world's democracies have adopted instead some form of **parliamentary government.**

How does parliamentary government differ from a constitutional system based on separation of powers?

The Framers were very much influenced by the British constitution, even though it differed in important respects from the model they eventually adopted. The British constitution featured a system of checks and balances, but its executive, legislative, and judicial branches were not separated. Parliament, for example, was considered an instrument of the Crown, rather than an independent branch of government.

During the last two centuries a system of government modeled on the British constitution has been widely imitated, not only in Britain's former colonies but in many other countries as well. In a parliamentary system, government ministers are also members of the legislature. The head of the executive branch, usually called a **prime minister,** is determined by whatever party or combination of parties has a majority in the parliament or legislature.

Unlike the American system, in a parliamentary arrangement the majority in the legislative branch decides who will head the executive branch. Many nations prefer the parliamentary system because they see the closer linkage of the executive and legislative branches as a more efficient form of government and one that is more reflective of the popular will.

What has been the influence of the U.S. Bill of Rights on constitutional government elsewhere?

Probably the single greatest contribution of American constitutionalism to the world has been its example of incorporating fundamental guarantees of individual rights into a written constitution. Nearly all national constitutions adopted since have included similar guarantees. The inspiring model of the U.S. Bill of Rights has become especially important during the latter half of this century, when interest in basic rights has increased around the world. As President Jimmy Carter observed in 1977:

> *The basic thrust of human affairs points toward a more universal demand for fundamental human rights.*

Before this century, individual rights were generally regarded as an internal matter, to be left to each nation to decide. The world-wide economic depression of the 1930s, and the unprecedented crimes against humanity committed by totalitarian governments before and during World War II, gave the issue of human rights a new importance.

It was an American president, Franklin D. Roosevelt, who anticipated a new era in the history of basic rights. In a speech to Congress in 1941, the president defined the **Four Freedoms** worth fighting for: freedom of speech and expression, freedom of worship, freedom from want, and freedom from fear. The charter that founded the **United Nations** in 1945, and subsequently led to the **United Nations Universal Declaration of Human Rights of 1948,** followed President Roosevelt's example. The Declaration and the charter proclaimed universal standards of basic rights, called **human rights,** because they were considered essential to the dignity of each human being.

In the decades since, the concern for human rights has become an issue of importance in the relations among nations. Regional agreements have expanded the United Nations Declaration. For example, in 1950 the countries of Western Europe agreed to a **European Convention on Human Rights.** They established a European Court to which the citizens of these countries could appeal when they believed their rights had been violated.

Increasingly, the protection of rights is also an important diplomatic issue among nations. The United States, for example, has sometimes restricted trade with countries considered to be violating human rights. In recent years our relations with the Republic of South Africa were influenced to a large extent by the issue of rights violations in that country.

How do other national guarantees of rights differ from the U.S. Bill of Rights?

As fundamental and lasting as its guarantees have been, the U.S. Bill of Rights is a document of the eighteenth century, reflecting the issues and concerns of the age in which it was written. The rights guaranteed to Americans are **civil** and **political rights.** They express a fear of government power. They protect the individual from wrongful acts by government and provide each citizen with ways to participate in public affairs.

Other national guarantees of rights also reflect the cultures that created them. Many of these cultures have values and priorities different from our own. In many Asian countries, for example, the rights of the individual are secondary to the interests of the whole community. Islamic countries take their code of laws from the teachings of the Koran, the book of sacred writings accepted by Muslims as revelations made to the prophet Muhammad by God.

In some countries freedom of conscience is considered less important than it is in the United States and other Western democracies. What constitutes cruel and unusual punishment, which is forbidden by our Eighth Amendment, differs greatly from country to country, depending on its particular history and culture.

Contemporary charters of basic rights also reflect the changes that have taken place in government and society during the last 200 years. Many guarantees of rights adopted since World War II have been modeled on the United Nations' Universal Declaration of Human Rights. They include many of the civil and political rights represented in our Bill of Rights. Most go further to include **social** and **economic rights.**

Examples of social and economic rights would be the right to choose a career, secure employment, health care, and education. Others might include certain societal rights, such as the right to responsible management of nonrenewable resources or a clean environment. The inclusion of such provisions in guaranteed rights reflects a change in the role government plays in society and the expectations its citizens place on it.

The Founders considered the role of government in people's lives to be very limited, as indeed it was in the eighteenth century. Governments play a much larger role today and that role has expanded the meaning of basic rights in most societies. The people in the former Communist states of Europe, for example, may appreciate their newfound civic and political rights, but many are reluctant to give up the economic security and social rights their former Communist governments provided.

What is the difference between negative and positive rights?

In the natural rights tradition, which provides the foundation of the United States Constitution, rights are seen as restraints on the power of government. They are sometimes called **negative rights** because they prevent government from acting in a certain way. The Bill of Rights generally requires the government not to act. For example, the First Amendment says, "Government shall make no law . . ."

The social, economic, and **solidarity rights** included in the United Nations' Universal Declaration of Rights, and in many national guarantees of rights adopted since, are what are sometimes called **positive rights.** Instead of preventing the government from acting, they require it to act, to ensure such things as economic security, health care, and a clean environment for its citizens.

There are other important differences between negative and positive rights. Negative rights prevent the government from taking away something its citizens already possess, for example, freedom of expression. Many positive rights, on the other hand, describe certain benefits that citizens should have. These rights express the objectives worthy of any just society.

Critical Thinking Exercise
Examining the Universal Declaration of Human Rights

Review the Universal Declaration of Human Rights found in the Reference Section and answer the following questions:

1. **What rights does the Universal Declaration of Human Rights proclaim that are in the U.S. Constitution and Bill of Rights?**

2. **What rights in our Constitution and Bill of Rights are not included in the Universal Declaration of Human Rights? Why do you suppose they are not included?**

3. **What appears to be the purposes of the rights in the Universal Declaration of Human Rights that are not protected by our Constitution or Bill of Rights?**

4. **Examine each of the rights in the Universal Declaration of Human Rights that is not protected specifically in our Constitution. Is the right you have identified protected in the United States by other means, such as civil rights legislation; civil or criminal law contracts between private parties; labor and management agreements on employment benefits, vacation pay, and sick leave; custom or tradition; other means not listed above?**

5. **What rights, if any, in the Universal Declaration of Human Rights should be established in the United States? How should they be established? Explain your position.**

6. **How do the rights listed in the Universal Declaration of Human Rights appear to reflect the history and experiences of the time in which it was written?**

Reviewing and using the lesson

1. Which aspects of American constitutional democracy have been particularly influential in other countries?

2. How would you describe the important features of a parliamentary form of government?

3. What is the difference between civil and political rights, on one hand, and social and economic rights, on the other? How is this difference related to the difference between "negative rights" and "positive rights"?

4. What are some important differences between the Bill of Rights and the Universal Declaration of Human Rights?

5. Research the work Eleanor Roosevelt did on behalf of passage of the United Nations' Universal Declaration of Human Rights.

Mandatory Core
Service Learning

Making a Difference with Service Learning

Lesson 1

Orientation to Service Learning

Key Terms

community service
debriefer
facilitator
orientation
recorder
reflection
reporter
service learning
timekeeper

What You Will Learn to Do

- Identify the components of service learning

Linked Core Abilities

- Apply critical thinking techniques

Skills and Knowledge You Will Gain Along the Way

- Compare the types of service opportunities within your community
- Identify the benefits of serving others within a community
- Associate the roles and responsibilities of service learning teams
- Define key words contained in this lesson

Introduction

You have probably noticed that people who seem to find the most satisfaction in life are those actively engaged in doing something to make the world a better place for everyone. They seem happy because they are making a difference. Have you ever helped a friend through a difficult time or done something similar to stopping to help change a flat tire or take food to a sick neighbor? Then you know why people who help others appear to be more genuinely content with their lives.

Unfortunately, although you know you will feel good, it is probably not easy for you to get started. You are not alone. Many people find it awkward to reach out. However, after you take those initial steps and begin making a difference, the difficulties disappear. Feelings of accomplishment and generosity of spirit make the effort and time you spent worthwhile.

So how do you get started in service? First, look around you. There are problems and people in need everywhere. You do not have to look very far to find hunger, illiteracy, pollution, illness, poverty, neglect, and loneliness. Decide on an urgent need or one that you find most compelling. What matters most is that you make a commitment to address the need in a positive way.

After you have chosen a need, select a project that will help you accomplish your goal of making a difference. President John F. Kennedy reminded everyone to, "Ask not what your country can do for you; ask what you can do for your country." Planning and carrying out the **service learning** project will help you selflessly "do" for your neighbor, your community, your state, your country, and the world.

The author Aldous Huxley said, "Experience is not what happens to you; it's what you do with what happens to you." Service learning takes that belief to heart. It is not enough to take positive actions, you must learn from your actions. For example, starting a paper recycling program is a worthy project; it can become more meaningful when you learn more about why it is important, reflect on your experiences, identify what you learned, analyze how you've changed, and decide other ways you can recycle and help others commit to recycling.

Service learning experiences can become the starting point for self-awareness, self-improvement, and self-fulfillment. In the process of making a difference for others, you make a difference in yourself.

Key Note Term

service learning – an environment where one can learn and develop by actively participating in organized service experiences within one's own community.

What Is Service Learning?

Key Note Term

orientation – the act or process of orienting or being oriented, such as being oriented onteh first day of college.

Service learning is an active and experiential learning strategy where students have a direct impact on an identified need that interests and motivates them. It requires sequential lessons that are organized so **orientation** and training come before the meaningful service activity and structured reflection follows the activity.

```
┌─────────────────────────────────────────┐
│          Orientation and Training         │
│           + Meaningful Service            │
│           + Structured Reflection         │
│                ─────────                  │
│            SERVICE LEARNING               │
└─────────────────────────────────────────┘
```

Structured Teamwork

Service learning requires active participation in structured teamwork. Working within small teams and solving problems together will help you become active participants. Each member is assigned a team role, including:

- **Facilitator** (The facilitator leads team discussions to identify needs and prepare service learning activities.)
- **Recorder** (The recorder takes notes for the team and organizes information.)
- **Reporter** (The reporter represents the team voice and reports team findings.)
- **Timekeeper** (The timekeeper keeps track of time and plans the schedule.)
- **Debriefer** (The debriefer encourages team members and leads discussion after presentation.)

Cadet teams should determine, plan, and execute service-learning activities with the aid of their instructor.

Orientation and Training

Orientation and training activities are necessary to prepare you and other participants for the service experience. Integrating what you are learning in class with the service activity is a key goal of service learning. This step requires in-class lessons, followed by selecting a service project that relates to the curriculum and meets academic standards.

You should be familiar enough with the material to conduct the service project you have selected. Part of the planning process will require you to determine what you need to know before the activity and to train yourself accordingly.

If possible, speak with representatives or others involved with the service you have selected to see what to expect. Orient yourself with the service goals, those you will be helping, other organizations or people that you may need to contact, and so on. In other words, learn what you need to know before starting the service experience and plan for all potential circumstances.

Key Note Terms

facilitator – one who facilitates; one who leads team discussion.

recorder – one who take notes for the team and organizes information.

reporter – one who represents the team voice and reports team findings.

timekeeper – one who keeps track of time and plans the schedule.

debriefer – one who encourages team members and leads discussions after presentation and team discussion.

Meaningful Service

It is your responsibility to initiate and plan service activities to correspond to the lesson material. Although there should be at least 15 cadets per service experience, you can either work in committees on one project or small teams on separate projects. For example, you may want to divide the project components among three teams of five cadets each. Learning should be an active and social experience that is meaningful to you and those involved. Within your teams, choose a service activity that:

- **Addresses a real and important need another group is not addressing**
- **Is interesting and challenging**
- **Connects you to others within the community or world**
- **Challenges you to develop new skills**
- **Requires little or no money**
- **Is achievable within the time available**
- **Has a positive effect on others**

Structured Reflection

Key Note Term

reflection – a thought, idea, or opinion formed or a remark made as a result of mediation; consideration of some subject matter, idea, or purpose.

Reflection, or taking time to observe, analyze, and integrate actions with learning, is an important part of the learning process. A strong reflection helps you develop skills and extend learning from the service experience. You may use many types of reflection: learning logs and essays; team and class discussions; performances; graphic organizers; and public presentations. Using learning logs throughout the experience to record thoughts, feelings, knowledge and processes will help you organize what you have learned.

Within your teams, share what you have learned by discussing your answers to open-ended questions before, during, and after each service experience. Reflection questions should encourage observation, analysis and integration.

Community Service Versus Service Learning

Key Note Term

community service – any form of service provided for the community or common good.

Community service in many states is dispensed by a judge or court system as mandatory work for infractions of the law. Some students and members of the community view this type of service as punishment. What students learn is that they don't ever want to be forced to do "service" again. Today, many high schools include community service hours as a graduation requirement and though intentions are good, sometimes the emphasis is on quantity of hours, not quality of the project.

Service learning, on the other hand, is a step up from community service; it brings academics to life and is driven by student involvement. You should identify essential needs in your school or community, and then decide on your own projects. In addition, you should plan and carry out your own projects and take responsibility for your own learning. Reflecting on the experience will reveal the importance of your service work and the impact you are making on yourself and others.

Why Use Service Learning?

Service learning is rapidly growing in popularity around the country. Students who are able to learn about the world around them and work to improve it as part of their education reap many benefits. Such students:

- **Learn more**
- **Earn better grades**
- **Come to school more often**
- **Demonstrate better behavior**
- **Become more civic minded**
- **Gain a first-hand appreciation and understanding of people from other cultures, races, and generations**
- **See the connections between school and "real life"**
- **Feel better about themselves**
- **Learn skills they can use after leaving school**

Service learning provides a safe environment where you can learn, make mistakes, have successes, and develop by actively participating in organized service experiences within your community. For example, such experiences might include:

- **Meeting actual community needs by providing meaningful service**
- **Coordinating in partnership with the school and community**
- **Integrating these service opportunities into an academic curriculum, thereby enhancing what your school teaches, extending your learning beyond the classroom, and offering unique learning experiences**
- **Providing you with opportunities to use previously and newly acquired academic skills and knowledge in real-life situations in your own community**
- **Providing structured time for you to think, talk, and write about what you did and saw during your actual service activity**
- **Helping you to develop a sense of caring for others**

Providing service can be a powerful tool in the development of attitudes and behavior. It can transform young adults from passive recipients into active providers, and in so doing, redefine the perception of their involvement in the community from a cause of problems to a source of solutions.

Important skills you will need to work successfully to accomplish each service learning activity are similar to those identified in the Secretary's Commission on Achieving Necessary Skills (SCANS) report. There are several important skills and qualities identified in the SCANS to ensure students are prepared for the workforce. The following are just a few of those skills service learning can help you strengthen.

- Being an effective team member
- Providing resource and time management
- Engaging in frequent and effective communication
- Making decisions
- Organizing and being responsible
- Effectively managing personal problems such as poor writing skills, lack of research skills, or stereotyping

Conclusion

When combined with formal education, service becomes a method of learning or "service learning." Learning is maximized by combining the three main service learning components: orientation and training, meaningful service, and structured reflection.

Service learning is the single learning strategy that can accomplish the most good for the greatest number of people. Studies suggest that service learning reinforces curriculum content and standards, and benefits participants academically, as well as personally and socially. By getting involved to help meet different needs, you have the potential to make a difference to someone specific or to the entire community.

Chapter 8

Lesson Review

1. Who do you know that might benefit from your participation in service learning?
2. Define the term "learning logs."
3. Compare and contrast community service and service learning.
4. List five benefits from your participation in service learning.

Lesson Review

Lesson 2

Plan and Train for Your Exploratory Project

Key Terms

experimental learning
exploratory project
field education
problem-based learning
training

What You Will Learn to Do

- Prepare for a service learning project

Linked Core Abilities

- Build your capacity for life-long learning
- Communicate using verbal, non-verbal, visual, and written techniques
- Do your share as a good citizen in your school, community, country, and the world

Skills and Knowledge You Will Gain Along the Way

- Select an exploratory project
- Identify the steps needed to conduct a service learning experience

- Identify the essential components of a chosen service learning project
- Develop a plan addressing various circumstances and outcomes of the project
- Define key words contained in this lesson

Introduction

There are several points to consider before undergoing service learning. Planning ahead will prepare you both mentally and physically to undertake the challenge. Before you select a service learning project in class, your instructor should familiarize you with service learning by guiding you in an **exploratory project** within the community. This will help you select a service project and demonstrate the steps to conducting a proper service learning experience.

Exploratory Project Purpose

The exploratory project is an introduction to a service learning activity that utilizes **experiential learning** and **problem-based learning** principles. The purpose of a teacher-planned exploratory project is to provide students with a meaningful experience, expose them to how it feels to serve, and to stimulate their thinking about possible service learning activities.

One of the primary benefits of engaging in an exploratory project is to understand what service learning entails. Service learning is not community service, although many confuse the two. Until you participate in service learning, you will not have a real-life experience to justify the difference.

Exploratory projects help you capture a vision of how to make a difference in the world. After you get involved, you may begin to see the world through different glasses. In addition, as you work to address one need in the community, several other unmet needs will begin to surface. Your vision of the world may change when you begin to see critical needs where you never saw them before.

Suggested introductory projects could include going to a hospital or nursing home to visit residents, distributing food at a food bank, or volunteering at a local Red Cross program.

Service Learning Steps

Before participating in service, familiarize yourself with the following steps to conduct a proper service learning experience:

Key Note Terms

exploratory project – a teacher-planned introductory project to service learning, intended to provide students with a meaningful experience, expose them to how it feels to serve, and to stimulate their thinking abut possible service learning activities.

experiential learning – gaining practical knowledge, skills, or practice from direct observation of or participation in events or in a particular activity.

problem-based learning – an instructional strategy that promotes active learning where problems form the focus and learning stimulus and problem-solving skills are utilized.

1. Complete a pre-assessment of skill level using the Personal Skills Map from the JROTC Success Profiler.

2. Determine a school, community, or national need you can fill relating to class curriculum.

3. Brainstorm and select a meaningful service project that meets proposed guidelines.

4. Start a learning log to record new knowledge, thoughts and feelings throughout all phases.

5. Plan and organize details of the service activity and discuss expectations.

6. Participate in a meaningful service activity that meets the service learning guidelines (Form 219-R).

7. Discuss and reflect on what you experienced (observation).

8. Discuss and reflect on what you gained from the experience (analysis).

9. Discuss and reflect on what you can do with the new information (integration).

10. Complete a project summary report and a final group evaluation form to judge teamwork and other activities.

11. Brief the experience to community members, administration, classmates, and so on.

12. Complete a post-assessment using the Personal Skills Map and related analysis to determine a plan of action.

Choosing a Service Activity

After participating in an exploratory project, you should be able to select your own service activity that meets an important need and integrates the curriculum.

It is very important that you participate in selecting a service activity that is meaningful to you and others. Brainstorm service ideas relative to the lesson curriculum and program at hand. Then as a class or team, select the service activity.

Service learning opportunities can use **field education** principles to incorporate scholastic programs with the curriculum. You can integrate programs such as:

- Lions-Quest Skills for Action®
- Groundhog Job Shadow Day®
- NEFE High School Financial Planning Program®
- You the People®
- Chief Justice®
- Cadet Ride®

Key Note Term

field education – performing service and training to enhance understanding with a field of study.

Key Note Term

training – to form by or undergo instruction, discipline, or drill; to teach so as to make fit, qualified, or proficient.

In field education, you perform the service as a part of a **training** program designed primarily to enhance understanding of a field of study while providing substantial emphasis on the service.

Besides integrating curriculum and service, you will learn more about the different types, models, and terms of service in the next lesson, "Project Reflection and Integration."

Planning the Service

After you have chosen an activity, you must plan the essential facets for project completion and prepare or train yourself for what is to come.

This is where service learning begins. Service learning efforts should start with clearly stated goals and development of a plan of action that encourages cadet responsibility. You can achieve those goals through structured preparation and brainstorming such as discussion, writing, reading, observation, and the service itself. Keep the goals consistent with the level of the activity planned and ensure that the goals and plan of action draw upon the skills and knowledge of your team. When corresponding goals to the curriculum, try to determine academic content standards you will address through the service.

Besides determining goals and standards, plans should be comprehensive to ensure adequate preparation for each step or task. Determine a description of the task(s) and answer the questions:

- **Who will be involved?**
- **What is involved and needs to be done?**
- **When will each step take place?**
- **Where will it all take place?**
- **Why will we do it?**
- **How will it work?**

For example, you might decide to visit a local veterans hospital. You could discover the needs of the elderly patients that reside there by discussions with the hospital's administrative personnel or possibly by meeting with the residents themselves. You should also determine where the project fits into the curriculum. Together, you might decide that the patients need to have younger people help them write letters to family members, assist with their wellness and fitness, or plan and lead activities.

If you are aware of children who have a hard time learning to read, you could plan a service activity to a local elementary school. Because teachers rarely have extra time on their hands to spend one-on-one with those children, certain schools may welcome JROTC cadets who could come and spend time reading or listening to the children read. You do not have to limit this service to reading.

Consider helping in mathematics or other subjects. Remember to maximize the use of your participating cadets' skills and knowledge. Contact your local Junior Achievement office at http://www.ja.org for more service learning suggestions to help teach elementary students. You can also find service learning project ideas by searching the Internet.

Do not forget to accomplish the administrative details during the preparation phase. Teams often overlook these requirements or assume that someone else will do them. You must obtain permission from school administrators to conduct the service learning activity as a field trip and arrange for transportation, lunch, and parental release/permission slips for participating cadets, and the necessary supplies and equipment to perform the activity. Invite administrators, counselors, community members, and so on to be on your Advisory Board so that they will become more involved with your project.

Training for the Service

Before participating in the service activity, prepare yourself for different circumstances or outcomes. This may involve learning about the subject matter you will be expected to know to complete the tasks you have laid out, or discussing different outcomes and expectations within your teams. Try your best to be prepared for different situations you may encounter. Within teams, or as a class, brainstorm and discuss potential hazards you may encounter, and precautions you should take to make the task run smoothly.

Pretend you are taking a bus to a children's hospital with a group of cadets to tutor sick children who cannot be in school. You may need to train yourselves on particular academic subjects/content, research what grade levels will be represented, and locate the hospital. Also, make sure to pair up and plan a meeting time and place.

Executing the Service

In this phase, there are a few rules to remember. Arrive on time and always be courteous. You are representing your school and you should act accordingly at all times. Also, ensure that you understand the task or goal at hand. If you are not sure, ask an authority. They should be able to point you in the right direction. If you are a team leader, make sure your team members feel completely comfortable with the tasks. Finally, if a situation or problem arises that needs an authority's attention (for example, an accident occurs and someone is hurt), take what actions you can and have someone contact the person in charge.

Being well organized and completely prepared are fundamental for a successful execution phase. For example, if you are going to build a garden such as the one mentioned earlier in this lesson:

Service Learning Success Story

During lessons on Planning and Social Responsibility, cadets in Gastonia, North Carolina, decided to plant a garden at a nursing home. Their pre-planning resulted in a specially designed, waist-high "no stoop garden" so seniors could help maintain the plants and flowers. This is a good example of how the needs of the elderly were taken into consideration when the garden plan was developed.

- Ensure you have the correct tools and supplies to complete the service.
- Know the name or names of the contacts for the particular service you are performing.
- Identify alternate group leaders in case there are absences.
- Assign cadets to work on projects according to their experience and abilities.
- Be thoroughly prepared to complete the task, but be flexible to make changes. Things may not go as you plan them.

Remember, you are there to render a service for your community.

Conclusion

The exploratory project will introduce you to service learning through active participation. From there, you will be ready to choose your own service activity. At that time, remember that good planning is the key to a successful service learning venture. Training may be necessary to complete the task, and learning should be the focus as well as making a difference through service.

You should now be prepared to use the proposed steps and planning procedures to conduct a proper service learning experience.

Chapter 8

Lesson Review

1. Define the term "problem-based learning."
2. Why is it important to participate in a service activity that means something to you?
3. What materials might you need if you were visiting children in a hospital?
4. Name three projects in your community you might want to join.
5. What are the steps needed to conduct a service learning experience?

Lesson Review

Lesson 3

Project Reflection and Integration

Key Terms

advocacy service
after action review
analysis
direct service
indirect service
integration
observation
placement
project

What You Will Learn to Do

- Evaluate the effectiveness of a service learning project

Linked Core Abilities

- Communicate using verbal, non-verbal, visual, and written techniques
- Apply critical thinking techniques

Skills and Knowledge You Will Gain Along the Way

- Relate the projected goals of a service learning project to the final outcomes
- Identify ways to integrate service learning into the JROTC curriculum
- Outline service learning objectives for the future
- Define key words

Introduction

Now that you have an idea of what service learning is all about, what comes next? After the exploratory project, you will be able to determine and conduct appropriate service learning activities. Before choosing activities, you should know about the models, terms, and types of service available, and how to integrate service with what you are learning in class.

After you have completed a service activity, you should follow it up with a structured reflection, demonstration of learning, and evaluation of the service learning.

Short-term Versus Long-term Service

You need to understand how to meet others' needs through either short-term or long-term service activities. Short-term service projects include:

- **Restoring a historical monument during history lessons**
- **Raising money at an event for charity during financial planning lessons**
- **Visiting a nursing home while discussing wellness and fitness issues**

Long-term service projects include:

- **Adopting a local waterway while studying environmental issues**
- **Setting up an advocacy campaign to raise financial resources for shelters during financial planning lessons**
- **Organizing an after-school tutoring program during lessons on teaching skills**

Models of Service

Service can be done anywhere to reinforce what you are learning in class; you do not even have to leave the school grounds. The two models of service include **projects** and **placements**.

Project Model

Service learning projects are initiated and planned by cadets with instructor guidance. Tutoring elementary children in subjects you are currently studying or starting a recycling program based on information from your geography lessons are examples of service projects.

Key Note Terms

projects – a task or problem engaged in usually by a group of students to supplement and apply classroom studies; service learning projects are initiated and planned by cadets with instructor guidance.

placement – service learning activities carried out beyond the classroom in a pre-existing, structured situation.

Placement Model

Service learning placements are activities carried out beyond the classroom in a preexisting, structured situation. The placement organization typically assigns responsibilities to students individually. Examples include: teaching lessons for Junior Achievement, or volunteering for Special Olympics during fitness lessons.

Three Types of Service

The three types of service are **direct**, **indirect**, and **advocacy**. These service types are described in the following sections.

Direct Service

Direct service involves face-to-face contact with those being served in either project or placement models of service learning. Examples of direct service include working in a soup kitchen or working with disadvantaged children while you are studying about group communication.

Indirect Service

Indirect service requires hands-on involvement in a service activity without any face-to-face contact with those served. An example would be raising money for a veterans hospital or e-mailing deployed soldiers during your military lessons unit.

Advocacy Service

Advocacy services do not require face-to-face contact with those served. Advocacy involves speaking out on behalf of an issue or cause. For example, starting a school-wide poster campaign to teach others about an issue would be an advocacy service.

Integrating Service Learning

Because the learning should equal the service in service learning, it is important to integrate classroom content with the chosen service. Service learning should reinforce curriculum content and standards for you to benefit academically, personally, and socially. Applying content standard material to real-life experiences will give you a better understanding of the curriculum.

When conducting a service learning project, take time to pinpoint the standards you should address and ways to assess your learning. As a team or class, consider:

- **What standards are we addressing?**
- **What should we know or be able to do?**
- **What assessments can illustrate our learning?**

Key Note Terms

direct service – involves face-to-face contact with those being served in either project or placement models of service learning.

indirect service – requires hands-on involvement in a service activity without any face-to-face contact with those served.

advocacy service – does not require face-to-face contact with those served; involves speaking out on behalf of an issue or cause.

Not only will you fulfill an important need with your service project, you will be learning the national standards in a more relevant and engaging manner.

Service Learning Examples

Field education integrates curriculum programs with service learning. This section presents examples of how you can integrate service learning with curriculum related programs, including:

- **Lions-Quest Skills for Action®**
- **You the People®/Chief Justice®**
- **Groundhog Job Shadow Day®**
- **Cadet Ride®**
- **Winning Colors®**
- **NEFE High School Financial Planning Program®**

Lions-Quest Skills for Action®

Lions-Quest Skills for Action (SFA) is a student-centered program based on combining learning with service. The program is divided into four parts and a Skills Bank. The program curriculum is an elective that advocates service, character, citizenship, and responsibility.

The Skills for Action curriculum helps guide you through the crucial steps of conducting service learning activities. Those steps include identifying needs, choosing and planning a project to address the need, carrying out the project, and reflecting on experiences and exploring what was learned throughout the project.

You the People and Chief Justice®

There are a variety of ways to incorporate service learning with You the People (YTP) and Chief Justice. After you are grounded in YTP citizenship skills and have formed groups, you can identify a service learning activity to integrate into the skill-building curriculum.

For example, you could create, circulate, and publicize a petition that addresses a community issue and create a videotape to document the issue for community officials.

Groundhog Job Shadow Day®

Groundhog Job Shadow Day (GJSD) is a nationwide effort to introduce students to the skills and education needed to make it in today's job market by letting them explore various career options.

For example, you may decide to start a Job Shadow effort to link the schools to the community; then organize a career day or GJSD to make it possible for high school students in the community to explore different career opportunities.

For details about the program, go to *http://www.jobshadow.org*.

Cadet Ride®

The Cadet Ride is an extension of American history that allows you to choose different historical characters to research. You can reenact them on site or in the classroom and then complete a related service learning activity.

You first need to identify issues that still relate to the community today, such as homeless veterans or victims of terrorist attacks; then take time to discuss how you can use what you have learned to improve the community/world issue. Finally, complete a related service learning activity, taking time to reflect on each phase of the experience.

Project examples used with the Cadet Ride include supporting war memorials or assisting in veterans' hospitals or shelters. Specifically, you could decide to educate others on the service of Lieutenant General Maude, who died in the line of duty at the Pentagon on 11 September 2001. In addition, you could plan a memorial for him and/or other victims to commemorate the acts of war that occurred at the World Trade Center, the Pentagon, and in Pennsylvania.

Winning Colors®

Winning Colors states that everyone is capable of developing decision-making, thinking, feeling, and action behaviors. One example of a service learning project would be to teach senior citizens or elementary students about Winning Colors, how to discover their personal needs, and develop a plan to help them achieve a successful balance.

Note

You can earn two hours of college credit with Winning Colors and a service learning project. Ask your JROTC Instructor for more details.

For more information about Winning Colors go to *http://www.winningcolors.com*.

NEFE High School Financial Planning Program®

The National Endowment for Financial Education (NEFE) High School Financial Planning Program® (HSFPP) is designed to teach practical money management skills to introduce financial planning through course work. Numerous service learning activities can be integrated into the NEFE HSFPP curriculum.

> **Note**
>
> You can earn two hours of college credit when you do the NEFE curriculum and a service learning project. Ask your JROTC Instructor for more details.

Suggested service learning activities related to the NEFE HSFPP include:

- **Teach elementary students Junior Achievement material in relation to HSFPP**
- **Provide a budget assistance program**
- **Host a Credit Awareness or Financial Fitness Fair**
- **Develop budgets and spreadsheets for local services**
- **Start an Investment Club in school**
- **Design, produce, and distribute informative posters**
- **Comparison-shop for homebound seniors' groceries**

For more information, call NEFE at (303) 224-3510, or visit *http://www.nefe.org*.

Integration with Additional Unit Content

Besides using applicable curriculum programs in service learning, you may decide to integrate additional content and services. The key is to connect the service activity with course curriculum.

For example, after studying harmful effects of tobacco/drugs, you could teach elementary school kids by putting together an anti-drug advocacy program. You could create banners, skits and instructional materials, then plan and coordinate the elementary program teachings.

After the Service

Key Note Term

after action review – reflecting on what was learned after an act.

After the service, you will participate in an **after action review** so you can reflect, demonstrate, and evaluate. This will be done in three phases, as described in the following sections.

Structured Reflection Phase

Remember, a strong reflection helps develop skills and extend your learning from the service experience. Besides keeping a running learning log of entries, you should hold team discussions to answer open-ended questions before, during, and after each service experience. Sharing what you learned with your teammates and listening to others, will add to your learning experience.

Types of reflection questions to ask about the service learning experience include:

- **Observation**/What—What did I do?

- **Analysis**/So What—What did it mean to me?

- **Integration**/Now What—What will I do because of what I accomplished or learned?

This phase provides you with a structured opportunity to think about what you just did for your community and to describe the feelings that stimulated your actions throughout this activity. Experience indicates that reflection is the key to successful service learning programs.

After you actually perform the service, you should come together as a group to contemplate your service experiences in a project summary report, learning logs, essays, and class discussions. In doing so, you should thoroughly describe what happened during the activity; record any differences your activity actually made; and try to place this experience in a larger context. Specifically, do you believe you successfully accomplished your service learning goals? If not, why? What can you do better the next time? Share your feelings and thoughts. Discuss experiences that made you happy, sad, or angry, events that surprised or frightened you, and other topics related to the activity.

Demonstration Phase

In the demonstration phase, you share with others your mastery of skills, creative ideas, and the outcomes from this project; then identify the next steps to take to benefit the community. The actual demonstration can take many different forms. For example, you might:

- **Give a presentation to peers, faculty, or community members about the activity.**

- **Write articles or letters to local newspapers regarding issues of public concern.**

- **Extend the experience to develop future projects that could benefit the community.**

EVALUATION PHASE: Evaluating Service Learning

A goal in JROTC is to couple high service with high integration of course content to maximize learning and skill development, as well as meet identified needs. When evaluating your service learning activities, reflect upon accomplishments and determine ways to improve.

High service meets a clear and important need and is organized and implemented by students. High integration with curriculum addresses classroom goals, incorporates classroom content, and improves course-related knowledge and skills. Use the following quadrants to rate your service learning experience.

Quadrant 1

Example: After studying financial planning lessons from the National Endowment of Financial Education, cadets teach Junior Achievement lessons to elementary students and assist them in making posters to advocate financial responsibility.

Key Note Terms

observation – an act or instance of examining a custom, rule, or law; an act of recognizing and noting a fact or occurrence.

analysis – a study of something complex, its elements, and their relations.

integration – the act or process or an instance of forming, coordinating, or blending into a functioning or unified whole.

Quadrant 2

Example: Cadets organize a drive for stuffed animals and blankets after learning about work skills and participating in Groundhog Job Shadow Day.

Quadrant 3

Example: Teacher directs cadets to send e-mail to deployed service members after studying a historic event through a cadet ride.

Quadrant 4

Example: Teacher assigns cadets to perform a color guard in the community after studying lessons in You the People.

Service Learning Authentic Assessments

Authentic assessments that evaluate the service activity and student learning are imperative to a successful service learning initiative. Choose assessment tools that measure and affirm learning, program goals, and impact on the need identified, to determine potential improvements.

Service learning lends itself to performance-based assessment, enabling you to exhibit what you have learned in a hands-on and meaningful context. Be sure to take advantage of college credits available through service learning and your curriculum.

Conclusion

In addition to teaching you the value of volunteering, service learning fosters your development of citizenship skills, as well as personal, social and thinking skills. It teaches service responsibilities and prepares future service commitments. Most importantly, service learning builds a spirit of cooperation among you, your peers, the school, and the community.

Chapter 8

Lesson Review

1. **List the three types of services and give an example of each.**
2. **Choose one service learning curriculum-related program and discuss it.**
3. **Define the term "placement."**
4. **State what you learn through the evaluation phase.**

Lesson Review

Index

Using the Classroom Performance System (CPS) to Enhance Your Teaching

Key Terms

engagement
interactive teaching
post-questions
pre-questions
transfer of learning

What You Will Learn to Do

- Use the Classroom Performance System (CPS) for teaching

Linked Core Abilities

- Communicate using verbal, non-verbal, visual, and written techniques

Skills and Knowledge You Will Gain Along the Way

- Explain why using CPS can make you a more effective instructor
- Develop CPS questions that will enhance your lesson
- Explain the location of resources for learning the technical aspects of CPS

Using the Classroom Performance System (CPS) to Enhance Your Teaching

Introduction

One of the most challenging parts of teaching is keeping your students focused, motivated, and on-task throughout the entire lesson. It is also important to know if your students fully understand the material. When used effectively, the Classroom Performance System (CPS) can be a very powerful tool to help you accomplish both of these goals.

In this lesson, you will consider several important elements of CPS use:

- **How CPS Works**
- **Effective Question Delivery**
- **Integrating CPS into the Four-Phase Lesson Plan**
- **Resources for Learning the Technical Aspects of CPS**

How CPS Works

Key Note Term

engagement – the degree of attention, focus, or motivation that a student displays during a learning experience.

Have you ever sat through a classroom lecture and struggled to stay focused? If you answered yes, chances are you are not alone. Lack of **engagement** is one of the main reasons students do not fully learn the material that is presented in class. The average attention span for students in a classroom setting is only about 7-12 minutes. Therefore, instructors must use a variety of methods, activities and even technologies to help students stay engaged with learning.

When using CPS, students hold a small response pad (clicker) while they are learning. Using specially designed software the instructor projects multiple-choice questions on a screen and student responses are collected through an infrared receiver that is plugged into the back of a computer. The results are displayed on the screen providing real-time feedback of the learning that is taking place. CPS can also be used to play games for team or individual competition, as well as grade tests or homework.

Using the Classroom Performance System (CPS) to Enhance Your Teaching

One of the main reasons CPS keeps students on-task is that it provides a way for immediate two-way communication. In other words, while your students are learning from you, you are now also learning from them. This style of instruction is known as **interactive teaching**. Are your students interested in your topic? Are they ready to learn? How much information do they already know? How many students understood the concept you just presented? Did the students really do the homework? These are all questions you can answer immediately when you use CPS.

Key Note Term

interactive teaching – a style of teaching where there is a consistent two-way flow of communication between the instructor and students.

Note

The resources available for learning the software and hardware aspects of CPS are presented at the end of this Appendix in the section titled "Resources for Learning the Technical Aspects of CPS."

Effective Question Delivery

The Classroom Performance System (CPS) is a teaching tool. Just as with any tool, it can be used well or it can be used poorly. There are several important questions that will help guide your thinking as you work to integrate CPS into your lesson.

What are my learning objectives?

Before you develop or select questions to deliver with CPS, you should review the learning objectives of your lesson. Each CPS question should enhance, support or relate to a learning objective. For example, if you have a learning objective about what students will *know* by the end of the lesson, then you may want to select or develop questions that will test students' knowledge of that objective. One way to do this might be to ask **pre-questions** before your lesson. Then, at the end of the lesson, ask the same questions (**post-questions**). The change in percentage of correct answers is a measurable indicator of the learning that took place during the lesson on that objective.

At what point during my lesson should I deliver my CPS questions?

The timing and spacing of your CPS questions is a very important consideration. A well-designed CPS lesson will typically follow this format:

- **Start with 2-4 *focusing questions* to get students ready to learn**
- **Deliver 2-3 *reinforcement questions* every 10-15 minutes to maintain attention**
- **Finish with 3-5 *review questions* to see if students can apply the material**

Key Note Terms

pre-questions – questions that are asked before a learning experience to measure student's knowledge of the material.

post-questions – questions that are asked at the end of a learning experience to measure the learning gains that were achieved.

Using the Classroom Performance System (CPS) to Enhance Your Teaching

Here are some examples of these three types of questions:

Focusing questions

What is your attitude about learning this morning?

a. **I am distracted or have low energy.**

b. **I am awake, but a little skeptical that this topic will interest me.**

c. **I have good energy and am ready to learn this topic.**

d. **I am so excited about this topic that other people often tell me to calm down and be quiet!**

The theory that leaders were born was prominent from the 1800s to the 1940s and was called the _____ approach.

a. **Hatching**

b. **Leadership**

c. **Succession**

d. **Traits**

In my opinion, leaders are mostly . . .

a. **born**

b. **made**

Reinforcement question

Feedback to subordinates is most effective when it is _____.

a. **immediate**

b. **delayed**

Review question

Which of the following analogies does not represent the purpose of a lesson plan?

a. **A lesson plan guides the teaching of a lesson as a recipe guides the creation of a meal.**

b. **A lesson plan guides the teaching of a lesson as a railroad track guides a train.**

c. **A lesson plan guides the teaching of a lesson as sheet music guides a musical performance.**

d. **A lesson plan guides the teaching of a lesson as map guides a traveler.**

Note

CPS questions are available for each Unit, Chapter, and Lesson in the Army JROTC curriculum. Ask your instructor for directions on how to access these question banks from the JROTC web portal.

How do I select/develop effective CPS questions?

To use CPS effectively, you must consider the quality of the questions. High quality questions will be:

- **Clear and well-written (rather than confusing)**
- **Challenging (rather than too easy)**
- **Designed to get students to think (rather than just to recall facts)**

Clear and well-written questions

Make sure that the questions you deliver with CPS are clearly written and easily understood. Here is an example of a confusing and poorly written question:

> **Which of the following is not one of the most important leadership principals that we will learn about?**
>
>   **a. Giving direction**
>
>   **b. Following orders**
>
>   **c. Being persuasive**

The wording of this question is awkward and difficult to follow. There are also at least two grammatical errors. Can you find them?

We recommend that you have another person review your questions for clarity and grammar before you deliver them in class.

Challenging questions

If questions are too easy, they will not create the same level of engagement or motivation for your students. For example, the following question is so easy that it may not be very interesting to most students.

> **The U.S. Constitution was written using a Venn Diagram**
>
>   **a. True**
>
>   **b. False**

However, the question below is more challenging and possibly more engaging.

> **Read the paragraph below and determine which of the options (A-D) is most correct:**
>
> **"Logan is preparing a lesson on the writing of the constitution. Students will follow the progress of the continental congress as they met to write the constitution and work through the various issues and challenges that arose. As part of the final report, students will create a *concept web* to illustrate the sequence of events in the writing of the constitution."**

     a. **Replace "concept web" with "Brace Map"**

     b. **Replace "concept web" with "Double Bubble Map"**

     c. **Replace "concept web" with "Bridge Map"**

     d. **Replace "concept web" with "Flow Map"**

Longer questions like this one should be used sparingly as they require time and are demanding for students. However, one or two higher-level thinking questions spaced throughout your lesson can greatly enhance both the instructional quality and level of difficulty of your lesson.

Note

When delivering a particularly challenging question to your students, you may want to divide them into teams. For example, have two or three cadets work on a question together and then click in on the answer. This will energize the room by making the learning experience feel more like a competition. We call this stealth learning. In other words, the learning is so fun that you don't even notice you are learning!

Questions designed to get students to think

Many people think that multiple-choice questions are limited to the realm of lower-level thinking such as recalling facts, defining terms, or answering trivia. However, when delivered through CPS, multiple-choice questions can not only bring students to higher-level thinking (e.g., application, analysis, evaluation) but can even encourage students to defend their opinions (debate), reflect on their thinking (meta-cognition), or create their own "clicker questions" (synthesis).

The following are just a few examples of how you can deliver CPS questions that encourage discussion or deeper-levels of thinking.

Example #1: Ask controversial questions and then facilitate student discussion. For example, "Malcolm X did more to harm civil rights in America than to help it." Choices range from strongly agree to strongly disagree. Once you see the results, ask students from various view-points if they would like to defend their positions.

Example #2: Scaffold your questions by following these steps: First, have students click in on a very difficult question without any discussion. Next, have students break into pairs, discuss the question, then click in again on the same question. Finally, move into groups of four and click in once again. Eventually more and more students will get the correct answer as the confident students share insights with their peers. Finish the activity by asking the students to share the highlights of what was discussed in their groups.

Example #3: Use videos or role playing activities that relate to your topic and then have cadets evaluate the presentation by "clicking in" on what they observed. For example, watch a video of a popular movie where one character mediates a conflict between two other characters. Ask cadets to select the type of conflict resolution strategy that was primarily used. This will allow you to see if cadets can analyze actual situations based on the knowledge they have learned in the lesson.

Integrating CPS into the Four-Phase Lesson Plan

As you have probably already learned in other sections of your text, JROTC lesson plans consist of four phases: Inquire, Gather, Process, and Apply. There are also three components that are common to each of the four phases: Direct Student Focus, Learning Activity, and Reflection. In this next section, we will consider various methods for integrating CPS into each of the three common components.

Using CPS to Direct Student Focus

CPS is an excellent tool for directing student focus because it increases an active rather than passive style of learning and promotes accountability for each student's learning. Here are a few examples of how you might us CPS questions to direct student focus:

Example #1: Display the learning objectives for the lesson. Ask cadets to select the learning objective that they think will be the most difficult for them to achieve. This will not only direct student attention to the objectives in a very active way, but it will also give you information that can direct your teaching.

Example #2: Before you watch a video, give cadets two questions ahead of time that they will answer immediately following the video. This will help students focus on the important parts of the film rather than irrelevant details. For example, if you were going to watch a 15-minute video on the civil rights movement, you may give these two questions to cadets ahead of time.

Question 1: Malcolm X and Martin Luther King Jr. were both civil rights leaders. Which of the following is NOT true of these two men?

    a. they were both religious men

    b. they were both assassinated

    c. they were both African-American

    d. they were both Christians

Question 2: Malcolm X did more to help civil rights than Martin Luther King Jr.

    a. strongly disagree

    b. disagree

    c. not sure

    d. agree

    e. strongly agree

Using CPS to Facilitate a Learning Activity

One of the most important aspects of any learning activity is that *everyone* participates. This can be very challenging for an instructor since some cadets are shy and withdrawn, while others are more active and talkative. By using CPS, you can be sure to involve every student during any learning activity. Here are a few examples:

Example #1: Let's say you were teaching a lesson on leadership. You might start with an activity to get students thinking about the idea of leadership by putting up pictures of four famous leaders and asking the class which one they think was the strongest leader (e.g., George Washington, César Chávez, Malcolm X, Queen Elizabeth). If you asked this question in a typical classroom with a raise of hands, only the most assertive students would participate. By using CPS, every student gets to participate in the evaluation. Therefore, the discussion that follows will be more personal and engaging for the entire class.

Example #2: For a lesson on health you might ask cadets to start by rating how "healthy" they think their own diet is. The results can become the starting point of a discussion on food groups, saturated fat, and sugar. At the end of the lesson you might then ask students to rate their own diet again and discuss any change in results.

Example #3: Asking a CPS question that highlights a misconception can be a very effective method for drawing students into a learning activity. For example, if you were teaching a lesson on map reading, you might start by asking the following question:

Which city is the farthest west?

a. **Las Vegas, NV**

b. **Reno, NV**

c. **San Diego, CA**

d. **Los Angeles, CA**

Most people will choose either C or D. However, the correct answer is "B" (Don't believe me? Look on a map.) This opening "gotcha" experience can draw students into a learning activity because it shows them what they don't know.

Using CPS for Reflection

One of the most important and challenging parts of any lesson is Reflection. This is when students and instructors are faced with question of "So what?" For example, I have learned about civil rights. What does this mean for me personally? I have learned how to read a map. How does this relate to anything else I have learned? These are critical questions because they measure the **transfer of learning** that did or did not take place as a result of the lesson. In other words, how much learning will actually transfer out of the classroom experience and into the life of each student?

Key Note Term

transfer of learning – the degree to which learning from a classroom experience carries over into real-life situations.

Using the Classroom Performance System (CPS) to Enhance Your Teaching

CPS is an effective tool to promote transfer of learning. Here are a few examples.

Example #1: ""What is the BEST thing you learned in this lesson?" And, "How could you APPLY this to a real life situation?" These are two powerful questions that can be used at the end of any lesson. In a typical classroom, you might ask these questions and then wait for a show of hands. However, you would then only engage the fastest or most active students. In a CPS classroom, we would ask this question and give each student 1-2 minutes to think and write out an answer. We would then use the Random Student Generator in CPS to pick 2-3 students to give an answer. Even though you only hear from 2-3 students, every student had to get ready with a response and struggle with the question about how to apply what they learned.

Example #2: Ask questions that relate the new topic to information that is already familiar. For example, if you just finished a lesson on orienteering, and you are about to start a lesson on teaching, you might start off with a question such as:

A compass is to orienteering as a lesson plan is to

a. learning

b. teaching

c. reading

d. studying

Your students may have a hard time with this question if they have not yet read or learned about lesson planning. Therefore, you may want to have them discuss in teams or groups before they click in on the answer. The key here is not to get the right answer, but rather to stimulate reflection and connection between the material they just learned with the material they are about to learn.

Example #3: For learning to transfer out of the classroom, students often need prompting to think about "next steps" that they might take. CPS can help facilitate this process. For example, on a lesson about health, you might end with this CPS question:

Which of the following next steps would be the most helpful for you in improving your health?

a. Eat more fruit

b. Eat more vegetables

c. Exercise more

d. Eat less sugar

e. Other

Notice that option "e" allows discussion of other actions that would be helpful. When you give students the chance to reflect on what is important to them you help to make the learning personal and challenge students to move the learning from thought into action.

Resources for Learning the Technical Aspects of CPS

In this Appendix we have taught you how to deliver CPS questions during a lesson. We have not addressed the technical aspects of how to use the CPS software or hardware. The resources for learning this part of CPS can be accessed through the resources listed below.

Print-based Instructions for CPS

Help menu: Inside the CPS software there is a "Help" menu that is organized by Chapter, Index, and Search. You can use this resource to learn CPS in a step-by-step manner (by Chapter) or to find features you would like to learn (by Index or Search). Each section in the Help menu can be printed for easy reference.

CPS User's Guide: If you install CPS from the install CD, the CPS User's Guide will automatically download to your computer in a PDF document. You can also download this resource from the eInstruction® Corporation website at *www.eInstruction.com.*

The CPS User's Guide is a 200+ page reference manual. It is designed to either be printed in sections or to be used as an electronic reference. Printing the entire CPS User's Guide for reference is not recommended.

On-line Training Resources

Free video training series: You may access a full range of video training clips any time from the eInstruction website. If you have a fast internet connection you can watch the videos live from the website. You can also download all the training videos from the eInstruction website for viewing off-line.

Free on-line training sessions: You may attend a live web-based training session registering at *www.einstruction.com.* During the training, you will be live with an instructor and other students for 45-minutes learning a specific aspect of CPS. You will be able to see the instructor's computer screen and speak with him/her on the phone during the session. There are 2–3 training sessions every weekday.

Technical Support

Phone: You may speak to a technical support team member by calling 888-333-4988. Phone support is available Monday–Thursday 7am–6pm / Friday 7am–5pm Central Standard Time.

Email or chat: You may send technical support questions to the tech support team via email or live chat at *http://www.einstruction.com/Support/index.cfm.* Chat is available Monday–Friday 8am–5pm Central Standard Time.

Knowledge Base: You may search the eInstruction knowledge base for frequently asked questions and answers at *http://www.einstruction.com/Support/ index.cfm.*

Sales Support and Point of Contact

Point of Contact: For sales support or help finding the correct resource, please contact Steve Huff at 720-261-2597 or *steveh@einstruction.com.*

Personal Skills Mapping—A New Way of Looking at Yourself

The results of the Personal Skills Map can provide you with a very interesting picture of where you are on your personal success journey and where you are going. The authors of the Personal Skills Map are more interested in what is right and healthy about you than what is wrong or incomplete. They prefer to help you get in touch with your strengths and provide you with an opportunity to learn new skills for personal problem solving and change. Think of it this way. A personal problem is identified by the Personal Skills Map as a low score. A low score is an indication of a "stuck place" in your personal growth. We prefer to work with you from a positive, proactive model, before personal problems become self-defeating and damaging to your emotional and physical health. The Personal Skills Map is a positive assessment approach that results in a guide that will suggest possible directions for skills training and learning experiences that foster healthy personal development and growth.

A Healthy Personality

For the most part, the feedback that we receive from other people seems to point out our limitations or the things we cannot do as well as others. We seem to be in touch with what is wrong or what is incomplete about ourselves. People with healthy personalities are able to view themselves at their best. Healthy personalities emphasize what we are capable of becoming by developing our potential to grow and to change in ways that we choose, and also to live more creatively.

Choose Your Life

Perhaps one of the most often overlooked theories that deal with personal development is this—we actively choose and create our lives each day. Once we understood this, we can learn to choose how successful we will be in life. The Personal Skills Map will provide you with an opportunity to see for yourself what you think of yourself in relation to personal success skills. Keep in mind that if you have a low score, you can choose to improve that skill at any point in your life. We can actively choose and create our lives rather than behave in line with determined patterns that were set down by family, friends, culture or society.

Self-Acceptance

Famous psychologists Carl Rogers and Abraham Maslow identified that healthy personalities have a common characteristic. That characteristic is self-acceptance. Self-acceptance is simply the ability to accept yourself as you are.

Fully-functioning people regard themselves as good and worthy. Healthy persons regard both themselves and others highly. Their behaviors and relationships are not compromising or controlling. Healthy persons are growth-motivated and view living as a process of becoming all that they are capable of becoming. They are aware of their weaknesses and accept them as problems to be solved. But healthy people are not overly aware or stuck on their problems. They know that they can work these problems out if they choose to do so.

Live in the Present

One of the key cornerstones of healthy people is their ability to live effectively in the present without being controlled by the past or scared about the future. Healthy people have the ability to create and to achieve meaningful personal goals, manage time in the present and complete tasks that are important as well as satisfying.

Case Study

Shawn is an 18-year-old senior at Edgewood High School. Throughout his years in school Shawn has been successful at not setting any goals for himself. Shawn has been able to get by with this process for some time however now he is faced with a new situation—high school graduation. Shawn must now deal with setting and then achieving his post-high-school goals. The results of his *Personal Skills Map* show relatively high scores in all areas except three: Drive Strength/Motivation, Time Management and Commitment Ethic. Because Shawn is not in the habit of setting and achieving goals, a low Drive Strength/Motivation score is the direct result of having no specific goals. How can Shawn be motivated when he has no goals? Time Management is another low score. Without

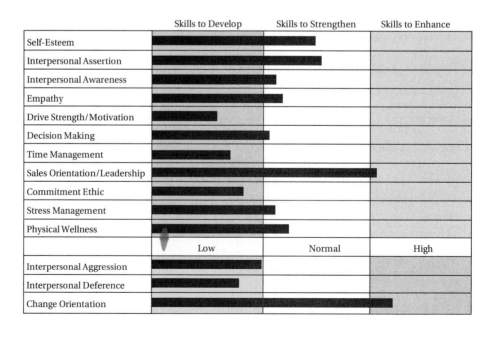

goals, time management is not necessary or important to Shawn. Finally the Commitment Ethic score is low. Commitment requires a commitment to something—to a goal. Without a goal, commitment is not possible. If goals are not set at this time in Shawn's life, stress management and physical wellness will become problems for him. The good news is that the Change Orientation score is quite high. This shows a person who wants to make personal changes and improvements in his life. Perhaps going through the *Personal Responsibility— Achieving Academic and Career Goals* program, along with the *Success Profiler— The Change Profile,* which will help Shawn to become more open to change as well as improve his goal setting and achievement skills.

Manage Stress

Another key factor to healthy and creative living is the ability to control self-destructive behaviors. Stress, when it is unmanaged in a person's life, is a self-destructive force. The *Personal Skills Map* helps identify the current level of ability to manage stress. The connection between managing stress and developing a healthy personality are clearly demonstrated in our society. Our mental health and physical health are directly related to our skills in knowing how to deal with the stress in our lives. Healthy people respond to stress in ways that are not destructive or damaging to their physical or mental health.

Case Study

Jose is a sophomore at Madison High School. Jose has been dealing with the stress of his parents' recent divorce. Jose was asked to take the *Personal Skills Map.* Here are his results:

These results indicate low Self-Esteem, Stress Management and Physical Wellness. Jose is not accustomed to having low self-esteem. The low Stress-

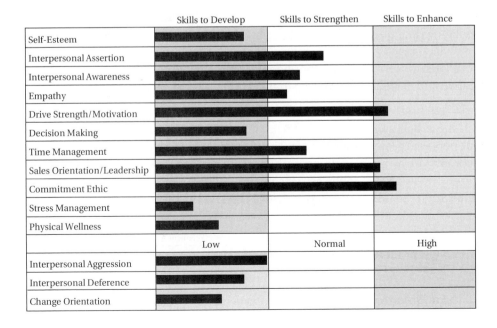

	Skills to Develop	Skills to Strengthen	Skills to Enhance
Self-Esteem	▉		
Interpersonal Assertion	▉▉		
Interpersonal Awareness	▉▉		
Empathy	▉		
Drive Strength/Motivation	▉▉▉		
Decision Making	▉		
Time Management	▉▉		
Sales Orientation/Leadership	▉▉▉		
Commitment Ethic	▉▉▉		
Stress Management	▉		
Physical Wellness	▉		
	Low	Normal	High
Interpersonal Aggression	▉▉		
Interpersonal Deference	▉▉		
Change Orientation	▉		

Management and Physical Wellness scales show a recent and unusual event in Jose life, his parents' divorce. Because this has created changes for Jose, something needs to be done soon to correct or to cope with the them. If Jose does not deal with the changes caused by his current situation, problems will continue to occur and poor decision making could result. Jose needs to acknowledge that things are happening in his life that he feels are out of his control. He needs to find someone to help him work through his thoughts and feelings and to help him learn to cope with his situation. Perhaps a mentor, a friend, a parent, a teacher, or a family member could help. Another issue is that Jose's Change Orientation scale is low which shows that Jose is not open to change and does not want to learn new coping skills. This resistance to change will cause him to continue to allow stress to build up in his life and suppress his stress management and physical wellness skills. His feelings about himself (self-esteem) will continue to deteriorate until he realizes that he needs to make some changes in his life (change orientation). Why is the above information important? Simply stated, it is a roadmap for self-awareness and self-improvement as well as a tool to help develop a healthy personality that is able to cope with current and future difficult situations in Jose's life.

Personal Skills Map Model of a Healthy Personality

The *Personal Skills Map* Model of a Healthy Personality is based on the assumption that healthier living is the result of learning essential personal skills in intrapersonal, interpersonal and career and life management areas. A healthy personality is viewed as possessing all of the creative resources necessary for healthy living. Personal growth and change is seen as a lifelong process of developing and learning new personal skills. A process of personal skills development that moves a person toward skilled and creative living, consistent with the values of the individual, is part of the healthy personality.

Destructive personality is viewed as the result of unresolved impasses to personal growth and a failure or lack of knowledge in the process of making personal changes. Personal change is difficult but not impossible. At sometime in our lives most of us need other people to help us learn and explore more creative and skilled ways of living in this world.

One of the first steps to moving toward a healthy and creative lifestyle is self-awareness. Self-awareness comes from identifying the factors that relate to your personal growth and success. The *Personal Skills Map* is a tool to help you become more aware of your strengths and limitations. The *Personal Skills Map* is a positive approach to the self-assessment of the personal skills that are important to healthy and creative living. The healthy person is one who claims the following creative living skills:

1. **A high positive feeling about self (Self-Esteem)**
2. **Assertive communication skills (Interpersonal Assertion)**
3. **An awareness of self and others (Interpersonal Awareness)**
4. **An understanding of how other people feel (Empathy)**

5. **High drive strength and a desire to grow as a person (Drive Strength/ Motivation)**

6. **Good decision making and problem solving skills (Decision Making)**

7. **Good time management skills (Time Management)**

8. **Leadership and the ability to sell ideas to others (Sales Orientation/ Leadership)**

9. **Ability to stick to a task until it is completed (Commitment Ethic)**

10. **Positive stress management skills (Stress Management)**

11. **Positive physical wellness skills (Physical Wellness)**

These eleven personal characteristics are reflective of the eleven skills assessed in the *Personal Skills Map*. Research shows that these eleven skills are directly related to positive and healthy personal development. Low scores are Skills to Develop on the *Personal Skills Map* and are specific indicators of the need for personal change. Taking this information and making a personal decision to change is key to personal growth and success. The decision to change is the start to finding healthier and more satisfying ways of thinking, feeling and behaving.

One of the major advantages of the *Personal Skills Map* is that the scales can be directly related to specific skill building and personal growth experiences. Upon completion of your *Personal Skills Map*, consider working on one or more of the skill building units that are part of *The Success Profiler*. Select the lowest scale score and begin working on changing that skill from a low to a high score.